Methods of Research into the Unconscious

The psychoanalytic unconscious is a slippery set of phenomena to pin down. There is not an accepted standard form of research, outside of the clinical practice of psychoanalysis. In this book a number of non-clinical methods for collecting data and analysing it are described. It represents the current situation on the way to an established methodology.

The book provides a survey of methods in contemporary use and development. As well as the introductory survey, chapters have been written by researchers who have pioneered recent and effective methods and have extensive experience of those methods. It will serve as a gallery of illustrations from which to make the appropriate choice for a future research project.

Methods of Research into the Unconscious: Applying Psychoanalytic Ideas to Social Science will be of great use for those aiming to start projects in the general area of psychoanalytic studies and for those in the human/social sciences who wish to include the unconscious as well as conscious functioning of their subjects.

Kalina Stamenova, PhD, FHEA, is a research fellow and a lecturer at the University of Essex. Her research interests involve psychoanalytic research methods, psychoanalysis and education, and psychoanalysis and organisations.

R. D. Hinshelwood is a British psychiatrist and psychoanalyst who has always had a part-time commitment to the public service (NHS and universities) and to teaching psychoanalysis and psychotherapy. He has written on Kleinian psychoanalysis and on the application of psychoanalysis to social science and political themes. He has taken an interest in and published on the problems of making evidenced comparisons between different schools of psychoanalysis.

Methods of Research into the Unconscious

Applying Psychoanalytic Ideas to Social Science

Edited by Kalina Stamenova and
R. D. Hinshelwood

LONDON AND NEW YORK

First published 2018
by Routledge
2 Park Square, Milton Park, Abingdon, Oxon OX14 4RN

and by Routledge
711 Third Avenue, New York, NY 10017

Routledge is an imprint of the Taylor & Francis Group, an Informa business

© 2019 editorial matter, introductory and concluding chapters, Kalina Stamenova and R. D. Hinshelwood; individual chapters, the contributors

The right of Kalina Stamenova and R. D. Hinshelwood to be identified as the authors of the editorial material, and of individual chapters, has been asserted in accordance with sections 77 and 78 of the Copyright, Designs and Patents Act 1988.

All rights reserved. No part of this book may be reprinted or reproduced or utilised in any form or by any electronic, mechanical, or other means, now known or hereafter invented, including photocopying and recording, or in any information storage or retrieval system, without permission in writing from the publishers.

Trademark notice: Product or corporate names may be trademarks or registered trademarks, and are used only for identification and explanation without intent to infringe.

British Library Cataloguing in Publication Data
A catalogue record for this book is available from the British Library

Library of Congress Cataloguing in Publication Data
A catalogue record for this book has been requested

ISBN: 978-1-138-32661-3 (hbk)
ISBN: 978-1-138-32662-0 (pbk)
ISBN: 978-0-429-44975-8 (ebk)

Typeset in Times New Roman
by Integra Software Services Pvt. Ltd.

Printed and bound in Great Britain by
TJ International Ltd, Padstow, Cornwall

Contents

Notes on the editors and contributors   viii
Acknowledgements   xiii
Foreword by Michael Rustin   xiv

Introduction   1
KALINA STAMENOVA AND R. D. HINSHELWOOD

PART I
An overview of qualitative methodologies   17

1 A psychoanalytic view of qualitative methodology: observing the elemental psychic world in social processes   19
KARL FIGLIO

PART II
Psychoanalytic methods in data collection   41

Interviewing   42

2 The socioanalytic interview   43
SUSAN LONG

3 Psychoanalytic perspectives on the qualitative research interview   55
NICK MIDGLEY AND JOSHUA HOLMES

4 Psycho-societal interpretation of the unconscious dimensions in everyday life   70
HENNING SALLING OLESEN AND THOMAS LEITHÄUSER

5 Using the psychoanalytic research interview as an
   experimental 'laboratory'   87
   SIMONA REGHINTOVSCHI

OBSERVATIONS   **105**

6 Psychoanalytic observation – the mind as research instrument   107
   WILHELM SKOGSTAD

7 The contribution of psychoanalytically informed observation
   methodologies in nursery organisations   126
   PETER ELFER

PART III
**Psychoanalytic methods in data handling and data
analysis**   **143**

Visual methods   **144**

8 Social photo-matrix and social dream-drawing   145
   ROSE REDDING MERSKY AND BURKARD SIEVERS

OPERATIONALISATION   **169**

9 Is it a bird? Is it a plane?: operationalisation of unconscious
   processes   171
   GILLIAN WALKER AND R. D. HINSHELWOOD

10 Comparative analysis of overlapping psychoanalytic concepts
   using operationalization   183
   KALINA STAMENOVA

NARRATIVE ANALYSIS   **197**

11 Psychoanalysis in narrative research   199
   LISA SAVILLE YOUNG AND STEPHEN FROSH

12 Researching dated, situated, defended, and evolving
   subjectivities by biographic-narrative interview:
   psychoanalysis, the psycho-societal unconscious, and
   biographic-narrative interview method and interpretation   211
   TOM WENGRAF

PSYCHO-SOCIETAL ETHNOGRAPHY — 239

13 Psychoanalytic ethnography — 241
LINDA LUNDGAARD ANDERSEN

Conclusion — 256
R. D. HINSHELWOOD AND KALINA STAMENOVA

Index — 259

Notes on the editors and contributors

Linda Lundgaard Andersen, PhD, is professor in learning, evaluation, and social innovation in welfare services at Roskilde University; director, PhD School of People and Technology, and co-director at the Centre for Social Entrepreneurship. Her research interests include learning and social innovation in welfare services, psycho-societal theory and method, ethnographies of the public sector, democracy and forms of governance in human services, voluntary organisations, and social enterprises. She is a founding member of the International Research Group in Psycho-Societal Analysis (IRGPSA).

Peter Elfer is principal lecturer in early childhood studies at the School of Education, University of Roehampton. He is also a trustee of the Froebel Trust and a vice president of Early Education. His research interests concern under-threes, their wellbeing in nursery contexts, and the support that nursery practitioners need to facilitate that wellbeing. He is currently investigating the contribution of work discussion groups, underpinned by psychoanalytic conceptions, as a model of professional reflection for nursery practitioners.

Karl Figlio is professor emeritus in the Department of Psychosocial and Psychoanalytic Studies, University of Essex. He is a senior member of the Psychoanalytic Psychotherapy Association of the British Psychoanalytic Council and an associate member of the British Psychoanalytical Society. He is in private practice. Recent publications include *Remembering as Reparation: Psychoanalysis and Historical Memory* (Palgrave Macmillan, 2017); 'The Mentality of Conviction: Feeling Certain and the Search for Truth', in N. Mintchev and R. D. Hinshelwood (eds), *The Feeling of Certainty: Psychosocial Perspectives on Identity and Difference* (Palgrave Macmillan, 2017, pp. 11–30).

Stephen Frosh is professor in the Department of Psychosocial Studies (which he founded) at Birkbeck, University of London. He was pro-vice-master of Birkbeck from 2003 to 2017. He has a background in academic and clinical psychology and was consultant clinical psychologist at the Tavistock Clinic, London, throughout the 1990s. He is the author of many books and papers on psychosocial studies and on psychoanalysis. His books include *Hauntings: Psychoanalysis* and *Ghostly Transmissions* (Palgrave, 2013), *Feelings* (Routledge, 2011), *A Brief Introduction to Psychoanalytic Theory* (Palgrave, 2012), *Psychoanalysis Outside the Clinic* (Palgrave, 2010), *Hate and the Jewish Science: Anti-Semitism, Nazism and Psychoanalysis* (Palgrave, 2005), *For and Against Psychoanalysis* (Routledge, 2006), *After Words* (Palgrave, 2002), *The Politics of Psychoanalysis* (Palgrave, 1999), *Sexual Difference* (Routledge, 1994), and *Identity Crisis* (Macmillan, 1991). His most recent book is *Simply Freud* (Simply Charly, 2018). He is a fellow of the Academy of Social Sciences, an academic associate of the British Psychoanalytical Society, a founding member of the Association of Psychosocial Studies, and an honorary member of the Institute of Group Analysis.

R. D. Hinshelwood is a fellow of the British Psychoanalytical Society, and a fellow of the Royal College of Psychiatrists. After 30 years working in the NHS, he was subsequently professor in the Centre for Psychoanalytic Studies at the University of Essex. His academic interest developed towards comparative methodologies for investigating psychoanalytic concepts, and he published *Research on the Couch* (2013) on the use of clinical material for this research.

Joshua Holmes is a child and adolescent psychotherapist working in the NHS. His book *A Practical Psychoanalytic Guide to Reflexive Research: The Reverie Research Method* was published by Routledge in 2018. He is a former winner of the *Journal of the American Psychoanalytic Association* new author prize. Two people who have inspired him are Thomas Ogden and Thierry Henry.

Thomas Leithäuser was professor for developmental and social psychology (1973–2004) at the University of Bremen, director of the Academy for Labor and Politics in Bremen (1996–2009), and is now honorary professor at Roskilde University, Denmark. He holds guest professorships in the Netherlands, Brazil, and China. His research focuses on the consciousness of everyday life, ideology and political psychology, and working with qualitative methods: theme-centred interviews/group discussions, psychoanalytically orientated text interpretation, and collaborative action research. His published works are both fundamental studies in psychosocial methodology and present results of major empirical research projects on topics including the consciousness of everyday life in workplaces and cultural institutions; the anxiety of war, stress, and conflict resolution; violation in public space and the experience of technology.

Susan Long, PhD, is a Melbourne-based organisational consultant and executive coach. Previously professor of creative and sustainable organisation at RMIT University, she is now director of research and scholarship at the National Institute for Organisation Dynamics Australia (NIODA). She also teaches in the University of Melbourne Executive Programs, INSEAD in Singapore, Miecat and the University of Divinity. She has been in a leadership position in many professional organisations: president of the Psychoanalytic Studies Association of Australasia (2010–2015), past president of the International Society for the

Psychoanalytic Study of Organizations and inaugural president of Group Relations Australia. She has published eight books and many articles in books and scholarly journals, is general editor of the journal *Socioanalysis* and associate editor with *Organisational and Social Dynamics*. She is a member of the Advisory Board for Mental Health at Work with Comcare and a past member of the Board of the Judicial College of Victoria (2011–2016).

Rose Redding Mersky has been an organisational development consultant, supervisor, and coach for over 25 years. She offers workshops in various socioanalytic methodologies, such as organisational role analysis, social dream-drawing, organisational observation, social photo-matrix, and social dreaming. She is an honorary trustee of the Gordon Lawrence Foundation for the Promotion of Social Dreaming. She has been a member of the International Society for the Psychoanalytic Study of Organizations (ISPSO) for 30 years and served as its first female president. Her publications have focused primarily on the practice of consultation and the utilisation of these methodologies in both organisational and research practice. She is currently writing a book on social dream-drawing, a methodology she has developed, extensively trialled, and evaluated. She lives and works in Germany.

Nick Midgley is a child and adolescent psychotherapist and a senior lecturer in the Research Department of Clinical, Educational and Health Psychology at University College London (UCL). He is co-director of the Child Attachment and Psychological Therapies Research Unit (ChAPTRe), at UCL/the Anna Freud National Centre for Children and Families.

Henning Salling Olesen is professor at Roskilde University, affiliated with the doctoral programme Learning, Work and Social Innovation, Department of People and Technology. He was formerly prorector and acting rector of the university, and founder and director of the Graduate School of Lifelong Learning. He was for 15 years the chair of the European Society for Research in the Education of Adults (ESREA), and is now co-editor of the *European Journal of Adult Learning and Education* (RELA). Henning Salling Olesen holds an honorary doctorate at the University of Tampere, Finland, and serves as advisory professor at East China Normal University, Shanghai. He led a major methodological research project on the life history approach to adult learning, and has developed methodology for psycho-societal empirical studies of learning in everyday life (Forum for Qualitative Social Research, 2012/2013, thematic issue). His work on policy and implementation of lifelong learning is focusing on the transformation of local and national institutions and traditions in a modernisation process perspective, and the interplay between global policy agendas and local socio-economic development.

Simona Reghintovschi is a psychoanalyst, member of the Romanian Society of Psychoanalysis. She studied physics and psychology in Bucharest, and received a PhD in psychoanalytic studies from the University of Essex. She is lecturer in projective methods and applied psychoanalysis at Titu Maiorescu University in Bucharest, and psychology/psychotherapy series editor at Editura Trei.

Burkard Sievers is professor emeritus of organisational development at the Schumpeter School of Business and Economics at Bergische Universität in Wuppertal, Germany. His research and scholarly publications focus on unconscious dynamics in management and organisations from a socioanalytic and systemic perspective. As organisational consultant, he has worked with a whole range of profit and non-profit organisations. He brought group relations working conferences to Germany in 1979, and has been a staff member and director of conferences in Australia, England, France, Germany, Hungary, and the Netherlands. He was president of the International Society for the Psychoanalytic Study of Organizations from 2007 to 2009. He has held visiting appointments at universities in Australia, Austria, Brazil, Canada, Chile, Colombia, Finland, France, Hungary, Poland, Russia, Sweden, Switzerland, the Netherlands, the UK, and USA. Building on his work with Gordon Lawrence on the development of social dreaming, he developed the social photo-matrix, which is an experiential method for promoting the understanding of the unconscious in organisations through photographs taken by organisational role-holders. He is an honorary trustee of the Gordon Lawrence Foundation for the Promotion of Social Dreaming. His last article is 'A photograph of a little boy seen through the lens of the associative unconscious and collective memory': https://link.springer.com/article/10.1057%2Fpcs.2016.3

Wilhelm Skogstad is a psychiatrist and psychoanalyst, and training analyst of the British Psychoanalytic Society. He worked for a long time as consultant and later clinical lead at the Cassel Hospital, a hospital for psychoanalytic inpatient treatment of patients with severe personality disorder. He is now in full-time private psychoanalytic practice. He is one of the founders and organisers of the British German Colloquium, a bi-annual conference of British and German psychoanalysts that has been running since 2006. He teaches and supervises regularly in Germany. He has published widely, in English and German, on psychoanalytic observation of organisations (including a book, co-edited with Bob Hinshelwood), on inpatient psychotherapy and on psychoanalytic practice.

Kalina Stamenova, PhD, FHEA, is a research fellow at the Centre for Psychoanalytic Studies (now Department for Psychoanalytic and Psychosocial Studies) at the University of Essex. Her research interests involve psychoanalysis and education, social trauma and psychoanalysis, and politics, and she has presented at numerous conferences.

Gillian Walker originally trained as a general nurse, becoming a nurse specialist in burns and trauma, and subsequently taught biology and psychology to student nurses. She is currently a psychoanalytic researcher with a specific interest in Freud's theory of masochism.

Tom Wengraf was born in London to a nineteenth-century-born father (b.1894) from Freud's Vienna, and he has always had, as Melanie Klein would say, a love–hate relationship with psychoanalysis. Along with intermittent psychoanalyses and therapies, he has also done a lot of studying on their workings. The breakup of his first marriage stimulated a lot of what he now sees as psycho-societal thinking, as has the breakup of planetary stability. He originally read modern history at Oxford, and sociology at the London School of Economics, and researched newly independent Algeria in post-colonial struggle. Teaching mostly at Middlesex University, he has been involved in left-wing political journals such as *New Left Review* and *The Spokesman*, and with the *Journal of Social Work Practice*, as well as the International Research Group for Psychosocietal Analysis and the new UK-based Association for Psychosocial Studies. Specialisation in sociology and qualitative research led to his interest in biographic-narrative interpretive method (BNIM) in which, with others, he has been training and exploring for the past 20 years.

Lisa Saville Young is an associate professor at Rhodes University in Grahamstown, South Africa, where she practises, teaches, and supervises trainee psychologists, primarily focusing on psychoanalytic psychotherapy. Much of her research has involved developing methodological/analytic tools that draw on psychoanalysis alongside discursive psychology in qualitative research. She has used this methodology to investigate the negotiation of identity in relationships, including adult sibling relationships, researcher–participant relationships, and, more recently, parent–child relationships in the South African context.

Acknowledgements

KS:
The idea for the book evolved from my research at the Centre for Psychoanalytic Studies at the University of Essex, which has formed me as a researcher open to diverse studies and applications of psychoanalysis, and I am deeply indebted to both Bob Hinshelwood and Karl Figlio as well as my many colleagues at the Centre for fostering such a culture of rigorous enquiry. And working with Bob on this book has been a truly satisfying and enriching experience. Trying to map a constantly changing and evolving diverse field is both a challenging and immensely rewarding task, so my deepest gratitude to all those who agreed to participate in the endeavour and who have helped us on the way – the contributors to the book and the numerous colleagues who commented, critiqued, and provided invaluable suggestions – Mike Roper, Mark Stein, Lynne Layton, and Craig Fees, among many others.

My son Marko and my daughter Anna have shared with me the various stages of the book's progress, and their affection and cheerfulness have helped me tremendously along the way. Finally, yet importantly, I thank Rositsa Boycheva, Raina Ivanova, and Emil Stamenov for their unflagging support.

RDH:
I am first of all grateful to the Centre for Psychoanalytic Studies at the University of Essex, where I spent 18 years learning to be an academic. And in particular, I thank the Director, Karl Figlio, for taking the risk and giving me the opportunity. But of course the biggest opportunity for learning about academic research methods came from the two dozen or so doctoral students I supervised. I must acknowledge too the editors of journals and publishers of books, who have given me the experience of entering the cut and thrust of enduring debate. Perhaps I should also recognise the important contribution of the field itself to my life, career, and this book, as it is responsible for the absorbing fascination of all those hardly solved obstacles to researching the human unconscious and human subjectivity. Lastly, I express my gratitude to Gillian for tolerating my fascination and who has in the process suffered a serious infection of that fascination as well.

And beyond lastly, thank you, Kalina, for being such a willing accomplice, in seeing this book through to its completion together.

Foreword

Michael Rustin

In the past twenty or so years, there has been a great deal of attention given to research methods and methodologies in the social sciences, as a distinct area of reflection and study. One early impetus for this was the wish to establish the legitimate range of social scientific methodologies, and in particular the value of qualitative and interpretative methods, in opposition to a previous hegemony of quantitative and 'positivist' approaches in the social sciences. Whereas for some disciplines, such as psychology, legitimacy had been sought primarily through proximity to the methods of the natural sciences, others, notably sociology, anthropology, and cultural studies, had come to emphasise the distinctiveness of human and social subjects as objects of study, and the specific forms of investigation that followed from that. Research methods have since became a substantial field of publication (see, for example, the extensive series of Sage Handbooks on social research) and a specialism in their own right.

Psychoanalysis and psychoanalytic research have until recently had only a very limited place in these debates. Psychoanalysis has throughout its history been mainly conducted as the work of a profession, rather than as an academic discipline. In particular, this has been as a clinical practice, outside the university system and the context of formal scientific research. In so far as the field did engage in the discussion of methods, these were more often clinical methods, or 'techniques', than methods of academically recognised investigation. But this situation is now changing, following the academic accreditation of programmes of psychoanalytic education and training in Britain, in a significant number of universities. One of these is the University of Essex, where the Centre for Psychoanalytic Studies, now the Department of Psychosocial and Psychoanalytic Studies, has been one of the leading centres for this work, and from which this book has come. (Others include University College London, Birkbeck College, the University of the West of England, and the University of East London through its partnership with the Tavistock Clinic in the UK, as well as a number of European universities with psychoanalytically oriented departments and programmes, such as Roskilde University in Denmark, the University of Milan-Bicocca in Italy, the University of Vienna in Austria, and the University of Jyväskylä in Finland.)

Psychoanalytically informed social and historical research has for many years been conducted at the University of Essex, for example, in the work of the late Ian Craib, Karl Figlio, Matt ffytche, Robert Hinshelwood, and Michael Roper. Hinshelwood has been deeply involved in the development of a doctoral research programme, and much of this book represents one of its significant outcomes.

Its editors, Kalina Stamenova and Robert Hinshelwood, came to the view that it was now time for the issues of method involved in undertaking psychoanalytic research to be systemically reviewed, and the field surveyed. This mapping by the editors provides the organising frame for the collection of methodological papers of which the book is composed. The resulting chapters are diverse in their topics. In this, they reflect, as its editors acknowledge, the fragmented state of what is still a new field of social research. Two essential dimensions of research method – those of data collection and data analysis – are properly assigned substantial sections in the book. The crucial issues explored here are those involved in capturing unconscious phenomena – individual and social states of mind and feeling – in accountable ways. Different approaches to the essential processes of interview are outlined. The implicit argument of the book is that only if such valid and reliable methods of research can be developed can the field of psychoanalytic social research achieve a coherence comparable to that which has been achieved within different traditions of psychoanalytic clinical practice – a connectedness that Hinshelwood has demonstrated in several earlier books. The contributors to this volume include many researchers, such as Karl Figlio, Stephen Frosh, and Susan Long, who are authorities in this field, as well as other writers who have recently made important and original contributions to it.

The range of research methods set out in this book is wide, including, for example, the socio-photo matrix and social dream-drawing, the psychoanalytic dimensions of narrative approaches, and the biographical narrative method, but it also devotes attention to some important topics which had been explored in earlier work by Hinshelwood and his colleagues. For example, attention is given here to the methods of psychoanalytic institutional observation, the subject of his and Wilhelm Skogstad's earlier influential book *Observing Organisations: Anxiety, Defence and Culture in Health Care Institutions* (2000). Chapters on the problems of 'operationalising' psychoanalytic concepts, and of testing specific psychoanalytic hypotheses in a rigorous, empirical way, develop the arguments that Hinshelwood set out in his recent book on this topic, *Research on the Couch: Single Case Studies, Subjectivity and Psychoanalytic Knowledge* (2013). This new collection of chapters is given a valuable focus through its development of these debates and through the work of the psychoanalytic research PhD programme at the University of Essex, which is represented in this book.

There are now many actual and prospective doctoral students in the field of psychoanalytic social research who are in need of guidance in regard to issues of research method. Gaining a clear understanding of methodological questions is an essential requirement of academic study in every social science, all the more so in a new field like this one in which research methods have so far been little discussed or defined. Stamenova and Hinshelwood's *Methods of Research into the Unconscious* should be of great value both for its mapping and for referencing of this emerging field, and for its presentation of a valuable and diverse range of specific research methods.

Introduction

Kalina Stamenova and R. D. Hinshelwood

This book was conceived following the research done by Kalina Stamenova in the course of a PhD at the Centre for Psychoanalytic Studies (CPS; now the Department of Psychosocial and Psychoanalytic Studies, DPPS) at the University of Essex, and under supervision from R. D. Hinshelwood.

Some thoughts to bear in mind for a reader

Psychoanalytic research is a hybrid; it exists between the clinical practice of psychoanalysis from which nearly all psychoanalytic knowledge has come, and on the other hand, social science. A clear qualitative methodology for psychoanalytic studies does not exist, but has been debated over many years at the CPS. The problem for psychoanalytic research is that it is about the 'unconscious' in human beings and their social groups. Obviously, the unconscious, by definition, cannot be known consciously. However, the assumption that conscious awareness is sufficient is made in most social science research, where interview and questionnaire methods seek conscious answers from samples of subjects! If you ask a conscious question, you get a conscious answer. It is assumed that the object of research is a 'transparent self'. In psychoanalysis, instead, the unconscious has to be inferred. This is not the particular problem, since science in general is a body of inferences about what cannot be seen. No-one has 'seen' an atom, but we know quite a lot about it from using special tools and instruments to generate data from which fairly firm inferences can be made. So too with inferences about the unconscious. The problem with the psychoanalytic unconscious is not the problem of knowledge by inference.

There are, however, several problems with accessing knowledge about the human unconscious from outside the clinical setting, which are specific to psychoanalytic studies. They need to be kept in mind while progressing through these chapters. The first of these problems is to understand what the unconscious is, and there is debate about that, a debate reflected across the chapters in this book. The second which reverberates also throughout the chapters is some concern with the nature of the instrument of observation.

The nature of the unconscious

If psychoanalytic studies are a small corner of psychosocial studies, then we gain our concepts from two different sources, one psychological and one social. Many in the field of psychosocial studies tend to insist on the social origins of psychological phenomena (Frosh, 2007; Parker, 1996). This does not fit well with Freud's attempts to generate explanations of social phenomena from psychological ones – for instance, his book *Totem and Taboo* (Freud, 1913). And later he wrote:

> In the individual's mental life someone else is invariably involved, as a model, as an object, as a helper, as an opponent: and so from the very first individual psychology, in this extended but entirely justifiable sense of the words, is at the same time social psychology as well.
>
> (Freud, 1921, p. 69)

Freud's easy elision of two disciplines is not very convincing. And indeed, it did not convince social scientists (e.g., Malinovski, 1923; Smith, 1923; River, 1923; and Jones' response, 1925). The dichotomy, even bad feeling, between the two disciplines reflects the difficulty in translating individual experience into social dynamics, and vice versa. The art of a psychoanalytic version of the psychosocial would be to integrate the forces from different directions (Hinshelwood, 1996). The fact that Freud notes the basic tendency for human beings to be object-related does not mean psychoanalysis is a social science, as we would understand it now. It is important to recognise the distinction between the impetus to behave that arises in bodily states – stimulus of the erogenous zones, as Freud (1905) would say – and, on the other hand, the 'associative unconscious', as it is called in some of the chapters in this book.

The associative unconscious

The idea of the associative unconscious is that we are all part of a matrix of relations in a social group, where certain ways of perceiving reality are impressed on the individuals without a proper conscious awareness of that influence. It is an idea (originally described in Long and Harney, 2013) that comes from the notion of a field of relations in which one emerges as an individual being, so that one's sense of self and being is formed in that context of a matrix external to the person. This has been developed by Foulkes and his followers (Schlapobersky, 2016), and may owe something to Jung's idea of the collective unconscious, a set of bedrock templates for thinking that we share from the outset with everyone else (Jung, 1969, called them 'archetypes').

Structure in language

This associative unconscious is sometimes seen as a product of the verbal representation humans have used to create civilisation. In the form of discourse analysis, it is possible to discern the way language instils assumptions into the individual mind without awareness. There is an unthought level of 'knowing' that informs our perceptions, thought, and behaviour. It is literally embedded in the syntax. This approach often seeks support from Jaques Lacan, a maverick psychoanalyst who drew upon Ferdinand de Saussure's theories of linguistics (de Saussure, 1916). Lacan saw the invisible influence of language as the ultimate source of the unconscious, rather than the Freudian unconscious arising in affective states. It is the case that Freud did indeed regard the conscious mind as capable of thought only in so far as its contents are verbalisable:

> The system Ucs. contains the thing-cathexes of the objects, the first and true object-cathexes; the system Pcs. comes about by this thing-presentation being hypercathected through being linked with the word-presentations corresponding to it.
>
> (Freud, 1915, pp. 201–202)

Saussure's linguistics is a relational one; meanings come from the relations between words. For instance, we are accustomed to using personal pronouns that indicate gender – 'he' and 'she' – but when we want to generalise, we use the male pronoun, as if the standard type is always male of which female is merely a variant. This implicit valuation of gender comes from the customary (and apparently arbitrary) relations we use between 'he' and 'she'. This is of course more pronounced in French, the language of Lacan (and de Saussure), in which there are no words for the neutral English pronouns 'it' or 'they'.

These implicit assumptions embedded in the customary use of language are a truly unconscious influence in the sense that they are unthought, and not consciously intended necessarily – merely that we have to use language, and cannot avoid what is hidden there. These influences become consciously intended by customary use – at least until a feminist polemic displays them. This kind of hidden syntactical influence is prevalent in languages in general. It is a social mechanism that was also held to support class differences, in an unthought way. Georg Lukács (1923) termed it a 'false consciousness', and saw it embedded in the culture, so that the class positions were socially constructed, as a product of the natural order, as it were, and not amenable to change. Lukács saw this influence as not primarily embedded in language, but in the dominant mode of industrial production. This was an idea taken up by Western Marxism (a form of Marxism that did not die with Soviet Marxism). But it is transmitted and instilled by its usage in customary relationships.

This idea of hidden social influences crops up in various places in social thinking. The prevalent social relations come to be accepted via an unthinking osmosis, via language or other forms of transmission. Despite Freud's emphasis on language, he did know that visual representations are important, and psychoanalysis started really from his discovery of the 'syntax' of visual dream symbols rather than verbal ones (though words have their place in dreams too). The syntax of visual representations we construct is the syntax of spatial relations.

These modalities of hidden influence from social sources have deeply internal effects. However, they do not have the dynamic structure of the psychoanalytic unconscious; that is quite different, and depends on the anxiety–defence dynamic – condensation and displacement in the mind, on one hand, and, on the other, the distance in social space between classes, genders, races, and so on. The inner dynamic influence is an affective structure dealing with painful experience and not, as the associative unconscious, a conceptual structure dealing with categories of perception and the relations between those categories (Hinshelwood, 1996). This distinction between two different forms of unconscious dynamic influence needs to be held in mind as we read these chapters.

The instrument of observation

Just as de Saussure described linguistics as moving from a study of the isolated word to the relations between words, so it is necessary to put aside the notion of the unconscious as a static thing to be studied. It is a 'thing' in relation to other similar ones. There is a constant unconscious-to-unconscious communication going on. We cannot study an unconscious mind without its being in relation to others. In particular, it is in relation to the researchers' unconscious minds. There is therefore a continuous process of unconscious communication flowing around the research setting.

This creates a problem for psychoanalytic studies research (probably for other studies in the human sciences as well, but that is not the issue here). There is a clear problem that if unconscious influences and communication go on in the research setting, then the research is not, as it is said, 'controlled'; that is, it is not consciously controlled. Influences impact on the researcher and team without their awareness. This makes psychoanalytic studies seem unscientific where the intention is to control all the variables. So by the admission of unconscious communication, we allow influences and variables that are not consciously known. The standard response to that problem has been to attempt a reduction to so-called objective research methods. In that pursuit, there is a move towards quantitative and standardised data, which can be shown to have validity and reliability. In other words, the aim is to reduce and exclude uncontrolled unconscious influences. However, there is, on the surface at least, a paradox in excluding the very thing one is studying: the activity of the unconscious on others. This is perhaps the single most important reason why it has been so difficult to establish a standard method for psychoanalytic studies research.

It remains a fact that the instrument for the investigation of the human unconscious can only be another human unconscious. As Freud put it, the analyst's mind has to be a delicate receiving apparatus. The awareness that the research may be invalidated by the impact on the research of the very thing that is being researched is unfortunate and paradoxical. We need, however, to confront it. As mentioned earlier, it is not a problem that we must infer our data and results; most scientists do not immediately perceive what they make conclusions about. However, we have to make inferences about the unconscious mind making inferences itself about the researcher's mind. It is the very impact on the unconscious mind in the research that we have to allow and of which we have to take notice. What you will find in many of these chapters is an awareness of this kind of problem and then a turn to finding ways of capturing the workings of this hidden interaction.

One of the important strategies for picking up the unconscious effects is to consider process *in the research activity* in contrast to the thematic analysis of what appears on the surface. Freud's dream analysis was thematic, picking up common threads in the various streams of associations that led from the different elements of the dream. Instead, moments of surprising *process* can occur, like the sudden emergence of avoidance that Hollway observed (Hollway and Jefferson, 2012) indicating a 'defended subject', who had, unconsciously, to skirt around a topic. The skirting around is the indicator and is picked up by the observing unconscious as a hiatus, an unexpected move that leaves a gap or a jump in continuity. It is not the new topic that is jumped to, but the fact of the jump itself. Variations in this method by which the unconscious both indicates and avoids itself will be found.

But the unconscious does more than mark a change of direction, it significantly affects the mind of the interviewer or observer. There has been a good deal of discussion in the literature of what has been, loosely, called 'countertransference', in parallel perhaps to the clinical literature, where countertransference has, also loosely, been discussed frequently in recent years. The term means now the collection of affective responses the clinician feels whilst in the context of working with his or her patient. It is indeed believed to be a product in the clinical setting of an unconscious communication. The issue, not yet decided perhaps, is whether the conception can be validly applied to the research setting. There are significant differences. In particular, in the clinical setting, the unconscious communication resulting in an affective position in the analyst is a communication made in the interests of some aim of the patient – either insight or a defensive enactment. In the research setting, does the subject engage unconsciously for the same purposes? The patient in analysis needs something from his or her analyst; in the research setting, the researcher needs something from his or her subject. The relations of need and power are reversed. Does this make a difference to what can be inferred from the data that the 'instrument' (the researcher's unconscious) is producing for analysis?

An easy kind of expansion of the term 'countertransference' within the clinical setting has not necessarily been helpful for academic/professional communication. Whatever the answers, the focus in psychoanalytic studies is the feeling states of the researcher, and the *process* by which they come about. So we must be wary of the impact on who is motivated for what.

An increasing number of social science research studies have tried to elaborate many of these aspects and challenges of using countertransference. Devereux (1967) early on called our attention to the use of countertransference to better understand what might be happening in research. A number of current studies discuss how countertransference might be used to discover previously unrecognised material (Hansson and Dybbroe, 2012; Roper, 2003, 2014; Theodosius, 2006; Morgenroth, 2010; Whitehouse-Hart, 2012; Price, 2005, 2006; Garfield et al., 2010; Martinez-Salgado, 2009; Arnaud, 2012; Franchi and Molli, 2012; Khan, 2014). Jervis (2012) points to the importance of the use of countertransference in research supervision, and Rizq (2008) discusses the use of both transference and countertransference in qualitative research paradigms. The studies of Froggett and Hollway (2010) and Hollway (2010) focus on the researcher's emotional response. There have also been certain critiques on the use of transference and countertransference in research (Frosh and Baraitser, 2008; Frosh, 2010), emphasising the danger of attributing researchers' feelings to research subjects and observational fields.

The current field

Social science has been engaged with psychoanalysis, and indeed social research studies making use of such psychoanalytic conceptualisations have been steadily developing over the last decade in various countries across the world. In preparation for the book, KS has conducted a scoping review to systematically map the existing studies by using a combination of web search, the electronic database PEP Web, twelve peer-reviewed journals in the area of applied psychoanalysis and qualitative methodology searched separately, as well as by contacting editors and researchers in the field. The results were then organised into categories of subfields, and we have tried to include studies that have particularly focused on and elaborated how they have used psychoanalytic thinking in developing their particular methods within the last ten to fifteen years. The review is intended for researchers and research students to survey the field of opportunities when they are choosing the method for their own projects.

A growing number of psychoanalytic anthropology and ethnography studies has used psychoanalysis as a complementary method in their discussions, ethnographic cases, and interpretations. Psychoanalytically oriented anthropologists adopt a wide range of psychoanalytic methods and practices to examine symbols, and relational and interactive processes. Mimica (2006, 2014) studies dream experiences, speech, and knowledge among the Yagwoia people of the Papua New Guinea highlands; Elliot et al. (2012) investigate identity transitions of first-time mothers in an inner-city multicultural environment; Chapin (2014) uses the analysis of researchers' dreams as a key to analysis of children's response to indulgence; Rae-Espinoza (2014) considered both a dynamic culture and a dynamic psyche and defence mechanisms in their study of children's reactions to parental emigration; Rahimi (2014) investigated the meaning and political subjectivity in psychotic illness; Prasad's (2014) field research explored how neo-colonial sites may significantly change researchers' conceptions of self and other; Stanfield (2006) studied the transformation of racially wounded communities and the role of psychoanalytic ethnography; Khan (2014) utilised psychoanalytic conceptualisations in an anthropological study of extreme violence in Pakistan; Ramvi (2010, 2012) elaborated how a psychoanalytical method can illuminate the collected data when researching school teachers as well as the need for anthropologists to remain open to the experience; Devisch (2006) advocated a type of post-colonial and psychoanalytically inspired anthropology in the study of poverty-stricken Yaka people in Congo. Martinez-Salgado (2009) discussed how a critical psychoanalytical perspective shapes the study of poor urban families in southern Mexico.

Studies using narrative methods have also integrated psychoanalysis. A major development in the UK is the free association narrative interview (FANI), also discussed by Nick Midgely and Josh Holmes in this book (Hollway, 2008, 2009, 2010; Hollway and Jefferson, 2012). Additionally, there have been various applications of the method. Urwin (2007) discussed its use in a study of mothers' identities in an inner London borough, while Lertzman (2012) used it alongside in-depth interviews exploring environmental awareness, and Garfield et al. (2010) and Whitehouse-Hart (2012) investigated the necessity of supervision in using FANI as well as the dynamics between supervisees and supervisors. Ramvi (2010) used the method to elicit stories about teachers' relationships and challenging situations.

Other studies have also used psychoanalytic methods alongside, for instance, biographic narrative methods, such as BNIM, presented in this book as well (Chapter 12). Aydin et al. (2012) employed psychoanalytic understanding in their narrative analysis of cancer patients; Tucker (2010) used BNIM and Bion's ideas of containment to understand the stresses on school head teachers; Schmidt (2012) integrated psychoanalytic thinking to understand the inter- and intrasubjective tension between interviewers and interviewees in narrative interviews. Alford (2011) used psychoanalytic conceptualisations in his analysis of recorded interviews with survivors of the Holocaust, and Hoggett et al. (2010) integrated a dialogic approach to observe the effects of interpretations in the interview process.

Psychoanalytically informed methods have also been used in discursive analysis and psychology. Parker (2013) discusses the role of psychoanalysis in psychosocial research; Hook (2013) elaborates on the contributions of Lacanian discourse analysis to research practice, a type of psychoanalytic discourse analysis focused on trans-individual operation of discourses; Taylor (2014) offers conceptualisation of psychosocial subjects within discursive analysis which draws on psychoanalysis; Gough (2009) advocates the use of both discursive and psychoanalytic perspectives in facilitating the interpretation of qualitative data analysis. Glynos and Stavrakakis (2008) explore the potential of subjectivity in political theory and psychoanalysis in their study of fantasy to enhance the understanding of organisational practices.

Organisational studies have used a number of psychoanalytically informed methods. In addition to major developments such as socioanalytic methods (Long,

2013) and social defence systems methodologies (Armstrong and Rustin, 2014), Arnaud (2012) provides an overview of the application of psychoanalysis in organisational studies. Stein (2015, 2016) has used psychoanalytic conceptualisations to study trauma and fantasies of fusion affecting European leaders as well as rivalry and narcissism in organisations in crisis. Tuckett and Taffler (2008) study financial markets, and Fotaki and Hyde (2015) examine organisational blind spots as an organisational defence mechanism. Clancy et al. (2012) develop a theoretical framework on disappointment in organisations informed by psychoanalysis; Nossal (2013) discusses the use of drawings as an important tool to access the unconscious in organisations. Kenny (2012) uses psychoanalytically informed interpretations and analysis of data in the study of power in organisations. Numerous studies in organisations have also used Lacan's ideas (Driver, 2009a, 2009b, 2012).

Despite the initial suspicion towards integrating psychoanalytic understanding in sociology, more and more fruitful connections and integrations have occurred. Rustin (2008, 2016) reflects on the relations between psychoanalysis and social sciences. The contributors to Chancer and Andrews' (2014) edited book look into a variety of ways psychoanalysis can contribute to sociology. Clarke (2006) elaborates the use of psychoanalytic ideas around sociological issues and research methodology informed by psychoanalytic sociology, and Berger (2009) integrates psychodynamic and sociological ideas to analyse social problems. Theodosius (2006) studies the unconscious and relational aspects of emotions and emotional labour.

There have been a number of developments in historical research as well, such as studying Holocaust survivors and trauma (Alford, 2011; Rothe, 2012; Frie, 2017, 2018; Kohut, 2012); in oral history projects (Roper, 2003); and in researching totalitarian states of mind (Pick, 2012; Wieland, 2015). Scott (2012) has argued about the productive relationship between psychoanalysis and history.

Another growing research field is in the application of psychoanalytically informed methods in education studies. A number of studies have used modifications of infant observation methods to study various aspects of educational life (Franchi and Molli, 2012; Datler et al., 2010; Marsh, 2012; Adamo, 2008; Bush, 2005; Kanazawa et al., 2009).

Other studies in education have used various psychoanalytic conceptualisations to study hidden complexities. Price (2006, 2005) used projective identification, transference, and countertransference to study unconscious processes in classrooms, and Ramvi (2010) to study teachers' competency in the area of relationships. Archangelo (2007, 2010), Ashford (2012), and Mintz (2014) employ Bick's and Bion's conceptualisations in educational research. Shim (2012) studies teachers' interactions with texts from a psychoanalytic perspective. Vanheule and Verhaeghe (2004) use Lacanian conceptualisations to inform their research on professional burnout in special education.

Different educational research questions and areas have also been studied. Carson (2009) explores the potential of psychoanalysis to broaden understanding of self in action research on teaching and cultural differences in Canada. Lapping and Glynos (2017) study the dynamics affecting graduate teaching assistants, and McKamey (2011) researches immigrant students' conceptions of caring.

The chapters of the book have been selected out of this review using the following criteria:

1. The studies elaborate the use of psychoanalysis as a method of data collection and/or analysis in social science research.
2. The research methods are innovative and developed by pioneers in the last ten to fifteen years.
3. Wherever possible, research methods from different subfields were selected to map the existing field.

The outline of the book

The book is arranged in three parts. Part I presents an overview of the field. Part II puts on the map methodologies that have used psychoanalysis mainly in the data collection phase of research, and Part III presents methods that have used psychoanalysis mainly in the data analysis. As with most qualitative methodologies, it is not always possible to draw a strict differentiating line between the data collection and the data analysis of a study, but for the purposes of classifying the existing methods, we have divided them into methods that have used psychoanalysis mostly in the data generation and collection phase of a research project and methodologies that have used psychoanalysis predominantly in the data analysis stage of research. To that end, we have adapted the classification model developed by Beissel-Durrant (2004).

The book starts with an introductory Chapter 1 by Karl Figlio in which he emphasises that the psychoanalytic object has its place in social science, the process of sociation is permeated by the psychic level, and individual actors are under the influence of unconscious irrational processes. We could also observe, he argues, social-level forces impinging on the psyche through a social superego, which could be socially embedded but structured by internal objects.

Part II of the book presents psychoanalytic methods used predominantly in the data collection part of the research investigation.

Chapter 2 on socioanalytic interviewing by Susan Long examines the concept of the associative unconscious (originally described in Long and Harney, 2013), the nature of socioanalysis, and the application of socioanalytic ideas to interviewing, mainly in studying organisations. A central feature of the thinking is the importance of the social field (similar to the concept of Foulkes), whereby the individual is constructed, in part, by the field of relations. Long describes the socioanalytic interview as giving access to the associative unconscious of the organisational system as a whole, which is the object of the research, and which could emerge and be observed through transference and countertransference between interviewers and interviewees.

Chapter 3 by Nick Midgley and Joshua Holmes provides an extensive overview of current developments in psychoanalytically informed qualitative interview methods such as free association narrative interviews (FANI) and theme-centred interviews, scenic understanding, and the use of notions of the defended subject, transference, and countertransference in the process of data collection/interviewing. The authors present an additional method of reverie-informed interviewing based on a concept of the unconscious matrix formed by the transference–countertransference interactions between interviewer and interviewee.

Chapter 4 by Henning Salling Olesen and Thomas Leithäuser discusses the use of psychoanalytic understanding of unconscious aspects of social life alongside a theory of subjectivity and interpretation methodology based on hermeneutic experiences from text analysis. The conceptualisations of scenic understanding, in which free-floating attention and emotional associations of the researchers are used during text analysis, and thematic group discussion, in which participants are encouraged to explore experiences in relation to a theme, including those that are not conscious, are elaborated.

The final chapter in this section, Chapter 5 by Simona Reghintovschi, presents another innovative methodology by applying Ezriel's conceptualisations of the psychoanalytic clinical interview as an experimental situation in which three types of relationships between interviewer and interviewee can be tested. She presents a study demonstrating the possibility to observe and pinpoint unconscious sources of chronic conflicts affecting psychoanalytic organisations themselves through psychoanalytically informed interviews combining hermeneutic and causal perspectives to test different psychoanalytic concepts.

The next two chapters discuss how psychoanalytic thinking and ideas can be applied in psychoanalytically informed observational studies.

Chapter 6 by Wilhelm Skogstad presents an overview of the method of psychoanalytic observations of organisations and examines the links with the clinical practice of psychoanalysis and the method of infant observation as well as the theoretical concepts of the anxiety/defence model, splitting, projection and projective identification, transference and countertransference, and psychosocial culture underpinning this observational method. He emphasises the use of the observer's subjectivity in the data collection and elaborates the specific conditions for conducting systematic observations.

Chapter 7 by Peter Elfer continues the exploration of the anxiety/defence model of psychoanalytic observations as applied to nursery research. He argues that psychoanalytic observation methods based on Bick's model of infant observation offer a means to access the unspoken aspects of the mind. Psychoanalytic observation draws from direct observation of behaviour from which unconscious communications can be inferred. Peter Elfer discusses the potential of the method for use by non-clinically trained observers as a research tool in data collection and also for enabling the exploration of current issues related to nursery organisation and practice.

Part III of the book presents methods that have used psychoanalysis predominantly in the data analysis stage of a research project.

Chapter 8 offers an exploration of integrating psychoanalytic thinking with visual methods for data collection. The chapter by Rose Mersky and Burkard Sievers presents two action research methods – social photo-matrix (SPM) and social dream-drawing (SDD) – that are part of the larger group of socioanalytic methods, and the chapter outlines their theoretical underpinnings. The methods can be used to access the hidden complexities in organisations, and they make use of research participants' dreams and free associations to photographs as raw material that allows for unconscious processes to resurface and become available for thinking and further analysis.

Chapter 9 by Gillian Walker and R. D. Hinshelwood discusses the possibility to operationalise psychoanalytic concepts. The chapter presents the steps needed to define operational features and illustrates how the operationalisation of the container–contained conceptualisations is used in empirical research.

Chapter 10 by Kalina Stamenova presents comparative analysis of overlapping psychoanalytic concepts by using operationalised sets of criteria of envy and frustration. The operationalisation allows for establishing differentiating features, first at a theoretical level, and then the two sets of observable criteria can be used to identify occurrences of such mental states in educational observation research.

Lisa Saville Young and Stephen Frosh advocate the integrated application of psychoanalysis alongside narrative methods in Chapter 11. The authors demonstrate how psychoanalytic understanding can enhance narrative analytic accounts of interview material by considering affective elements expressing interpersonal and societal interconnected subjectivities. The methodology allows for the analysis of continuously entwined interpersonal, intersubjective, and social and socio-political processes while at the same time allowing for reflexive space for the research project itself.

Chapter 12 by Tom Wengraf presents biographical narrative interview method and interpretation (BNIM). The narrative expression of the biographical subject situated in a social culture and an historical period can be analysed to illuminate both conscious anxieties and also unconscious cultural, societal, and historical tendencies. The chapter demonstrates how a twin-track case interpretation methodology can be used to avoid focusing exclusively on the inner world of the research participants or on the social world only, thus fostering a genuine psycho-societal understanding of situated subjectivities.

The final chapter, Chapter 13 by Linda Lundgaard Andersen, develops the tradition of using a psychoanalytic eye to analyse ethnographic records. She works in a psycho-societal tradition, which considers research data in relation to specific political-ethical attitudes of the contextual society that envelope the social entity focused on.

We hope readers will find the chapters informative, inspiring, and helpful with their own research endeavours.

References

Adamo, S. (2008), Observing educational relations in their natural context. *Infant Observation*, 11(2): 131–146.
Alford, F. (2011), Is the Holocaust traumatic? *Journal of Psycho-Social Studies*, 5(2): 14–44.
Archangelo, A. (2007), A psychoanalytic approach to education: 'problem' children and Bick's idea of skin formation. *Psychoanalysis, Culture and Society*, 12(4): 332–348.
Archangelo, A. (2010), Social exclusion, difficulties with learning and symbol formation: a Bionian approach. *Psychoanalysis, Culture and Society*, 15(4): 315–327.
Armstrong, D., and Rustin, M. (2014), *Social Defences against Anxiety: Explorations in a Paradigm*. London: Karnac.
Arnaud, G. (2012), The contribution of psychoanalysis to organization studies and management. *Organization Studies*, 33(9): 1121–1135.
Ashford, E. (2012), *Learning from Experience: The Case Study of a Primary School*. Unpublished PhD thesis, Canterbury Christchurch University.
Aydin, E., Gullouglu, B., and Kuscu, K. (2012), A psychoanalytic qualitative study of subjective life experiences of women with breast cancer. *Journal of Research Practice*, 8(2): 1–15.
Beissel-Durrant, G. (2004), *A Typology of Research Methods within the Social Sciences*. NCRM working paper.
Berger, L. (2009), *Averting Global Extinction: Our Irrational Society as Therapy Patient*. New York: Jason Aronson.
Bush, A. (2005), Paying close attention at school: some observations and psychoanalytic perspectives on the educational underachievement of teenage boys. *Infant Observation*, 8(1): 69–79.
Carson, T. (2009), Teaching and cultural difference: exploring the potential for a psychoanalytically informed action research. In S. E. Noffke and B. Somekh (eds.), *The SAGE Handbook of Educational Action Research*. London: SAGE, pp. 347–357.
Chancer, L., and Andrews, J. (2014), *The Unhappy Divorce of Sociology and Psychoanalysis: Diverse Perspectives on the Psychosocial*. Basingstoke: Palgrave Macmillan.
Chapin, B. (2014), Dreamwork and fieldwork in Sri Lanka. *Clio's Psyche*, 20(4): 395–399.
Clancy, A., Vince, R., and Gabriel, Y. (2012), That unwanted feeling: a psychodynamic study of disappointment in organizations. *British Journal of Management*, 23(4): 518–531.
Clarke, S. (2006), Theory and practice: psychoanalytic sociology as psycho-social studies. *Sociology*, 40(6): 1153–1169.
Datler, W., Datler, M., and Funder, A. (2010), Struggling against a feeling of becoming lost: a young boy's painful transition to day care. *Infant Observation*, 13(1): 65–87.
Devereux, G. (1967), *From Anxiety to Method in the Behavioral Sciences*. The Hague: Mouton & Co.
Devisch, R. (2006), A psychoanalytic revisiting of fieldwork and intercultural borderlinking. *Social Analysis: The International Journal of Social and Cultural Practice*, 50(2): 121–147.
Driver, M. (2009a), From loss to lack: stories of organizational change as encounters with failed fantasies of self, work and organization. *Organization*, 16(3): 353–369.
Driver, M. (2009b), Struggling with lack: a Lacanian perspective on organizational identity. *Organization Studies*, 30(1): 55–72.

Driver, M. (2012), The lack of power and the power of lack in leadership as a discursively constructed identity. *Organization Studies*, 34(3): 407–422.

Elliot, H., Ryan, J., and Hollway, W. (2012), Research encounters, reflexivity and supervision. *International Journal of Social Research Methodology*, 15(5): 433–444.

Fotaki, M., and Hyde, P. (2015), Organizational blind spots: splitting, blame and idealization in the National Health Service. *Human Relations*, 68(3): 441–462.

Franchi, V., and Molli, A. (2012), Teaching and implementing classroom observations in France and Italy: a preliminary review. *Infant Observation*, 15(3): 281–296.

Freud, S, (1913), Totem and taboo. In *The Standard Edition of the Complete Works of Sigmund Freud, Vol. 13* (pp. 1–161). London: Hogarth.

Freud, S. (1915), The unconscious. In *The Standard Edition of the Complete Works of Sigmund Freud, Vol. 14* (pp. 159–215). London: Hogarth.

Freud, S. (1921), Group psychology and the analysis of the ego. In *The Standard Edition of the Complete Works of Sigmund Freud, Vol. 18* (pp. 65–144). London: Hogarth.

Frie, R. (2017), *Not in My Family: German Memory and Responsibility after the Holocaust*. New York: Oxford University Press.

Frie, R. (2018), *History Flows Through Us: Germany, the Holocaust, and the Importance of Empathy*. Abingdon, Oxon, and New York: Routledge.

Froggett, L., and Hollway, W. (2010), Psychosocial research analysis and scenic understanding. *Psychoanalysis, Culture and Society*, 15(3): 281–301.

Frosch, S. (2007), Disintegrating qualitative research. *Theory and Psychology*, 17(5): 635–653.

Frosh, S. (2010), *Psychoanalysis Outside the Clinic*. Basingstoke, UK: Palgrave Macmillan.

Frosh, S., and Baraitser, L. (2008), Psychoanalysis and psychosocial studies. *Psychoanalysis, Culture and Society*, 13(4): 346–365.

Garfield, S., Reavey, P., and Kotecha, M. (2010), Footprints in toxic landscape: reflexivity and validation in the free association narrative interview (FANI) method. *Qualitative Research in Psychology*, 7(2): 156–169.

Glynos, J., and Stavrakakis, Y. (2008), *Lacan and Political Subjectivity: Fantasy and Enjoyment in Psychoanalysis and Political Theory*. Swansea, paper presented at the 58th PSA Annual Conference.

Gough, B. (2009), A psycho-discursive approach to analysing qualitative interview data, with reference to a father–son relationship. *Qualitative Research*, 9(5): 527–545.

Groenewald, T. (2004), A phenomenological research design illustrated. *International Journal of Qualitative Methods*, 3(1): 42–55.

Hansson, B., and Dybbroe, B. (2012), Autoethnography and psychodynamics in interrelational spaces of the research process. *Journal of Research Practice*, 8(2).

Hinshelwood, R. D. (1996), Convergences with psycho-analysis. In I. Parker and R. Spiers (eds.), *Psychology and Society* (pp. 93–104). London: Pluto Press.

Hoggett, P. et al. (2010), Working psycho-socially and dialogically in research. *Psychoanalysis, Culture and Society*, 15(2): 173–188.

Hollway, W. (2008), The importance of relational thinking in the practice of psychosocial research: ontology, epistemology, methodology and ethics. In S. Clarke, P. Hogget, and H. Hahn (eds.), *Object Relations and Social Relations* (pp. 137–162). London: Karnac.

Hollway, W. (2009), Applying the 'experience-near principle to research: psychoanalytically informed methods. *Journal of Social Work Practice*, 23(4): 461–474.

Hollway, W. (2010a), Conflict in the transitions to becoming a mother: a psycho-social approach. *Psychoanalysis, Culture and Society*, 15(2): 136–155.

Hollway, W. (2010b), Preserving vital signs: the use of psychoanalytically informed interviewing and observation in psycho-social longitudinal research. In R. Thompson (ed.), *Intensity and Insight: Qualitative Longitudinal Methods as a Route to the Psycho-Social*, Timescapes Working Paper, Series No. 3.

Hollway, W., and Jefferson, T. (2012), *Doing Qualitative Research Differently*, second edn. London: SAGE.

Hook, D. (2013), Discourse analysis: terminable and interminable. *Qualitative Research in Psychology*, 10(3): 249–253.

Jervis, S. (2012), Parallel process in research supervision: turning the psycho-social focus towards supervisory relationships. *Psychoanalysis, Culture and Society*, 17(3): 296–313.

Jones, E. (1925), Mother-right and the sexual ignorance of savages. *International Journal of Psycho-Analysis*, 6(2): 109–130. [Reprinted in E. Jones, *Essays in Applied Psychoanalysis*. London: Hogarth, 1951.]

Jung, C. (1969), *Archtypes and the Collective Unconscious*. London: Routledge.

Kanazawa, A., Hirai, S., Ukai, N., and Hubert, M. (2009), The application of infant observation technique as a means of assessment and therapeutic intervention for 'classroom breakdown' at a school for Japanese-Koreans. *Infant Observation*, 12(3): 348–355.

Kenny, K. (2012), 'Someone big and important': identification and affect in an international development organization. *Organization Studies*, 33(9): 1175–1193.

Khan, N. (2014), Countertransference in an anthropological study of extreme violence in Pakistan. *Clio's Psyche*, 20(4): 408–411.

Kohut, T. A. (2012), *A German Generation: An Experiential History of the Twentieth Century*. New Haven and London: Yale University Press.

Lapping, C., and Glynos, J. (2018), Psychical contexts of subjectivity and performative practices of remuneration: teaching assistants' narratives of work. *Journal of Education Policy*, 33(1): 23–42.

Leininger, A. (2014), Participant observation in toxic interactions. *Clio's Psyche*, 20(4): 399–403.

Lertzman, R. (2012), Researching psychic dimensions of ecological degradation: notes from the field. *Psychoanalysis, Culture and Society*, 17(1): 92–101.

Long, S. (2013), *Socioanalytic Methods*. London: Karnac.

Lukács, G. (1923), *History and Class Consciousness*. London: Merlin, 1971.

Malinowski, B. (1923), Psychoanalysis and anthropology. *Nature*, 112: 650–651.

Marsh, A. (2012), The Oedipal child starts school: some thoughts about the difference in the experience of starting school for boys and girls at four years of age. *Psychodynamic Practice: Individuals, Groups and Organisations*, 18(3): 311–323.

Martinez-Salgado, C. (2009), Qualitative inquiry with women in poverty in Mexico City: reflections on the emotional responses of a research team. *International Journal of Qualitative Studies in Education*, 22(3): 297–313.

McKamey, C. (2011), Uncovering and managing unconscious ways of 'looking': a case study of researching care. *Psychodynamic Practice*, 17(4): 403–417.

Mimica, J. (2006a), Descended from the celestial rope: from the father to the son, and from the ego to the cosmic self. *Social Analysis: The International Journal of Social and Cultural Practice*, 50(2): 77–105.

Mimica, J. (2006b), Explorations in psychoanalytic ethnography. *Social Analysis: The International Journal of Social and Cultural Practice*, 50(2): 1–24.

Mimica, J. (2014), A psychoanalytic ethnography among the Yagwoia. *Clio's Psyche*, 20(4): 427–431.

Mintz, J. (2014), *Professional Uncertainty, Knowledge and Relationship in the Classroom*. London: Routledge.

Morgenroth, C. (2010), The research relationship, enactments and 'counter-transference' analysis: on the significance of scenic understanding. *Psychoanalysis, Culture and Society*, 15(3): 267–280.

Nossal, B. (2013), The use of drawing as a tool in socioanalytic exploration. In S. Long (ed.), *Socioanalytic Methods* (pp. 67–91). London: Karnac.

Parker, I. (2004), *Qualitative Psychology: Introducing Radical Research*. London: Open University Press.

Parker, I. (2010), The place of transference in psychosocial research. *Journal of Theoretical and Philosophical Psychology*, 30(1): 17–31.

Parker, I. (2013), Discourse analysis: dimensions of critique in psychology. *Qualitative Research in Psychology*, 10: 223–239.

Pick, D. (2012), *The Pursuit of the Nazi Mind: Hitler, Hess and the Analysts*. Oxford: Oxford University Press.

Prasad, A. (2014), You can't go home again; and other psychoanalytic lessons from crossing a neo-colonial border. *Human Relations*, 67(2): 233–257.

Price, H. (2005), Lutfa, a 'slow' learner: understanding school literacy learning in its social and emotional context. *Journal of Infant Observation and Its Applications*, 8(1): 45–57.

Price, H. (2006), Jumping the shadows: catching the unconscious in the classroom. *Journal of Social Work Practice*, 20(2): 145–161.

Rae-Espinoza, H. (2014), Culturally constituted defence mechanisms for globalisation. *Clio's Psyche*, 20(4): 411–422.

Rahimi, S. (2014), Meaning and political subjectivity in psychotic illness. *Clio's Psyche*, 20(4): 435–438.

Ramvi, E. (2010), Out of control: a teacher's account. *Psychoanalysis, Culture and Society*, 15(4): 328–345.

Ramvi, E. (2012), A psychoanalytic approach to fieldwork. *Journal of Research Practice*, 8(2).

Rivers, W. H. R. (1920), *Instincts and the Unconscious*. Cambridge: Cambridge University Press.

Rizq, R. (2008), The research couple: a psychoanalytic perspective on dilemmas in the qualitative research interview. *European Journal of Psychotherapy and Counselling*, 10(1): 39–53.

Roper, M. (2003), Analysing the analysed: transference and countertransference in the oral history. *Oral History*, 31(2): 20–32.

Roper, M. (2014), The unconscious work of history. *Cultural and Social History*, 11(2): 169–193.

Rothe, K. (2012), Anti-Semitism in Germany today and the intergenerational transmission of guilt and shame. *Psychoanalysis, Culture and Society*, 17(1): 16–34.

Rustin, M. (2008), For dialogue between psychoanalysis and constructionism: a comment on paper by Frosh and Baraitser. *Psychoanalysis, Culture and Society*, 13(4): 406–415.

Rustin, M. (2016), Sociology and psychoanalysis. In A. Elliot and J. Prager (eds.), *The Routledge Handbook of Psychoanalysis in the Social Sciences and Humanities*. London: Routledge.

de Saussure, F. (1916), *Course in General Linguistics*. New York: Philosophical Library. [English translation, 1959.]

Schlapobersky, J. (2016), *From the Couch to the Circle: Group Analytic Psychotherapy in Practice*. London: Routledge.

Schmidt, C. (2012), Using psychodynamic interaction as a valuable source of information in social research. *Journal of Research Practice*, 8(2).

Scott, J. (2012), The incommensurability of psychoanalysis and history. *History and Theory*, 51(1): 63–83.

Shim, J. M. (2012), Exploring how teachers' emotions interact with intercultural texts: a psychoanalytic perspective. *Curriculum Inquiry*, 42(4): 472–496.

Smith, E. (1923), Preface. In W. H. R. Rivers, *Psychology and Politics*. London: Kegan Paul, Trench and Trubner.

Stanfield, J. (2006), Psychoanalytic ethnography and the transformation of racially wounded communities. *International Journal of Qualitative Studies in Education*, 19(3): 387–399.

Stavrakakis, Y. (2007), *The Lacanian Left: Psychoanalysis, Theory, Politics*. Edinburgh: Edinburgh University Press.

Taylor, S. (2014), Discursive and psychosocial? Theorising a complex contemporary subject. *Qualitative Research in Psychology*, 12(1): 8–12.

Theodosius, C. (2006), Recovering emotion from emotion management. *Sociology*, 40(5): 893–910.

Tucker, S. (2010), An investigation of the stresses, pressures and challenges faced by primary school head teachers in a context of organisational change in schools. *Journal of Social Work Practice*, 24(1): 63–74.

Urwin, C. (2007), Doing infant observation differently? Researching the formation of mothering identities in an inner London borough. *Infant Observation*, 10(3): 239–251.

Vanheule, S., and Verhaeghe, P. (2004), Powerlessness and impossibility in special education: a qualitative study on professional burnout from a Lacanian perspective. *Human Relations*, 57(4): 497–519.

Whitehouse-Hart, J. (2012), Surrendering to the dream: an account of the unconscious dynamics of a research relationship. *Journal of Research Practice*, 8(2).

Wieland, C. (2015), *The Fascist State of Mind and the Manufacturing of Masculinity*. London and New York: Routledge.

Part I

An overview of qualitative methodologies

Chapter 1

A psychoanalytic view of qualitative methodology
Observing the elemental psychic world in social processes

Karl Figlio

Introduction

In this chapter, I will not survey this vast field, but stick to a defined project. I define qualitative methodology as a means of getting to know a particular kind of object, one that does not exist in three-dimensional space, cannot be seen, and cannot be characterised in material terms. It is a virtual object, one perceived inside a field of imagination. Social examples might include 'the people', 'public opinion', 'nation', 'society', 'government', 'parents/parenting'. Individual examples might include 'the individual', 'mind', 'personality', 'character', 'conscience'. They are real and have objective qualities, but they can be viewed only inside an observing mind. Take public opinion, with its two unknowns: public and opinion. In a social analysis, one could point to surveys in an attempt to capture public opinion, or even the idea of a public, but they become objects in their own right only in the interpreting activity of the observer. The cohesiveness of a 'public' is an experience of a mind aiming for internal coherence as it observes a social object that, to be an object, is also coherent.

Psychoanalysts speak of a psychoanalytic object (Andrade De Azevedo, Bion, Sandler), a non-sensuous object, recognised by the analytic working unit in the analytic setting as an observation of transference and countertransference. It is a crystallisation of a process in the moment, but it can be recreated and can achieve stability as an object. An example of a psychoanalytic object is the dynamic relationship among the agencies of the psyche, as in Freud's structural model. The relationship between superego, id, ego, perceptual reality congeals into a structure, projected into the analytic relationship, held in being there, and observable in the analytic collaboration. These solidified structures can lie unnoticed in the unconscious, but flash into the observational field in moments when these internal, dynamically based structures are stressed. I call such moments transferential moments. Suddenly, one sees what was there, now thrown into relief. These moments form the basis of the methodology I am proposing.

I am further proposing that the concept of a psychoanalytic object can be – and must be – carried over to the social. It forms an essential ingredient of a psychoanalytic social methodology, a methodology that is inherently qualitative, as I have defined it above. It implies that the basis of this methodology – the place to confirm its existence and study it in detail – is to be found where one might least expect it: in the psychoanalytic consulting room, or, as I will explain later, in a social equivalent. The reason for looking there is that we need the mind – two minds, or a few more – to grasp the qualitative features of the psychoanalytic social object.

We need two minds because this object has certain features that are quite different from the features captured in sociological analysis. They are experiences, often irrational and, therefore, incomprehensible. And just as the square root of $-X$ is incomprehensible, but has knowable consequences, so too is, for example, ambivalence: holding, simultaneously, two contradictory thoughts or feelings. Unconscious, irrational ambivalence is expressed as anxiety, which is trapped in a 'social defence' system that forms the inner surface of the social structure observed by sociologists. Two or more minds are needed to make the observation because these irrational features can be known only through their consequences, principally through their being parsed out into their components, now apparent in the relationships between the parts. I will take up this example later.

The phenomenological tradition in sociology

The sociological traditions loosely called 'phenomenological' or 'mico-sociological' come close to psychoanalysis in defining an object of study akin to a psychoanalytic object. The theoretical and methodological approaches in sociology, ranging from phenomenology to ethnomethodology, share the view that society is not external to the members of society, but is created and sustained by them; and not only by their interactions, but by their subjectivities and by their interpretations of each other's subjectivities. These approaches share an interest in the formation of individual and social identity through jointly held expectations about how life proceeds, in jointly held meanings and in the idea of the social as a continuous process of aligning individuals with each other and interpreting each other.

The phenomenological lineage, leading from Husserl through Simmel, Schutz, Mead, and Goffman, to Garfinkle's ethnomethodology, is concerned with a 'natural attitude' towards the everyday life of both social actors and social scientists. Natural attitude was a term invented by Husserl and developed by Schutz and Garfinkle (see Leiter, 1980, pp. 7–11, 42). The idea that the world was seen through the eyes of observers, and could not be broken down into facts that lay outside their view, seen as if from a universal point of view, also had roots in American pragmatism (Dewey, James) and in the holistic philosophy of Whitehead (to whom Schutz often referred). Social actors invest meaning in their lives and interpret the meanings invested by others. Phenomenologists base this interpretive capacity on the idea of the interchangeability of social actors: standing in place of an other and seeing the world as the other would. They seek to describe units of 'sociation' (Simmel), which are based in face-to-face relationships in a common-sense world of commonly held ideas, expectations, and attitudes: the 'natural attitude' of Husserl, Schutz, and Garfinkle.[1] This interpretive process is called the *Verstehende* approach to the world (Weber).

In this tradition, social events that build up society occur between 'wide-awake' adults (Schutz, 1945, pp. 212–214, 1953a, p. 7). Their 'natural attitude' towards the world, understood in common-sense terms, takes what is unconscious to be simply what is out of awareness because it is not an object of attention. Acting in situations that are always about to happen, with incomplete knowledge, social actors necessarily anticipate each other's behaviour and subjectivity – interpret it – in a field of pragmatic action.

To observe the unobservable experiences of sociation, one must interpret. And to interpret, one must accept some form of identification or comparison of the observer's experience with the experience of the observed. Schutz simply calls it an assumption that one's fellows share one's own subjectivity, and that, therefore, their point of view is like one's own, giving a sense of objectivity to observations (Heritage, 1984, p. 55; Schutz, 1945, pp. 218–222).[2] The subject, including the social scientist, reaches over the gap between them, to speak as the other would speak if he or she could convey an awareness of their situation.

The elements of social life are units of inference between individuals, whose subjectivity and agency are only realised in these inferences. They come to experience themselves as actors, and along with conferring an identity to others, others confer their identity on them. At a more rudimentary level, one might say that others see themselves in the eyes of the observer, by inferring what the observer sees; and the observer sees him- or herself in the eyes of the other, by inferring what the other sees.

Georg Simmel, a central figure in this tradition, sought to define fundamental elements of 'sociation', as abstract forces of association, which were the proper object of a discipline of sociology. He based these abstract forces on the senses of vision, hearing, smell, and functions such as eating through which individuals relate themselves to others. For Simmel, a simultaneous sensory impression is a social bond, a 'construction of a sociated existence' (1907, p. 110). We can imagine how that might occur: everyone sees the same sunset or hears the same music or speech, and they feel themselves to be as one, in sharing that event.[3]

The defining feature of this phenomenological tradition was the human capacity to recognise an other as a person, like oneself: *zu verstehen* the other as a person by inference and interpretation. In ethnomethodology, for example, one looks for the interaction that shows the creation and maintenance of a common world of everyday experience. One looks for the moments in interactions at which an *et cetera*, an anticipated pattern, might render a situation intelligible as one of a range of '"ad hocing" practices [that] have been an important theme of ethnomethodological research' (Wieder, 1974, p. 157, n. 5).

What distinguishes the observing social scientist from other members of society is the capacity to maintain a distance from the observed. The *Verstehende* observer is only partially immersed in the commonly constructed social world, not wholly assimilated to it, and must interpret. Referring to Mead and

Simmel, Schutz refers to the essential incompleteness of the commonly embraced world as the basis for social roles and the driving force for a structured society of actors who sustain a common-sense and essentially imaginative shared world of 'consociates' (1953a, pp. 15–19). Equally, Schutz argues that one must not impose a mechanical, causal order on the social world, which would mistake the *behaviour* of others for the *meaning* of their behaviour (Schutz, 1945, 1953a, esp. pp. 16–19; 1953b; Simmel, 1918, p. 125; Weber, 1906, pp. 120–122).

Social scientists can stand back from the action, and construct models of social activity, based on assuming one's fellows are like oneself. Models, expectations, and hunches, based on a common-sense world shared with other social scientists, establish an objectifying difference from the social actor. The 'normal' relationship of the social-scientist-observer to the observed is one based on an expectation of predictable behaviour along with interpreted intention, in which intention acts as a force (Schutz, 1953b).

The sociology of relating as the fundamental constituent of the social

In his treatment of 'micro-sociology' – the sociology of relating – the eminent sociologist and psychoanalyst Neil Smelser (1997) says that trust is the essential ingredient of relationships, and that it extends into institutionalised trust as the systemic dimension of the sociological element of relating. He concludes his discussion by saying that every level of human interaction includes a sociological component (p. 27). His list of the higher level of organisation that must be included in any account of a lower level of organisation is interesting in this respect.

> My own effort to resolve this problematic [of the temptation in the social sciences to fall into an individualist reductionism] has always been to insist on the conceptual validity of higher levels of formulation... [I]t is impossible to understand and explain events, situations, and processes of 'lower' units without appealing to some higher organization by which they are constrained. Physics requires its chemistry, chemistry its biochemistry, biochemistry its biological organism, biological organism its integrative mental processes, and individuals their social organization, if we are to proceed beyond atomistic characterizations and understand more complex behaviors and sequences.
>
> (1997, p. 31)

In Smelser's hierarchy of explanation, there are particular conditions of the 'higher' into which the 'lower' must fit. The properties of water cannot be derived from the properties of the hydrogen and oxygen that make up water, and hydrogen and oxygen form water under the constraint that two hydrogen atoms bond with one oxygen atom. We have to add additional information to what we know of hydrogen and oxygen, in order to get from the elements to the molecule of water, and then from the molecule of water to the macro-structure of water as a solid, liquid, or gas. The same is true of amino acids bonded into proteins and all higher-order structures.

There is, however, a break in this hierarchical sequence when mental processes appear, both at the interface between biological organism and individual and at the interface between individual and social. At these junctures, the psyche is our main concern, in a way that the bonding valences of atoms and molecules are not. No new kind of knowledge is added in the case of valences; but something new is added in the case of the psyche, and that something new is the main focus of our intense interest. If we are not aware of it, we can assert that it is not there, but we can also say that it is there and that we are unaware of it, because it is profoundly unconscious in the psychoanalytic meaning of unconscious. Then we have a domain to study, at one with the subjective drive to be interested. We know what it feels like to be interested, to be curious, to have an urge to know, to be animated, and we take the other to be similarly animated. We have direct evidence of a core feature of the psyche, the subject and object of our study; and psychoanalysis specialises in that dual knowing, providing a theoretical and empirical base for this unique study.

I would, therefore, also reverse Smelser's hierarchy, and claim that there is no sociological level that is not permeated by psyches in relationship with each other and with a collective dimension, and I propose that it can be described and theoretically and empirically grounded in psychoanalysis. Psychoanalysis adds an essential ingredient to what is missing in a sociology grounded within a dimension described as inherently and irreducibly social: the processes by which individuals are drawn into the systemic patterns called 'social' by sociologists (on micro-sociology, see Stolte, Fine, and Cook, 2001).

Psychoanalytic sociology

Not only is the sociated level permeated by the psychic level, but also the 'wide-awake' adult of a phenomenological analysis sits on an unconscious that is the core of the psyche – an unconscious profoundly different from the unawareness described by the phenomenologists, which is simply a lack of organised attention (Schutz and Luckman, 1983, pp. 314–317). It is unconscious by repression and other defences. Relationships built on this unconscious base are not attributable to a wide-awake adult, but to a conflicted personality in a conflicted social world. Indeed, psychoanalytically, 'individual' is not the element of sociation: rather, the elements that combine into social 'molecules' are the agencies of Freud's structural model (superego, ego, id) or later refinements of the model of the internal world. The jointly held, common-sensical, phenomenal world would be seen as an organised defence against the anxiety that would irrupt if individual actors were actually consciously to experience what they were thinking and doing, in the sense of the 'wide-awake' awareness of the phenomenological tradition. I will briefly illustrate three forms of this peculiar, non-common-sensical *Lebenswelt*: 1) irrational aspects of the unconscious, as in ambivalence; 2) the projection of primal elements of the psyche; 3) social behaviour as a defence against anxiety – a 'social defence system'.

Ambivalence

In his treatment of ambivalence, Neil Smelser (1998) gets to the heart of the essentially psychic dimension of the social as well as the individual. Ambivalence is a core psychoanalytic concept. It refers to loving and hating the *same* object, *simultaneously*. He argues that ambivalence is silently weeded out of sociological methodology, producing a grounding assumption that the social comprises assessable – ultimately measurable – components. The typifying methodology is the social survey, in which, for example, one ranks a range of attitudes across a sample population, from which one composes a portrait of a social group. The nation is one such group, with a profile that refers to degrees of allegiance to its various characteristics. The very structure of the survey eliminates ambivalence:

> Surveys often depict the world as though it is divided into people who are for and against someone or something – a clear distortion of the social-psychological reality of public feelings. This representation is then reified into an imagined 'public opinion'... Following this reasoning, we must regard attitude surveys not as revealed preferences but as a distorted structure of reality that minimizes and – in the process – delegitimizes both ambiguity and ambivalence.
>
> (1998, pp. 186–187)

Although one can express this idea quite simply in a grammatically faultless sentence, it is irrational. I cannot do justice to its complexity without appealing to a body of theory and clinical examples of the mood and thinking that accompanies ambivalence: mourning, reparative urges, restoration of aliveness, depression, despair, obsessional correction of dangerous thoughts, manic relief, retreat into paranoia, dividing the world into friends and enemies. In addition, ambivalence is an internal contradiction: it cannot exist over time. Instead, it drives defensive processes that crystallise into structures both of the psyche and of the social. We see ambivalence through these defences, and they provide us with a methodology for the study of the social.

Beneath the common-sense world of inference through which the social is built up, the other – unconscious – layer is neither common-sensical nor known to the actors. The process of sociation is not a smooth interaction that builds up a world held in common, including the sense of being an individual amongst others like oneself: it is a result of opposing forces, which makes sociation both desired and feared, the fundament of life and the extinguisher of life (primal ambivalence). Sociation includes paradoxical, delusional states that substitute for, yet appear to be, ordinary reality, as framed in social defence analysis. To the extent that processes of these sorts operate, everyday reality is an insecure basis for observation and theorising (on psychoanalysis as an exploration of subjectivity within a naturalistic framework, see Figlio, 2007; on delusion inside reality, see Figlio, 2017).

Here is a clinical vignette.

> A male patient complained of tension, which he fought to control by trying to impose relaxation upon himself – a demand for relaxation, which he inflicted on himself with self-hatred and fury at his tension. His tension seemed to be an embodied conflict – two sets of opposing muscular movements. The greatest tension was around his throat, mouth, neck, shoulders, and one side of his face. The tension around his throat and neck, he explained, started when he fell ill with glandular fever, then lost his girlfriend. These symptoms were frozen scenarios. Fragments of this sort comprised a conscious account, as pieces lodged in the mind without connections and without significance. One might infer that he used the pain and swelling from his glandular fever as a painful, conflicted relationship by identification with her. The swollen glands of the 'kissing fever' were erotised and felt to be physically held as part of him, through which he was punishing himself and his ex-girlfriend for a relationship that he desired, enacted, and repudiated.

In a psychoanalytically defined dimension, ambivalence is a force with social consequences. Not only does it stand beneath the range of conditions I mentioned above, it also drives the formation of groups. Ambivalence is inconceivable. It is a psychic catastrophe, which is recognised in its effects. The ambivalence in individual psychic reality is intensified as individuals gather, and finds a resolution by the compacting of individuals into at least two groups, which divide internal, contradictory aspects between them. The relationship between groups replaces contradiction inside the psyche with conflict between groups and with efforts either to subdue each other or to find forms of collaboration that diffuse the ambivalence.

The projection of primal elements of the psyche

I want to introduce the idea of primal elements of the psyche with a vignette from a psychodynamic observation of a two-week-old baby boy with his mother.[4]

> His mother sat him on her lap facing away from her. The observer could see his face clearly, but mother and baby could not see each other's faces. He held his left thumb effortlessly in his mouth and gummed it vigorously but not greedily. His fingers were extended towards his right eye. His mother, saying he mustn't get his fingers in his eyes, brushed gently over his forehead. It wasn't clear whether she actually pushed his hand away and his thumb out of his mouth, but

that was the effect. His left hand now moved to the same place on his face, as if repeating, with his hand, the movement she had just made. She wiped his lips with a cloth. His left hand went to the right side of his face, fingers extended and palm outwards, as if warding off a blow. He settled and yawned. She yawned and said he was making her sleepy.

One might infer from this observation that the baby displayed two forms of perception: 1) an imitation of his mother's gestures towards him – psychoanalytically, his imitative gestures repudiated the external reality of his mother; 2) an introjection – an eating – of his thumb as if it were his mother, an external object, now inside him as an internal object; therefore, partly external and partly of his own making. His imitative and introjective performances led to a peaceful re-settling in both baby and mother, as he became mother to her and to himself, just as she was mother to him. In his imitative tracing with his hand, coupled with his thumb-sucking, we can see his imitation as the origin of development into a capacity to perceive himself as an object, as if from mother's viewpoint. It extends into an identification with mother's care of him, then into a recognition of mother's mothering him. So, his awareness of mother, of himself, of his mothering mother, and of her mothering him, develop together.

Mother shows herself to be as if seized by his psyche: at first disturbed, then calmed. He makes use of her psychic capacity to develop his own (Bion's concept of 'containment'; Bion, 1962; Hinshelwood, 1989, pp. 246–253). A disturbance in the baby – hunger, discomfort, need, wish – simultaneously disturbs mother. This dissonance generates an urge to calm it. In this vignette, all was anticipation. The baby inferred the incipient disturbance of its quiet sucking through the mother's inference that he might poke his eye and her reaction to it; and, reciprocally, the mother's calm was restored by the baby's restoring his own calm, which he did through his mother's removing the danger to him.

These shared states are forms of primitive communication based on a phantasy of occupying the object with part of the self. In psychoanalysis, it is called 'projective identification'.[5] The baby's own urge to reduce his disturbed feeling of strangeness would, by projective identification, be equivalent to the mother's urge to reduce her own sense of strangeness to herself and to her baby; that is, the baby would be reaching into his mother's intentions as he sought to reduce his own feeling of strangeness in himself.[6] Her response, including her capacity to calm the baby, is inwardly brought towards being the same as the baby's own capacity to restore his composure.

Here is a model of an urge to relate, which starts with a psychosomatic pull towards imitation that subsumes the other as it garners an experience of being oneself. This tendency becomes a reading of the intentions of the other. One could say that we are always looking for indicators of an other's way of thinking, mostly unconscious, as an intuition into what we think. The search for meaning is based on the attribution of one's own state of mind – at base, the intrusion of one's own mind – (in)to the other. The aim is to dwell in the intention of the other – the flow of feeling and the line of thinking – as an objectifiable form of our own intention and line of thinking. It is a fundamental inferential process; not one based on common sense but on the occupation of one mind by another.

The projection of primitive elements of the psyche bonds the individual into a social group. As in the case of ambivalence, individual parts of psyches coalesce and are housed in groupings that are then brought into relationships with each other, and in that way, the 'individual' is re-assembled through these group relationships. Groups magnify the projection of primitive elements of their members' psyches, making it easily observable. For example, where two individuals might be inclined to reach an accord, their inclusion in a group tends towards radical division, a form of splitting in psychoanalytic terms. Now the perhaps visible positions each might hold appear, magnified, as a dispute between groups.

This observation also follows directly from Freud's model of the psyche (the 'structural model'): if individual ego ideals are held in common, the individual egos will be held in common; that is, the members will identify with each other (1921, pp. 105–116). In that sense, the group becomes a large psyche with the properties of a psyche. But note: the unit is not the individual of the historian or social scientist. The units are the id, superego or ego ideal, and the ego. The unit of consciousness – the individual of the historian and social scientist – is drawn into an irrational, affective sense of belonging or not belonging by these unconscious forces. This sense of a social being has little to do with a declared, conscious self-experience of a person or of chosen group membership.[7]

In a Freudian formulation, 'sociated existence' or 'communalising socialising effect' is reduced to 'identification', 'people' are reduced to 'ego' in relation to 'ego ideal', 'impression' becomes 'introjection'. Let it suffice to say that the ego is the psychic institution closest to 'I'; the ego ideal is the psychic institution closest to figures, such as parents, to whom one aspires, based on infantile residues of perfection; identification refers to a process of assimilation. A leader becomes the ideal part of each of the members of the group, by each member projecting into the leader his or her 'ego ideal'. With the ideal held in common for the group by its leader, outsiders projectively become a denigrated part of members and of the group as whole. These collective projective processes coalesce members into a group, which then idealises itself and attacks outsiders. Because the group is in effect led by its own idealised versions of reality, which correspond to wishes, it can be delusional in its conviction of the reality and justice of its views and actions (Chasseguet-Smirgel, 1985, pp. 76–93; Freud, 1921, esp. pp. 105–116; on the 'absolute' tendency in individuals and groups, see Figlio, 2006; on 'delusional enemies', see Figlio, 2017, pp. 73–100).

Following Freud's model, we can see that groups divide in order to preserve an internal homogeneity based on the perfection of the ego ideal. There is space for only one ego ideal in a group. Conflict within the group pushes towards a division, producing two groups, each with its ego ideal. In this process, conviction leaps to a new level because the ego ideal of each group has been returned to its purity. The ill-defined unease of the parent group becomes the 'rational' conflict between the groups produced by the splitting. The ambivalence, anxiety, and psychotic loss of secure identity – which cannot be borne – become conflict. It may be frightening, but it seems rational.

Without such a bond of inclusion, we have no idea of what makes a group. Without it, the historian and the social scientist are left reporting facts awaiting interpretation. To say that 90 per cent of a population voted for the same leader cannot be translated into, say, nationalist sentiment. It would need either the common-sense notion that such a majority implies a nationalist sentiment, or a psychoanalytic theory that speaks directly to the unconscious, affective bond. Such a bond underlies the experience of conscious individuality, drawing individuals unconsciously into a social formation without regard to their individual, conscious experience.

Social defence systems

In this model of group formation, the forces that hold groups together are the same forces that offer relief from bearing an emotional burden and complexity in the individual. But there is a difficulty, in that groups are built on a narcissistic architecture – nationalism in the case of societies (Wirth, 2009). Tolerating truth brings disillusionment and fracturing of narcissism, against which pride is retrenched as arrogance that can seem normal. A group picks out unacceptable features in another group, which invites projection of hurt pride and makes antipathy reasonable. What would seem to be a manic defence in the individual becomes reasonable social comfort or even a belief in superiority in the group. Systematic organisations of defences build up the structure of groups, which function as 'social defence systems' to protect individuals from ambivalence and anxiety. Freud (1927) proposed the germ of this idea, arguing that religion was a collective neurosis, and observed that 'devout believers are safeguarded in a high degree against the risk of certain neurotic illnesses; their acceptance of the universal neurosis spares them the task of constructing a personal one' (p. 44). The concept was formulated by Elliott Jacques (1953), and is now part of a psychoanalytic group theory and practice. A 'social defence system' refers to a collective defence against anxiety, protecting the individuals in a group. It simultaneously structures an unconscious culture of a social organisation, thereby becoming a cohesive force (see Hinshelwood, 1989, pp. 430–432).

In the 'social defence' model, groups cohere, not just consciously to make a common world, but unconsciously to organise a defence against anxiety. The common-sense view of groups – of their identity, of the identities of their members, of the group's avowed aims and of the roles of its members – does not recognise this function. The disparity between conscious purpose and unconscious function means that the behaviour of groups is the surface manifestation of an unconscious process that has a subject-like quality, and as in the case of understanding any subject, it has to be interpreted. Moreover, this subject-like quality is based, not on the individual of everyday life, but is the resultant of systems of projection of primitive parts of the psyche.

The classic social defence analysis was carried out by Isabel Menzies (1959), who studied nurses in a London hospital. She noticed that nursing was organised as 'task nursing', in which nurses performed specified tasks on several patients, rather than all the nursing tasks with fewer patients. Her hypothesis was that this partial nursing disrupted the nurses' reparative aims. They were deprived of the sense of making anyone better, and therefore also could not make reparation for their own destructive impulses. The sense of being unable to confirm their reparative impulses and to mitigate the attendant guilt were carried in the hospital society, magnified by the environment of damaged people.

The unconscious defensive strategy minimised anxiety arising from the phantasy of damaging one's object world (Melanie Klein's 'depressive anxiety'; Klein, 1935). The unstated means to achieve this unconscious aim was to displace accountability downwards in the staff hierarchy, and responsibility upwards. In other words, staff more junior were always to blame for what was done, while being deprived of opportunities for responsible decision-making, and staff more senior were always responsible for decisions, which they did not implement. This vacancy of agency created a stability, albeit fragile, because it left any one staff member always vulnerable to feeling guilty: either about to be blamed or to be held responsible for a bad decision. In the absence of a sense of agency, the blame in the system reinforced the very defence that could not address the original vulnerability to guilt.

With a hypothesis of this sort in mind, one can make observations. Vivid examples of such a strategy were the rituals of working to task lists and to checking and double-checking even in situations with minor consequences from mistakes (pp. 54–56). Of course, scrupulous accuracy was important, and was the conscious aim of the rituals. But Menzies observed an additional feature: that these moments were also enactments of an obsessional avoidance of responsibility and accountability, exacerbated by the anxiety of being held accountable and responsible in a system that did not provide opportunities for mitigating guilt through reparative work. Organisational coherence might have been the manifest aim of the hospital, but it was reinforced by a defence against anxiety.

Methodological implications

This chapter began with the idea that the social level is based on relating among subjects, even when its regularities suggested a lawfulness that could not be reduced to the individual level. The phenomenological tradition on which this thinking is based has used the concept of *Verstehen* to turn the epistemological and methodological principle, that social life has to be understood through the intentions and meanings of social actors, into a working sociological method. In my view, the notion of a common-sense *Lebenswelt* is a model, not a self-evident description, of social functioning. It is an idea that it is sustained by the 'wide-awake' adult. From a psychoanalytic angle, it has to be analysed into its unconscious and non-common-sensical elements, psychotic anxieties, and defences. It includes the psychoanalytic recognition that the individual is a composite of dynamic forces. The agencies in these dynamic relationships, not just the individuals of conscious awareness, coalesce in forming groups.

The psychoanalytic model leads to a different theory of social formation. From a methodological angle, the place to study it is in the consulting room, delving into individual psychic reality, supplemented by group observation, such as carried out by Menzies. Analysis of the individual reveals the dynamic forces surrounding disintegration and cohesion displayed in transference and countertransference; psychoanalytic group observation traces the consequences of this dynamic play of forces as they coalesce through splitting and projection in stable group relations. The projection is really projective identification, in that groups now bear, by attribution, parts of the subjectivity of each other, just as the subjectivity of the individual is parsed into the relationships between internal objects.

Moreover, just as the analyst works with a subject in the consulting room, in the living relationship of the transference, so too the analyst can work with the social world, in its subject-like character. Both inside and outside the consulting room, the psychoanalyst attends to moments of change, when the dynamics of the relationship between analyst and subject are suddenly exposed and made available to analytic work by the discontinuity. They are moments when the object relations change. At a whole-object level, for example, the analyst might become more father-like in the sudden appearance of an attitude towards him or her that enacts that experience of being fathered. The analyst as that father-object is the father in the transference, and there will be many shifts that bring into view an array of other object relations. In particular, primitive elements enter the stage. For example, moments of change may bring out, not father as an historical figure, but the superego as an authoritarian and/or protective agency in relation to the ego. This relationship, forced into the open, informs the thinking, feeling, and behaviour of the individual subject, and through a social superego, it similarly informs the thinking, feeling, and behaviour of the social subject.[8]

Transferences have a delusional aspect, but their very unreality opens a window to psychic reality. As an object in the internal world of the patient, the analyst is presented with the unconscious of the patient, revealing what the ego feels about, thinks about, tries to do with, this ego-fashioned object. It is the route to discerning and interpreting the irrational unconscious.[9] Such a method relies on interpretation, based on the object-analyst's private apperception of the subject-patient's private psychic state. Although the private world of the psyche refers to personal psychic experience, which is not ostensive in the same way as external objects, psychoanalysis takes it as an object of continuous investigation – a psychoanalytic object – assured that transference/countertransference make up a determinate field that can be systematically tracked. It provides a systematic analysis of unconscious inference, to supplement phenomenological inference.

I am proposing that we look for the opportunities for transference-based observation. It is certainly possible for all forms of organisational and social observation in the phenomenological tradition; also for oral history and interviewing, and as an adjunct to large-scale studies.[10]

It is also possible to observe social-level forces impinging on the psyche in the consulting room. One can, for example, speak of a social superego, whose characteristics can be linked to institutional, historical, and sociological phenomena. In this case, one can observe the breaking up of the psyche along cleavage planes that are socially embedded, yet structured by the internal world. I want to give an example of such a case, because such cases satisfy the psychoanalytic preference for the living moment of transference as well as the social scientist's preference for social-level information. The methodological principle is to search for 'transferential moments', the moments of shift in the transference.

In a case reported by an East German psychoanalyst living in West Berlin (Kothe-Meyer, 2000), a six-year-old boy from the German Democratic Republic (GDR) was adopted by parents who had moved to the West just before the fall of the wall. The parents described him as 'wicked, constantly fighting and thieving', which, they feared, would lead to his having to leave school and to their humiliation as a problem family. This sort of severe description of a child by parents from the GDR was a common experience for the analyst, who saw in it the imprint of the severity of GDR authority. But more immediately, her own reactions to the mother, who brought the boy, and to mistakes that followed on from her reactions, could be understood as an unconscious superego interchange between her and the mother.

The severe description of the boy was that of a parent seeking approval from severe – GDR – authority, transferred to the analyst. Though born in the GDR, the analyst had lived in West Berlin for many years. She found herself uncharacteristically judgemental and hostile. When the parents failed to bring the boy to a session, she searched for her clinical notes, but found them missing. She became the mistrustful target of the same mistrusting, severe – GDR – surveillance and severity. The unconscious, disorientating impact of a GDR superego was confirmed when she found her clinical notes and discovered that she had given the parents a different date.

The analyst's social and educational history gave her an insight into the difficulties faced by migrants from one side to the other, specifically the maintenance of prior collectively instilled psychic structures from the GDR; so she was interpreting in the social in both the immediacy of the transference and in the dependence of her ego on the social superego. What she witnessed in the parents' denunciations of their children were 'highly moralistic, judgmental remarks of the GDR superego', which also 'often held an uneasy, fearful undertone' of anxiety in the face of children who showed an autonomy from authority (an autonomy they also feared in themselves). The GDR superego, with which they identified and which they feared would say, for example: 'He lies often – nearly always.' 'She never does what she should, only what she wants.' 'She is remarkably malicious.' 'He will not accept any duties or take any responsibilities' (2000, p. 419).

The detection of this cultural incompatibility, produced by the social superego, was a clinical finding in psychoanalytic work with migrants. It built on the anthropological-psychoanalytic tradition based on Mario Erdheim's concept of the 'social production of unconsciousness' (Erdheim, 1984; Kohte-Meyer, 1994; also Parin, 1977 on social adaptation as a process by which the ego is relieved of conflict unless this harmonious relationship is challenged). The ego of the migrant, challenged by coming into conflict with the social superego of the home culture, retreats, pushed by the persecutory side of the superego and allured by its protective side. This superego can be retained, producing the judgemental parents, or projected into the analyst, who becomes a threatening figure. Kohte-Meyer experienced anxiety and loss of competence, as her ego was crippled by the 'social superego, acquired in the cultural space of the old GDR... In the failed correspondence between [analyst and patient and] the prevailing "inner management plan" the ego-identity of the patient was shattered, [and the] ego, under the superego anxiety that broke out, was unable to function. An irritated feeling of disjointed harmony of the situation arose in me' (Kothe-Meyer, 1994, p. 255; my translation).

This analysis makes sense only with Freud's structural model of the psyche (superego/ego ideal, ego, id). The parents were identified either with egos subservient to a punitive and all-embracing superego, or with the superego itself. For Kohte-Meyer, the object of study was not the parents as individuals or their conscious experience of the GDR, but the eruption of a social superego. The positioning of analyst or patient as an agent in the internal world depended on who in the moment would transferentially enact the complementary agency: ego to superego or superego to ego. This unconscious structure defended against the anxiety of ego consciousness should anyone begin to see what was going on. And this superego was fashioned in social environments that carried the unconscious defence: the GDR formed from resistance to the West Germans and from being unable to depart from a superego intolerance of West German individuality. The persecutory dimension stands out in this vignette, but the analyst also emphasises the importance of the protective umbrella offered by the GDR state.

At a social level,

> These almost unbearable emotions of rage, grief, depression, and even shame are usually avoided, so that, through the individual denial of emotions on both sides, the dialogue between 'East' and 'West' Germans may quickly become derailed. Consistent misunderstandings and consolidation of the splitting processes result, and dialogue and possible beginning of a sympathetic relationship come to an abrupt end.
>
> (2000, p. 427)

She continues:

> It is just this derailed dialogue [for me, a transferential moment] that should be recognized and understood, and it is the continual switching of roles between 'hunter' and 'hunted,' [transferred into the analytic relationship] induced by persecuting and paranoid fantasies, that should be revealed. I am convinced that development and integration can only begin through this psychoanalytical process.
>
> (p. 427)

The social superego of the GDR both protected and persecuted: the GDR did provide welfare, and it enforced the socialist ideal through the teaching of children, which had both the persecutory and the protective sides. Introjected, it offered a collectively reinforced stability to the subservient ego, but at the cost of splitting and projecting whatever did not fit its ideology. Next to the GDR-stabilised ego, West German individualism was 'ego-oriented and narcissistic' (2000, p. 426). The outcome was an irrational, accepted, mutual hostility between two societies, the roots of which remained unconscious and persisted into reunited German society. In Kohte-Meyer's words:

> With the turning away from the old traditional cultural space and moving towards the cultural space of the new social territory something essential can be lost to the ego: consciousness and capacity for scenic phantasies and role identifications, which concerned the socially allowed drive satisfactions and, as identifications, were part of the old ego-identity [in a] process ... comparable intrapsychically to the process ... described for whole societies and groups in Mario Erdheim's concept of the 'social production of unconsciousness'.
>
> (1994, p. 257; my translation)

Conclusion

I could add many examples of the dramatic eruption of socially informed features of the unconscious (see Figlio, 2017, pp. 45–72, for a more detailed treatment).

Here are some examples of entry points into the shifts in the social world, which can engage the psychoanalyst in an interpretive dialogue with sociologists and historians.

1. The fundamental research setting is the psychoanalytic consulting room, as in the example above, in which the GDR as a social superego erupts between analyst and patient. Although the analysis focuses on an individual, perhaps with extension to the family, the social-level analysis is clear (see Figlio, 2017, pp. 45–72, for other examples).

2. Conflict among actors, whether contemporary or historical, observed by whatever means; for example, conflict between politicians and the press, as in interviews.
3. A special case of the above would be eruptions of indignation (for an example, see the press reporting of the self-righteous attack on the house of a *paed*iatrician, because she was a *paed*o...; Allison, 2000).
4. Conflict among intellectuals and other observers about a specific social or historical issue (in Figlio, 2017, pp. 119–144, I work through in detail the 'historians' debate', a public debate in the 1980s among historians about revisionism in German historiography).
5. Conflict and partisanship among current scholars, whose transferential relationships to different historical actors and their social superegos drive them into dispute with each other, producing shifts in their positions.

Whether as historians, sociologists, or psychoanalysts, we are drawn into a first-person, living relationship with our subjects, including the same factional identifications. They provide the points of entry for psychoanalysis. The psychoanalysis of these identifications must focus on the unconscious agencies – the internal worlds – of the objects, not their conscious, individual presentations. There are two versions of the individual in society and, therefore, in social analysis. There is the 'wide-awake' individual of everyday life, who struggles with conflictual internal and external forces, sometimes more divided, sometimes more coherent, usually aiming for the latter and for feeling internally individual and harmonious. There is also the schismatic individual, whose internal agencies are pulled asunder and deposited unconsciously in various groups. The individual in this case is recomposed in two or more forms through the relationships between those groups: in the individual's own multiple identifications, which cohere to a greater or lesser extent; and as a participant in a social subjectivity, which we have to attribute to a social group to understand it. To go back to Smelser's criticism of sociology, for example, we can only capture the idea of social ambivalence through ascribing to it a subjectivity, and we can only sustain such an analysis by thinking of group relations as a parsing out of the psyches of individuals (see also Figlio, 2017, pp. 45–72).

In any event, the object of my proposed psychoanalytic methodology is the transferential moment, which exposes the eruptions of primitive object relations. They structure the internal dimension of sociated life, the stable crystallisation of which we call social structure.

Notes

1 According to Schutz (1953b), there was a broad agreement on the unquestioned nature of common-sense knowledge.

> Philosophers as different as James, Bergson, Dewey, Husserl, and Whitehead agree that common-sense knowledge of everyday life is the unquestioned but always questionable background with which inquiry starts and within which alone it can be carried out. It is this *Lebenswelt*, as Husserl calls it, within which, according to him, all social science and even logical concepts originate....
>
> (p. 57)

All 'facts' are interpretations.

> Strictly speaking, there are no such things as facts, pure and simple. All facts are from the outset facts selected from a universal context by the activities of our minds. They are, therefore, always interpreted facts, either facts looked at as detached from their context by an artificial abstraction or facts considered in their particular setting. In either case, they carry along their interpretational inner and outer horizon.
>
> (Schutz, 1953a, p. 5)

    This tradition has been called 'micro-sociology' in recent work (Stolte, Fine, and Cook, 2001).

2 Simmel aims to limit the intrusion of imagination in this process, and cautions against the notion of a 'psychological isomorphism' between the interpreter and the object of interpretation. His thinking is akin to the concept of projection in its psychoanalytic meaning: the attribution of one's own psychic states to another, as if they were, in reality, the attributes of the other; indeed, he uses the concept of projection (1918, p. 99).

3 Simmel says

> every sense delivers contributions characteristic of its individual nature to the construction of sociated existence... What I am presenting here is only the attempt... to openly reveal certain form-creating factors in the mere structure of our sensory functions for the simple everyday relations as well as the complex circumstances of human beings... [A]n extraordinary large number of people can have the same auditory impression [which, for example] connects a concert audience sociologically into an incomparably closer unity and commonality of mood [than does vision, but w]here, exceptionally, the eye also provides such an identity of impressions for a great number of people [e.g., the sun], then the communalizing sociological effect also occurs... One will no longer be able to consider as unworthy of attention the delicate, invisible threads that are spun from one person to another if one wishes to understand the web of society according to its productive, form-giving forces....
>
> (1907, pp. 110, 114–115, 116, 120; on the meal, see 1910, pp. 130–135 in this collection; on sociability, 1911, see pp. 120–130)

4 Observations of this sort are common in psychoanalytically orientated trainings. They are carried out on a regular basis, in which the observer becomes part of the emotional atmosphere, but refrains from doing anything other than observing, including the observer's own responses; writing up the observations as accurately and completely as possible, avoiding judgements or theoretical structuring ('process notes'); reporting and discussing the observation in a psychodynamically sensitive

setting (Miller and Miller,1989; Waddell, 2006). I have reported this observation previously (Figlio, 2000/2001, p. 117).

5 It is a form of imitation, which, taken to the extreme, moves from an apparently passive accommodation to an other, over to an active assimilation of an other. This unconscious stance, first described by Karl Abraham in 1919, seems to be based on what Melanie Klein later called projective identification. Projective identification is an identification based on the phantasy of occupying the other with part of the self and thereby commandeering the other, as if it were part of the self's own bio-psychological equipment. The other is an object in the sense of a repository for projection, but is really a subject, a part of the projector's subjectivity. That is what makes it a projective *identification*. Wilfred Bion (1959) introduced the idea that projective identification was an early form of communication, in which the infant maintained an intrinsic connection between its psyche-soma and its mother. Any disturbance in its own psyche-soma was, in phantasy, simultaneously a disturbance in the mother. Her response was, simultaneously, the baby's own nascent response, based on its nascent sense of agency (containment).

6 Careful observation of mothers and babies shows the minute interlocking of their gestures, the baby's attempts to elicit responses from the mother and the apparent despair and cut-offness into which they fall if there is no response. Observations have been made of infants only a few hours old, who unmistakably imitate the facial gestures of the experimenter. Within seconds, the keen little subject assumes a similar expression, though his muscles are barely able to carry out the gesture (Beebe, Lachmann, and Jaffe, 1997). But they do not necessarily refer to inner states, since these states are not observable. Psychoanalytic research, especially in the Kleinian tradition, has focused in great detail on projective identification in the transference/countertransference relationship in the clinical setting (Hinshelwood, 1989, pp. 179–210). Feldman (1994) has described the pressure exerted on the analyst towards conformity with the patient's unconscious thinking and feeling, as expressed in the transference. Seligmann (1999) bridges intersubjective studies and the theory of projective identification with detailed psychoanalytically interpreted observations of parents and babies or young children, documenting the subtle but powerful influences of one mind upon another. For an overview of psychoanalytic intersubjective research into pre-symbolic development and capacities, see Beebe, Lachmann, and Jaffe (1997). What is striking about the imitation that I reported is that it reproduced gestures that the baby did not see, as if he could create the gesture of his mother's gesture as the sort of thing that must have happened. It was as if, at least, he inferred his mother's intentions, but noteworthy that he seemed to insert himself into mother's movements, whether we say of body or of mind. On imitation and perception, see Gaddini (1969).

7 Anzieu (1975) has elaborated on this model, proposing that the groups as a whole can become the group ego ideal, akin to the leader in Freud's analysis of the mechanism of group cohesion. Chasseguet-Smirgel (1985) considers the same system from a different angle. Individuals acting in concert produce the same group cohesion, in that their synchronised movement constitutes an identification in their egos and posits a leader ego ideal in the group as a whole. Interestingly for a dialogue between history and psychoanalysis, the historian William McNeill (1995) has extensively documented the binding force of coordinated activity – a 'muscular bonding' – in religious and military groups.

There are indicators of these internal processes in social psychological research. For example, in classic research into the strength with which men who had been drafted into the US army retained an identification with civilian life, the researchers found that a single indicator, their uniform, was an adequate index of their identification with the army: 62 per cent of regular soldiers said they preferred to wear their uniforms while on furlough, while 30 per cent of drafted men said they preferred to wear their uniforms (Kendall, 1950). Thinking psychoanalytically, one could say that to wear the army uniform is to be seen by others on the street, but particularly by other men in uniform. Each man is therefore like the other, but also as a huge uniformed individual, and that individual, along with all the people who coalesce to compose it, are seen by the imagined eyes of primal figures in the abstract form of the army. With Freud, we can say that when they identify with each other in their egos, they project their ego-ideals onto the same leader – the army – and therefore share a common ego-ideal (Chasseguet-Smirgel, 1985, pp. 76–93; Freud, 1921). They would see themselves both as individuals and as a group, and each is seen by his own internal observer who is also identified with the group, both as a collective of other individuals and, abstractly, as the army, the nation, the cause, God.

8 This attention to change as a moment of discontinuity, which pushes underlying dynamics into the open, accessible to observation and interpretation, is akin to Lorenzer's (1986) 'scenic understanding' (Bereswill, Morgenroth, and Redman, 2010). Rothe (2009, 2012) has used it to explore forms of not-remembering in a group of Germans who, in childhood, observed the deportation of Jews.

9 The conceptual refinement, investigation, demonstration, and clinical management of transference and countertransference make up a major area of technical concern in psychoanalysis (three seminal papers from this vast literature are Brenman Pick (1985), Joseph (1985), and Money-Kyrle (1956); for a critical overview, see Sandler, Dare, and Holder (1973, pp. 37–98)). This method has been extended to psychoanalytic social observation, primarily of infants and of institutions, which can be seen as small, bounded societies (Hinshelwood and Chiesa, 2002; Miller and Miller, 1989; Waddell, 2006). In particular, the model of countertransference monitoring has been extended into the psychoanalytic observations of small societies. Extensive 'process notes' are recorded by the observer, and they are orally presented to a monitoring observer or group, with the aim of establishing the transference characteristics of the small society, and therefore, of its unconscious structure. Although the link is not usually made, this method is an extension and a deepening of participant observation, which is well known to sociologists, and might be extended into fields in which the subject is not immediately present, such as history (the original formulation of participant observation resulted from a collaboration of sociologists and psychoanalysts; see Figlio, 1987; on history and psychoanalysis, see Figlio, 1998).

10 The project of Stephen Frosh and his co-workers on masculinity among young males in inner-city schools might serve as a model (Frosh, Phoenix, and Pattman, 2005).

References

Abraham, K. (1919), A particular form of neurotic resistance to the psychoanalytic method. In *Selected Papers on Psychoanalysis* (pp. 301–311). London: Hogarth.
Allison, R. (2000), Doctor driven out of home by vigilantes. *The Guardian*, 29 August.
Andrade De Azevedo, A. (1994), Validation of the psychoanalytic clinical process: the role of dreams. *International Journal of Psychoanalysis*, 75: 1181–1192.
Anzieu, D. (1975), *The Group and the Unconscious*. London: Routledge & Kegan, 1984.
Beebe, B., Lachmann, F., and Jaffe, J. (1997), Mother–infant interaction structures and presymbolic self and object representations. *Psychoanalytic Dialogues*, 7: 133–182.
Bereswill, M., Morgenroth, C., and Redman, P. (2010), Alfred Lorenzer and the depth-hermeneutic method. *Psychoanalysis, Culture and Society*, 15(3): 221–250.
Bion, W. (1959), Attacks on linking. *International Journal of Psychoanalysis*, 40: 308–315. [Reprinted in *Second Thoughts* (pp. 93–109). London: Heinemann, 1967.]

Bion, W. (1962), A theory of thinking. *International Journal of Psychoanalysis*, 33: 306–310. [Reprinted in *Second Thoughts* (pp. 110–119).]

Bott Spillius, E. (ed.) (1988), *Melanie Klein Today: Developments in Theory and Practice*, vol.2: *Mainly Practice*. London and New York: Routledge.

Brenman Pick, I. (1985), Working through in the counter-transference. *International Journal of Psychoanalysis*, 66: 157–166. [Reprinted in Bott Spillius (ed.), *Melanie Klein Today* (pp. 34–47).]

Chasseguet-Smirgel, J. (1985), *The Ego Ideal: A Psychoanalytic Essay on the Malady of the Ideal*. London: Free Association Books.

Erdheim, M. (1984), *Die gesellschafliche Produktion von Unbewusstheit: Eine Einführung in den ethnopsychonalytischen Prozess*. Frankfurt aM: Suhrkamp.

Feldman, M. (1994), Projective identification in phantasy and enactment. *Psychoanalytic Inquiry*, 14: 423–440.

Figlio, K. (1987), The lost subject of medical sociology. In G. Scambler (ed.), *Sociological Theory and Medical Sociology* (pp. 77–109). London: Tavistock.

Figlio, K. (1998), Historical imagination/psychoanalytic imagination. *History Workshop Journal*, 45: 199–221.

Figlio, K. (2000), *Psychoanalysis, Science and Masculinity*. London: Whurr; Philadelphia: Bruner-Routledge, 2001.

Figlio, K. (2006), The absolute state of mind in society and the individual. *Psychoanalysis of Culture and Society*, 11(2): 119–143.

Figlio, K. (2007), A new naturalism: on the origins of psychoanalysis as a social theory of subjectivity. In C. Bainbridge, et al., *Culture and the Unconscious* (pp.24–40). Houndmills, Basingstoke: Palgrave Macmillan.

Figlio, K. (2017), *Remembering as Reparation: Psychoanalysis and Historical Memory*. London: Palgrave Macmillan.

Freud. S. (1921), *Group Psychology and the Analysis of the Ego. Standard Edition*, 18: 67–143.

Freud, S. (1927), *The Future of an Illusion. Standard Edition*, 21: 1–56.

Frosh, S., Phoenix, A., and Pattman, R. (2005), Struggling towards manhood: narratives of homophobia and homosexuality. *British Journal of Psychotherapy*, 22(1): 37–56.

Gaddini, E. (1969), On imitation. In *A Psychoanalytic Theory of Infantile Experience: Conceptual and Clinical Reflections* (pp. 18–34). London: Tavistock/Routledge, 1992.

Heritage, J. (1984), *Garfinkle and Ethnomethodology*. Cambridge: Polity.

Hinshelwood, R. D. (1989), *A Dictionary of Kleinian Thought*. London: Free Association Books. [Second edn., 1991.]

Hinshelwood, R. D., and Chiesa, M. (2002), *Organisations, Anxieties and Defences: Towards a Psychoanalytic Social Psychology*. London/Philadelphia: Whurr.

Jacques, E. (1953), On the dynamics of social structure. *Human Relations*, 6: 3–23. [Republished as, Social systems as a defence against persecutory and depressive anxiety. In M. Klein, P. Heimann, and R. Money-Kyrle (eds.), *New Directions in Psychoanalysis* (pp. 478–498). London: Tavistock, 1955.]

Joseph, B. (1985), Transference: the total situation. *International Journal of Psychoanalysis*, 66: 447–454. [Reprinted in Bott Spillius (ed.), *Melanie Klein Today* (pp. 61–72).]

Kendall, P. (1950), A review of indicators used in 'The American Soldier'. In P. Lazarsfeld and M. Rosenberg (eds.), *The Language of Social Research* (pp. 37–39). New York: The Free Press, 1955.

Klein, M. (1935), A contribution to the psychogenesis of manic-depressive states. In *The Works of Melanie Klein*, vol. 1 (pp. 262–289). London: Hogarth and the Institute of Psycho-Analysis.

Kohte-Meyer, I. (1994), 'Ich bin fremd, so wie ich bin': Migrationserleben, Ich-Identität und Neurose. *Praxis der Kinderpsychologie und Kinderpsychiatrie*, 43: 253–259.

Kohte-Meyer, I. (2000), A derailed dialogue: unexpected difficulties in the psychoanalytic work with patients from East Germany. *Psychoanalytic Review*, 87: 417–428.

Leiter, K. (1980), *A Primer on Ethnomethodology*. New York and Oxford: Oxford University Press.

Lorenzer, A. (1986), Tiefenhermeneutische Kulturanalyse. In A. Lorenzer (ed.), *Kultur-Analysen: Psychoanalytische Studien zur Kultur* (pp. 11–98). Frankfurt aM: Fischer.

McNeill, W. (1995), *Keeping Together in Time: Dance and Drill in Human History*. Cambridge, MA: Harvard University Press.

Menzies, I. (1959), The functioning of social systems as a defence against anxiety: a report on a study of the nursing service of a general hospital. *Human Relations*, 13: 95–121. [Reprinted in *Containing Anxiety in Institutions: Selected Essays*, Volume I (pp. 43–85). London: Free Association Books, 1988.]

Miller, J and Miller, L. (1989), *Closely Observed Infants*. London: Duckworth.

Money-Kyrle, R. (1956), Normal counter-transference and some of its deviations. *International Journal of Psychoanalysis*, 37: 360–366. [Reprinted in Bott Spillius (ed.), *Melanie Klein Today* (pp. 22–33).]

Parin, P. (1977), Das Ich und die Anpassungs-Mechanismen. *Psyche – Zeitschrift für Psychoanalyse*, 31(6): 481–515.

Rothe, J. (2009), *Das (Nicht-)Sprechen über die Judenvernichtung: Psychische Weiterwirkingen des Holocaust in mehreren Generationen nicht-jüdischer Deutscher*. Giessen: Psychozial Verlag.

Rothe, K. (2012), Anti-Semitism in Germany today and the intergenerational transmission of guilt and shame. *Psychoanalysis, Culture, and Society*, 17(1): 16–34.

Sandler, J., Dare, C., and Holder, A. (1973), *The Patient and the Analyst: The Basis of the Psychoanalytic Process*. London: George Allen and Unwin. [Second edn., London: Karnac, 1992.]

Schutz. A. (1945), On multiple realities. In M. Natanson (ed.), *Collected Papers*, vol. 1: *The Problem of Social Reality* (pp. 207–259). The Hague: Martinus Nijhoff, 1962.

Schutz. A. (1953a), Common-sense and scientific interpretation. In M. Natanson (ed.), *Collected Papers*, vol. 1: *The Problem of Social Reality* (pp. 3–47). The Hague: Martinus Nijhoff, 1962.

Schutz. A. (1953b), Concept and theory formation in the social sciences. In M. Natanson (ed.), *Collected Papers*, vol. 1: *The Problem of Social Reality* (pp. 48–66). The Hague: Martinus Nijhoff, 1962.

Schutz, A., and Luckmann, T. (1983), *The Structures of the Life-World*, vol. 2. Evanston, IL: Northwestern University Press.

Seligman, S. (1999), Integrating Kleinian theory and intersubjective infant research. *Psychoanalytic Dialogues*, 9: 129–159.

Simmel, G. (1907), Sociology of the sense. In D. Frisby and M. Featherstone (eds.), *Simmel on Culture: Selected Writings* (pp. 109–120). London: Sage.

Simmel, G. (1910), Sociology of the meal. In D. Frisby and M. Featherstone (eds.), *Simmel on Culture: Selected Writings* (pp. 130–135). London: Sage.

Simmel, G. (1911), The sociology of sociability. In D. Frisby and M. Featherstone (eds.), *Simmel on Culture: Selected Writings* (pp. 120–130). London: Sage.

Simmel, G. (1918), On the nature of historical understanding. In *Essays on Interpretation in Social Sciences*, translated, introduced, and edited by G. Oakes (pp. 97–126). Manchester: Manchester University Press, 1980.

Smelser, N. (1997), *Problematics of Sociology: The Georg Simmel Lectures, 1995*. Berkeley/Los Angeles/London: University of California Press.

Smelser, N. (1998), *The Social Edges of Psychoanalysis*. Berkeley/Los Angeles/London: University of California Press.

Stolte, J. F., Fine, G. A. and Cook, K. S. (2001) Sociological miniaturism: seeing the big through the small in social psychology. *Annual Review of Sociology*, 27: 387–413.

Waddell, M. (2006), Infant observation in Britain: the Tavistock approach. *International Journal of Psychoanalysis*, 87: 1103–1120.

Weber, M. (1906), The logic of historical explanation. In W. Runciman (ed.), *Weber: Selections in Translation* (pp. 111–134). Cambridge: Cambridge University Press.

Wieder, D. (1974), Telling the code. In R. Turner (ed.), *Ethnomethodology: Selected Readings* (pp. 144–172). Harmondsworth: Penguin.

Wirth, H.-J. (2009), *Narcissism and Power: Psychoanalysis of Mental Disorders in Politics*. Giessen: Psychosozial-Verlag.

Part II

Psychoanalytic methods in data collection

Interviewing

Chapter 2

The socioanalytic interview

Susan Long

Socioanalysis

Socioanalysis is the study of group, organisational, and societal dynamics using a depth psychology approach. It has a focus on unconscious dynamics following psychoanalysis and integrates this with systems theory. Its object of study is the dynamic field of human systems.

Socioanalysis takes the view that the psychology and behaviours of individual persons can be best understood from within their social contexts. This does not deny personal characteristics or experiences, but considers these to be long-term introjected aspects of the social environment and of relationships with others, within the constraints of general and personal biology. From this perspective, the individual person can be regarded as 'holding' particular aspects of the social environment at various times and for various lengths of time, or even throughout their life. Moreover, because it is the person who can act, speak, sense, feel, intuit, and think, it is through the person and through interactions between persons that the dynamics of the social system can be expressed consciously or enacted unconsciously.

But beyond the behaviour and interactions of persons, socioanalysis regards the group or system-as-a-whole as having its own dynamics. For example, basic assumption behaviour in groups (Bion, 1961), social defences in organisations (Menzies-Lyth, 1960; Armstrong and Rustin, 2014), and country romances in nations (Boccara, 2013, 2014) each demonstrate system-as-a-whole dynamics that affect the behaviours, thoughts, and emotions of those in the system. Different from the personal unconscious, there are unconscious systemic processes that may not be easily accessible to the people in the group, organisation, or social system, yet have strong effects on those people. Ideas about a systemic unconscious have been developed over many years. Jung refers to a collective unconscious that he believed was similar in each person and reached into the historical experiences of humans across cultures. Fromm (1962) describes a social unconscious, referring to the notion that societies determine which thoughts and feelings are permitted to come to consciousness. This idea is taken up by Foulkes (1975), who conceptualised an unconscious mental field across all members of an interacting group. Maurita Harney and I (2013) gather evidence for an associative unconscious which is a form of such an unconscious mental field. It consists of all the associations implicate (Bohm, 1980) in the signs, symbols, and signifiers available to any set of interacting thinkers, limited only by biological impediments, personal and social repressions, cultural constraints, and technological limitations.

The idea of an unconscious matrix is evident in psychoanalytic thinking, and many authors, including Freud, have alluded to the metaphor of the mycelium in an attempt to describe this matrix: 'a dream wish arises like a mushroom from its mycelium' (Freud, 1900). The idea that the matrix is social rather than individual acknowledges humans as fundamentally group animals.

Interviews and their object of study

Interviews have many, diverse purposes. These include: to gather information or do research; to query a respondent around particular issues; to enquire into a topic; to use as a basis for selecting new employees or entrants into training programmes; to advise; to use as part of a performance review; to influence a respondent; to use as part of a therapeutic programme. The interview normally involves enquirers (the interviewers) and interviewees. They may involve only two people or be conducted with groups.

I will focus primarily on research and enquiry interviews, although many of my points will also be relevant to other types of interviews. I include, for example, interviews as part of studies such as organisational cultural analyses carried out by organisational consultants or coaching interviews conducted with managers or professionals. The general assumption, at least of a research interview, is that the interviewer has a set of questions to ask and the interviewee will respond. The implicit model is of a social interaction that is primarily one-way, where one party holds the rules. The whole idea of a 'respondent' is that the interviewee rarely initiates. This is in contrast to a discussion.

The socioanalytic interview, however, challenges assumptions about those traditional research interviews that regard an interview as simply a method for collecting facts.

1. The socioanalytic interview concerns the *accounts* of people, that is, what they say *about* the object of the research. For example, what they say about their organisation and their experiences in the organisation. By referring to accounts, we recognise that these are personal perceptions and ideas, not necessarily facts. Also, accounts may be coloured by psychological defences against the material discussed (see Hollway and Jefferson, 2000).
2. The socioanalytic interview also concerns the *here and now* of the interview situation. For instance, how the participants behave, respond, and feel during the interview; what they think during the interview. These data may

point to issues within the organisation that are mirrored in the interview; re-enacted at a less than conscious level. This follows the idea of projective identification at a systemic level whereby thoughts and feelings belonging to one part of the system emerge in other parts of the system through projective and introjective processes (Long, 2000).
3. *Socioanalytic* research methods in general take a different stance to research from general social science enquiry. The ideas of reliability and validity of research, for example, must be approached from the perspective of the system as-a-whole rather than from the perspective of multiple individuals. Traditional research, for instance, might argue that for results to be reliable and valid, all individuals in a study should be approached in exactly the same way and asked exactly the same questions. This is regarded as standardised practice. However, the object of study for socio-analysis is neither the individual nor an aggregate or average. The object is the system-as-a-whole – whether a group, an organisation, or a society.

In relation to the third point, a metaphor will help. An organisation, for example, can be seen as like a jigsaw puzzle. Each of the pieces – people, departments, sections – is uniquely shaped. Yet they fit together to give a picture of the whole. They cannot be approached in exactly the same way because their shapes are different, and it is that difference that allows the researcher to see where and how each fits in relation to any other piece. Moreover, while examination of any one piece can only give a hint of the whole, that hint is important for the overall picture. The uniqueness of the piece, its colour and lines, is what allows the whole to become a thing in itself.

Consequently, when our object of study is the organisation as a whole, the interview must (i) discover the uniqueness of that part of the organisation represented in the interviewee, and (ii) discover the ways in which that part is interrelated to other parts. The whole idea of unconscious representation is crucial to understanding socioanalytic methods. We disclose about ourselves, our groups and organisations that which we don't realise we are disclosing because we are steeped in their culture.

What then does the interviewee represent in terms of the organisation as a whole? The most easily discriminated smallest part of an organisation is a person-in-a-role. One might argue that it is a person, but that is misleading because it is the person *in role* who makes decisions and takes actions (Long, 2016a). The organisation as a whole is constituted by many interacting roles, where many interacting decisions are made and actions taken. Winnicott says there is no such thing as a baby – there is only a mother (and father) and a baby. They only make sense in their relation to one another. So too, an organisation has roles that are in relation to one another. The roles and their relatedness may not always be self-evident; they can be discovered. One part of that discovery can be through the socioanalytic interview.

As well as a role, an interviewee may represent an aspect of a group or a department; or a value or set of behaviours; an aspect of the culture and its beliefs. They may represent a group in its entirety, either consciously, as when they are a chosen representative, or unconsciously through identifications with the group. It is difficult for people by themselves to discern exactly when and how they are doing this. There are many systems in the organisation. Primarily, there is the task system – a set of interacting tasks that support the purpose of the organisation. But also there is the social system of interacting people rather than work-roles. There is the political system – a system of power and authority relations that impact decisions and behaviours. There are technical systems and procedural systems and the systems where these interact – the socio-technical systems. Importantly, there are emotional systems where different people take up different emotional roles such as 'the bossy one' or 'the nurturer', 'the extravert' or the 'street wise one'. So there are many systems and sub-systems that interviewees may be representing. These are not always easily discerned by either the interviewer or interviewee. The interview must allow a space for them to emerge.

The socioanalytic interview

The socioanalytic interview is a space where both interviewer and interviewee can together discover the various roles, systems, and sub-systems that the interviewee is 'holding' or represents (that is, the structures of the system) and the conscious and unconscious dynamics and cultures linked to them. It is a space of potentials – what is not known – as much as actuals. In our metaphor, it is a space to discover the shape and colours of the particular jigsaw piece that is the respondent's experience. Consequently, following several such interviews, a representation of the organisation-as-a-whole emerges. This will be explored more fully later in the chapter when the analysis of interview material is discussed.

In defining the socioanalytic interview as a potential space, we must consider the nature of this space and the conditions whereby such a space can be created and sustained. To do this, we should consider the various social and emotional systems operating in the interview, and perhaps by extension, in the social system that is the object of the research.

First considered is the social-emotional system. Humans are relational animals and the interview engages them in role relations – interviewer and interviewee – and person-to-person relationships. This means there will be transferences and countertransferences involved. That is, the interviewer and his/her questions will raise thoughts and feelings in the interviewee from past similar situations. Similarly, thoughts and feelings will be raised in the interviewer. Rather than seeing these thoughts and feelings as distracting, irrelevant, or even dangerous, we need to understand them as data about the situations being discussed – that is, about the research object.

In order for new learning to be achieved in the research or consultancy, the interview must be a collaborative process. Otherwise, the past certainties of either or all participants are simply confirmed. Each, in that case, holds to his or her habits and nothing new can emerge. Collaboration cannot be regarded as a given but is built and grows alongside trust. Moreover, trust need not be generalised. The situation requires that the people involved can be trusted to take up the roles of interviewer and interviewee ethically and with authenticity, to learn as they proceed, and to agree to the task at hand. None of these conditions can be achieved perfectly, certainly not at first, although the research interviewer should be bound by professional and research ethics and should strive to be accountable to the task.

The discovery within the interview is necessarily collaborative or at least co-created, whether or not this is consciously apprehended. The 'right' questions to ask are gradually discovered rather than known at the outset by either the interviewer or interviewee. They emerge as the enquiry proceeds. This does not mean that the interview should not be carefully planned. Initial questions should be constructed in light of the research or consultancy purpose. Secondary questions and answers arise during the interview. Unconscious collaborative and also collusive processes between the interview participants are always present and affect the way that data emerges. Collusion occurs when the players simply re-establish past beliefs without question. In the mind, they merge on the points at issue. For true collaboration, the other must be seen as distinct and different so true dialogue is present. For traditional interviews, the presence of collusion and sometimes collaboration is regarded as error or bias and is guarded against through standardised procedures. For the socioanalytic interview, they are data.

Second, the interview will be experienced through the political system. Power relations within the interview are worth understanding. Let's think about how these normally proceed. The conditions for the interview are normally negotiated: where and when it will take place, who will be the participants, what will be the topics/areas covered. Good ethical practice dictates that the interviewer negotiates a safe setting where the participants will be undisturbed, and confidence and confidentiality can be maintained. Initial rapport must be established and the interviewer should outline the intent of the interview, its personal confidentiality, how the data will be handled and analysed, and who will have access to findings and whether they include de-identified material.

Normally, for research interviews a plain language statement about the research is produced and discussed, and the interviewee may be asked to sign a statement that he or she has read and understood the plain language statement and agrees to the interview. Included is an understanding that the interviewee can withdraw from the research at any time without fear or favour and a process for any complaints is outlined. It might improve the practice of organisational consultants also to follow such ethical guidelines.

Such a formal approach to the interview sets it within an institutional authority outside the personal authorities of the particular participants. This authority establishes a formal 'container' for the research or the consultancy. The socioanalyst is aware of the contextual authority and conditions within which the interview takes place because this adds to the meaning of the interview data.

The socioanalytic interviewer will gather data from the initial contacts with the interviewees. A collaborative tone should be set and some simple ideas about the interviewer and interviewee roles should be discussed: in particular, the collaborative nature of the enquiry. This is an attempt to establish the equivalent of the analytic third (Ogden) or what can be described as a position outside each of the individuals: a third space that allows some independence both of thought and power. However, in my experience, despite this initial discussion, the interviewer initially holds the power through (i) setting the conditions of the interview, (ii) representing the institutional authority for the research or consultancy, and (iii) holding the desire and accountability for the research or consultancy activity.

For a truly collaborative effort to be achieved, and hence for the truth to be revealed, the power in these three areas needs to be shifted into the interview system rather than lying solely with the interviewer. The 'truth' in this sense is that knowledge of and by the group or organisation that leads to learning. This new learning is contrasted to the tendency to cling to past certainties that no longer have a hold in reality.

Very often for the novice interviewer, the weight of responsibility to 'get it right' means that they are internally focused on what their next question will be, or on finding exactly the right words at the expense of listening to the interviewee. Responsibility for finding the right questions should not lie solely with the interviewer. If a collaborative effort is achieved, then the questions emerge. The experienced interviewer learns to subtly shift the responsibility for the success of the interview away from themselves as a sole player onto the interaction between themselves and the interviewee(s). The basis of this skill is curiosity.

The genuinely curious interviewer will engage the interviewee through his or her interest and capacity to attentively listen; to ensure that he or she really understands what the other is saying by summarising, clarifying, and playing back their understanding with a willingness to be corrected; to respectfully challenge complexities and ambiguities; to show empathy without false agreements or collusions; as far as possible to gain concrete examples about what is being said; and to allow for free associations to the interview material (see Long and Harding, 2013). Genuine curiosity leads to learning and supports the interviewee's own curiosity.

At times, the interviewee may assume a powerful position in the interview. A sense of power is gained through attending to the task and pursuing the truth within the interview. This is positive, appropriate authority. But a sense of power may be achieved through defensive manoeuvres and be displayed in attempts to deflect the curiosity of the interviewer by avoiding questions or challenging the interviewer. Often this is because the curiosity of the interviewer is experienced as intrusive or personalised. The interviewer must be willing to reflect internally on his or her own intents, but also willing to withstand the fears and anxieties of the interviewee; naming them with a willingness to explore what they might mean for the research object.

Unconscious process in the interview

Third, attention must be paid to unconscious processes in the interview. These may take the form of unconscious wishes or defences at a personal level, but they may reflect also the unconscious social defences of the organisation or social system against the anxieties or other unbearable emotions aroused by the task or the cultural assumptions and behaviours of the organisation or social system (Armstrong and Rustin, 2014). Unconscious processes may be recognised by the interviewer through sensitivity to the operation of projections and transferences from the interviewee. Should the interviewer begin to experience strong feelings or thoughts that seem not to be their own – or at least not to be typical of the emotions and thoughts they have in similar situations – then the possibility of projective mechanisms is raised. For example, the interviewer might become frightened with no obvious cause. This might indicate a projective identification whereby it is the interviewee who feels frightened but unconsciously stimulates this emotion in the interviewer. Issues around fear might then be explored. It should be stressed that not all emotions felt by the interviewer are the result of unconscious projections. They should be noted and can form the basis of a working hypothesis which might be tested through additional and repetitive examples. The identification of unconscious processes relies on noting repetitions and patterns in behaviour; single incidents might give an alert, but persistent patterns give confirmation. Defensive unconscious patterns indicate the presence of repressed ideas, or ideas that are not permitted to come to consciousness.

The latter indicates the operation of a social unconscious (Fromm, 1962; Foulkes, 1975; Hopper, 2003). Social systems operate so as to prevent certain ideas coming to consciousness or, if they do become conscious to some members, they cannot be acted upon. These are ideas that are counter-cultural or challenge the ruling elite. They challenge the establishment of the system and challenge the internal establishment of the mind (Bion, 1970). Such unconscious ideas are extremely hard to access in an interview, not least because interviewee and interviewer most likely share similar cultural assumptions. Reflection on all that is assumed is a corrective. The socioanalytic interviewer should provide pauses within the interview when this can be done. Again, this practice helps to develop a collaborative and reflective mind-set in the interview.

Other unconscious processes at a systemic level include splitting and denial. Whenever black and white opinions are expressed about particular groups or others with little modification, these defences may be operating. It is as if all the bad characteristics of the organisation are located in one person, or role, or department and all the good in another. Splitting and denial as systemic defences are most readily identified and considered during the analysis of multiple interviews, to be discussed later in this chapter. Quite normally when doing research or consulting interviews, quite some time may be spent by the interviewee 'letting off steam'. At this time, they may report all the 'bad' things about their experience in the organisation and may identify many people or areas to 'blame'. This initial splitting appears to be a way of venting built-up grievances. It may be that the interviewee has not really had anyone so interested in their experience before. While this provides a lot of data, two things emerge. First, the interviewee may later feel guilty about some of the things they have said. It is worth having enough time in the interview for the interviewee to work through this stage and provide modified accounts, and it is ethically responsible for the interviewer to recognise this. Once more, a review and reflection space is helpful. Second, the interviewer should recognise the grievances and their modifications as part of a process so that the facts are distinguishable from the emotional experiences surrounding them. This is where it is helpful to get concrete examples of the issues raised in the interview, rather than generalised ideas and opinions.

Some unconscious dynamics, however, are not defensive. In the long history of the development of the idea of the unconscious, it has often been regarded as a source of creativity (McGrath, 2012; Long, 2016b). Jung's collective unconscious, for instance, includes the archetypes that lie at the basis of those cultural myths and stories that give meaning to human experiences in groups and societies. The associative unconscious (Long and Harney, 2013) is understood as an unconscious mental network that links people through thoughts within a communicating system and is described as:

> a mental network of thoughts, signs, and symbols or signifiers, able to give rise to many feelings, impulses and images . . . . The associative unconscious as a system holds a set of processes of symbolisation constrained only by current expressions.
>
> (Long and Harney, 2013, p. 8)

This network is accessed through free associations. The socioanalytic interview, by admitting the validity of free associations as well as focused thinking, can have access to the associative unconscious of the organisation (see, for example, Lawrence, 1988, 2001, 2007; Long, 2013, 2016; Mersky, 2017). This enables the researcher to discover the 'unthought known' in the organisation and to aid members to consciously work with the ideas that were hitherto latent in their culture. One has just to think of the experience of Henri Poincaré, for whom a mathematical solution came in an image while he was thinking of nothing in particular, or the many dreams that have guided individuals and societies in their decision-making. Creativity has long been seen to have an unconscious phase in its overall process. Further to this, actual examples and stories about experiences should be encouraged during the interview because (i) they give more articulate and deeper meaning to any abstract ideas raised, (ii) they engage the interviewee more fully in the process, and (iii) they allow for the emotional content of experience to be expressed. It is useful in this regard to gain a picture of events across time.

In order to access the unconscious processes in an interview that may be either defensive or creative, an atmosphere of curiosity, collaboration, and trust is developed. It is good practice to leave at least ten minutes at the end of an interview to review the interview experience itself. This often throws more light on the here and now of unconscious processes, as the participants can reflect on what has emerged and how the ongoing process of the interview unfolded. In practice, the review becomes a third space slightly different to the more intense 'here and now' where both interviewer and interviewee can together look at the process they have experienced.

Analysing the interview

Interviews can be recorded (with permission) and transcribed for analysis. If not recorded, the interviewer should take notes, explaining to the interviewee that these are for purposes of recall and that from time to time the interviewer may have to pause to catch the interviewee's meaning. Taking notes, however, can distract from the process. A good way to use this method is to have two interviewers, where one engages in the discussion and the other takes notes. Two interviewers are also valuable when it comes to analysis because each has a different perspective and may receive different conscious impressions and different unconscious projections from the situation. Socioanalytic interviewers should train themselves in process notes taken immediately after the interview to capture their observations of the atmosphere of the interview, what stood out and grabbed attention in what was said, and their own thoughts and feelings. With two interviewers, a post-interview discussion of these is helpful to understand what each of the interviewers is 'holding' in terms of the various systems that the interviewee might be representing.

The first step in analysis is to become familiar with the material (interviews and process notes) by reading it through several times. In this way, the researcher internalises the thoughts and feelings present. There are several software packages for analysing transcripts and these are useful if the number of interviews is large and the data must be rendered manageable. However, these packages should not be used as a substitute for the process of internalisation of the material. This is because the socioanalyst uses him- or herself as an instrument for analysis. Internal work and the recovery of meaning may be done at an unconscious level because the interviewer, through the very nature of their intervention, joins the associative unconscious of the system being explored. Emergent patterns from the data may then become more readily accessible.

Individual interviews can be analysed by attending to major themes in the material. One way of doing this is to mark transcribed interviews or interview notes with different coloured markers for different themes. This is done across several interviews. Themes can then be ordered in terms of their strengths, the number of interviewees who raise them, and whether or not they occur in particular groupings of interviewees. This gives rise to discerning patterns amongst themes. The discovery and analysis of patterns is fundamental to socioanalytic enquiry and abductive logic (Long and Harney, 2013).

As well as particular themes in the material, interviews should be analysed for the processes occurring during the interview. What was the atmosphere and climate of the interview? What were the dynamics between interviewee and interviewer? What seemed to be avoided or left unsaid?

In addition to themes and processes, another cut into the data is to consider narrative analysis. Here, particular events and stories emerge. While thematic analysis gives a picture of the present state of the system (individual, group, organisation, or social system), narrative analysis tends to capture the evolution of experience across time.

Multiple interviews

Returning to the previously used metaphor of the jigsaw puzzle, multiple interviews in organisations, groups, or social systems should each be seen as a part of the whole. How might we put them together to glimpse the whole? This is where the initial purpose and design of the interview is important. It may be that different groupings are to be contrasted, for example department A and department B; or men and women; or those who have been in the organisation for different numbers of years; or different roles or professions. Depending on what is to be explored, interviews will contain basic questions that address such 'demographical data' in the first instance. The interviewee may be told that the demographic data is to be collected for this purpose while individuals' comments, as part of our ethical approach, will be de-identified so that group themes only will emerge in the research. In the analysis, then, the themes from various groupings of interviews can be considered. These groupings themselves are then each considered as one piece in the jigsaw of the overall system.

Hypothesis formation

Once themes, patterns, and narratives are discovered, and different demographics are compared, the researcher might formulate working hypotheses as an explanatory tool. The working hypothesis is a device to attempt to explain the data in causative terms. I briefly diverge here to explain this. We tend to think of causation in terms of A leading to B in a consistent manner. I kick the ball (A) and it moves (B). But this is just one causative model. Aristotle noted four forms of causation that we still recognise today.

1. *Material causation.* An object or function is caused by its material essence. Hence my written chapter is caused by my body and brain together with my computer's metals, wires, and plastics arranged in intricate ways. A tree is caused by its wood and leaves.
2. *Efficient causation.* This is the A leads to B type. It is causation of dynamics across time. My written chapter is caused by my thinking and activating the keyboard of my computer, which activates electronic

messages and so on until I have a document arranged into letters and words and sentences. A tree is caused by its growth from a seed.
3. *Formal causation.* An object or function is caused by a pattern. My written chapter is caused by my thoughts which may not be linear but jump around so that I backtrack and change or delete something. My argument comes as a whole, and I have to break the pattern into parts. It might come as a dream or a picture. It is only later that I turn it into a linear piece of work. A tree is caused by its structural pattern; a pattern already in its DNA.
4. *Final causation.* An object or function is caused by its 'final place' or its maturity in a system. My written chapter is caused by my vision of it in this book. I desire it to be and the cause is my desire.

We can see here that although the physical sciences primarily use material and efficient causation as a basis for hypotheses, the sciences concerning human symbolic functioning primarily use formal and final causative models. Our human psychology and organisational systems are predicated on our desires and the patterns and forms that these take.

In developing working hypotheses that look for patterns, motives, and desires, we use the abductive logic outlined by Peirce, that is, the logic underpinning psychoanalytic and socioanalytic practice (Long and Harney, 2013).

Working hypotheses can then be tested with new evidence, from new or secondary interviews.

Socioanalytic interviewing is used when an in-depth interview is required. As it is a collaborative process, it is not successful if coercion is used or if the interviewer takes a biased stance.

Closing

This chapter has outlined the nature and practice of socioanalytic interviewing. This is a style of interview that aims at discovering facts, dynamics, patterns, and desires within groups, organisations, and social systems. It does this through discovering the experience of the interviewee or multiple interviewees below the surface of conscious everyday discourse. Through a collaborative process, the interviewer aids the interviewee to enter a reflective space that aids in the discovery of themes, patterns, narratives, and desires in the interviewee's experience. Moreover, both interviewer and interviewee can become increasingly attentive to the dynamics within the interview that may parallel the dynamics being discussed or may give deeper insight into that material.

References

Armstrong, D., and Rustin, M. (2014), *Social Defences against Anxiety: Explorations in a Paradigm*. Tavistock Clinic Series. London: Karnac.
Bion, W. R. (1961), *Experiences in Groups*. London: Tavistock Publications.

Bion, W. R. (1970), *Attention and Interpretation*. London: Tavistock Publications.
Boccara, B. (2013), Socioanalytic dialogue. In S. D. Long (ed.), *Socioanalytic Methods* (pp. 279–300). London: Karnac.
Boccara, B. (2014), *Socioanalytic Dialogue: Incorporating Psychosocial Dynamics into Public Policies*. New York: Lexington Books.
Bohm, D. (1980), *Wholeness and the Implicate Order*. London: Routledge.
Foulkes, S. H. (1975), *Group Analytic Psychotherapy: Method and Principles*. London: Karnac, 1986.
Fromm, E. (1962), *Beyond the Chains of Illusion: My Encounter with Marx and Freud*. New York: Simon & Schuster.
Hollway, W., and Jefferson, T. (2000), *Doing Qualitative Research Differently*. California: Sage.
Hopper, E. (2003), *The Social Unconscious: Selected Papers*. International Library of Group Analysis Series. London: Jessica Kingsley.
Lawrence, W. G. (ed.) (1988), *Social Dreaming @ Work*. London: Karnac.
Lawrence, W. G. (ed.) (2007), *The Infinite Possibilities of Social Dreaming*. London: Routledge.
Long, S. D. (2000), Conflict and co-operation: two sides of the same coin. In R. Wiesner and B. Millet (eds.), *Current Issues in Organizational Behaviour*. Jacaranda: Wiley.
Long, S. D. (ed.) (2013), *Socioanalytic Methods*. London: Karnac.
Long, S. D. (ed.) (2016a), *Transforming Experience in Organisations: A Framework for Organisational Research and Consultancy*. London: Karnac.
Long, S. D. (2016b), The transforming experience framework and unconscious processes: a brief journey through the history of the concept of the unconscious as applied to person, system and context with an exploratory hypothesis of unconscious as source. In S. D. Long (ed.), *Transforming Experience in Organisations: A Framework for Organisational Research and Consultancy*. London: Karnac.
Long, S. D., and Harding, W. (2013), Socioanalytic interviewing. In S. D. Long (ed.), *Socioanalytic Methods* (pp. 91–106). London: Karnac.
Long, S. D., and Harney, M. (2013), The associative unconscious. In S. D. Long (ed.), *Socioanalytic Methods* (pp. 3–22). London: Karnac.
McGrath, S. J. (2013), *The Dark Ground of Spirit: Schelling and the Unconscious*. London and New York: Routledge.
Menzies-Lyth, I. E. P (1960), Social systems as a defence against anxiety. *Human Relations*, 13: 95–121.
Mersky, R. (2017), *Social Dream Drawing*. Unpublished doctoral thesis, UWE England.

Chapter 3

Psychoanalytic perspectives on the qualitative research interview

Nick Midgley and Joshua Holmes

Interviewing is the most commonly used method of data collection in qualitative research (Briggs, 1986; Silverman, 2013). Yet despite clinical psychoanalysis being a particular kind of conversation between analyst and patient, which could potentially contribute to how qualitative researchers approach these encounters, the majority of psychological studies within the Anglo-Saxon research literature 'scarcely contain references to Freud and the psychoanalytic research interview' (Kvale, 2000, p. 13).

In-depth interviewing involves a number of expected components (e.g., Gubrium and Holstein, 2001; Kvale and Brinkmann, 2008). A researcher meets with a participant, aiming to elicit the latter's thoughts and feelings about a research topic (e.g., bereavement, depression, etc.). Sampling is often 'purposive': participants will have been invited to take part because they have some degree of experience of this topic, and are felt to be in a position to throw some light on the research topic. Interviewees are thought of as 'experts by experience' (Ramon, 2009, p. 80). Interviewers usually ask participants questions which may be open-ended (i.e., to encourage elaboration on an experience and avoid simple yes/no answers), and the interview schedules used are usually 'semi-structured' (i.e., mostly pre-determined, but flexible as to order, phraseology, etc.). In addition to questions, the interviewer makes statements or offers other cues, such as showing genuine interest and leaving space for ideas to develop, with the hope of encouraging the participant's responsiveness and helping them to speak openly and explore their personal experience in some depth.

Steiner Kvale (1986, 1996, 1999, 2000, 2003) has argued that psychoanalysis has overlaps with 'existential, hermeneutic, dialectical and postmodern philosophical positions' and is 'relevant for enriching and deepening the use of qualitative interviews in the social sciences' (Kvale, 2000, pp. 9, 11). He points out the incompatibility of the psychoanalytic approach with the positivist epistemology on which most *quantitative* research is based, and sets out a number of areas in which it has potential to contribute to a qualitative model, especially the focus on the interpersonal relations of the interview when constructing knowledge.

Kvale describes aspects of the psychoanalytic, clinical interview which he believes make it of interest to qualitative researchers: it takes place in a structured setting, which is free and non-directive and proceeds in an open manner, led by the patient's free associations and the analyst's 'free-floating attention'; knowledge is built up over a considerable period of time, allowing for deeper and more informed understandings; it involves a human, emotional interaction between two people which promotes the generation of new knowledge; it is in this respect a true 'inter-view', in which the knowledge constructed between the two participants is 'inter-subjective', in contrast to academic psychology, which he characterises as a 'psychology of strangers' (Kvale, 2000, p. 22).

However, Kvale's work is limited in not offering many examples of how psychoanalytically informed interviews might be carried out in practice, and insufficiently considering the difference between the clinical and the research setting. Other researchers have developed ways of researching inspired by the psychoanalytic interview. Some such approaches will now be explored.

The 'free-association narrative interview method'

Hollway and Jefferson's book, *Doing Qualitative Research Differently*, offers a psychoanalytically informed model of qualitative research structured around an investigation of 'the fear of crime'. This topic is suitable for study from a psychoanalytic point of view because of its subjective and anxiety-provoking nature. They begin by noting that the levels of anxiety about crime often bear little relation to the actual levels of crime in a particular setting. Hollway and Jefferson discuss why traditional research methods – using variables such as gender, age, and social deprivation – are unlikely to explain the meaning of this phenomenon. They go on to say that qualitative approaches have also been limited because of their 'tell it like it is' assumption, which leads them to believe that research participants are self-conscious about what motivates their fear of crime, and are able to understand and articulate the nature and origins of this fear. Hollway and Jefferson call this the assumption of a 'transparent self' able to provide a 'transparent account' of their own psychological world, while in reality what people know and what they say is often contradictory and complex (2000, pp. 2, 3). For research to reflect this complex psychological reality, the idea of the 'defended subject' helps researchers see their participants as human subjects who are not fully aware of the meaning of their own behaviours, and consider the effects of defences against anxiety in the narratives that people produce (Hollway and Jefferson, 2000).

When taking such a position, in what way would this change how a researcher might conduct an interview? Like many other qualitative researchers, Hollway and Jefferson advocate interviews that involve open questions (e.g., 'what do you most fear?' rather than 'how safe do you feel?'); and the eliciting of stories (so even better than 'what do you most fear?', 'can you tell me about a time when you were fearful?'). They also suggest avoiding 'why' questions that can encourage intellectualisation; following the participant, even when they appear to be going 'off-topic'; and using the respondent's own ordering and phrasing in order to transmit the value of a participant-led conversation, akin to free association in the analytic setting. By adapting the traditional qualitative interview in these ways, allowing unconscious dynamics to become foregrounded (especially the emergence of anxiety and the narrative processes by which these anxieties could be defended against), Hollway and Jefferson argue that interviews are enriched (for examples of how, see Hollway and Jefferson, 2012).

The credibility of their case for interviewing in this way is helped by the inclusion of the false-starts and failures. In their pilot interviews, for example, the authors used an interview schedule, asking about areas of theoretical interest, for specific examples and probing for accounts of both events and the respondents' feelings – in other words, a typical, semi-structured question-and-answer interview. When the authors piloted this interview, however, they discovered that this approach, rather than eliciting, tended to suppress the very narratives that they had wished to explore, while the participants themselves seemed to comply to the researcher's implicit agenda. This indicated that if researchers plan interviews with too much of an idea of what they are trying to find, their own spontaneity and that of the participants will be hindered, and the research may end up lacking depth.

Making use of the 'defended subject' concept to interpret interview data, Hollway and Jefferson build up a series of 'psychosocial case studies'. Highlighting the limitations of traditional models of generalising the results of quantitative studies, which tend to rely on the assumption that simple variables have the same meaning for all people, they suggest that studies of psychosocial subjects can be used – however cautiously – to help construct more meaningful theories about the fear of crime (chapter 6).

Hollway and Jefferson are indebted to psychoanalysis 'both theoretically and methodologically' (p. 77): through their theoretical model of anxiety and the 'defended subject'; their approach to data production based on Freud's free association method; and their emphasis on the interpretive aspect of data analysis. In the first iteration of their book, however, Holloway and Jefferson (2000) warn against in-interview interpretive comments. This was reconsidered in the second edition of their book (Hollway and Jefferson, 2013) and is discussed further later in this chapter. Hollway and Jefferson are also careful to highlight one key difference between psychoanalysis and the research interview: the fact that the object of clinical psychoanalysis is the particular person, whereas the researcher usually has a wider social/research interest. This leads Hollway and Jefferson to write about the 'psychosocial', rather than the purely psychological, subject.

Hollway and Jefferson's method pays some attention to the intersubjective dynamics of the interview setting itself (pp. 44–52) and recognises theoretically that the research interview is always an encounter between *two* anxious, defended subjects. They argue for the importance of the researcher recording their fantasies and feelings at the end of the research interview (although little data of this kind is presented in the book), and give an example of how the encounter can be thought about in terms of the psychoanalytic process of transference–countertransference, and recognition and containment (see also

Gadd, 2004). However, we must turn to the Central European tradition of psychoanalytically informed research for a fuller recognition of countertransference in interviewing.

The 'theme-centred interview' and scenic understanding

More than in the UK and the Anglo-Saxon tradition, in Germany, qualitative research – however marginal it might be in relation to 'mainstream' psychology – has maintained links with psychoanalysis, particularly in its overlaps with the hermeneutic tradition within philosophy and the social sciences (Mruck, 2000; Apitzsch and Inowlocki, 2000; Frommer, Langenbach, and Streek, 2004). Two such examples of this cross-over between hermeneutics, psychoanalysis, and qualitative research have been the methods of analysis known as 'objective hermeneutics' (Oevermann, 1993) and 'in-depth hermeneutics' (Leithäuser and Volmberg, 1988), both of which draw on Freud's distinction between the 'manifest' and the 'latent' meaning of communication to attempt an analysis of the unconscious aspects of communication, while putting the researcher's emotional responses within the interview setting at the heart of the data collection and data analysis process.

In-depth (or 'deep-structure', as it is sometimes translated into English) hermeneutics draws on a form of literary interpretation developed by Lorenzer (1986), in which the effect of the text on the researcher is thought about as a way of accessing latent – or unconscious – levels of meaning.

For Lorenzer, understanding comes through enactment, or the 'scenic drama' which inevitably becomes activated when an 'evenly suspended attention' is offered by the researcher and his or her affective reactions are noted. König gives the example of a study of media representations of right-wing extremism, where attention to moments of such 'irritation', when discussed in a group setting, led to disagreements among members of the discussion group, a conflict that could in itself be understood as a 'scenic enactment' and therefore, when analysed, be used as part of the process of interpretation.

The 'scenic' refers to an affective register of meaning, with its origins in the early phases of life, operating initially below the surface and verbal level, yet continuously present. These scenic phenomena are inscribed in the body and brain in the form of 'engrams'. As development proceeds, scenic phenomena typically become symbolised through language. But, either through the traumatic nature of experience, or because of social forces antipathetic to symbolisation, this process may be aborted or remain incomplete. Here, emotional responsiveness does not merely capture participant projections, rather it is an intersubjective consideration, where the emotions expressed by the participant interact with those brought forth in the interviewer.

Because the researcher, in Wellendorf's terms, is always being pulled into the dynamics of the individual (or the organisation) being researched, he or she acts like a 'projective surface', and a scenic interpretation of the 'usage of the relational-space of the interview' can lead to insight into the research phenomena itself (Tietel, 2000). In order to make use of this affective response of the researcher, some form of discussion or reflection becomes vital, again influenced by the psychoanalytic model of clinical supervision.

Marks (2001) describes a process of what he terms 'inter-vision', in which the researcher, having conducted an interview and made notes on his or her emotional responses to it, then has an 'inter-vision' with two colleagues, in which the thoughts, feelings, impressions, and associations of the researcher are discussed and explored. In addition, each of the interviews is evaluated by two small research groups, each working directly from the audio recording of the interview rather than a transcript. Whenever a particular interruption, contradiction, or fantasy is noted in the interview – or in the mind of the group of researchers – the audio is stopped and this observation is itself explored by the group (see also Dieckmann, 1976). Selected interviews (those that were in some sense the most 'difficult') are in turn evaluated by a team discussion, moderated by a supervisor, allowing a gradual process of hypothesis formation. These hypotheses are then examined by means of a computerised textual-analysis system, so allowing a 'triangulation' of data-analytic processes to strengthen the credibility of the final analysis.

As a brief aside, it is worth noting that working from transcripts is probably the most common form of data analysis used in qualitative research, perhaps because it adds an element of 'objectivity' to the research process. But due to the close connection between voice and emotion, Marks and Mönnich-Marks argue that tape recordings themselves should be used (2003, para. 27). Similar to this process of 'inter-vision', Drapeau (2002) describes a process of working with what he calls '*le tiers*' (or 'the third party') – someone who is able to see the unconscious dynamics being enacted from a position both inside and outside the research setting. The use of this concept of 'the third' hints at the link to the oedipal triangle, and in particular its importance for providing a self-reflexive position (see Britton, 1989).

It is perhaps not coincidental that such intensive attention to the researcher's own emotional responses has taken place when dealing with topics that are likely to create strong feelings among researchers themselves. Germany's Nazi history is a topic fraught with anxiety and contradiction, both for those involved in that history and those (mostly younger) people attempting to research it. Marks (2001) and Marks and Mönnich-Marks (2003) describe the way in which many of the manifest testimonies of people involved with Nazism whom they interviewed as part of a study attempting to understand what motivated so many ordinary German people to tolerate – or actively support – the Nazi movement, were quite banal; yet powerful dynamics took place within the interview setting itself. Many of those interviewed were dominating and self-opinionated, and the researchers doing the interviews could feel 'overrun, bulldozed, emptied, saddened, confused, sickened, abused or knocked down' (Marks and Mönnich-Marks, 2003, para. 8), and following the interviews, researchers reported nightmares about war or persecution.

Marks and Mönnich-Marks note that there was a central emotional reaction that those doing the interviews gradually began to describe through the process of 'inter-vision': shame. At first, it was experienced as a sense of failure – a feeling that they had not done a 'good' interview, or that they had been weak, and had failed to challenge comments dismissing the Holocaust or other Nazi atrocities. Significantly, these feelings were at first unacknowledged or excluded from discussions about the research process, and only began to be spoken about when a sufficient degree of trust within the research team had been established (para. 20/21). As well as the personal dynamics involved, this reflects the depersonalised assumptions of the university culture (which encourages the 'avoidance of the first person pronoun in scientific texts') which tend to mitigate against the expression of subjective experience (Marks and Mönnich Marks, 2003).

In this case, the analysis of the countertransference reaction of shame helped the researchers to identify a 'cycle of victimisation', in which shame was being passed from perpetrator to victim, while being re-enacted through a process of what Klein would have called 'projective identification'. Returning to the interviews in the light of this insight made it possible to detect a multitude of subtle processes by which the interviewees produced such a sense of shame in the researchers, often touching on their own personal vulnerabilities (para. 32). In this way, the countertransference reaction became a way of identifying a key (but latent) theme in their object of study itself – the support for Nazism as a way of defending against unconscious feelings of shame (see also Jureit, 2000; Tietel, 2000; L. Andersen, 2003). The latter two papers refer to psychoanalytically informed interviews taking place in an organisational setting. It is likely that such complex organisational changes working at both a personal and a social level, and the dynamics involved with studying them, are also appropriate for this kind of emphasis on 'scenic understanding', and offer a good example of the ways in which psychological and sociological factors inter-relate.

Hollway, and colleagues (e.g., Froggett and Hollway, 2010; Hollway and Froggett, 2012) have further developed the concept of 'scenic understanding', encouraging the creation of 'scenic compositions' in 'a process by which researchers reflect on their affective and embodied experience of their data' (Redman, Bereswill, and Morgenroth, 2010, p. 217), in order to provide 'a vivid, visualised rendering of a data extract that preserves its emotional resonance during data analysis and for the reader' (Hollway and Froggett, 2012, no page number, online article).

Here is an example of a scenic composition, describing a research participant:

> Darren is pale, gangly, shaven headed; slouchy shoulders in slouchy, street-cool clothes… he is childlike – waiting to be led, or entertained, or told what to do. His feet shuffle as if they don't quite belong to him… Darren rubs his head, stressed.
>
> ibid.

The aim of the 'scenic composition' is to enable the person to come to life in the mind of the reader, so that it is easier to identify with him, or to 'traverse imaginatively the distance' (ibid.) between researcher and participant. This description incorporates researcher subjectivity, with imagined feeling states ('Darren rubs his head, stressed'); colloquial and evocative language ('gangly'); emotive, rather than purely descriptive, words ('slouchy, street-cool clothes'). This is a different imaginative creation for the reader, contrasting with a 'standard' 'clinical' preamble such as: 'Darren is a white 17-year-old from a working-class family in Dalston. He studies computer programming at college.' Scenic composition aims to capture the emotional atmosphere in the presence of a participant, which is not only omitted but possibly defensively avoided through conventional demographic descriptions (see also Hollway, 2010, in thinking about motherhood; and Bereswill, Orgenroth, and Redman, 2010, in analysing a young woman's reaction to an episode of the television programme *Big Brother*).

In summary, Lorenzer's (1983) concept of 'scenic understanding' points towards a) the omnipresence of unconscious forces which shape everyday life (including research interviews), and b) their relationality. In his psychosocial model, the latter is reflected both in the unconscious preconceptions and defences which the participants bring to their interactions, but also to the ways in which prevailing social forces reinforce or discourage different elements in the interaction. In the research setting, the prevailing socio-political dominance of the 'masculine' and instrumental may chime with emotional diminishment in researchers and participants to generate affect-impoverished data and banal conclusions. Here, the research interview becomes a *commodity exchange* in a utilitarian framework in which participants become little more than sources of information, plundered to fulfil research aims, and duly rewarded with financial incentives.

Problems and criticisms of psychoanalytically informed qualitative interviewing

Criticisms have come not only from *quantitative* researchers working from a more traditional positivist perspective (who may see psychoanalytically informed interviewing as an exaggerated version of most qualitative research, i.e., in especially lacking objectivity and as especially weak in the areas of reliability, validity, and generalisability), but also from *qualitative* researchers, whether those working from a more critical realist perspective, or those working from a more social constructionist position.

Hollway and Jefferson's work, for example, has been criticised by discursive psychologists, for its tendency to 'reproduce the essentialist, individualist and normative characteristics of traditional psychology' (Georgaca, 2005). Ian Parker writes 'Beware the free-association narrative interview' (2005, p. 108), arguing that, in this approach, 'psychoanalysis rather than qualitative research . . . is in command'. He argues that Hollway and Jefferson's method creates a number of dangers in the research process: of *individualising* (seeing society purely as an 'aggregate of individual psychological processes'); of *essentialising* ('when the researcher thinks they really know what the "emotional logic" of the free association is pointing to'); of *pathologising* (unearthing the 'reprehensible things' from the past which will explain why they think or behave in the way they do); and of *disempowering* (with the researcher as 'the expert who only tells other experts what has been discovered'; Parker, 2005, p. 108).

Yet in other respects, psychoanalysis and discursive psychology appear to have much in common. Indeed, Parker has claimed in his earlier writing that psychoanalysis is one of the four 'key resources' (alongside Marxism, feminism, and post-structuralism) that has most informed his work and that of his colleagues at the Discourse Unit in Manchester. This seeming contradiction becomes clearer when one looks more closely at what Parker means by 'psychoanalysis'. While arguing that 'classical' (especially ego-psychological) psychoanalysis is 'inimical to the whole project of discursive qualitative research' (3.4), Parker argues that the Lacanian re-reading of Freud, in which the unconscious is an 'Other' site of discourse, has a great deal more to offer. For Parker (like a number of other discursive psychologists, such as Wetherell and Burman), Lacan's work emphasises the way in which subjectivity is structured in and by discursive relations, which in themselves are inherently cultural.

Parker (2003) offers his own ideas about what a psychoanalytic research strategy could look like, while simultaneously treating psychoanalysis as a powerful discourse that has to be treated with great caution (see also Parker, 1997). As a discourse that both structures how we think about ourselves in modern society, and simultaneously offers a critical position to analyse that positioning, Parker sees psychoanalysis as 'part of the problem and part of the solution' (2005, p. 108). The tone of his work is predominantly suspicious of – and hostile to – psychoanalysis, especially as it is manifested in most clinical practice and training in Britain today. Yet in so far as psychoanalysis stands as the 'repressed other of psychology' (Burman, 1994), he sees it as a potentially valuable tool within his vision of a 'radical' qualitative psychology.

The apparent dichotomy between Lacanian and 'classical' (or object relations) psychoanalysis, like the dichotomy between different discursive and other approaches to qualitative psychology, is questioned in the work of Stephen Frosh, whose interview-based study of young masculinities tried to build bridges between these different versions of psychoanalysis and of qualitative psychology (Frosh et al., 2002).

Frosh's work recognises that Lacanian psychoanalysis appears 'more promising' in the contribution it can make to the practice of qualitative psychology because of its emphasis on discourse. In contrast, a more object relations theory of the 'inner world' is at risk of 'losing the great contribution that discursive psychology has made in emphasising the performative nature of language in constructing identities' (2003, p. 42). Yet Frosh also recognises that the object relations version of psychoanalysis used by Wendy Hollway and others gives attention to 'individual biography and emotional subtexts' in a way that discursive psychology often fails to do. In particular, Frosh argues that discursive psychology fails to offer conceptual tools for explaining why individuals take up particular positions in relation to dominant discourses, and suggests that psychoanalysis is in a particularly strong position to help explore the emotional investment that subjects have in particular discursive positions.

Drawing on interviews with a group of 11- to 14-year-old boys in London schools during the 1990s, he shows how discursive positions taken up by young people in relation to topics such as 'masculinity' or 'racism' can be seen as attempts to negotiate unconscious conflicts (2003, p. 46). As an example, he describes how a 12-year-old boy negotiates a 'counter-hegemonic' model of masculinity in his discourse about 'being with girls', while arguing that such a discourse is underpinned by a 'strong sense of loss and exclusion', as well as anxiety (Frosh et al., 2003, pp. 44–46). It is not simply enough to say, as other (non-psychoanalytic) discourse analysts may do, that Oliver performs such a counter-hegemonic identity through various discursive strategies; Frosh and his colleagues go on to argue, using an explicitly psychoanalytic model, that this positioning by Oliver may be an 'attempt to use the available discursive possibilities to deal with a set of powerful unconscious conflicts' (p. 46). While recognising that the interpretations offered are speculative, Frosh et al. argue that bringing in such a psychoanalytic perspective allows a 'move which goes "beyond" or "beneath" discourse to explore the needs which are being met, the "enjoyment" created, by the position which is taken up' (2003, p. 52). (See Frosh and Emerson, 2005, who follow up this work with a 'discursively driven interpretative' approach to explore questions of power, interpretative validity, and the subsequent differences or possibilities for collaboration between the two approaches.)

Reverie-informed research interviewing

Let us return to the process of conducting in-depth interviews, and in particular the question of drawing on one's own emotional experiences as part of the interview process, and in particular *whether* offering psychoanalytically informed interpretations may be appropriate in the course of interviewing a research participant. One argument against doing this is that it could lead to a kind of 'wild analysis', and impose the interviewer's own point of view on what the participant is speaking about. There is also concern that research participants have not consented to engage in a therapeutic encounter, and so offering interpretations in the course of the interview (as opposed to during the process of analysis) may be at best inappropriate, and at worst unethical. Yet to not do so may feel like a lost opportunity to bring a depth to the interview encounter, and hence to our understanding of the topic of research.

A cautious approach might involve recording post-interview reflections and feelings in the form of a self-interview. Shakow (1960, p. 84) has suggested recording 'the immediate... associations of the therapist's own unexpressed processes – the feelings, thoughts, and the intuitive impressions... during the therapy hour'. One can imagine an interview analogy. Although this may be helpful as we begin to interpret the data, the trouble with this method is that without in-the-moment engagement we may miss an opportunity to help a participant feel understood and thus enhance rapport, and hence the chance to explore interesting material. Shakow acknowledges that psychoanalytic data are generated in 'the fleeting and momentary' (p. 90). A bold approach may attempt to find a way to remain research-oriented yet engaged in the moment, paying equal attention to one's own internal responses as to the participant's words. For example, one psychoanalytically informed interviewer notes his mismatch of feelings – fearful as his interviewee speaks about his philanthropic deeds – in a research interview (Cartwright, 2004). This is useful research information, informed by his clinical stance. But if not taken up within the interview itself, it represents an opportunity lost.

It has been suggested that the psychoanalytic notion of reverie may offer a way in which interviewers can form and use interpretation-like responses in the moment in interviews (e.g., McVey et al., 2015; Holmes, forthcoming). The word 'reverie' implies a state of day-dream. These states have been described as 'autistic' (e.g., Chessick, 1982, p. 160), inward-looking, and thus the antithesis of relational. But when Bion (1962) asserted that mother's 'love is expressed by reverie' (p. 36), he moved the definition from autistic to viewing reverie as the means by which the mother responds to and understands the communications of her infant. Post-Bion, reverie has become relational.

Bion's reverie theory led to the description of a countertransference–transference amalgam, an unconscious matrix mutually created between analyst and patient (e.g., Aron, 1995; Ogden, 1995), in which the analyst's reverie becomes a clue to the inner world of the patient, and especially to disavowed elements of their affective life. Some post-Bionian analysts (Ogden, 1994; Ferro, 2002) have suggested that reverie is the analyst's principal means of accessing this realm.

How can Bion's ideas inform the research setting? Holmes (in press) has suggested that interviewers may formulate interpretation-like responses in the interview setting, based on reverie experiences, then scrutinise them with a degree of conscious awareness, then attempt to incorporate them into a response. Below is a brief example that attempts to convey both a scenic composition style of capturing the essence of an interview interaction through writing, while also illustrating a reverie-informed comment, which was made to the participant 'live' during a research interview. The example comes from an interview that took place in the context of a study called 'Improving Mood with Psychoanalytic and Cognitive Therapies – My Experience' (IMPACT-ME; Midgley, Ansaldo, and Target, 2014). NM was principal investigator in this study and JH worked as a qualitative interviewer. The 'My Experience' part refers to the qualitative sub-study associated with the main IMPACT randomised controlled trial. IMPACT-ME explored the experiences of therapy for adolescents with depression. As these were often extremely reticent participants, creative methods of engaging with them in interviews were required. These were some notes that JH made soon after one face-to-face interview with Karl, a 17-year-old depression sufferer:

> Karl speaks about the difference between his depression and sadness. Sadness 'was' (using the past tense) 'the opposite of happy' but depression... he pauses. 'I dunno' – another pause... 'just sort of...', the tone conveys progression – he will know soon – an empty glass about to be moved towards and filled from running water. And now stumbling towards a close-enough fit: 'it's like it goes over all your feeling as a whole thing'. With my own inward glance, I imagine a field which snow has blanketed – 'gone over' it. I see stillness, and hear silence. 'And it sort of governs your thoughts as well.' Now I wonder if an internal authoritarian figure has made Karl's bed (put the blanket in place). A few seconds of quiet, beholding the snowscape, before we are aware of it. 'I'm imagining a blanket covering everything', I say. With the word 'blanket', Karl has said 'yeah', then he rests, and perhaps needs to dismiss exploration in this moment with appraisal: 'that's some incre- good example'.

In this example, we glimpse how a reverie-influenced within-interview comment may help with emotional awareness during moments of over-articulacy. Drawing on reverie during a research interview may open up new areas of conversation, and create richer interviews. A reverie-informed approach may also be informative about research questions themselves, and thus may provide new forms of data which would otherwise have been inaccessible. In this brief example, we see an early stage hypothesis that Karl's depression may be linked to feeling controlled by a 'harsh superego', and once this is seen, there is the chance for further exploration. This information is helpful if, for example, we were setting out to explore understandings of adolescent depression and we wanted to compare manifest verbalised data and latent data accessible through interviewer reverie (for more in-depth examples of how reverie both helped with impasse and was informative about research questions, see Holmes, forthcoming).

Reverie is often accessible through awareness of general feeling states, accessed through awareness of the 'pit of the stomach'. Indeed, Ogden (1997, p. 572) describes reverie as experienced first as 'physical sensations as opposed to verbal narratives'. The notion of reverie-informed research is in its infancy, but interviewers interested in making use of it may wish to focus their awareness on the following:

- *Anticipation*: attunement to the usefulness of reverie. Rather than dismissing unexpected thoughts, feelings, images, or other manifestations of reverie while conducting interviews.
- *Non-directive facilitation of thoughts and fantasies*: allowing reverie to take its shape or direction.
- *Overcoming barriers to reverie*: including tolerance of anxiety, allowing it to arise, but for it not to become overwhelming. A partially drifting and de-

focused engagement seems necessary, which may not be possible with a very structured interview.
- *Reflection*: paying attention to bodily and emotional states.
- *Linking*: thinking about how these states might relate to the participant and/or research topic. Links to the research question or the participant's emotional world may not be immediately apparent. The researcher must withstand the anxiety associated with *not* understanding.
- *Utterance*: the researcher may, if appropriate, incorporate the above into a verbal response.
- *Writing:* through talking with colleagues, listening to the recording, and writing, the reverie may be further adjusted (cf. 'inter-vision' as described in the summary of Marks and Monnich-Marks, above).

Criticisms of within-interview interpretation

Qualitative research interviews may inevitably develop a 'clinical' – that is, confidential, emotionally engaged – atmosphere. Indeed, the more clinical-seeming the interview, perhaps the more 'successful' it will be, in that it will have facilitated hitherto latent emotional expression. This argument can be viewed as a reversal of Freud's view that every psychoanalysis was a species of research (Freud, 1912) – that is, every research interview can also be 'therapeutic'.

The argument for the usefulness of within-interview, reverie-guided comments draws on intersubjective psychoanalytic theory, namely that 'the analyst's associations to the patient's dreams are no less important than the patient's associations' (Ogden, 2001, p. 12). In the example above, the interviewer's impressions, observations, and reveries interact with Karl's responses to generate mutual understanding: '*that's some incre-good example*'.

However, it could be argued that the interviewer strayed from the researcher role to that of a therapist. Talking about a blanket in the midst of what Karl was saying was clearly *not* using a word he had used, although his phrase that depression 'goes over all of your feelings' is linked to the image of a blanket (indeed, perhaps this is a good way of thinking about the reverie method; it aims to harness the imagination of the interviewer as it links into the imagination of the participant and see how one can influence the other and build towards meaning). Nevertheless, the notion of an interpretation *within* a research interview may jar because there are enduring differences between research and clinical settings:

a) *Aims*: the aim of eliciting spontaneous conversation is only one strand of psychoanalysis, which also may aim to alleviate psychic suffering of patients. Qualitative research's aims are different: that is, information gathering and deepening understanding of the participant's experience of a

particular phenomenon. This difference lessens if reverie interviewing enhances the garnering of relevant information.
b) *Continuity*: psychoanalysis takes place over a number of years and between four or five times a week, while qualitative research interviews are typically one-off meetings. But this quantitative measure does not stand up, given that even a single session of a long-term analysis will be psychoanalytically informed.
c) *Privacy*: apart from extreme cases, such as potential violence or child protection, psychoanalysis is a private matter, and patients have the final say about whether data from their analysis may be shared or published. In the context of 'consent', the same applies in research, but there is an understanding from the outset that the aim is dissemination. This means that the endeavours will be entered into in different states of mind.
d) *Training*: The psychoanalyst undergoes a rigorous training involving his or her own psychoanalysis, supervised clinical work, and theoretical input over a number of years. Most qualitative interviewers have not undergone such a training. This raises the danger of 'wild', or even unethical, reverie.

Conclusion

This chapter has outlined some ways in which qualitative researchers have drawn on psychoanalysis to inform their interviewing strategies. Notions of the defended subject helped reframe the interviewing process with a respect for unconscious dynamics. Lorenzer and his notion of the 'scenic' has been usefully taken up in incorporating a consideration of the role of countertransference in interviewing. One way in which within-interview 'interpretation' may be employed has been discussed. Criticisms of psychoanalytic approaches to qualitative research interviewing have been outlined, as well as ethical challenges.

References

Apitzsch, U., and Inowlocki, L. (2000), Biographical analysis: a 'German' school? In P. Chamberlayne, J. Bornat, and T. Wengraf (eds.), *The Turn to Biographical Methods in Social Science*. London: Routledge.
Andersen, L. (2003), When the unconscious joins the game: a psychoanalytic perspective on modernization and change (44 paragraphs). *Forum Qualitative Sozialforschung/ Forum: Qualitative Social Research* (on-line), 4 (3). Available at: http://www.qualitative-research.net/fqs-texte/3-03/3-03andersen-e.htm
Aron, L. (1995), The internalized primal scene, *Psychoanalytic Dialogues*, 5: 195–237.
Bion, W. (1962), *Learning from Experience*. London: Karnac.
Briggs, C. (1986), *Learning How to Ask: A Sociolinguistic Appraisal of the Role of the Interview in Social Science Research*. Cambridge: Cambridge University Press.
Britton, R. (1989), The missing link: parental sexuality in the Oedipus complex. In J. Steiner (ed.), *The Oedipus Complex Today: Clinical Implications* (pp. 83–101). London: Karnac.

Burman, E. (1994), *Deconstructing Developmental Psychology*. London: Routledge.

Cartwright, D. (2004), The psychoanalytic research interview: preliminary suggestions. *Journal of the American Psychoanalytic Association*, 52: 209–242.

Chessick, R. (1982), Metaphysics or autistic reverie. *Contemporary Psychoanalysis*, 18: 160–172.

Dieckmann, H. (1976), Transference and countertransference: results of a Berlin research group. *Journal of Analytical Psychology*, 21/1: 25–36.

Drapeau, M. (2002), Subjectivity in research: Why not? But.... *The Qualitative Report*, 7/3. Retrieved from http://www.nova.edu.ssss/QR/QR7-3/drapeau.html

Ferro, A. (2002), Some implications of Bion's thought: the waking dream and narrative derivatives. *International Journal of Psycho-Analysis*, 83: 597–607.

Freud, S. (1912), Recommendations to physicians practising psycho-analysis. *Standard Edition*, 12: 109–120. London: Hogarth.

Froggett, L., and Hollway, W. (2010), Psychosocial research analysis and scenic understanding. *Psychoanalysis, Culture and Society*, 15: 281–301.

Frommer, J., and Langenbach, M. (2000), The psychoanalytic case study as a source of epistemic knowledge. In J. Frommer and D. Rennie (eds.), *Qualitative Psychotherapy Research – Methods and Methodology*. Lengerich: Pabst.

Frosh, S., and Emerson, P. (2005), Interpretation and over-interpretation: disputing the meaning of texts. *Qualitative Research*, 5: 307–324.

Frosh, S., Phoenix, A., and Pattman, R. (2002), *Young Masculinities: Understanding Boys in Contemporary Society*. Basingstoke: Palgrave.

Georgaca, E. (2005), Lacanian psychoanalysis and the subject of social constructionist psychology: analysing subjectivity in talk. *International Journal of Critical Psychology*, 4: 74–94.

Gubrium, J., and Holstein, J. (2001), *Handbook of Interview Research: Context and Method*. London: Sage.

Hollway, W., and Froggett, L. (2012), Researching in-between subjective experience and reality. *Forum: Qualitative Social Research*, 13: 3.

Hollway, W., and Jefferson, T. (2000), *Doing Qualitative Research Differently: Free Association, Narrative and the Interview Method*. London: Sage.

Hollway, W., and Jefferson, T. (2013), *Doing Qualitative Research Differently: A Psychosocial Approach*. London: Sage.

Holmes, J. (2017), Reverie-informed research interviewing. *International Journal of Psycho-Analysis*, 98(3): 709–728.

Jureit, U. (2000), Patterns of repetition: dimensions of biographical memory. *Trauma Research Newsletter*, 1, Hamburg Institute for Social Research, July. Retrieved from: http://www.TraumaResearch.net/focus1/jureit.htm

Kvale, S. (1999), The psychoanalytic interview as qualitative research. *Qualitative Inquiry*, 5(1): 87–113.

Kvale, S., and Brinkmann, S. (2008), *InterViews: Learning the Craft of Qualitative Research Interviewing*. London: Sage.

Leithäuser, T., and Volmberg, B. (1988), *Psychoanalyse in der Sozialforschung*. Opladen: Westdeutscher Verlag.

Lorenzer, A. (1986), Tiefenhermeneutische Kulturanalyse. In H. Konig, A. Lorenzer, H. Lüdde, S. Naghol, U. Prokop, G. Schmid-Noerr, and A. Eggert (eds.), *Kultur-Analysen. Psychoanalytische Studien zur Kultur*. Frankfurt aM: Fischer.

Marks, S. (2001), Research Project 'History and Memory'. In M. Kiegelmann (ed.), *Qualitative Research in Psychology*. Schwangau: Verlag Ingeborg Huber.

Marks, S., and Mönnich-Marks, H. (2003), The analysis of counter-transference reactions is a means to discern latent interview-contents (38 paragraphs). *Forum: Qualitative Social Research* (online), 4/2. Available at http://qualitative-research.net/fqs-texte/2-03/2-03marks-e.htm.

McVey, L., Lees, J., and Nolan, G. (2015), Practitioner-based research and qualitative interviewing: using therapeutic skills to enrich research in counselling and psychotherapy. *Counselling and Psychotherapy Research*, 15(2): 147–154.

Midgley, N., Ansaldo, F., and Target, M. (2014), The meaningful assessment of therapy outcomes: incorporating a qualitative study into a randomized controlled trial evaluating the treatment of adolescent depression. *Psychotherapy*, 51(1): 128–137.

Mruck, K. (2000), Qualitative research in Germany (54 paragraphs). *Forum: Qualitative Social Research* (online), 1/1. Available at http://qualitative-research.net/fqs

Oevermann, U. (1993), Die objective Hermeneutik als unverzichtbare methodologische Grundlage fur die Analyse von Subjektivitat. In T. Jung and S. Muller-Doohm (eds.), *Wirklichkeit im Deutungsprozeß. Verstehen in den Kultur- und Sozialwissenschaften*. Frankfurt aM: Surhkamp.

Ogden, T. (1994), The analytic third: working with intersubjective clinical facts. *International Journal of Psycho-Analysis*, 75: 3–19.

Ogden, T. (1995), Analysing forms of aliveness and deadness of the transference–countertransference. *International Journal of Psycho-Analysis*, 76: 695–709.

Ogden, T. (2001), Conversations at the frontier of dreaming. *Fort Da*, 7B: 7–14.

Parker, I. (1997), *Psychoanalytic Culture: Psychoanalytic Discourse in Western Society*. London: Sage.

Parker, I. (2003), Discursive resources in the Discourse Unit. *Discourse Analysis Online*, 1/1: http:www.shu.ac.uk/daol/articles/v1/n1/a2/parker2002001.html

Parker, I. (2005), *Qualitative Psychology: Introducing Radical Research*. Maidenhead: Open University Press.

Ramon, S. (2009), Comparative methodology in mental health research: its relevance in social work and social policy. In S. Ramon and D. Zavirsek (eds.), *Critical Edge Issues in Social Work and Social Policy* (pp. 79–96). Faculty of Social Work, University of Ljubljana.

Redman, P., Bereswill, M., and Morgenroth, C. (2010), Special Issue: Alfred Lorenzer and the depth-hermeneutic method. *Psychoanalysis, Culture and Society*, 15(3): 213–214.

Shakow, D. (1960), The recorded psychoanalytic interview as an objective approach to research in psychoanalysis. *Psychoanalytic Quarterly*, 29: 82–97.

Silverman, D. (2013), *Interpreting Qualitative Data* (4th edition). California: Sage.

Tietel, E. (2000), The interview as relational space (20 paragraphs). *Forum: Qualitative Social Research* (online), 1/3. Available at http://qualitative-research.net/fqs/fqs-eng-htm.

Chapter 4

Psycho-societal interpretation of the unconscious dimensions in everyday life

Henning Salling Olesen and Thomas Leithäuser

In this chapter, we present an approach to researching subjective dimensions of everyday life. Rather than a single well-defined method, it is a bundle of theoretical assumptions and methodical practices that are used in research of different areas of social life that places the understanding of subjectivity at the centre of interest. This approach has been developed jointly by researchers from different paradigmatic backgrounds, conducting research in a wide and varied range of specific empirical fields. However, they share the ambition of understanding the unconscious dimensions of social life and social relations, drawing on psychoanalytic theory and interpretative practices, while at the same time theorising these unconscious dimensions as imprints of societal relations mediated through social interaction. It combines a theory of subjectivity and an interpretation methodology based on hermeneutic experiences from text analysis and psychoanalysis. One element is a theory of socialisation which conceptualises subjectivity as an individually specific capacity, with conscious as well as unconscious levels built on experience of social interactions. The other element is a methodology for empirical research of social agency and communication in everyday life which takes advantage of hermeneutic experiences from psychoanalysis, condensed in the notion of scenic understanding, attending to conscious meanings as well as unconscious meanings that may relate to sensual and bodily experiences.

The approach emphasises the bodily-ness of socialisation, but extends it to the understanding of language acquisition and language use, working out an unconscious dimension within the Wittgensteinian notion of language games. Finally, the chapter describes a practical implementation of scenic understanding, and gives a couple of examples of interpretation of mundane cases.

Introduction

In this chapter, we present an approach to researching subjective dimensions of everyday life.

It is an approach that combines a theory of subjectivity and an interpretation methodology based on hermeneutic experiences from text analysis and psychoanalysis. The term 'approach' indicates the intrinsic connection between the theorising of the empirical object and the interpretation method. In line with Adorno's methodological position, we believe that the object of study in each case sets premises and conditions which call for specific methodological practice (Vorrang des Objekts; Adorno, 1976), and requires a reflection of the epistemic subject. This approach revives themes that have received much attention in the wider literature of qualitative methodology, for example in a thematic issue of *Forum for Qualitative Social Research (FQS) around fifteen* years ago: *Subjectivity and Reflectivity in Qualitative Research* (Breuer, Mruck, and Roth, 2002; Breuer and Roth, 2003). The concrete researcher plays a significant role. Its particular focus is on subjectivity, as an aspect of the 'research object', that is, what we study, and also as an aspect of the research process.

The particular contribution of our approach to this discussion was presented in more detail in a thematic issue of FQS (Salling Olesen, 2012). It is based on a psycho-societal understanding of subjectivity. Here, the assumption is that the individual psyche with its conscious and unconscious dimensions is socially produced in a lifelong dialectic interaction with the social environment, and that the unconscious dimension of this socialised psyche is active in feelings and consciousness of the individual subject, as well as in an implicit layer of meaning in social interaction and social relations. The distinction between conscious and unconscious is deliberately simplified here as a dichotomy; in reality, we believe it to be an interactive continuum of more or less conscious meanings that are permanently shifting. The basic application of the psychoanalytic idea of the unconscious as a socialised and changing dynamics draws on traditions of psychoanalysis from Ferenczi, Lorenzer, and Klein. These have been adopted in different versions of cultural and social psychology, but are not uncontested within psychoanalysis, and are often unknown outside psychoanalysis; we will therefore point out the basic elements in our method.

One element is a theory of socialisation that combines materialistic theory of society (Marxism) and psychoanalysis. It conceptualises subjectivity as an individually specific capacity, with conscious as well as unconscious levels which build on experience of social interactions. We assume that it is influenced (but not determined) by interaction in general societal circumstances and specific life courses, and in turn is involved in any social interaction and any symbolic meaning. A particular point in this theory is the understanding of the relation between the bodily and sensory experience of the material world, and the experiences of symbolic interaction which emerge with language acquisition. It provides a framework for studying everyday life processes in the span between individual bodily experience and social and cultural processes mediated in language use. Subjectivity is thus not seen as an individual attribute but as a relational and dynamic lifelong experience of the social world, in which the relation between conscious and unconscious levels are continuously reconfigured. This has very direct consequences for our methods, involving data production as well as interpretation.

The other element is the adoption of a methodology of cultural analysis which takes advantage of hermeneutic experiences from psychoanalysis, condensed in the notion of scenic understanding. By interpreting texts or similar material, it seeks to understand subjective dimensions of cultural artefacts, agency, and communication in a holistic and concrete way. We have developed its wider application in empirical research of social agency and communication in everyday life, attending to conscious meanings as well as unconscious meanings that may relate to sensual and bodily experiences. Besides being aware of transference and countertransference in the field being studied (the epistemic object), we have also used it as a tool in the interpretation procedures (the relation between empirical material and interpreters).

Researching subjectivities in their specific mundane and societal context

The development of qualitative empirical methods in social science has its roots in the critique of positivism. In order to avoid the reifications following from behaviourism and the quantitative regime in methodology, a range of qualitative methods for social inquiry were developed from the 1960s onwards. They give prominence to the subject in the empirical data, typically in the form of semi-structured or narrative interviews which directly invite the agents in the field (epistemic objects) to become subjects by giving them voice, and/or in the form of participatory observation in which it is an accepted fact that the observations are shaped by the researcher subject's interaction with the subjects studied. Critical sociology and cultural studies had already integrated with an ethnography in which the originally quite positivistic scientific ideals were replaced by a more interactive and interpretative understanding of fieldwork. We build on, but are also critical of, these traditions because they allow but do not conceptualise, least of all theorise, subjectivity.

Our psycho-societal approach also owes a great deal to critical reformulations of Marxism and psychoanalysis (Leithäuser, 2012; Salling Olesen and Weber, 2012). However, the psycho-societal approach as a research practice has emerged as a response to and a result of empirical studies of everyday life and specific social practices. It has been a response to the challenge of developing a flexible and sensitive approach which is valid in discovering the dynamics and potentials of mundane social phenomena, that is, those aspects of the social which the development of qualitative social science has addressed but mostly in a way that neglected the psychodynamic dimensions.

Let us illustrate with our own respective research areas of learning and work life.

Leithäuser and his group at Bremen University researched work life from the perspective of the workers' life world. They adopted a method from experimental social psychology and developed it into a thematic group discussion. This method has some similarity with focus group interviews: a group discussion is directed by a prescribed theme. But whereas the focus group moderator supports consensual elements in the group, and thus helps the group produce a joint and possibly clearer view of the prescribed theme, here the moderator of the thematic group discussion will seek to challenge the tendency to build joint opinions. Instead, (s)he will encourage the participants to explore their different and possibly ambiguous experiences in relation to the theme. The theme is prescribed by the researchers on the basis of background knowledge and theoretical assumptions about the group and is intended to open discussions that are latent and may be problematic in the group or for the group members individually.

The creative idea in this way of producing data is that the language use in a group becomes dynamic and refers to participants' life experiences, including those that are not conscious or already established in articulate opinions. In this way, the dynamics of the group discussion can, if the theme is well chosen, provide an insight into the dynamics of unconscious and conscious dimensions of life experience which become relevant in relation to the discussion. In this context, we were drawing on the work of Thomas Leithäuser and his group and also Regina Becker-Schmidt's research into female workers (Becker-Schmidt, 1982).

In educational and learning research, we experienced a drift from educational philosophy, which was mostly quite holistic but also very normative, to an 'industrial' modernisation of formal education from the mid-twentieth century, using learning psychology and didactic rationalisation, in order to meet new societal demands. This was replaced around the end of the century by output-oriented thinking, less connected with institutional training and education, and more interested in learning as an integrated aspect of everyday life, under the headline of lifelong learning. One way of addressing this challenge has been to focus on the life history of the learner subjects, in an attempt to understand their history and societal circumstances. Some researchers have adopted biographical research methods, based on autobiographical narratives, influenced by both narrative structural semantics and symbolic interactionism, while others are more oriented to psychodynamic interpretations of life histories (Marotzki, Alheit, von Felden, and Nohl, 2002; Salling Olesen, 2004; L. R. West, Alheit, Andersen, and Merrill, 2007). This type of empirical social research gains its plausibility and relevance by focusing on specific individuals: how can we understand a person's present in the light of the person's memory of the past and imagined future? But the critical research interest is not in the *individual* processes of learning and knowing. It is to use individual cases to theorise learning as an aspect of social practice, a moment in a subjective life history embedded in the symbolic and social environment, and contributing to societal processes of reproduction as well as innovation. In some cases, one may discover collective learning processes in which new knowledge or new practices, or even utopian dimensions, emerge. Societal knowledge-building and cultural dynamics are mediated on the micro level in individual learning. Against this background, materialistic socialisation theory and psychoanalytic insights in subjectivity and the subjective have become crucial.

As a result of the challenges in our respective research areas, we became interested in the idea of a method of interpretation suitable to discover the social unconscious in mundane everyday life. In practical terms, we established the International Research Group for Psycho-Societal Analysis in 2001, the so-called

Squid Group (Salling Olesen, 2012a, 2016). This research group gathered psychoanalytically trained scholars from Germany, the UK, and Denmark as well as people from social science and education who were not trained in psychoanalysis but were interested in developing research into subjectivity.

Socialisation: sensory experience and language use

The psycho-societal approach understands the unconscious as an individual psychic dynamics, which is at the same time basically a societal phenomenon. The fundamental idea in the method is to theorise the interweaving of society and psyche, and to pursue the entanglement in interpretations. Alfred Lorenzer's materialist theory of socialisation and symbolisation, and his methodology for interpreting cultural phenomena became strong inspirations, decisive for our method. We will briefly highlight his most important ideas about the early societal influence in the psyche, and the framework for interpreting the connection between this early social genesis of the psyche and later interaction with social environments throughout the life course. According to Lorenzer, interaction experiences become embodied already during the embryonic phase and the first few months of life, in what he calls 'engrams'. Through the body's sensomotoric reactions, these remain for the entire lifetime a dimension of the dialectic with the social environment. The important aspect is their connection with language and language use.

The start of this development in very early childhood is a holistic physical process based entirely on sensory perceptions:

> The 'visual', 'tactile' and 'acoustic' denote modes of sensory reception, which are directed by the central nervous system from the periphery of the body and which are then stored as engrams in precisely defined areas of the brain (...). These engrams are 'memory traces' in Freud's terms (...). Just as Freud had pointed out, in advance of his time, in his book 'On aphasia' (Freud and Stengel, 1891 1953), that cerebral physiological functions and 'psychological' content cannot be separated ... Although this process is naturally common to all infants, the engrams of a single person are the memory traces of his or her experience as a particular individual. They have an individual profile (...) which means that the content of memory (which is, of course, social) modifies the brain's physiological structures of the nervous system. The memory traces combine into ideas of objects. Like the sensual impressions (visual, tactile and acoustic), they combine into an idea of an object; similarly, the objects that are perceived in different situations will combine to form definite and concrete scenes (....). An awareness of individual objects only emerges gradually, and may later, in differing situations combine to form well defined poles and stable figures within the scenic gestalt.
>
> (Lorenzer, 1986, pp. 41–42; our translation)

Lorenzer emphasises the bodily-ness of these processes. A child's early experiences of stimulus-response games with his mother and other close individuals are based on efforts to achieve pleasure and avoid unpleasure, and they are retained as memory traces, which Lorenzer calls interaction forms. They become, in his terms, 'socialised nature'.

But how do single memory traces become a configuration of many which evolve into life experiences and a complete life world? The idea of the scenic primacy poses the question the other way round: 'It is the scene which is the immediate subject of the infant's experience. An awareness of individual objects only emerges from the scene gradually, and may later, in differing situations, combine to form well-defined poles and stable figures within the scenic Gestalt' (Lorenzer, 1986, pp. 41–42, our translation). The undifferentiated scenic experience oriented by the subject-to-be evolves gradually through differentiation to become more detailed and stable object images. This conception aligns with empirically based knowledge about infant development (Stern, 1985).

The scene is shaped by the bodily referent inherent in it from the outset. A child's earliest perception, no doubt while still in the womb, is a holistic experience. The perceptive instruments are an ensemble of receptors which give the external world in intra-psychical space a scenic structure. Hence, this describes the scenic unit between the organism and its environment. The scene always encompasses both, and 'this interplay is the foundation for everything' (Lorenzer and König, 1986, p. 43). Such interplay provides the basis for human experience, it remains both active and necessary one's whole life long, and it constitutes an ever more discerning ability to take in new experiences.

> The basic human state of vulnerability is the source of the drive towards exchange and interplay: the first fundamental content of this drive is directed towards satisfying interactions and the defense against unsatisfying and damaging ones. The drive is therefore the urge both to accept and seek out specific interactions fulfilling and satisfying needs. It is clear that such requirement and needs have their origin in bodily metabolism. The need for human contact evolves from this. Sexual needs bear witness to these bodily origins.
> (Lorenzer and König, 1986, p. 44)

This theory fruitfully combines the biological dimension of the drive theory by emphasising the pleasure–unpleasure principle and the socio-cultural understanding of the subject by stressing the importance of early social interactions. The dialectic between biological needs and the social relations in which they can be satisfied and are reconfigured gives rise to a lifelong development dynamics of the subject in interaction with other subjects and the world. This is why we name his socialisation theory materialistic.

Several years later, Alfred Lorenzer developed the interpretation method that he called in-depth hermeneutics, which inspired our psycho-societal interpretation. This interpretation method depends on the theorising of the next step in the socialisation process: language acquisition and language use. The early preverbal, scenically stored interaction experiences, the 'specific interaction forms', gradually include verbal images which appear in the interaction. Simple (pre-symbolic) interaction forms and spoken words, which are in themselves holistic and situated entities of meaning, defined in social interaction, are the material for the development of a symbolic level, 'a language-symbolic interaction form' (Sprachsymbolische Interaktionsform). Lorenzer adopted and developed the notion of language game from Wittgenstein. The latter defined the language game as a dialectic unit of life practice, language use, and world view (1953). Wittgenstein's language game notion was in fact primarily critical of previous *philosophical* ideas of language and scientific statements, by pointing out that language meaning is a result of language use and the social practices in which language use is embedded. He saw language games not as mere conventions but as dynamic results of a negotiation between language users, which therefore contain different social experiences from specific practices. As it appears, this aligns with the understanding of the psyche as a result of interaction experiences (practice). Language acquisition adds a new quality to interaction experience: it enables the regulation of practice.

> The 'power of language to regulate practice' when oriented outwardly encompasses what we term 'action' or 'conscious perception'. However, the 'power of language to regulate practice' when oriented inwardly, also encompasses 'internal reflection', 'conscious emotion' etc.... Only when a complex of sounds has found its appropriate place in the context of the language-sign, and the syntactic level of language links with the pragmatic and semantic nature of language, only when this is accomplished has a full language figure (Sprachfigur) that corresponds with the scenic practice figure been established.
>
> (1986, pp. 51–52)

However, the unity of interaction form and language use can also be re-excluded from the language context. This happens, for example, with the aid of resistance mechanisms: by repressing them, they are excluded from the conscious relationship between language and practice. Although this turns them back into unconscious interaction forms, the very fact of this reversion allows them to retain their energetic, dynamic relevance. They act as behaviour drivers, albeit in the form of blind action and reaction which is not open to conscious self-reflection. For the individual, the recurring unconscious re-enactment of a scene whose structure is similar to a particular conflict appears in the form of a need for repetition. The destruction of this symbolic unit reverses symbolisation, hence the term 'desymbolisation', and it may occur during (subjective) conflicts later in life. This means that once achieved, the ability to symbolise (verbal expression of a subjective structure) is withdrawn in relation to a specific problem which the individual experiences as an inner conflict. The ability to express an experience or an emotional process in words is lost in connection with the issue causing the conflict. Conflict in this sense is seen as the situated clash of irreconcilable, contradictory interaction forms.

Symbolisation through language has the advantage of being brought to mind independently of the immediate real situation and thus fulfils an important function in the regulation of emotion. In other words, it assists the subject's independence (tentative action, hesitation). By separating the language from the interaction form, the person is again made dependent on the effects of unconscious conflict. In the worst case, these are the type of problems that appear in the clinical psychoanalysis from which Lorenzer started his theorising.

As social researchers, we are more interested in understanding more generally how unconscious dynamics of the psyche influence subjective structures and their forms of experience. This differs from symbolised, verbal forms in the subject's inability to reflect on those forms of experience, and the subject loses control of practice. At the same time, as Lorenzer repeatedly emphasises, the non-verbal interaction form is always linked to subsequent language symbolic forms.

> When integrated into a theory of individual structures, the model of the language game – embracing its constituents practice and language – provides us with a useful backdrop that renders visible what was previously opaque, namely the active making of configurations of consciousness as they emerge in practices (both being realized in concrete interactions).
> (Lorenzer, 1977, pp. 34ff)

With the concept 'Language-symbolic interaction forms' (*Sprachsymbolische Interaktionsform*), Lorenzer provides a theoretical extension to the theory of language games, incorporating unconscious dimensions which were not addressed in Wittgenstein's concept. It means that the 'negotiation' of meaning also involves non- and pre-verbal experiences and harbours elements that are products of a destroyed symbolisation of experience. Language as an instrument of symbol-building is not simply *based on* the pre-symbolic interaction form, but actually *contains it*. For this reason, the pre-symbolic interaction form remains virulent one's whole life long, and, if it is being excluded from the language symbol spectrum, seeks out non-verbal ways of finding expression.

In Lorenzer's work, we learned that individual psychic structure is an expression of real interaction experiences from early life onwards. Language games can thus only be understood in the context of the social practice in which they were established. They assume a common practice-based agreement on meaning and are always the result of social practice (Lorenzer, 1970b). If the language game is the link between a specific interaction form and a societal (cultural) language figure, then potential disturbances and interferences in the language game can be identified. The symbolic unit is dissolved when it is subject to repression.

From this insight in desymbolisation, Lorenzer developed his distinction between emotionless empty signs, with no basis in sensual experience, and clichés. A cliché is an interaction engram that becomes 'unconscious again losing all the characteristics which it had gained from its relation to the word, i. e. through its introduction into the meaning system of language. In other words, what is lost is: - the capacity to reflect upon behavior patterns' (Lorenzer and König, 1986, p. 53).

The term 'language game' here thus refers to and connects three dimensions of the social: the individual psychic structure of the subject, the socialisation process, and forms of social practice. This complex interconnection is the background for tracing the mediation between society and psyche in the interpretation of specific, unique empirical cases.

Scenic understanding and interpretation

The basic methodological ambition in the psycho-societal approach is to understand the genesis of subjectivity and the way subjectivity mediates societal dialectic. We seek to overcome the individualistic and idealistic ideas of the rational subject and society as the result of rational and transparent agency. By tracing and interpreting psychic meanings, conscious as well as unconscious, we seek to understand social relations that are not immediately accessible to the conscious reflection of agents. Based on Lorenzer's socialisation theory, we can see language games as the connection between interaction experiences, conscious as well as unconscious, mediated in individual life histories and societal structures, transparent as well as non-transparent, mediated in the interaction of the life world. His concept of scenic understanding provided inspiration to learn from the hermeneutic procedure involved in psychoanalysis but to relocate it to the understanding of the social.

Social relations and practices will appear in language use in spoken language, interviews, and texts, and tracing what is not directly understandable, revealing distortions and limitations in symbolic units, is a key to understanding aspects of the social that are not conscious or intended. A means of access is needed that re-identifies the scenic unit, including when there is no, or only an altered, form of verbal expression because the unit of language-symbolic interaction form has been lost. This is where Lorenzer's idea of scenic understanding has its methodological significance. It provides the possibility to learn from the type of hermeneutic process in psychoanalysis for the analysis of cultural phenomena.

> In the psychoanalytic process, all understanding centers on and is related to the mode of 'scenic understanding'. In this mode understanding is attuned to two specific objects: the 'scenic drafts', i.e. the 'interaction forms' of the analysand. Particularly hereby psychoanalysis provides us with a model example. If we want to understand the analysand's life-practice, which does

not exclude his concrete social reality, we must follow the path laid down by his subjective phantasies and outlines of relations. This means we must become attuned to his scenic interaction forms as these unfold before us.
(Lorenzer, 1977, p. 125)

What this quotation describes as a therapeutic approach in the analyst's consultation room can be transferred to understanding texts, language, and human behaviour. It resembles Adorno's statement about the role of social theory in critical social analysis in his critique of positivism:

But if theory is not to fall prey to the dogmatism over whose discovery scepticism – now elevated to a prohibition on thought – is always ready to rejoice, then theory may not rest here. It must transform the concepts which it brings, as it were, from outside into those which the objects has of itself, into what the object, left to itself, seeks to be, and confront it with what it is.
(Adorno, 1976, p. 69)

Immediately, the question arises as to how to practise a mode of understanding which explores the scenic in a non-clinical context. In other words, how could qualitative social research understand unknown subjective content and processes which include the unconscious and draw attention to non-verbal messages?

Lorenzer and his colleagues have demonstrated the approach in relation to literary texts and cultural phenomena (Lorenzer and König, 1986; Prokop, Friese, and Stach, 2009). We have taken it somewhat further into qualitative social research in a number of more mundane contexts (Dybbroe, 2002; Liveng, 2010; Salling Olesen, 2007, 2012; Salling Olesen and Weber, 2002; Weber, 2010). In the following, we shall describe a practical implementation of scenic understanding. Like every hermeneutic approach, it is about understanding the meaning in agency and expressions in practical social research. Although some measures can be taken to make the data suitable for this type of interpretation, scenic understanding can be applied to almost any text or phenomenon referring to agency and subjective expression. The prototypical material is, however, a text, or can be seen as a text. Less frequent ways of producing the data in the first place are videos or conversations held while observing videos (second-order field observation). Very often, the text is a transcript of a focus group discussion or thematic group discussion. In other cases, it may be an individual or collective interview, or a field diary from an observation.

To identify the meaning structure of a text, we may distinguish different levels of interpretation:

1) The obvious referential content of the text: What is being talked about? What is being told?

2) How do people talk to one another? This question on the meta-communicative content of a text takes us to the level of scenic understanding.
3) Why are the characters talking in precisely this way? How can we understand it by means of theoretical knowledge combined with background factual knowledge?

The first of these levels is the same as in most types of qualitative method. The form of the third level might be reminiscent of an explanatory approach which seeks a causal or rule-based understanding of the observations on the first and second levels. Since it is a hermeneutic methodology, this is not the case; instead, it is a more comprehensive multi-layered interpretation enabled by the second level. The 'scenic understanding' focuses on the ongoing tense relation between the manifest and the unconscious meanings of a text which requires an imagination of the unconscious as a collective reservoir of culturally rejected patterns, forbidden yearnings, and suppressed desires. In-depth hermeneutic interpretation thus focuses on the characters in the relationship described in the text and on the dynamics of the relationship between a text and its interpreter(s) in order to trace the subjective structure of cultural constraints.

The reference point in the scenic interpretation is the language used in the text, with particular attention being placed on how scenes in the text point to unexpressed desires and tensions, on how the text arranges 'forms of communication which make the "unspeakable" understandable', or 'secures it an un-negligible position in public space', as Lorenzer says about the task of the poet (1986, p. 24).

The three levels are not the same as a sequence. The initial reading seeks to apply the same type of free-floating awareness (*gleichschwebender Aufmerksamkeit*) as is known from the clinical situation: one's own reactions and irritations are noted without coming immediately to any particular conclusions or forming theoretical definitions. Indications of such hidden conflict dynamics include gaps, inconsistencies, unusual use of language, jumps in the story, or sudden changes of subject, and remarkable ways of relating to the subject or to each other (in the case of group interaction texts). But also the reactions, emotional states, and associations of the readers/interpreters may be indications of the dynamics we are looking for, even if they are not immediately comprehensible.

In practice, an interpretation procedure is most often organised in a group. Some procedures go line by line, seeking to understand each unit of text, and revising the understanding gradually as the later segments are taken into consideration. Other procedures start with an open conversation conveying 'first impressions' and reactions from the members of the interpretation group. In some cases, one will find that controversies and conflicts arise within an interpretation group, evoked by the text. Using these observations and reactions as a base, particularly powerful passages are subjected to in-depth analysis in interpretation groups. What has already been described as transference between the individual reader and the text is now transferred to a collective understanding process: the transference and countertransference dynamics multiply. This procedure may lead very directly to 'holistic' but preliminary interpretations that are discussed, or it may produce several 'loose ends'. In a particular case, the whole situation to which the interview was referring was difficult to understand for the interpretation group and it led to emotionally charged reactions towards the interviewee, breaking out of the interpretation procedure. In turn, this can also open the primary interpretation, in this case via the interviewer's compassion with the difficulties of the interviewee ((Raae, 2018). The interpretation discussion most likely includes reference to the concrete text and its manifest meaning, and it may very well also draw on theoretical frameworks and on background knowledge which initially may support or contradict the interpretations suggested. The discussion gradually moves into a validation discussion. In principle, the validation will refer to the usual criteria and procedures for validation of qualitative analysis. In the first place, it will refer to the manifest text, on the one hand, and, on the other hand, a theoretical reflection of the whole complex of subjective agency and expression in the text and in the relation between the text and the interpreters.

The assumption of unconscious meaning components makes the language game an instrument with which to analyse individual structures and identifies collective social processes. Language figures and language-symbolic interaction forms always possess a social character which goes beyond the individual, because they assume social understanding processes within the language community. As a result, they can be analysed for the social meaning they contain and give an insight into the social configurations and their unconscious, not-yet-conscious component. This is the methodological bridge which enables the unconscious dimensions of experience to be accessed from language. They can also be observed from the subjective perspective of the speaker and shed light on the individual meaning contained in a specific scene. The language figure then reports on the subjective structures and the associated experiences of social life practice.

A couple of interpretation examples

Let us end with a research example to illustrate how the theory and the interpretation model can be applied in practical research. Clearly, the method is adapted to the research topic and issue, so there is no standard example.

The research is about professional identity and learning of general practitioners. We interviewed doctors about their lives and their experiences from everyday practice, and transcribed and interpreted what they said in these contexts. We worked with the transcripts in different ways, both by cross-case recollection of important themes, and with close text analysis of single cases, trying to understand the person, her/his identity process and its rooting in life experiences, recent as well as more distant. The interviews provide informative description and narration combined with reflection on difficulties and ways of handling difficulties in everyday life practice. A number of themes surface immediately across cases; for most interviewees, one is the feeling of time pressure, which limits their possibilities to work optimally. Many are preoccupied with techniques and strategies for the management of time and the feeling of pressure. Sometimes this feeling comes out in the form of general complaints about work conditions, and in other cases, it appears to explain a strong irritation, sometimes even aggression, with patients. Many narratives and reflections are related to feelings of insufficiency in concrete situations or in relation to particular tasks.

A female doctor tells about a visit to a cancer patient in a hopeless condition, being invited by the daughter of the patient because her mother (the wife of the patient) was suffering very much from the situation and from the anger of the patient. It is understandably a painful situation for everyone. The patient himself has previously asked the doctor to stay away because her visits exposed his newly dependent situation in relation to the family. This is one of the cases where the interviewee narrates with some resignation, interspersed with reflections. The time schedule of the contacts and communications becomes quite blurred in the interview; clearly, it is not a structured situation for the GP. But she gradually realises (or has realised during a longer trajectory) that she is unable to handle the situation in a satisfactory way. Our analysis demonstrates that this has to do with her relationship with the family members.

It appears obvious that the GP identifies with the man's feeling of having lost control; she has worked with suggestions about how to give him back a more active role (teaching his wife to use computers, which was among his professional competences). We can see this as a way of relating positively to the patient in spite of being unable to do anything. She reveals negative feelings towards the two women in the situation. This could be because of her identification with the man's anger, or it could be because she feels she is being played around with (maybe the family members actually called her because they want her to hospitalise the patient to relieve them), and she feels the object of angry reactions from the family members at the same time. But it could also be seen as a reversed gender reaction, where the two women have taken the female roles of care and compassion in the situation, and left the impossible male role – to do something – to her. There is hardly any doubt that she feels obliged to be able to do something. The request or desire for omnipotence appears in this interview as in many others.

This is an important situation for the doctor where her professional skills were not (felt to be) sufficient. She has, as a consequence of this experience, registered for a course in palliative (pain relief) medicine. This is a very typical professional reaction, seeking necessary knowledge from a course in order to handle the situation better, but it is also misplaced; the problem is not palliation, but care, social psychology, and the ability to handle relationships. It is a clear sign of the willingness to learn, which also appears in other passages of this interview, and in many other cases. During the process, she has already been thinking of the need to learn something more to handle this type of situation. But the options available and maybe the demand for omnipotence makes her take what is offered.

Another example, also a female doctor, is commenting more generally on her experience of being a GP. This interview is more disjointed, jumping between many topics and situations which relate somehow to conflicts and identifications, some of which are retrospectively related to her experiences of a hospital before she went into general practice. She is mostly not very specific, bringing few narratives and references to concrete events and time. We interpret this structure of the text as a manifestation of her loss of control and struggle to define herself. During the interview, several references to patients' behaviour occur: patients are 'demanding and rude'. In one passage, the feeling of flooding is condensed in telling about patients' use of their cell phones in her consultation/clinic. The clinic takes on a specific importance as a private room, in which she offers her full attention to people, and yet they intrude into it with technical devices which are entirely alien to this function. The clinic seems to become a metaphor for the particular hybrid relation between doctor and patient, in which she (professionally) makes herself (personally) available, in order to provide a space in which they can place their worries and anxieties. The partly aggressive feeling of being offended in this space reveals a real identity crisis, which is certainly produced by real changes in patients' expectations (and means of communication), and workload, but produces a split relationship to patients.

Close analysis of language use seems to reflect her conflict and positions it as a conflict of professional identity. The interviewee changes her use of personal pronouns between 'I' and 'we' in a significant way to represent being inside or outside in relation to gender. She partly indicates that she is a member of the doctors' community as opposed to a women's community (in relation to the hospital where female nurses prevail), but also appears as partly a member of the profession and defining herself out of the profession, referring to her own limits of tolerance. Her uncertainty comes out in an untranslatable way of talking about giving up the profession; she wants to 'lay off the key', which is in Danish a linguistic novelty, maybe combining 'laying off' and 'turning the key'. We may interpret this as a result of the fact that she has never dared to think about this possibility before; it comes as a consequence of the reasoning and the emotional expressions of the difficulties during the interview.

These examples illuminate the conditions for professional learning in the confrontation between complexity and habitual routines. Tasks and experiences in everyday life, with their rich and complicated meaning for the individual practitioner, cannot always be understood in the available knowledge discourses, much less mastered in a practical routine that is possible in the work situation. This is, however, what the professional must do. Under this imperative of practising which is built into any profession, the maintenance of a routine is not passive as the notion seems to suggest, it is an active editing of perceptions and knowledge in accordance with possible practices – a defence mechanism.

The academic knowledge base of the profession is a language game in which relatively stable meanings are institutionally regulated. But to the extent that individuals' experiences, from professional practice or from previous life history, are not covered by or cannot be communicated in this dominant language game, they may still be manifest in their concrete language use. A 'halo' of surplus meaning representing aspects of present experience, with its conflicts and the practice imperative, that are not covered in the established language game links them to and/or differentiates them from past experiences of conflicts and relations. Interpretation of language use is a key to the dynamics of the borderlines of possible meaning-making in everyday life within a certain professional discourse and a certain professional practice. This domain is individually a potential for learning (or defence). But it is also societally a terrain for potential professional development, which is then mediated in conscious as well as unconscious psychic dynamics.

Thomas Leithäuser and his colleagues use the concept 'everyday life consciousness' (*Altagsbewusstsein*) (Leithäuser, 1976; Salling Olesen, 1989) for an active, psychic, and collective organising of everyday life which makes it practicable and emotionally relieving. The function is to prevent everyday life conflicts from constantly evoking deep feelings and anxieties. I believe we can see the subjective function of knowledge discourses for professionals in this perspective. They have a selective and reductive influence on perception, and enable the professional practitioner to fulfil the imperative of practising. In the professional monopoly of the field of work, the knowledge discourse serves as a defence by defining the observations and problems to be understood and solved.

Elements of *defence* help professionals to stabilise self-understanding and the feeling of mastering certain practices under conditions that may seem contradictory and threatening. But there are also elements of *curiosity* and *responsibility*, in which they face challenges and try to learn from them. Professionals are often aware of the limitations of their professional knowledge and competence. This sensitivity to reality is subjectively supported by more or less idealised ideas of the mission of the professions, of being able to perform rational and useful practice. The dynamics of defence and curiosity may be related to external conflicts of professional ideals and challenges, but it may also be related to their own life experience. In the defensive function of knowing is also embedded a preconscious 'awareness' of conflicts and difficulties which in the first place evoke the defence. This awareness of alternative 'unlived lives' that were blocked in life history may be a reservoir for learning, which goes together with professional responsibility in forming new ideas and objectives.

More generally, this means that the defensive subjective functions of knowing and reality-oriented learning are dialectically interrelated.

Summary

To summarise some of the particular outcomes of a psycho-societal approach:

- It enables a richer understanding of concrete, everyday life experiences of specific people in societal contexts (such as profession or gender) and psychological contexts (here, defence against the feeling of failure to live up to omnipotence and the feeling of invasion); they are thus understood as entangled in the specific cases (individuals and agency).

- It provides a theoretical contribution: here, theorising learning in general as a cognitive and emotional process, and providing a way to handle some of the key issues of professional learning, such as understanding how the relationship between discursive (bio-medical) knowledge and practical challenges is mediated in the psychodynamics of individual doctors (Salling Olesen, 2007).
- It offers a window to understand the latent openness in the dynamics of social life: here, work life dynamics (learning, organisational change, and political agency) as mediated in defences and ambivalences in everyday life (Volmerg, Senghaas-Knobloch, and Leithäuser, 1986).

The common denominator of these (unreasonably briefly) condensed points is that they emphasise empirical interpretation, appreciating the uniqueness of each topic and setting.

References

Adorno, T. W. (1976), *The Positivist Dispute in German Sociology*. New York: Harper & Row.

Becker-Schmidt, R. (1982), *Nicht wir haben die Minuten, die Minuten haben uns : Zeitprobleme und Zeiterfahrungen von Arbeitermüttern in Fabrik und Familie: Studie zum Projekt 'Probleme lohnabhängig arbeitender Mütter'*. Bonn: Verlag Neue Geselschaft.

Breuer, F., Mruck, K., and Roth, W.-M. (2002), Subjectivity and reflexivity: an introduction. *Forum: Qualitative Social Research/Forum Qualitative Sozialforschung*, 3 (3), Art. 9. Retrieved from http://nbn-resolving.de/urn:nbn:de:0114-fqs020393

Breuer, F., and Roth, W.-M. (2003), Subjectivity and reflexivity in the social sciences: epistemic windows and methodical consequences. *Forum: Qualitative Social Research/ Forum Qualitative Sozialforschung*, 4 (2), Art. 25. Retrieved from http://nbn-resolving.de/urn:nbn:de:0114-fqs0302258

Dybbroe, B. (2002), 'You've got to give all the love you have, and yet consider it to be a job' – care work in a gendered and life-historical perspective. In Chr. H. Jørgensen and N. Warring (eds.), *Adult Education and the Labour Market, VIIb*. Roskilde: ESREA/ Adult Education Research Group, Roskilde University.

Freud, S., and Stengel, E. (1953), *On Aphasia: A Critical Study*. New York: International Universities Press.

Leithäuser, T. (1976), *Formen des Alltagsbewusstseins*. Frankfurt/Main and New York: Campus-Verlag.

Leithäuser, T. (2012), Psychoanalysis, socialization and society: the psychoanalytical thought and interpretation of Alfred Lorenzer. Alfred Lorenzer at the University of Bremen: a personal foreword. *Forum: Qualitative Social Research*, 13 (3). http://nbn-resolving.de/urn:nbn:de:0114-fqs1203176

Liveng, A. (2010), Learning and recognition in health and care work: an inter-subjective perspective. *Journal of Workplace Learning*, 22: 41–52. Retrieved from http://www.worldcat.org/oclc/593798392

Lorenzer, A., and König, H.-D. (1986), Tiefenhermeneutische Kulturanalyse. In *Kulturanalysen*, Vol. 7334 (pp. 11–98). Frankfurt: Fischer Taschenbuch Verlag.

Marotzki, W., Alheit, P., von Felden, H., and Nohl, A.-M. (2002), Education research. *Zeitschrift Für Qualitative Bildungs-, Beratungs- Und Sozialforschung*, 2: 185–300.

Prokop, U., Friese, N., and Stach, A. (2009), *Geiles Leben, falscher Glamour: Beschreibungen, Analysen, Kritiken zu Germany's Next Topmodel.* Tectum-Verlag.

Raae, P. H. (2018), Effective leadership? A case of the psychodynamic of work. In H. Salling Olesen (ed.), *The Socially Unconscious.* Rotterdam: Sense.

Salling Olesen, H. (1989), *Adult Education and Everyday Life.* Roskilde: Adult Education Research Group, Roskilde University.

Salling Olesen, H. (2004), The learning subject in life history: a qualitative research approach to learning. In M. H. Menne Abrahaõ Barreto (ed.), *A Aventura (Auto) biografico. Theoria & Empiria* (pp.419–464). Porto Alegra, Brasil: EDIPUCRS.

Salling Olesen, H. (2007), Be(com)ing a general practitioner: professional identities, subjectivity and learning. In L. West (ed.), *Using Biographical and Life History Approaches in the Study of Adult and Lifelong Learning: European Perspectives.* Frankfurt am Main: P. Lang.

Salling Olesen, H. (2012), The societal nature of subjectivity: an interdisciplinary methodological challenge. *Forum Qualitative Sozialforschung/Forum: Qualitative Social Research*, 13(3). http://nbn-resolving.de/urn:nbn:de:0114-fqs120345

Salling Olesen, H. (2016), A psycho-societal approach to life histories. In I. Goodson, A. Antikainen, P. Sikes, & M. Andrews (eds.), *The Routledge International Handbook on Narrative and Life History.* London: Routledge.

Salling Olesen, H., and Weber, K. (2002), Chasing potentials for adult learning: lifelong learning in a life history perspective. *Zeitschrift für Qualitative Bildungs-, Beratungs- Und Sozialforschung*, 2: 283–300.

Salling Olesen, H. and Weber, K. (2012), Socialisation, Language and Scenic Understanding. Alfred Lorenzer's Contribution to a Psycho-Societal Methodology. *Forum : Qualitative Social Research*, 3 (3). http://nbn-resolving.de/urn:nbn:de:0114-fqs1203229

Stern, D. N. (1985), *The Interpersonal World of the Infant: A View from Psychoanalysis and Developmental Psychology.* New York: Basic Books.

Volmerg, B., Senghaas-Knobloch, E., and Leithäuser, T. (1986), *Betriebliche Lebenswelt. Eine sozialpsychologie industrieller Arbeitsverhältnisse.* Opladen: Westdeutscher. Verlag.

Weber, K. (2010), Professional learning between past experience and future work. *Frontiers of Education in China*, 5(3).

West, L. R., Alheit, P., Andersen, A. S., and Merrill, B. (eds.) (2007), *Using Biographical and Life History Approaches in the Study of Adult and Lifelong Learning: European Perspectives.* Frankfurt am Main: Peter Lang.

Chapter 5

Using the psychoanalytic research interview as an experimental 'laboratory'

Simona Reghintovschi

In efforts to design methods suitable for researching unconscious aspects outside the clinical setting, some authors proposed different variants of psychoanalytically informed research interviews (Kvale, 1999, 2003; Hunt, 1989; Hollway, 2009, 2015; Cartwright, 2004; Holmes, 2013; Strømme, 2010). In clinical psychoanalysis, the knowledge is derived from different occurrences: contiguity, thematic affinity, genetic continuity, and triangulation give material for formulating interpretations (Hinshelwood, 2013). In a psychoanalytically informed methodology, free associations (Hollway and Jefferson, 2000), dreams, jokes, and parapraxes (Hunt, 1989), transference and countertransference relationships (Cartwright, 2004), the researcher's countertransference (Holmes, 2013), and reverie (Hollway, 2015; Holmes, 2017) give the researcher access to the material for psychoanalytically informed interpretation. Different analytic tools have been used to analyse data collected in psychoanalytically informed research interviews: 'relational scenarios' (Strømme, 2010), 'core narratives' (Cartwright, 2004), and 'scenic understanding' (Hollway, 2015).

In this chapter, I present an approach to the psychoanalytically informed interview as an experimental situation. This approach to interview is based on Ezriel's description of the psychoanalytic session as an experimental situation (Ezriel, 1956), and Hinshelwood's (2013) design for research in the clinical setting combining hermeneutic with causal approaches.

The psychoanalytic session as an experimental situation

In Ezriel's (1956) view, the psychoanalytic session is a here-and-now process, and has 'a ready-made setting for experimentation' (p. 34) in which one can observe the effect of the analyst's interpretations in the here-and-now reactions of the patient. 'The psycho-analytic session thus becomes an experimental situation in which hypotheses can be tested through direct observation of the patient's behaviour' (Ezriel, 1956, p. 38). The dynamics underlying the patient's behaviour can be made explicit in the here-and-now interpretations by selecting antecedent variables from pre-interpretation material, including them in the interpretations, and making predictions about the patient's reactions to these interpretations.

According to Ezriel (1956), it is possible to treat all session material as transference material. Describing the unconscious dynamics operating during the analytic session, Ezriel (1956) points to three types of unconscious object relations which 'can be linked up in a rational pattern by assuming that the patient feels compelled to adopt a certain course of behaviour and to avoid another because he fears the latter's supposedly disastrous consequences' (p. 39). Ezriel (1951) mentioned a patient who started the session that took place after the Christmas break complaining about having been let down by her grocer, her laundryman, and her milkman, and being betrayed by her husband. While speaking, she was scratching the couch, and she was pulling fiercely at the buttons of the couch. She adopted a critical attitude toward the men outside (required relationship) and avoided criticism towards her analyst for having let her down for Christmas (avoided relationship) because she feared that her criticism would turn the analyst against her, and he would retaliate by dropping her as a patient (calamity).

Ezriel (1956) formulated two laws of the experiments carried out in the session. The first law reads:

> if we set up a field by putting together a patient in need of treatment and a therapist presumed to be capable of satisfying this need, and if the therapist assumes a passive, non-directive role, then the patient will display in his words and actions a manifest form of behaviour from which, by applying certain operational rules, three kinds of object relations can be inferred: (i) **the required relationship**, which he has to adopt to escape from (ii) the **avoided relationship**, which he believes will lead to (iii) a **calamity.**
>
> (Ezriel, 1956, p. 40; emphasis mine)

The second law formulated by Ezriel is:

> if the analyst then gives a here-and-now interpretation – that is, points out the hidden dynamics of the patient-analyst relationship in terms of these three object relationships and their connection, by means of a 'because' clause –the subsequent material produced by the patient will contain the avoided object relationship in a clearer, i.e. less repressed, form.
>
> (Ezriel, 1956, p. 40)

A clearer manifestation of the avoided relationship in the here and now of the session after the interpretation is predicted; the reactions of the patient to the interpretation validate or do not validate the hypothesis regarding dynamics underlying the patient's behaviour.

For example, in the case mentioned above, Ezriel interpreted the underlying dynamic of patient's behavior in the session:

> I therefore pointed out to her that she seemed rather inclined to blame men outside instead of criticizing me for apparently having let her down at

Christmas, because she felt as dependent on her doctor as on her grocer and thought her criticism might turn me against her.

(1951, p. 32)

In response, the patient remarked she had called in her GP and told him that the analysis was making her worse instead of better, knowing that the GP was against psychoanalysis. The avoided relation (criticism towards the analyst) was expressed in a less repressed form. The interpretation enabled her to better reality test, she understood the imaginary nature of her fears, and the consequences of the unconscious impulse were no longer feared (Ezriel, 1951).

In Ezriel's view, psychoanalysis is 'a dynamic science concerned with the interaction between the analyst and his patient in the "here and now" of the analytic situation' (Ezriel, 1951, p. 34). The analyst can use the psychoanalytic session as an experimental situation by studying the analytic interactions 'both during the analytic session when he presents his patient with the dynamic interpretation of his behaviour, and after the event when he or other investigators study the record of that session as a pathologist might study a microscopic slide' (Ezriel, 1951, p. 34).

Hinshelwood (2013) presents a design for psychoanalytical research in a clinical setting 'retaining the same rigour of investigation as the natural science model' (Hinshelwood, 2013, p. 103). He argues that this design could be used to test a theory of metapsychology by making predictions hypothesised on the basis of the theory under test.

In order to avoid the risk of circular argument, Hinshelwood (2013) makes a distinction within psychoanalytic theory, distinguishing 'clinical theory' for selecting occurrences in the flow of clinical material from theory of metapsychology under test used to understand the way patients construct meanings. Type 1 theories (clinical theories) 'are used to select cause–effect links (sequences) from the clinical flow – we can list resistance, defence against anxiety, conflict, object-relations, and transference/countertransference – those theories that are experience-near (as Wallerstein called them) in the psychoanalytic session' (Hinshelwood, 2013, p. 120).

Type 2 theories are 'the narrative or discursive theories of metapsychology with which we understand the way the patient constructs and manages his meanings, and his experiences' (Hinshelwood, 2013, p. 120). The interpretation is based on meanings inferred in the material using this type of theory. This type of meaning occurrences needs to be found before and after the interpretation. Hinshelwood (2013) describes a few kinds of meaning occurrences used by clinicians: contiguity, thematic affinity, genetic continuity, and triangulation.

The research design could be briefly described as follows:

Formulating a prediction

The theory of metapsychology under test offers the basis for interpretation. The meaning occurrences are selected using triangulation – 'a convergence of meaning from two perspectives, the contents of the free associations produced by the patient, and the relationship as experienced by the psychoanalyst' (Hinshelwood, 2013, p. 147) – that should be part of a protocol.

Hinshelwood (2013) uses the Ezriel (1951, 1956) understanding of the structure of the transference relation as having three levels, and implying three object relations: the required relation, the avoided relation, and the calamitous relation. The prediction is that the interpretation incorporating all three object relationships (required, avoided, and calamitous) is followed by a movement in the transference toward a less repressed avoided relation.

Testing the formulated prediction

Clinical theories, different from theories of metapsychology that informed interpretation, are used to select a causal change sequence from pre-interpretation to post-interpretation (preferably also a triangulation) that is evaluated for the impact of interpretation on the transference–countertransference relationship.

Hinshelwood (2013) mentions:

- a shift in the post-interpretive material in line with the prediction, as indicated by the theory, will give a confirmation of the interpretation, and thus the validity of the theory in this instance;
- some other shift, after an interpretation, however apparently productive, will not confirm the interpretation;
- no shift at all, or the need for different theories to understand the two different sets of material, will be a disconfirmation of the prediction, the interpretation, and the theory.

(Hinshelwood, 2013, p. 142)

Psychoanalytically informed interview as an experimental situation

The researcher's intention to focus on a particular area inevitably limits the process of free associations during the interview. Although the interviewee cannot freely associate in the classical sense, 'the idea that thoughts are associated with one another through unconscious forms of psychic determinism holds great importance for understanding the interview dialogue' (Cartwright, 2004, p. 218). Hollway and Jefferson (2000) emphasise the idea that all research subjects are 'meaning-making' and 'defended subjects' who 'are motivated, largely unconsciously, to disguise the meaning of at least some of their feelings and actions' (Hollway and Jefferson, 2000, p. 26). They suggest that the process of storytelling contains significances beyond the teller's intentions, similar to the method of free association. 'The particular story told, the manner and detail of its telling, the points emphasised, the morals drawn, all represent choices made by the story-teller. Such choices are revealing, often more so than the teller suspects' (Hollway and Jefferson, 2000, p. 35).

As in any other encounter in everyday life, transference and countertransference are present in some degree during any interview. Some oral historians (Figlio, 1988; Roper, 2003) consider that the interview does not simply provide external evidence of social life, and emphasise the importance of understanding the verbal material of the interview as always informed by unconscious dynamics of transference and countertransference. As Roper (2003) argues, transference in interviews operates in all the material, influencing what the interviewee is telling to the interviewer at one particular moment in the encounter, eliciting a particular emotional reaction in him or her. Based on the idea that internalised object relationships tend to be played out in every person's relationship with another person, the transference and countertransference reactions could be considered useful data for drawing conclusions 'about the relational attitude of the participants and their defence processes, not just by analysing what they say but also from what they do in relation to the interviewer' (Strømme, 2010, p. 215). Different from the therapeutic setting where the transference and countertransference feelings are fully developed, in the interview setting only brief emotional impressions of the interaction are recorded (Cartwright, 2004). In Cartwright's (2004) view, they represent a 'corroborative source of information that confirms or disconfirms analytic impressions' (Cartwright, 2004, p. 226), giving clues to the nature of object relations activated during the interview that should be compared and checked against object relations discerned from interview text (see also Kvale, 2003; Strømme, 2010; Holmes, 2014, for the use of countertransference feelings in research interview as relevant research data).

Similar to the perspective on the analytic session as an experimental situation (Ezriel, 1956; Hinshelwood, 2013), I suggest that the psychoanalytically oriented interview requiring that the interviewer's intervention to be reduced to a minimum in order to allow the flow of free associations could be considered as an experimental situation, a 'laboratory setting' in which the interaction between the interviewer and the interviewee takes place in the here and now of the interview. We can assume that in the psychoanalytically oriented interview, a similar transference–countertransference field exists between the interviewer and interviewee as in the analytic session. The material produced by the interviewee is seen as being unconsciously determined and having something to do with the relationship between the interviewer and the interviewee.

Following Ezriel (1956), we can consider three kinds of object relations – the *required relationship*, the *avoided relationship*, and the *calamitous relationship* – that determine the interviewee's behaviour towards the interviewer. Everything the interviewee says or does would be considered as the idiom used by him or her to give expression to his or her need for a particular relationship with the interviewer in order to avoid another relation that ends in a calamity. The basic questions used in the 'microanalysis' of interviews are: what makes this interviewee behave (speak or act) towards me in this particular way at this moment?, what role does he or she unconsciously push me into?; what sort of relationship is he or she unconsciously trying to establish between us?

'Counterassumptive' and 'counterprojective' remarks instead of psychoanalytic interpretation

Some authors consider that the researcher should offer an interpretation in the interview (Kvale, 2003; Strømme, 2010) as a way of 'allowing the object to object' to the researcher's interpretation (Kvale, 2003, p. 291). Kvale (2003) suggests that 'intersubjective agreement' 'in the form of "member checks" is possible when the therapeutic or the academic interviewer checks his or her interpretations with the interviewee' (p. 290). Also in the study of Strømme and colleagues (2010), the interviewer uses interpretations in the form of 'thinking aloud' (p. 217), introducing her own comments to the interviewee's stories and 'giving them opportunities to reflect upon the researcher's hypotheses' (p. 229).

To avoid the dangers of 'wild analysis', (Freud, 1910) of the research subjects (here-and-now interpretations to them; while these could be perceived as aggressive and intrusive acts) the interviewer's interventions could point to the existence of the hidden dynamics of the relationship by using 'counterassumptive' and 'counterprojective' remarks (Havens, 1976, 1986) similar to Sullivan's (1970) approach of 'parataxic' distortions in psychiatric interview. Sullivan's technical advice is spread throughout his clinical writings, often expressed in anecdotes. Havens (1976, 1986) developed these bits of clinical advice into a systematic technique called 'participant observation' requiring 'that we sense what others are doing to and with us and that we be free to act in that social field' (Havens, 1976, p. 95).

The ego of interpersonal theory is not autonomous from society, and

> is not a rational executive presiding lucidly over the relations between id, superego, and the world. The ego has learned roles; in addition, it is at least partly composed of introjects, parts and wholes of significant others, who therefore continue to stand between the patient and reality. One result is that transference becomes parataxis: the distorting process is present and ubiquitous from the start.
>
> (Havens, 1976, p. 96)

The therapists don't have to wait for the transference neurosis; they are already 'victims' of it, and their task is to not be 'taken in'.

Sullivan considers the interviewer as being participant-observer, and he describes the communicative processes and the dynamic interplay of forces in the interview situation. In his view, the interviewer has 'an inescapable, inextricable involvement in all that goes on in the interview; and to the extent that he is unconscious or unwitting of his participation in the interview, to that extent he does not know what is happening' (Sullivan, 1970, p. 18). The social field created is composed of two real people, the participants, plus 'other people in the room' – the different transference figures. The patient's reactions to transference interpretation could be influenced by the relationship between analyst and patient. 'The patient may look honest, sound honest or even be honest, but the honesty may spring from an honest desire to please the therapist, not the truth. [...] Then the realistic ego has proved to be a dependent and obedient child, which therapy has reinforced' (Havens, 1976, p. 105). To avoid the deepening of transference neuroses, the interpersonal therapist use counterassumptive and counterprojective statements to clear the interpersonal field of the various projections brought by both participants in the interpersonal interaction.

The insight as an increased awareness into interpersonal relationships is in the centre of Sullivan's approach, resembling Strachey's (1934) concept of the mutative interpretation (Evans, 1996). However, the interpretation in Sullivan's approach is 'drastically different, in that it was an investigation directed toward mutual discovery. Instead of the detached, silent stance of psychoanalysis, Sullivan actively shared impressions with the clients, conceptualising them as hypotheses to be tested and worked out through consensual validation' (Evans, 1996, p. 172). Instead of interpretation of intrapsychic conflict, Sullivan offers different statements that 'gently shake the established fantasy system' (Havens, 1976, p. 46). The patient's expectations and projections are rendered inoperative through 'counterassumptive' statements, that is, 'comments made by therapists that unsettle assumptions they feel being made about them by their patients' (Havens, 1986, p. 111), and 'counterprojective statements', that is, comments that move attention, place critical figures 'out there' 'on the projective screen before the therapist and patient' (Havens, 1980, p. 55) and to some measure 'some part of the patient's feelings about those figures must be expressed by the therapist' (Havens, 1980, pp. 55–56).

These statements could have the form of a single exclamation:

> 'Great!' – Said directly after the patient's account of something he or she has done, it is directly encouraging. The purpose is to put down any inward or projected criticism of the act. Said sarcastically after the patient's description of something someone else has done, it would place the therapist squarely against the other person; it is then counterprojective. The feared obstruction is any tendency the patient has to identify the therapist with the other person and then to feel criticized by both.
>
> (Havens, 1976, p. 107)

In the psychoanalytically oriented interview, instead of transference interpretation resulting, in the long term, in dissolution of transference, some counterassumptive and counterprojective statements could be used with the same aim – to clear the interpersonal field of the 'other people in the room', and to gain insight into the interpersonal relationship created.

The assumption is that counterassumptive and counterprojective statements are similar in effect to psychoanalytical interpretation, resulting in better reality testing (Ezriel, 1956; Strachey, 1937).

The research design

Formulating a prediction

A prediction is formulated on the basis of the theory of metapsychology under test (type 2 theories) using the understanding of the relation between the interviewer and interviewee as implying three object relations: required relation, avoided relation, and calamitous relation.

The prediction is: the counterprojective/counterassumptive remark pointing to the hidden dynamic of the relation between the interviewer and interviewee is followed by a movement toward a less repressed avoided relation.

Meaning occurrences are selected using triangulation, a convergence of meaning from two perspectives, the content of free associations produced by the interviewee, and the relationship as experienced by the interviewer.

Testing the formulated prediction

Only a shift in the post-counterprojective/counterassumptive intervention material in line with the prediction will give a confirmation of the validity of the theory in this instance. The confirmation of the validity of the theory is given only by a shift in the post-intervention material according to the prediction. Some other shift, or no shift at all, will be a disconfirmation of the prediction, and the theory.

The causal change sequence from pre-intervention to post-intervention is selected using clinical theories (type 1 theories). Preferably, the post-intervention is also a triangulation. This change sequence is evaluated for the impact of counterassumptive/counterprojective remarks on the interviewer–interviewee relationship.

Example: sibling rivalry in psychoanalytic institutions

The aim of this research was to explore the unconscious elements that fuel the 'radioactive atmosphere' of psychoanalytic institutions – those unconscious sources of the chronic conflicts that sometimes plague the relationships between members of psychoanalytical societies and obscure the path of a constructive resolution of conflicts. As a result, this creates a toxic climate that stultifies members' creativity – hindering progress and further development. Kernberg (1986) refers to the 'radioactive atmosphere' of institutes, and the specific problems of psychoanalytic training. However, the 'radioactive' atmosphere is perpetuated also after the graduation, as the new members of the psychoanalytic society are still dependent on the institute for subsequent evaluations for becoming full members and training analysts (see also Thompson, 1958; Erlich, 2016).

Hinshelwood's (1999) idea that stressful relations between the analysts are due to displacement of pain derived from aggression in transference was the starting point of this research. Indeed, the practice of psychoanalysis puts a strong emotional pressure on the analyst, requiring openness to what is coming from the patient to foster understanding, and the responsibility of keeping and maintaining professional boundaries of analytic relationship. To suggest that the analyst is not affected by the destructiveness of the patient would not represent neutrality, but falseness. Naturally, there are situations when, in countertransference, following the aggression in transference, the analyst feels hate for his patient. This situation can generate in the analyst a particular conflict – conflict between his need to repair, to help, to be near the patient and the hate he feels towards the patient.

In his description of the 'indirect countertransference' related to the patient as an important factor within the analyst's professional relationships in the psychoanalytic society, Racker (1988) emphasised the impact of the analytic community as an internal object on the analyst's countertransference. Is this a one-way dynamic? Are the relationships between analysts influenced by the specifics of analytic work? The first hypothesis was formulated: one source of the conflicts between analysts is the displacement of negative countertransference from one's patients to one's colleagues.

In the next step, as understanding of countertransference represents a central aspect of the analytic attitude as an element at the crossroads between clinical practice and institutional recommendations and a guarantor of analytical identity, the previous hypothesis was reformulated in terms of analytic attitude and attitude towards colleagues. Consequently, I supposed that the analytic attitude used defensively is indicated by the tendency of the analysts to consider that they are invulnerable to the feelings expressed by the patients, to consider countertransference as being only the result of the patients' problems, to idealise their own training and their preferred theoretical model. An arrogant attitude towards their colleagues would parallel an omniscient attitude towards the patients.

The pilot study that set out to investigate the correspondence between the omniscient attitude towards patients and an arrogant attitude towards colleagues using thematic analysis of psychoanalytically informed interviews did not confirm this hypothesis. Nevertheless, the idea that a psychoanalytic institution could provide a scene for acting out the countertransference feelings and become a fighting arena needs to be further investigated using a different research design.

However, the pilot study pointed to 'sibling rivalry' as a common pattern of interaction between the interviewer and interviewees that signalled a hidden dynamic between colleagues in the psychoanalytic institution studied. A new hypothesis could be formulated: conflicts in psychoanalytic institutions are effects of complicated relations between members during a long training – 'sibling rivalries' and conflicts with 'parental' authority (Freud, 1913). Further, this hypothesis was empirically investigated using the experimental approach to psychoanalytically informed interviews, presented above.

The research design

The setting

The psychoanalytically oriented interview requires that the interviewer interventions be reduced to a minimum to allow the flow of free associations. The rules of free association and abstinence from the clinical setting are applied to the interview.

Hypothesis

Conflicts in the psychoanalytic society are due to the effects of complicated relations between members during a long training – 'sibling rivalries' and conflicts with 'parental' authority.

Prediction

In Freud's view, the relationship of the group members with authority is an ambivalent one, composed of affectionate and hostile impulses. Aggressive impulses could manifest in acts of rebellion against authority, or could arouse guilt feelings alleviated in great submissiveness toward authority, over-affectionate attitude, or displacement of hostility towards authority/father in the form of sibling rivalry.

The *predicted required relationship* between the interviewer and interviewee (two colleagues) will be sibling rivalry in order to avoid a hostile alliance against authority and the catastrophe of being responsible for 'murdering the father'.

The *predicted avoided relationship* in the interview will imply an alliance against authority.

The *predicted avoided catastrophe* implies the state of being responsible for 'murdering the father' and the consequences of this action.

The *predicted change* after the 'counterprojective'/'counterassumptive' remark is a movement in the here and now of the interview from the required relationship towards the avoided relationship.

Research question

Is there a 'sibling rivalry' between the interviewer and interviewee used to avoid the expression of hostility toward authority and the catastrophe of being responsible for excluding the authority figure?

Subjects

The research subjects are psychoanalysts with at least fifteen years of clinical experience, not directly involved in the researcher's training, not in an intimate relationship with the researcher. The researcher is also a psychoanalyst, a member of the studied group.

Test data

The selection of the material (the 'occurrence' in Hinshelwood's model of research) is informed by the Freudian theory about 'primal horde' (type 2 theory). Freud pointed out the ambivalent relationship between siblings and their father, and the inevitable competition among the surviving brothers (Freud, 1913). In order to avoid the catastrophe of being responsible for murdering the leader-father, the horde will cling together in great submissiveness to the leader. We will have:

a. a meaning occurrence of a sibling rivalry (required relation) identified by a triangulation process of content of interviewee's associations and interviewer's countertransference;
b. a counterprojective/counterassumptive remark pointing to the underlying dynamics in the interview session;
c. a post-remark occurrence that involves a change in the here and now from sibling rivalry towards hostile relation to authority observed using the clinical theory of transference–countertransference.

The sequence of change in the here and now of the interview session from pre-intervention remark to post-intervention is observed based on psychoanalytical clinical theories. For the sequence of change following the 'counterprojective' or 'counterassumptive' remark, only a shift in the post-remark material indicating a manifestation of hostility against authority figures in a less repressed form will give a confirmation of the validity of the theory.

Results

For confidentiality reasons, I am unable to include here a full case study. I could select only two small fragments from two different interviews, one to show how the method works, and another one to present a situation when the method didn't work.

How the method works

During the first interview session, the **required relation** seemed to be that of an alliance between us, an alliance of the 'good psychoanalysts' against the 'bad psychoanalysts', as the interviewee implicitly included me in her group, speaking about 'us' the whole time. At first sight, this required relation seemed to point to the narcissism of minor differences, with the emphasis on 'our' qualities and on the flaws of 'the others'. However, my colleague required me to ally with her in submissiveness toward the leaders of 'our group', exaggeratedly respecting them, waiting for and obeying their decisions.

The second interview session elucidated the **avoided relation** – alliance against our training analysts/parents, and the feared **calamity** – killing our training analysts/parents and becoming orphans unable to care for ourselves.

I take a closer look at the interaction in the here and now of the interview, selecting a sequence before and after my counterassumptive intervention.

Pre-intervention occurrence

The required relation was that of sibling alliance in submissiveness towards our leaders. We began the second session of the interview acting like two jealous 'sisters', furious that another 'sibling' was favoured by 'our parents', and discussing different colleagues being appointed in different high-status positions in the society.

Triangulation

My countertransference at that moment indicated identification with her – I was annoyed when I heard that my own interpretation on the recent conflict in our group was presented as being another colleague's idea. I felt like she had 'stolen' my 'brilliant' idea and now she was undeservedly appreciated. My anger feelings reflected also my interviewee's anger feelings toward another colleague 'undeservedly' appreciated. We were like two sisters jealous of the third one, unable to openly confront the authority and express our anger.

The counterassumptive intervention

The predicted avoided relationship derived from Freudian theory was an alliance in hostility against authority and the catastrophe of being responsible for 'murdering the father'. I found room for a counterassumptive intervention in the following situation.

At that moment, she was talking about our leaders: 'we give them [to our analysts] our endorsement and respect and support them as leaders, not to mention that its already set in stone that we would not repudiate our predecessors! The thought doesn't cross our mind! We are just very concerned with their opinion...'

I said: 'A bit exaggerated!'

With this remark, I presented myself being different from the 'fictitious' submissive person she assumed and required me to be. Also, the remark implies that something else – hostility towards authority – is added to our respect and endorsement, resulting in the 'exaggerated' quality of our behaviour.

Post-intervention occurrence

After my counterassumptive remark, her next association was: 'A bit exaggerated, so we're extra careful, so it doesn't seem as if we're disrespectful...!' This meaning was further developed in the next association, pointing to an adult son who can hit the parent in the face. 'My best friend has an adult son. She doesn't always ask for his opinion! She doesn't always want to know! (she laughs) At one point, you have to give to your adult son a fair chance to show that he is a grown-up and he can hit you in the face if you are unaware that he knows more than you or at least as much as you know.'

There was a movement towards a less repressed form of avoided relation – the hostility against the analyst/parent. The story of the son who can hit his mother in the face represents a less repressed form of the avoided relation. After that, the avoided relation was more freely expressed, in an imagined alliance against the training analysts/parents.

Triangulation

A change in countertransference feelings parallels the change in content of associations. The atmosphere became relaxed, we laugh, satisfied by the fantasy of a parent being beaten. The alliance against the analysts/parents evokes in me feelings of anxiety and guilt towards my analyst.

During the interview, my colleague required her and I to form a sibling alliance in submission towards our training analysts/parents in order to avoid an alliance against the parents because of the fear that we would kill them and we would become helpless orphans. After the counterassumptive remark, there was a movement in the here and now from the required relationship towards the avoided relationship and towards no other. The hypothesis was confirmed in this case.

An instance when a counterprojective intervention did not seem to work

In the first two minutes of another interview, my interviewee was asking me details about the research hypothesis, suggesting that I had better have used the hundreds of emails sent and received by all members during the escalation of the conflict in our society. Then she told me that when she is furious, she wants to leave this profession because there is no group where one can 'professionally' discuss different issues. The required relation seemed to be competitive sibling rivalry.

Triangulation

As mentioned above, during the beginning of the interview I felt enviously attacked and deserted. I was frustrated and angry. It was as if she invited me there to refuse me; she didn't seem to be available to share with me something about her experience of being an analyst, but she sent me to my computer to read emails, or attempted to lure me in 'falsifying' the interview material and destroying my study by implicitly communicating that she would tell me what I wanted to hear. I felt the need to be protected, and I evoked an authority figure (the Research Ethical Committee).

Counterprojective intervention

The predicted avoided relation was hostile alliance against authority. She mentioned a former colleague who resigned from our society, and she was convinced that she was expelled.

'Well, Anca was expelled from IPA.... As soon as she left, she was excluded from IPA, and yet, you need the support of an organisation. Especially for us, here, where there are so many other types of therapies.'

'I thought that something major had happened...'

'No, this is what I was referring to...'

'I was thinking that I was better off not signing, but no one told me that if you sign, you can no longer be a Direct Member of IPA....' (I try to emphasise this part of reality... as I know it. If you resign, your membership naturally ends...)

'Yes well... I don't know if it was stated somewhere, but if it was, then it's all right, because it means we didn't read it. But I'm convinced that some people knew.'

My intervention was intended to shake the fantasy about our colleague being punished and expelled from IPA, pointing out that she really resigned, and she was not excluded. At the same time, by revealing my regret about signing the documents, I was trying to place myself 'side by side' with her, and to look at the society from the same place.

Post-intervention occurrence

To all appearances, her next association was to good authority representatives of the IPA, which bound the members and alleviated the conflict between them – and not to the avoided relation in a less repressed form. Without their presence, she is afraid of future unfair evaluations. This is a long story, and what is significant for this study is that these good authority representatives were at the same time 'parents' dethroned and banished by their 'children'. This fragment of associations could be seen as a coming out from the avoided relation emerging in a less repressed form.

Triangulation

However, in countertransference I did not identify any change in the atmosphere of the interview. As she was talking, I remembered an unfair situation when she received a favour of 'flexibility' that was refused to me. At that moment, I felt frustrated and angry for this injustice, and my annoyance in the interview was related to failing in sibling competition.

I can offer two possible explanations for this situation. Maybe the intervention was taking place too soon, after two minutes of the interview, when we were still 'negotiating' the relationship and our particular roles. Another reason could be related to the specific form of that intervention – a self-revelation statement. It seems that the disclosure of my feelings blocked the interaction in the pattern of required relationship – competitive sibling rivalry – and did not allow the movement towards avoided relationship. The other interventions that worked in this interview expressed not my personal view about some events in the group, but they were things known and accepted by all the members of our psychoanalytic community. They had an impersonal quality, similar to proverbs, recommended by Havens (1986) as good instruments for shaking assumptions.

Empirical findings

The hypothesis was confirmed in two of three cases. These findings suggest that unconscious sibling rivalry should be added to the sources of conflict in psychoanalytic institutions discussed in the literature, along with narcissism of minor differences (Freud 1921, 1930; Benedek, 1954; Rothstein, 1980; Werman, 1998; Gabbard, 1993), envy and its vicissitudes (Erlich, 2016), social defence systems related to the nature of the work (Menzies-Lyth, 1959; Eisold, 1994), and the dynamics of political power (Kirsner, 2009).

Discussion

Hinshelwood's design for research in a clinical setting was extended to the research outside the clinical setting. Usually the psychoanalytically informed interview is approached from a meaning-centred perspective. One of the advantages of using this approach is the combination of the hermeneutic perspective with the perspective of scientific causality, opening the opportunity to use the interview as a 'laboratory' for testing different psychoanalytic theories. The pilot application of this approach could prove useful in testing psychoanalytic theories. The re-application of this method in further studies is needed to investigate the utility of this method of research in different areas of study.

Another advantage of this approach to the psychoanalytically informed research interview is that it could be used in insider research. In these cases, the methods frequently used by researchers are participant observation in communities within which they were previously members: for example, a jazz musician observing his professional group (Becker, 1963), an industrial worker-researcher studying boring work (Molstad, 1986), or grounded theory (van Heugten, 2004).

There are some limitations of the method itself, and also some limitations related to the researcher. As Rioch (1972) notes, in Ezriel's model of three object relations involved in the transference situation, the chosen required relation is not completely understandable in terms of avoidance alone. There is also the problem of the observer bias, which is present to some extent in all research situations. To overcome these difficulties, Hunt (1989) argues for exploring the researcher's motivations and conflicts related to the research topic as a preliminary part of the research study (Hunt, 1989). Also a reflexive attitude of the researcher is required to understand how data is constructed by both interviewer and interviewee (Holmes, 2013; Clarke, 2002).

This method works with psychoanalysts as subjects. Further studies are needed to test if it also works with subjects less trained in reflexive thinking.

Acknowledgement

This chapter is based on my PhD thesis in psychoanalytic studies (Emotional Radioactivity Behind Conflict in Psychoanalytic Institutions, University of Essex, Centre for Psychoanalytic Studies, 2016). I am grateful to my thesis supervisor, Bob Hinshelwood, for his support and contributions to the work reported here. My sincere thanks to my colleagues who shared their thoughts and feelings with me, for making this research project possible. I also thank Bob Hinshelwood and Kalina Stamenova for their comments on the first version of this text.

References

Becker, H. (1963), *Outsiders*. New York: Free Press.
Benedek, T. (1954), Countertransference in the training analyst. *Bulletin of the Menninger Clinic*, 18: 12–16.
Cartwright, D. (2004), The psychoanalytic research interview. *Journal of the American Psychoanalytic Association*, 52: 209–242.
Clarke, S. (2002), Learning from experience, psycho-social research methods in the social sciences. *Qualitative Research*, 2: 173–195.
Eisold, K. (1994), The intolerance of diversity in psychoanalytic institutes. *International Journal of Psycho-Analysis*, 75: 785–800.
Erlich, S. (2016), Envy and its in vicissitudes in psychoanalytic organizations. Paper presented at the EPF Annual Conference, Berlin, 19 March.
Evans, B. (1996), *Harry Stack Sullivan: Interpersonal Theory and Psychiatry*. New York: Routledge.
Ezriel, H. (1951), The scientific testing of psychoanalytic findings and theory. *British Journal of Medical Psychology*, 24(1): 30–34.
Ezriel, H. (1956), Experimentation within the psycho-analytic session. *The British Journal for the Philosophy of Science*, 7(25): 29–48.
Figlio, K. (1988), Oral history and the unconscious. *History Workshop Journal*, Vol. 26, No. 1 (pp. 120–132). Oxford: Oxford University Press.

Fox, R. P. (2003), Thoughts on authority and leadership. *Journal of the American Psychoanalytic Association*, 51S: 57–72.

Freud, S. (1910), 'Wild' psycho-analysis. *The Standard Edition of the Complete Psychological Works of Sigmund Freud*, Volume XI: *Five Lectures on Psycho-Analysis, Leonardo da Vinci and Other Works*, pp. 219–228.

Freud, S. (1913), *Totem and Taboo. The Standard Edition of the Complete Psychological Works of Sigmund Freud*, Volume XIII: *Totem and Taboo and Other Works*, pp. vii–162.

Freud, S. (1921), *Group Psychology and the Analysis of the Ego. The Standard Edition of the Complete Psychological Works of Sigmund Freud*, Volume XVIII: *Beyond the Pleasure Principle, Group Psychology and Other Works*, pp. 65–144.

Freud, S. (1930), *Civilization and its Discontents. The Standard Edition of the Complete Psychological Works of Sigmund Freud*, Volume XXI: *The Future of an Illusion, Civilization and its Discontents, and Other Works*, pp. 57–146.

Gabbard, G. O. (1993), On hate in love relationships: the narcissism of minor differences revisited. *Psychoanalytic Quarterly*, 62: 229–238.

Havens, L. (1976), *Participant Observation*. New York: Jason Aronson.

Havens, L. (1980), Explorations in the uses of language in psychotherapy: counterprojective statements. *Contemporary Psychoanalysis*, 16: 53–67.

Havens, L. (1986), *Making Contact: Uses of Language in Psychotherapy*. Cambridge, MA: Harvard University Press.

Hinshelwood, R. D. (1999), Countertransference. *International Journal of Psycho-Analysis*, 80: 797–818.

Hinshelwood, R. D. (2013), *Research on the Couch*. London: Routledge.

Hollway, W. (2009), Applying the 'experience-near' principle to research: psychoanalytically informed methods. *Journal of Social Work Practice*, 23(4): 461–474.

Hollway, W. (2015), *Knowing Mothers: Researching Maternal Identity Change*. London: Palgrave Macmillan.

Hollway, W., and Jefferson, T. (2000), *Doing Qualitative Research Differently: Free Associations, Narrative and the Interview Method*. London: Sage.

Holmes, J. (2013), Using psychoanalysis in qualitative research: countertransference-informed researcher reflexivity and defence mechanisms in two interviews about migration. *Qualitative Research in Psychology*, 10(2): 160–173.

Holmes, J. (2014), Countertransference in qualitative research: a critical appraisal. *Qualitative Research*, 14(2): 166–183.

Holmes, J. (2017), Reverie-informed research interviewing. *International Journal of Psycho-Analysis*, 98(3): 709–728.

Hunt. J. C. (1989), Psychoanalytic aspects of fieldwork. *Series on Qualitative Research Methods*, vol. 18. Newbury Park, CA: Sage.

Kernberg, O. F. (1986), Institutional problems of psychoanalytic education. *Journal of the American Psychoanalytic Association*, 34: 799–834.

Kirsner, D. (2009), *Unfree Associations: Inside Psychoanalytic Institutes*. New York: Jason Aronson.

Kvale, S. (1999), The psychoanalytic interview as qualitative research. *Qualitative Inquiry*, 5: 87–113.

Kvale, S. (2003), The psychoanalytical interview as inspiration for qualitative research. In P. Camic, J. Rhodes, and L. Yardley (eds.), *Qualitative Research in Psychology: Expanding Perspectives in Methodology and Design*. American Psychological Association.

Menzies, L. (1959), The functioning of social systems as a defence against anxiety. In *Containing Anxiety in Institutions: Selected Essays*, vol. 1. London: Free Association Books, 1988.
Molstad, C. (1986), Choosing and coping with boring work. *Journal of Contemporary Ethnography*, 15(2): 215–236.
Racker, H. (1988), Transference and countertransference. *International Psycho-Analysis Library*, 73: 1–196. London: Hogarth Press and the Institute of Psycho-Analysis.
Rioch, M. J. (1972), Discussion. *Contemporary Psychoanalysis*, 8(2): 246.
Roper, M. (2003), Analysing the analysed: transference and counter-transference in the oral history encounter. *The Journal of the Oral History Society*, 31(2): 20–32.
Rothstein, A. (1980), Psychoanalytic paradigms and their narcissistic investment. *Journal of the American Psychoanalytic Association*, 28: 385–395.
Strachey, J. (1934), The nature of the therapeutic action of psycho-analysis. *International Journal of Psycho-Analysis*, 15: 127–159.
Strømme, H., Gullestad, S. E., Stänicke, E., and Killingmo, B. (2010), A widened scope on therapist development: designing a research interview informed by psychoanalysis. *Qualitative Research in Psychology*, 7(3): 214–232.
Sullivan, H. S. (1970), *The Psychiatric Interview*. New York: Norton.
Thompson, C. (1958), A study of the emotional climate of psychoanalytic institutes. In *Interpersonal Psychoanalysis: The Selected Papers of Clara M. Thompson*. New York: Basic Books, 1964.
Van Heugten, K. (2004), Managing insider research: learning from experience. *Qualitative Social Work*, 3(2): 203–219.
Werman, D. S. (1988), Freud's 'narcissism of minor differences'. *Journal of the American Academy Psychoanalysis*, 16: 451–459.

Observations

Chapter 6

Psychoanalytic observation – the mind as research instrument

Wilhelm Skogstad

Introduction

Psychoanalytic observation is rooted in the practice of psychoanalysis itself. There, observation is a main part of the work: observation, that is, of both the patient and the analyst himself. The importance of the capacity to observe the other, and oneself as relating to the other, is one of the reasons why Esther Bick introduced the method of infant observation as a training exercise for child psychotherapists and psychoanalysts (Bick, 1964). Meanwhile, infant observation has also become an important, if limited, research method (Rustin, 1989, 1997, 2002). Hinshelwood took up this method and changed it into one for observing institutions, again initially as a training exercise for psychiatric trainees and medical psychotherapists (Hinshelwood, 1989, 2002; Hinshelwood and Skogstad, 2000, 2002). Hinshelwood and I have argued, however, that it could also be used as a method of research into the dynamics of institutions (Hinshelwood and Skogstad, 2002). Psychoanalytically based observational methods have also developed out of a different tradition of human science. Starting with Devereux (1967), anthropology has adopted psychoanalytic concepts, thus deepening its scientific approach and developing methods not too far off from the one I am presenting here (Hunt, 1989; Heald et al., 1994).

The main research instrument in psychoanalytic observation is the mind, the mind of the observer and the collective minds of a study or research group. It is the mind that takes in what is seen and heard, registers feelings in the observer and other people, and processes what has been observed. Psychoanalytic observation outside of clinical practice, however, lacks one important tool: interpretation. Interpreting to the patient is not only the most important instrument of therapeutic technique in psychoanalysis; it is also part of the observational process, as the patient's conscious and unconscious responses to interpretations provide further material for a deepening of one's understanding which the purely observational methods have to do without. This limits its research value, unless other ways of validation are found, a point I will come back to later in the chapter.

Psychoanalytic concepts as the basis of psychoanalytic observation

I would, first of all, like to describe those psychoanalytic concepts that I see as most relevant for the context of observation. These are: the unconscious; anxiety, defence, and conflict; splitting, projection, and projective identification; transference and countertransference; as well as other concepts such as psycho-social culture. I will try to spell out their significance for the method of observation and will illustrate them with case material from institutional observations. While I will do this in a rather schematic way, it has to be borne in mind that it will normally need much more material and context to verify whether the processes I am talking about are actually taking place.

The most fundamental concept in psychoanalysis is, of course, the notion of the *unconscious* which assumes that much of human behaviour is determined not by conscious thoughts but by unconscious phantasies, motives, and anxieties, and that all human activities are imbued with unconscious meanings. This model of individual psychology has been taken further, and it has been assumed that unconscious phantasies can also be shared within groups or institutions (e.g., Jaques, 1955; Menzies, 1959; Menzies Lyth, 1990; Hinshelwood and Skogstad, 2000). For the method of observation, the concept of the unconscious implies, of course, that these meanings and motives cannot be directly investigated but can only be inferred on the basis of careful observation. What is directly observed needs further processing through another mind (and its unconscious) or through a group of minds in order to get beyond the level of pure observable behaviour.

Particularly important psychoanalytic notions are those of *anxiety* and *defence* and of *intrapsychic conflict*. Many experiences cause pain and anxiety, but as it is inherently human to wish to avoid the experience of pain and anxiety, these are often dealt with by various mechanisms of defence, such as splitting, projection, or denial, so that they need not be felt. Conflicts between different internal demands can be a particular source of anxiety. Due to the effects of defence mechanisms, pain, anxiety, or conflict may not be directly observable but may only be inferred. Jaques (1955) and Menzies Lyth (1959, 1990) have taken this model of anxiety and defence into the realm of institutions. Jaques suggested that social systems could be used by the individuals to support their defences against anxieties. Menzies showed that the system as a whole could function in such a way that the anxieties and conflicts inherent to the institution's primary task could be evaded by the individuals. The unconscious defence mechanisms are, in her view, reflected in shared, socially accepted attitudes and working practices, which she called 'defensive techniques'. These practices can be observed directly, whereas the unconscious phantasies and anxieties motivating the defensive techniques can only be inferred.

Of the various defence mechanisms found in psychoanalysis, the most important ones for understanding the dynamics of groups and institutions are those of *splitting* and *projection* and the related one of *projective identification* (see, e.g., Hinshelwood,

1991). Through splitting, opposing aspects of experiences or the different sides of conflicts are completely separated in the mind and may then be projected into different people or groups. In projective identification, aspects are disowned in one's own mind and are instead, in phantasy, lodged in others; these others are then often influenced in such a way that they actually come to feel what has been disowned and to behave accordingly.

Any work involves conflicts, but a common feature of social institutions is that such conflicts are spread between different groups within the institution so that an internal conflict is turned into a conflict between different groups who may then fight against each other (e.g., Bott Spillius, 1976; Hinshelwood, 1993; Menzies, 1959; Miller and Gwynne, 1972; Roberts, 1994). Menzies, for example, described in her study of a nursing service how the conflicts around responsibility were avoided by attributing all the irresponsible impulses to junior nurses and all the harshness and strictness to the senior ones. And she showed that these splits did not remain in the realm of phantasy but became a reality, because, as she put it, 'people act objectively on the roles assigned to them' (Menzies, 1959, p. 57), an early formulation of projective identification.

I would like to give some brief observation material from a chronic psychiatric ward (Donati, 2000) to illustrate the concepts I have described so far, first of all that of defensive techniques:

> On that ward, there was a sense of deadness that the nurses were quite aware of. The observer noticed that contact between nurses and patients was usually made by brief questions such as 'Is it time for OT?', 'How are you feeling today?' or by challenging or jokey comments, and that the contact was then quickly broken off again. In ward meetings, patients would be encouraged to bring things up and yet, whatever they brought, was met with dismissal or rejection.

While staff on this ward consciously wanted to enliven the contact and atmosphere, in their actual working practice they were engaged in a behaviour that Donati came to describe as 'touch-and-go'; that behaviour allowed no real contact to develop and in fact contributed to the deadening of the atmosphere. Thinking about this repeatedly observed pattern led to the hypothesis that the contact itself caused anxiety: staff might be terrified of the patients' madness and its effect on themselves and afraid of their feelings of inadequacy which closer contact would evoke. Their working practice of 'touch-and-go behaviour' helped, as a defensive technique, to avoid such fears.

I want to continue with a further vignette from the same ward to give an example of the processes of splitting, projection, and projective identification. It has to be added that the ward had only male patients and male nurses, whereas the observer was a young female doctor:

> The nurses came back and went on chatting to the observer about 'how much better the female chronic wards are since women are capable of making wards their home, they are always doing something, looking after themselves and their environment. The atmosphere is much more alive, cleaner ... more at home. Male patients neglect themselves, need continuous encouragement, the place is boring and the nurses alone have to try to make the ward like at home.'
>
> (Donati, 2000, p. 36)

First of all, what is being said here suggests a split between male and female: all care and homeliness is located in women, and all neglect and un-homeliness in men. In thinking about that, it is striking that this was said by male nurses; one might assume that they had an inkling in themselves of what they were speaking about in male patients. In the context of other observation material from the same ward, one could arrive at the hypothesis that there was a deep sense of inadequacy and impotence in the male nurses which was felt to be intolerable and was therefore projected into the patients. This assumption was further supported by the observation of behaviour that could actively engender those feelings in the patients, such as in the following vignette:

> A patient, who was sitting near the observer and a nurse, asked three different questions of the nurse, about his exams, about their industrial action and about ward matters. The nurse gave monosyllabic answers and then started to talk only to the observer. He moved from enquiry about the observation project to describing how very bored he was with the ward's life, how difficult if not impossible it was to capture the patients' interest and promote interaction. Some patients were sitting around them and appeared to be listening.
>
> (Donati, 2000, p. 35)

Here, the nurse actively shut out the patient who showed a lively interest and then talked disparagingly about the patients in their presence. Such a behaviour might actually make the patients feel useless and impotent, therefore engendering in them the feelings unwanted by staff: an observable manifestation of projective identification.

This sense of impotence in the ward staff might even have had a wider institutional significance: the male back ward may have become a repository for the feelings of inadequacy and impotence within the hospital as a whole, in contrast to the chronic female wards or the acute wards. By allowing others in the hospital to project these feelings into this part of the institution, it might have served a purpose for the whole institution. To establish whether this was the case would however require further information or observation material from other parts of the institution.

Of particular importance in psychoanalysis and psychoanalytic observation are, of course, the concepts of transference and countertransference. In its initial conception, Freud saw *transference* (see, e.g., Sandler et al., 1992) as a kind of misperception by which the analyst was experienced as a figure of the patient's childhood, but it was soon recognised as a major tool for understanding the patient's internal world. We now have a much wider concept of transference: it is seen as a phenomenon that occurs all the time in everyday life, not just in the psychoanalytic situation, and as a mechanism by which aspects of oneself – more accurately, aspects of one's internal object relationships – are projected into another person or group and experienced in them. Internal relationships relate back to childhood but never truly reflect actual infantile experiences.

The phenomenon of transference, of course, also affects the way an observer is viewed by those he observes and, as in clinical psychoanalysis, this can be used for understanding unconscious anxieties, defences, and phantasies. Modern anthropological fieldwork has taken this into account and now also recognises transference manifestations as an important tool for understanding in their research (Hunt, 1989).

In my examples of the chronic psychiatric ward, and in that observation as a whole, one can see manifestations of a transference from the male nurses towards the young female observer and the sexuality that she represented. On the basis of the observation material, one could assume in these men both a desire for this woman and, linked with their sense of inadequacy, a fear of being viewed as impotent. The observed behaviour, of emphasising the inadequacy of male patients, of praising female patients, and of making contact with the observer while actively excluding the patients, may all be understood as attempts to assert themselves, internally and externally, as potent men towards a desirable and threatening woman figure. An important point for the method of observation is that such an interpretation would have greater conviction if it were supported by a concordant subjective experience in the observer. This brings me to the concept of countertransference.

Countertransference (see, e.g., Gabbard, 1995; Hinshelwood, 1999; Sandler et al., 1992) was initially seen by Freud as the analyst's transference to the patient, a reflection of the analyst's own neurotic problems and an unwelcome interference with the analytic task. Later, the concept was widened, initially by Heimann (1950), to include *all* the analyst's feelings towards his patient. It was recognised that many of the emotions and impulses felt by the analyst in the analytic situation reflected unacknowledged or unconscious aspects of the patient's internal life which, however, were picked up by the analyst's mind, often, as we would now see it, through the process of projective identification. Heimann saw the analyst's emotional response to his patient as 'one of the most important tools for his work' and as 'an instrument of research into the patient's unconscious' (Heimann, 1950, p. 81), and this remains the view in modern psychoanalysis.

A similar development has taken place in anthropology, where the researcher's subjectivity was initially seen 'as a hindrance to the scientific endeavour' (Hunt, 1989, p. 17). Nowadays, however, it is acknowledged that 'the researcher's subjective experience ... provides the medium through which the raw data is gathered' (p. 14), and the researcher's subjectivity is viewed 'in terms of unconscious processes that mediate the relationship between researcher and subject' (p. 27).

What the analyst feels can vary in the degree to which it reflects mainly an aspect of the patient or the analyst's own transference response to the patient, and countertransference has been described as 'a joint creation of contributions from both patient and analyst' (Gabbard, 1995, p. 482). It therefore needs working out what belongs to the patient and what to the analyst. The same task, of course, applies to the psychoanalytic observer who will experience powerful emotions while observing, and phantasies, memories, and dreams may be engendered by the experience of observing. For a fuller understanding of those, psychic work needs to be done to distinguish what originates in the observed and what may belong more to the observer.

In psychoanalysis, the capacity in the analyst to make this distinction comes from long training analyses but may still also require a corrective view from outside, such as through peer supervision. In psychoanalytic observation, particularly if carried out by people not themselves in analysis, the group, in which the observations are presented and discussed, has a vital role in this task. This is particularly important, because the corrective function provided in analysis by the patient's responses is lacking in the observation setting. The group may be helpful in exploring and understanding the conscious reactions of the observer to his experience, but may also detect clues to the observer's unconscious countertransference response. In this way, the group may not only help to differentiate the thoughts and feelings that are engendered, but may help to access parts of the observer's mind otherwise not utilised.

I would like to give an example to illustrate countertransference. An observer of a hospice for terminally ill patients had the following dream about the unit:

> I was in the corridor near to where I usually sat, but I was lying on the floor, being held up by my arms and feet by two nurses. My body was floppy and my limbs hung useless as a rag doll's as they tried to drag me along the floor. The feeling was of complete helplessness.
>
> (Ramsay, 2000, p. 146)

Many aspects of this dream may be related to the observer's own history but some clearly relate to the observation itself. Her paralysis in the dream, I think, may capture the immobility she had to adopt in her role of observer, in contrast to the nurses who 'rarely sat still, pacing the corridor vigilantly' (p. 150). More striking is the complete helplessness she experienced: this may have been what the dying patients felt and what the nurses could not tolerate being aware of in themselves and so needed to find ways of avoiding. The busy activity was a way of avoiding such experience for the nurses. The observer, however, picked up in her countertransference the sense of utter helplessness, which was then depicted in her dream. Her forced immobility as an observer, while uncomfortable, may have actually helped her to be more receptive to an experience which the nurses were able to defend themselves against.

I want to stay with this observation to give a further illustration of defensive techniques. In this hospice, patients were isolated in single rooms, with closed doors and signs 'Do not disturb' on them; nurses only entered the rooms when called by the patient ringing the bell. The communal area was hardly used, and if a patient died, everything was shuttered off to get the corpse out, away from anyone's gaze. While the conscious intention was to give death and dying a humane place, in practice the emotional experience of dying was shut out and the patients were left alone with it. The working practices that the observer found were therefore part of a defensive system that allowed staff to avoid the anxieties connected with their work, particularly the experience of deep helplessness in the face of death. It is curious that in its culture the hospice thus repeated the defensive shutting out of death that hospices were set up to counteract. The unrecognised deep helplessness, however, then appeared in the observer's dream and in her subjective experience.

In the 1950s, Trist (1959) brought up the notion of *psychosocial culture* as a conceptual bridge between the personal and the social realm. Hinshelwood and I (Hinshelwood and Skogstad, 2000) have taken the notion of culture up and have located an essential element of institutional culture in the *unconscious assumptions, attitudes, and beliefs* about the work and how to perform it, that is, in collectively shared unconscious phantasies which can only be inferred from observations. The shared unconscious assumption in the hospice that I have just described may be inferred as: helplessness in the face of death is unbearable and needs to be avoided at all cost.

We have also included the *emotional atmosphere* as a very important element of culture. Unlike the cultural assumptions which are unconscious and can only be inferred, the atmosphere can be registered consciously by the observer, through his sensitivity. For instance, the atmosphere that the observer picked up in the hospice was one of superficial brightness; and this quality of atmosphere was concordant with the hypothesis that the experience of death was being isolated and avoided.

The method of observation

Having described the theoretical concepts, I would now like to turn to the actual method of observation. One might ask whether, with this method, we do not just insert our preconceptions and theoretical models into the field that we observe. Surely, that risk exists, and we need to find ways of avoiding or at least minimising it. Being aware of this problem in psychoanalysis, Bion suggested that the analyst approach the patient 'without memory and desire' (Bion, 1970). He used Keats' phrase of 'negative capability' (Bion, 1970) to describe the need for the capacity in the analyst to tolerate not-knowing and not-understanding in order to come to a deeper understanding, out of one's own imaginative experience. A similar attitude of open-mindedness would be desirable for an observer outside of the psycho-analytic situation, if he is not to look just for confirmation of his preconceptions. And yet, we can't do away with our preconceptions and theories completely.

Rustin writes about this dialectic:

> Psychoanalytical observation methods ... require observers both to have in mind a range of conceptions and latent expectations, by which they can give coherence and shape to their experience, and to remain open-minded and receptive to the particular situations and events to which they are exposed. They cannot know in advance which of the conceptions of which they are already aware will turn out to have a useful application. Nor can they be sure that any of their preconceptions will fit. They may be confronted with experiences that, initially at least, fall altogether outside the bounds of their ability to understand them. What this method requires of its practitioners is the ability to hold in mind a loose cluster of expectations and conceptions, while remaining open to the experiences of the observation as it develops.
>
> (Rustin, 1989, p. 57)

In order for the observation to be as rigorous as possible, whether for training or for research purposes, it is essential to separate three different stages within the observational process:

- the actual observation;
- the writing up of the observation; and
- the processing and interpreting of the observed material.

In the *observation* itself, the focus should be on the task of observing alone. The observer should be as open to the experience as possible; therefore, no notes are taken, as this would interfere with the free-floating attention and the use of one's subjectivity. When observing, one's attention should be directed at three different areas at the same time:

- what one can see and hear outside: i.e., what people do, how they move, how they interact, little gestures, facial expressions, what is said, their tone of voice, etc.;
- what one can perceive empathically outside: i.e., the quality of the general atmosphere and how it might change during the observation, the emotional state of the people observed, etc.; and
- what one can observe inside, in oneself: i.e., one's own feelings and impulses, associations, mental images, memories, etc.

As soon as possible after the observation, all that has been registered needs to be *written up*, so that as much as possible of it is retained. When doing that, one needs to refrain from interpretations and, instead, one should only write down what one has seen, heard, and felt, in everyday language and as accurately as possible. Only in this way can a seminar group be allowed to approach the material with as open minds as possible. It also gives the observer him- or herself the chance to go back to his or her own material with a fresh mind and potentially find things in it that he or she hadn't been aware of initially.

The third step is that of *processing and formulating interpretations*. This is much better done within a group than by the observer alone. That is for various reasons: a group of minds of course provides a wider range of cognitive and emotional processing than just one mind alone. Other members of the group will be able to provide different perspectives, through their own different backgrounds, experiences, and ways of thinking. This perspective will be of particular value and greater depth if members of the group have experience in doing observations themselves and if the leader or some members are embedded in psychoanalytic practice. As members of the group are not directly affected by the experience in the way the observer is, they may also notice aspects that have eluded the observer and recognise shapes and patterns in the material that are otherwise missed.

The group may also be able to pick up clues from the observer's unconscious, in distortions in his write-up, in his use of language or his way of talking, in an ironic comment or a slip of the tongue, and thereby find access to feelings, phantasies, and associations that may deepen the picture. Material implicit in the observation but not directly accessible to the observer thus has a greater chance of being accessed through a group than by the observer alone. Furthermore, when the discussion in the group in this way helps to reduce the observer's internal resistance, forgotten observation material may emerge. In these ways, the group's mind may not only function as an additional 'research instrument' in the process, but may enable a better use of the original 'research instrument', the observer's mind.

Hinshelwood (2013) describes that the observer of a fracture clinic was bringing very inadequate protocols of his observations, with only general themes rather than any detailed material. This turned out to come not from a misunderstanding of the task, but out of some inner inability. With the group's observation and non-critical persistence, a deep sense of inadequacy in him as observer emerged. When this could be spoken about, he was able to bring vivid images of a disturbing situation at the clinic, where there was a lot of pain and disability and yet hardly any verbal communication. As it could then be understood, 'the thin and uninformative process records … were actually a very eloquent expression of the patients' experience of being lost in a bewildering place that made no effort to address the individual's plight' (Hinshelwood, 2013, pp. 62–63).

When trying to process the objective and subjective material of the observation, the material available will often appear overwhelming and confusing at first, to the observer and to the group. In order to eventually arrive at hypotheses and interpretations, it is important to look out for *ordering patterns* (Rustin,

2002) in the observed behaviour and relationships and the emotional experience. Such patterns may emerge only after some time. It would certainly be wrong to base hypotheses about a complex institution on brief vignettes alone (the use of such brief vignettes for illustration in this chapter might easily give the wrong impression that one would be justified in doing that). In order for interpretations of the underlying psychological processes in the organisation to have real conviction, there are, in my view, three requirements:

- there needs to be a concordance between different areas of the observation, such as the observed behaviour and the subjective experience of the observer;
- one needs to see repeated patterns rather than just a single event;
- interpretations arrived at through earlier observation material should normally remain meaningful when looking at later material.

The impact on the observer and on the observed

Observation methods differ in the degree to which they allow or encourage participation in the field that is being observed. Anthropological fieldworkers, for example, will usually participate in certain roles in the culture they study (Hunt, 1989). Participation may, as Jorgensen (1989) points out, reveal meanings and connections that escape the pure observer. Sufficient distance, on the other hand, may, in my view, allow more internal freedom to observe.

In psychoanalytic observation, one usually tries as much as possible to be in an observing role alone, although this can never be purely so. This may involve, although not necessarily so, finding a place from which to observe and remaining there. The role of observer does not mean, however, becoming mechanical and unresponsive. If addressed, one will need to respond, but in a way that neither encourages nor rejects and that avoids getting too involved. If one experiences an impulse, for example, to get up and help or stop someone, this may be registered without acting upon it. Being restrained in this way can be very difficult, as one is left without some of the familiar ways of relieving tensions. The emotional response is therefore intensified, but one's mind is also allowed better access to one's own subjective experience, which is so essential for the observation and can otherwise get lost.

An observer of an acute psychiatric ward described his experience of the role:

> The most difficult feelings were the ones evoked by the stilted and impersonal atmosphere which permeated the ward most of the time... The flattening of human contacts, the stifling of creative activities and the predominance of apathy evoked in me feelings of depression and hopelessness that were difficult to tolerate. After a while of sitting in my chair I would feel restless inside, wanting to move and do something active, or get

up and leave out of exasperation. At other times I realised I was coping by absenting myself mentally, caught up in phantasies and thoughts that had no connection with the task in hand.

(Chiesa, 2000, pp. 57–58)

In this case, the observer's emotional experience was presumably very similar to the feelings the ward staff were having to struggle with. Unlike the observer, however, they were able to 'do something active', even though what they did often seemed to be aimed at relieving themselves of such feelings rather than at helping the patients.

Being an observer can also arouse deep anxieties and conflicts of a more personal nature: the observer might feel uncomfortably like a voyeur or find it extremely difficult to be excluded from the relationships he observes. This might prevent him from being able to watch from what Britton (1989) has called a 'third position', which depends on a successful oedipal development within the observer. Such a position will enable the observer to be open to the experience of different participants at the same time. Otherwise, he might identify completely with one participant, say, a patient on a ward, against another, say, a nurse, and then become very critical instead of being able to explore.

Helping the observer find and maintain an internal position from which he can observe is another important function of a seminar or research group. This may need to involve discussing the observer's anxieties and powerful personal reactions that get in the way of observing. For this to be possible, an open and trusting atmosphere in such a group is essential. It will also involve noticing the particular roles to which the observer gets enlisted, of which he may be unaware, and helping him find a more neutral position again.

The observer may also be concerned about his impact on the observed, for scientific reasons. The influence of the analyst on his patient has been a serious criticism of psychoanalysis as a method of gaining knowledge (e.g., Grunbaum, 1984, 1993) and the same criticism could be made for psychoanalytic observation. In dealing with this criticism, Rustin writes that it is 'the contention of object-relations theory that mental life is organised in an ongoing relationship to others, and that there could never be any way of apprehending psychic reality which did not involve a relationship with an observer' (Rustin, 2002, p. 261). He argues that in psychoanalysis, this relationship becomes, via transference and countertransference, 'an explicit dimension of the description and explanation of the phenomena being observed, not an unnoticed distortion of what would otherwise be an "objective" account' (Rustin, 2002, p. 261).

No doubt, the observer's presence and the awareness of being watched can have a considerable effect on those who are being observed. The nature of the influence, however, cannot be generalised. In infant observation, the observer frequently seems to have a helpful, at times even therapeutic, effect through his or her non-judgemental and thoughtful presence and through containing what is being projected into him or her, such as a persecuting superego (H. Skogstad,

1999). An observer may unconsciously even be sought for that reason. On the other hand, it has also been shown that important conflictual material may be actively withheld from an observer (Diem-Wille, 1997).

The impact will, of course, be different when observing a loosely connected group of people working together than in such an intimate situation as infant observation. And in a fairly consistent group situation, where the observer is recognised as such, the impact may be different than in the hustle and bustle of a hectic ward, where he may hardly be noticed. The observer may be experienced as a persecuting, critical judge or may be given the status of a rescuer who will come up with a solution to their difficulties. The observer is experienced in some way, and whatever influence he or she has, the impact will always be based on the transference of a whole group or of individuals within the institution and on the unconscious phantasies active in the group. What is being observed may therefore be different from what would have happened without the observer's presence, but it will, in my view and following Rustin's argument, still reflect the very object that is being studied, that is, unconscious phantasies and their manifestations in transference phenomena.

An example of an observation

I would now like to give a more detailed example of an observation (Skogstad, 2000), with which I hope to show some of the aspects I have discussed in this chapter.

This was a general medical ward with a focus on heart problems, although, as it was not a real specialty ward, for all special investigations, such as angiography, patients had to be sent to a larger hospital. Because of the nature of the patients' illnesses, there were on the ward frequent sudden deaths, sometimes occurring just before the observation sessions.

> My entry into this observation was through meeting the lead nurse, then the ward manager and eventually part of the ward's nursing staff in a team meeting. The lead nurse was extremely accommodating which surprised me, given the pressure I was hearing about. She told me at length about the pressure they were under from their only purchaser, their need to break even financially, how their performance was being checked, and that they were not 'one of the big names' like that other hospital. Suddenly she asked me suspiciously, whether I was going to write something in the British Medical Journal about how bad the nurses were. The ward manager, too, was accommodating and invited me to the staff meeting, where I was treated pleasantly, and yet at one point I was asked by her 'This is not about spying?' Another nurse joked that I could sit at their desk and answer the phone. A counsellor offering a staff support group attended the same meeting and so nurses talked to her about being under a lot of stress and dealing with it by forgetting, sleeping and smoking. Somehow all the

agenda items seemed to be dealt with in a pressured and unthinking way that left no room at all for proper discussion.

This entry already gave some clues which, however, made more sense in the context of later observations. Behind an accommodating surface emerged a persecutory transference of the observer as a spy who would find them inadequate. The joke that I answer the phone revealed a serious meaning later on when I saw how often the telephone announced new patients, which often meant terrible stress, trouble finding a bed, and anxiety about whether they could keep the person alive. Thus, they were expressing more than a sense of strain: namely, an awareness of the lack of a protective boundary in the face of overwhelming pressures from the institution and a fear of being inadequate and being condemned for it. Their pleasant, accommodating attitude may therefore have partly been fed by such underlying fears. There may also have been the hope that I, for one, would recognise their distress.

In observing the ward, I found a particular atmosphere very characteristic: one of superficial friendliness, joking, and excitement which often tipped over into flirtatiousness and erotisation. Staff were frequently overtly sensual and flirtatious among themselves, calling each other 'Darling' and stroking each other. In dealing with patients, they were jolly and often joking. I noticed a pattern of friendly contacts with patients which, however, were usually very fleeting and superficial. At times, there was a sexual undertone in how nurses spoke to patients and not rarely did they call them 'Darling' as well. When it was quieter, staff were mostly engaged with each other rather than with the patients, but they were visible to them, on the corridor to which the patients' bays opened. I want to illustrate some of these aspects with a brief vignette that reflects a pattern that emerged in the course of the observations:

> In a bay that I could see into from my place in the corridor, a patient was sitting up in her bed with a bowl in front of her, trying with great difficulty to cough up. She was sweating and clearly suffering but didn't call anyone. At one point she looked at me and seemed to feel ashamed that she was being seen. At the entrance of that bay, a male nurse was at the same time chatting with a young female doctor who put her arm around his waist and caressed his neck. Observing this, I felt anger towards the nurse and doctor but also a sense of guilt for not attending to the patient myself.

I think one can see vividly here that the patient's suffering was not attended to, while staff were meanwhile engaged with each other in an excited way. Difficult feelings such as pain, anger, guilt, and shame were not only left with others, like the patient and the observer, but were also actively projected into them by this open erotic display. My countertransference experience reflected feelings that might partly be attributed to the patient, like the anger, and partly to staff, like the sense of guilt. Such a sense of guilt emerged not only in my subjective experience, but at some points also in direct observation of staff, such as in another brief vignette:

> After some very hectic and stressful period on the ward, nurse Nancy was sitting at the desk in the corridor, having a chat with another nurse, Ann. She was going tenderly through Ann's hair with her hand, which Ann seemed to enjoy and she made some appreciative comments. Suddenly Ann realised that I was watching and said to Nancy, obviously feeling uncomfortable: 'He's observing our conversation,' and they stopped.

Another pattern that emerged as characteristic for the culture of this ward was one of constant moving. Patients were often transferred to the other hospital for a few days or moved to other wards when a bed was needed, they were also moved within the ward, partly because patients who were more at risk were kept in two central bays, but often for no apparent reasons. I felt that patients were treated almost like furniture that could be rearranged without sufficient regard for their feelings about it. Sometimes staff showed some sensitivity, like when a nurse said to a patient: 'Sorry about all the moving. Now you won't be moved again.' More frequently, their sensitivity seemed to be drowned by their distress. Once,

> I observed how a doctor had to ask a patient to leave abruptly to make space for a new admission, even though his medication wasn't sorted out yet. He told him in the corridor, in a tone of voice that suggested this was completely natural. However, at the same time the doctor seemed to be perturbed by my observing presence and eventually asked me in a critical and hostile way: 'who are you, what are you doing, what is your profession?' This made me feel attacked and extremely uncomfortable.

Like the previous vignette, this is an example of the observer's direct impact changing the situation. It shows that the observer was experienced as a transference object representing the doctor's own sense of guilt or shame for having to do something rather insensitive as well as his fear of criticism. These feelings were initially not observable but came out through the observer's presence and what was stirred up in his subjective experience, via projective identification.

There was a lot of busy activity on the ward, often necessary, but in quiet times, too, nurses frequently seemed to seek this activity, and quiet sustained contact with patients was rare. Once, when I came, I was greeted: 'You should have been here an hour ago, we had such an activity'; another time: 'You've come too late, it's been chaos here, we had two arrests.' When a nurse enquired how long I would be observing for and I replied 'for four months, an hour each week', she replied 'Agony!' Observations such as these indicated to me that high activity was valued, whereas calmness or quiet thinking were not.

I have only touched briefly on some aspects out of a long and detailed observation, but I think they have already given an impression of the culture and dynamics on this ward. In coming to hypotheses about the dynamics on the ward, one needs, of course, much more than such brief impressions but detailed material in which repeated patterns can be seen. The following thoughts are therefore based on much more extensive material and the processing of the observations in the seminar group.

Staff were visibly under great strain from the various pressures of their work and had, at least unconsciously, major anxieties which could only be inferred: of being inadequate in the face of fatal diseases and overwhelming tasks and of being condemned for that, of being in touch with patients' suffering and of facing death. They dealt with these anxieties by a superficial jolliness and flirtatiousness and by a busy activity that seemed to deny their own worries. This left patients often unattended in their distress and sometimes even carrying the distress of staff. Staff seemed to function collectively with the assumptions:

- Friendliness can wipe out pain, guilt, and anxiety; and:
- Busy activity and sexual excitement can master death.

The defensive techniques deriving from these assumptions, however, helped them only partially, as the sense of guilt for their behaviour was often near the surface and staff felt burdened and overstretched.

Research application

Like infant observation, institutional observation was initially conceived and developed by Hinshelwood as a training method. The training aspect has been focused on more specifically elsewhere (Hinshelwood, 1989; Hinshelwood, 2013; Hinshelwood and Skogstad, 2002; Skogstad, 2002), but it may have also become apparent in this chapter that an observation project of this kind, with regular discussions in a seminar group, is an apt training exercise to hone one's sensitivity to institutional processes. But is it also justified as a method for research?

First of all, the question arises whether such a subjective method can make any scientific claims. Since Kuhn (1962) wrote about the structure of scientific revolutions, we have been aware that science needs to be diverse and requires different approaches depending on the specific topic of study. Even within social sciences, different methods are required to study different things, and Rustin (1989) argues that these different methods of research are complementary. Quantitative methods such as social surveys or experimental designs can study variables of behaviour and their causal relations in order to establish generalisations or causal laws but cannot discover subjective meanings. Case-study, life-history, and ethnographic methods, on the other hand, which study individuals or groups going about their normal lives, are specifically aimed at the subjective experience and subjective meanings constituting social relationships and therefore at the whole context of behaviour.

Very recently, complexity theory has been applied as a new paradigm transcending the dichotomy between deterministic and hermeneutic methods, and through its search for ordering patterns, psychoanalytic observation has been seen as a method bridging that dichotomy (Rustin, 2002).

The method described in this chapter may first of all be used for single case-study research to explore and bring to light aspects of an institutional culture, such as subjective experiences and meanings, unconscious anxieties and assumptions, and institutionally applied defensive techniques. However, subjective findings arrived at through the lens of a single observer may be seen as too unreliable for research purposes. Jorgensen (1989) argues that in participant observation, conventional notions of reliability (defined as the extent to which a procedure produces the same result with repeated usage) are not particularly appropriate. Instead, an observational method is concerned with dependable and trustworthy findings, and reliability is therefore very much interrelated with validity. Especially for the purpose of research, it needs to be considered how the validity of this very subjective method can be enhanced.

With a single case study, this may be done in a number of ways (Hoggett, 2003):

- by presenting and discussing the findings within a group, thereby widening the 'research instrument' from a single mind to a group of minds;
- by clearly separating observation material and interpretation and, in a research paper, presenting detailed observation material, thereby allowing a critical appraisal of the interpretations by others;
- by using the observational material in combination with data from other methods, such as interviews or findings from consultancy to the institution;
- by comparing the findings to other research done on similar institutions which may enable more confident claims to be made.

The question remains whether it could also have wider research implications, beyond a single case study. Rustin (1989) has argued for infant observation that such 'case-study research is most likely to be fertile in producing descriptions of new phenomena, in finding hitherto unrecognised links between their different aspects, and in generating new hypotheses', but that it is 'not ... well adapted to the testing of causal hypotheses' (pp. 70–71). He suggested that 'there is scope for adapting this observational method for more focused studies,' for example 'if observations were concurrently and collaboratively undertaken on the basis of a shared research interest, with samples selected to fit these aims' (p. 71). Briggs, for example, has researched infants at risk by doing a number of infant observations simultaneously and has thereby found particular aspects in parents that constitute risk and different aspects in children in their way of dealing with these aspects, which in turn enhance or reduce the risk (Briggs, 1997a, 1997b).

Similarly, I think, there would be scope for doing wider research into institutions with the method of psychoanalytic observation, in a way that could claim greater validity than single case studies can do. For example, one could do a number of observations of similar institutions, for example psychiatric hospitals, and, through finding similarities and differences, arrive at new hypotheses of the dynamics of such institutions. Or one could observe different parts of a wider institution, for example different wards as well as parts of the management structures within one hospital, and thus arrive at hypotheses about the dynamic functioning of a complex organisation.

To give just one example of such a potential project: through the observation of an acute psychiatric admission ward, Chiesa (2000) came to the hypothesis that the hopelessness and demoralisation which used to occupy the chronic psychiatric wards before major structural changes in mental health services took place had now moved to the acute admission wards. This could imply that in the care particularly of chronic psychiatric patients, hopelessness and demoralisation are unavoidable and have to find a place somewhere and that the closure of the asylums only led to a relocation of these emotions (Hinshelwood and Skogstad, 2002). However, different models of care may also be more or less containing for such feelings within the current overall structure, and these may therefore not necessarily have to be so prominent in psychiatry. In comparing different parts within one mental health service (in-patient wards, CMHTs, etc.) and differently structured services with each other, one could arrive at a better understanding of these issues. In this way, the method could be used for wider research yielding meaningful results that one would be unlikely to arrive at through other methods.

References

Bick, E. (1964), Notes on infant observation in psychoanalytic training. *International Journal of Psycho-Analysis*, 45: 558–566.

Bion, W. (1970), *Attention and Interpretation*. London: Tavistock.

Bott Spillius, E. (1976), Asylum and society. In E. Trist and H. Murray (eds.), *The Social Engagement of Social Science* (pp. 586–612). London: Free Association Books, 1990.

Briggs, S. (1997a), Observing when infants are at potential risk: reflections from a study of five infants, concentrating on observations of a Bengali infant. In S. Reid (ed.), *Development in Infant Observation* (pp. 207–227). London: Routledge.

Briggs, S. (1997b), *Growth and Risk in Infancy*. London: Jessica Kingsley.

Britton, R. (1989), The missing link: parental sexuality in the Oedipus complex. In R. Britton, M. Feldman, and E. O'Shaughnessy (eds.), *The Oedipus Complex Today* (pp. 83–101). London: Karnac.

Chiesa, M. (2000), At a crossroad between institutional and community psychiatry: an acute psychiatric admission ward. In R. D. Hinshelwood and W. Skogstad (eds.), *Observing Organisations: Anxiety, Defence and Culture in Health Care* (pp. 54–67). London: Routledge.

Devereux, G. (1967), *From Anxiety to Method in the Behavioural Sciences*. The Hague: Mouton.

Diem-Wille, G. (1997), Observed families revisited: two years on, a follow-up study. In S. Reid (ed.), *Development in Infant Observation* (pp. 182–206). London: Routledge.

Donati, F. (2000), Madness and morale: a chronic psychiatric ward. In R. D. Hinshelwood and W. Skogstad (eds.), *Observing Organisations: Anxiety, Defence and Culture in Health Care* (pp. 29–43). London: Routledge.

Gabbard, G. O. (1995), Countertransference: the emerging common ground. *The International Journal of Psycho-Analysis*, 76: 475–485.

Grunbaum, A. (1984), *The Foundations of Psychoanalysis: A Philosophical Critique*. Berkeley: California University Press.

Grunbaum, A. (1993), *Validation in the Clinical Theory of Psychoanalysis: A Study in the Philosophy of Psychoanalysis*. Madison: International Universities Press.

Heald, S., and Deluz, A. (1994), *Anthropology and Psychoanalysis*. London: Routledge.

Heimann, P. (1950), On counter-transference. *The International Journal of Psycho-Analysis*, 31: 81–84.

Hinshelwood, R. D. (1989), Comment on Dr Donati's 'A psychodynamic observer in a chronic psychiatric ward'. *British Journal of Psychotherapy*, 5: 330–332.

Hinshelwood, R. D. (1991), *A Dictionary of Kleinian Thought* (2nd enlarged edition). London: Free Association Books.

Hinshelwood, R. D. (1993), Locked in a role: a psychotherapist within the social defence system of a prison. *Journal of Forensic Psychiatry*, 4(3): 427–440.

Hinshelwood, R. D. (1999), Countertransference. *The International Journal of Psycho-Analysis*, 80: 797–818.

Hinshelwood, R. D. (2002), Applying the observational method: observing organizations. In A. Briggs (ed.), *Surviving Space: Papers on Infant Observation* (pp. 157–171). London: Karnac.

Hinshelwood, R. D. (2013), Observing anxiety: a psychoanalytic training method for understsanding organisations. In S. Long (ed.), *Socioanalytic Methods: Discovering the Hidden in Organisations and Social Systems*. London: Karnac, pp. 47–66.

Hinshelwood, R. D., and Skogstad, W. (2000), *Observing Organisations: Anxiety, Defence and Culture in Health Care*. London: Routledge.

Hinshelwood, R. D., and Skogstad, W. (2002), Irradiated by distress: observing psychic pain in health-care organizations. *Psychoanalytic Psychotherapy*, 16(2): 110–124.

Hoggett, P. (2003), Personal communication.

Hunt, J. C. (1989), *Psychoanalytic Aspects of Fieldwork*. London: Sage.

Jaques, E. (1955), Social systems as a defence against persecutory and depressive anxiety. In M. Klein, P. Heimann, and R. Money-Kyrle (eds.), *New Directions in Psycho-Analysis* (pp. 478–498). London: Tavistock.

Jorgensen, D. L. (1989), *Participant Observation: A Methodology for Human Studies*. London: Sage.

Kuhn, T. S. (1962), *The Structure of Scientific Revolutions*. Chicago: Chicago University Press.

Menzies, I. (1959), The functioning of social systems as a defence against anxiety: a report on a study of the nursing service of a general hospital. In I. Menzies Lyth, *Containing Anxiety in Institutions: Selected Essays*, Volume I (pp. 43–85). London: Free Association Books, 1998.

Menzies Lyth, I. (1990), A psychoanalytic perspective on social institutions. In E. Trist and H. Murray (eds.), *The Social Engagement of Social Science* (pp. 463–475). London: Free Association Books.

Miller, E. J., and Gwynne, G. V. (1972), *A Life Apart*. London: Tavistock.

Ramsay, N. (2000), Sitting close to death: a palliative care unit. In R. D. Hinshelwood and W. Skogstad, *Observing Organisations: Anxiety, Defence and Culture in Health Care* (pp. 142–151). London: Routledge.

Roberts, V. Z. (1994), Till death us do part: caring and uncaring in work with the elderly. In A. Obholzer and V. Z. Roberts (eds.), *The Unconscious at Work* (pp. 75–83). London: Routledge.

Rustin, M. (1989), Observing infants: reflections on methods. In L. Miller, M. Rustin, M. Rustin, and J. Shuttleworth (eds.), *Closely Observed Infants* (pp. 52–75). London: Duckworth.

Rustin, M. (1997), What do we see in the nursery? Infant observation as 'laboratory work'. *Infant Observation*, 1(1): 93–110.

Rustin, M. (2002), Looking in the right place: complexity theory, psychoanalysis, and infant observation. In A. Briggs (ed.), *Surviving Space: Papers on Infant Observation* (pp. 256–278). London: Karnac.

Sandler, J., Dare, C., and Holder, A. (1992), *The Patient and the Analyst*. London: Karnac.

Skogstad, H. (1999), The observer as containing object. Unpublished paper.

Skogstad, W. (2000), Working in a world of bodies: a medical ward. In R. D. Hinshelwood and W. Skogstad, *Observing Organisations: Anxiety, Defence and Culture in Health Care* (pp. 101–121). London: Routledge.

Skogstad, W. (2002), Kein Platz für Angst und Schmerz – Psychoanalytische Beobachtungen von medizinischen und psychiatrischen Einrichtungen. *Freie Assoziation*, 5(2): 143–150.

Trist, E. (1950), Culture as a psychosocial process. In E. Trist and H. Murray (eds.), *The Social Engagement of Social Science* (pp. 539–545). London: Free Association Books, 1990.

Chapter 7

The contribution of psychoanalytically informed observation methodologies in nursery organisations

Peter Elfer

The chapter first briefly describes the psychoanalytic observation method developed by Esther Bick and its development from its original use in family contexts to institutional contexts. The chapter then reviews and illustrates the depth of understanding of children's interactions that the data enables by reference to an observation vignette of an 18-month-old boy. The chapter concludes by arguing that psychoanalytically informed observation has an essential contribution to make in explaining aspects of nursery culture, organisation, and subtle interaction.

Introduction

This chapter argues that psychoanalytically informed observation methods have a particular contribution to understanding organisations and the interactions that occur within them. Such observation methods are especially of interest when attempting to access the unspoken aspects of the mind, the psychoanalytic unconscious. I want to propose the value of these methods by referring to the example of children's nurseries and illustrate the breakthrough they have enabled in the conceptualisation of a number of critical issues in nursery organisation and practice.

The chapter first briefly describes the psychoanalytic observation method developed by Esther Bick in 1948 as part of the training of child psychotherapists (Rustin, 2009). Bick herself described the purpose of the training as primarily:

> because it would help the students to conceive vividly the infantile experience of their child patients...
>
> (Bick, 1964)

The chapter draws on the work of Rustin (1989, 2006) to review what has been learned about early development from the use of such methods. Next, the chapter discusses the development of the observation methodology from its original use in family contexts to institutional contexts. The chapter then turns to review a number of contemporary themes of inquiry and progress in the theorisation of nursery organisation and practice that have been enabled through the use of psychoanalytically informed observation methods. Key to the further exploration of these is an understanding of the young child's own perspective and responses in relation to these themes. Here, the chapter argues that psychoanalytically informed observation offers a distinctive way of enabling us to access the feelings and emotional experiences of babies and young children who, unable to verbalise these, may nevertheless communicate much of their experience in the feelings they evoke in sensitive and receptive observers and educators.

The chapter then gives an illustration of the data gathered using an adapted form of the observation methodology and highlights the depth of understanding of children's interactions that the data enables. The chapter concludes by arguing that both as a research tool and as a pedagogic approach, psychoanalytically informed observation should now be included as an essential and distinctive but complementary observation methodology if we are to adequately explain aspects of nursery culture, organisation, and subtle interaction.

Psychoanalytic infant observation in family contexts

The psychoanalytic method of infant observation, as part of the training for child psychotherapists, was started in 1948 by Esther Bick. A detailed description of the method and discussion of its methodology has already been set out by Rustin (1989), but it is perhaps helpful to restate its essential elements here. A baby or young child and his close interactions are observed for around one hour at a regular weekly time and over a period of one to two years, starting as soon as possible after birth. The observations are conducted without recording device and written up immediately after the observation as a narrative holistic account. The observer provides as much detail as possible of context, sequences, interactions, and the child's responses, as well as her own feelings as they evolve throughout the observation. Care must be taken to avoid editing out any details that may at first be considered as irrelevant.

A sample of the observation narratives is then scrutinised and discussed in a group with other observers led by an experienced facilitator. The group helps the observer think about the observation record alongside the possible significance of her own emotional responses in understanding the child's emotional experience.

The method relies on a number of underpinning theoretical ideas introduced here.

Anxiety and defence

The experience of anxiety and unconscious defences against it are fundamental in psychoanalytic theory and to the processes of psychoanalytic observation.

They are an essential part of the infant's interactions with others and the interactions of observer with the observed, as the observer brings her own anxieties and defences to the observation situation.

The defensive capacity of the mind to block out painful or disturbing emotion is an essential part of ordinary human functioning. In this context, the term 'anxiety' does not refer to conscious and rational fear that may be experienced in the face of a real external threat. Rather, it refers to an unconscious internal psychic process that prevents a conscious experience that would feel too threatening or overwhelming. External behaviours may be deceptive in representing internal states:

> Infants have a limited mental capacity to deal with overwhelming sensory experiences, they need their parents to bear a large part of their feelings for them... when the mother cannot perform this function... babies may give up on trying to 'get through' to the mother..... An alternative response ..... is the infant's unconscious turning away from states of dependency by becoming precociously self-sufficient and controlling.
>
> (Emanuel, 2006, pp. 251–252)

The paranoid-schizoid split and the depressive position

Klein drew attention to the intense and rapidly fluctuating emotional experience of the baby:

> Klein understood the utterly dependent baby to inhabit a world of deep gratification and extreme discomfort, even terror; in the grip of passionate feelings of love and hate... He inhabits a polarized world...
>
> (Waddell, 1999, p. 27)

Waddell describes the 'paranoid-schizoid' position as a normal early developmental position in which 'paranoid' refers to the 'fear of persecution' (of being disliked), whilst 'schizoid' refers to the polarisation:

> people and events are experienced either as unrealistically wonderful or as unrealistically terrible. It is a natural and necessary state at this very early stage..... In the 'depressive position', a more considered attitude prevails.
>
> (1999, p. 6)

These intense emotional states and their transformation from one extreme to another are commonplace in babies. Klein's contribution was a model of how these extreme states were managed and became integrated in the baby's personality.

These concepts may appear as 'highly conjectured' (Rustin, 2001, p. 192). Yet they do describe common human experience, for example, the 'split' common in fairy stories between good (heroes) and evil (villains). Even in adulthood, there can be a tempting retreat to split 'good' and 'bad', 'virtue' and 'blame'.

Klein held that the instinctive demands of the baby for food and comfort and the satisfying or frustrating ways in which these were met provided a first experience of the existence of another mind capable of thought. This was held to be the basis of the baby's own capacity for independent thought and developing a 'depressive position' (Shuttleworth, 1989, p. 25).

Projection and containment

In the quotation above, Emanuel says infants need their parents to bear a large part of their feelings for them. Projection here refers to the process of an infant or young child making an attentive and receptive adult experience emotions approximating to those he himself is experiencing.

In 'good enough' care, the carer is able to think about and manage a baby or young child's distressed communications through emotional attunement, eye contact, voice, rhythmic rocking, and other actions based on attention to what may be wrong. The carer's capacity to do this depends on her own freedom from too much anxiety and her own resources for emotional containment, drawing on her own early experience and on emotional support from close adults (Bion, 1962, p. 90).

In psychoanalytic observation, the observer needs a capacity to receive and be able to think about the complex emotions that may be projected into her. It is partly the function of the seminar group to facilitate the observer's containment so that she is better able to be sensitive, receptive, and thoughtful to these projected emotions (Rustin, 1989).

Transference and countertransference

Transference, a central form of unconscious communication in psychoanalytic work (Rustin, 2001, p. 39), entails the attribution by one person to another of roles and dispositions associated with interactions from the first person's past. The observer's capacity to register and record her own emotional responses during the observation, her countertransference, is an essential part of her skill. It is again the function of the seminar group to help the observer think about and understand her reactions in the observation. Continual monitoring of the countertransference may, beyond controlling for subjectivity, richly enhance the data and their possible meanings (Urwin, 2006).

What has been learned about earliest development from psychoanalytic observation methods?

Observations in developmental psychology and attachment research have focused on the details of directly observable behaviours and their sequences.

These observations have been used to conceptualise early interactions and their role in shaping development. By contrast, psychoanalytic observation, drawing on directly observable behaviours from which unconscious communications can be inferred,

> studies the process of individuation from its earliest days, not its outcome in childhood and adulthood. Infant observation is the study of the earliest formation of the psyche, not of the fully-formed developed psyche itself.
> (Rustin, 2006, p. 39)

An enormous psychoanalytic observation literature has now been accumulated. From this, Rustin identifies four areas of inquiry and knowledge development (Rustin, 2006, p. 43).

First, he describes the emergence of new understandings about the development of the infant psyche and the integration of body and mind. Miller has shown how daily aspects of an infant's physical care, such as feeding, holding, and cleaning, each have psychological counterparts (1999). As the baby takes in milk, he also takes in the experience of an interaction, a carer motivated to feed him by her concern for his growth and well-being. The feed constitutes, at a somatic level, an experience of the capacity to take inside physical nourishment but also an experience of feeling thought about and attended to.

Second, Rustin refers to the development of new understandings of different patterns of emotional containment and its failures. The theory of 'second skin' (Bick, 1964) models a defensive developmental response to insufficient attention and containment. The skin, as a physical organ, is also a physical boundary for the baby. Bick proposed that the psychological counterpart of this physical boundary was the experience it provided of what is 'me', inside, and what is 'not me'. Alongside acting as a physical container, in healthy development, the skin is understood as functioning as an emotional container, an experience of feeling held together. Bick proposed the possibility of the 'faulty development of this primitive skin function' (p. 484) if, for example, the baby did not have sufficient experience of being held or was held aggressively or intrusively. In such cases, a psychological development occurs that can be represented as a 'second skin'. A baby excessively extending his body, stretching, straining, reaching, arching may be indicating the struggle to find a boundary, an experience of containment, in the absence of an attuned physically holding response from an attentive adult.

Third is the development of work on the therapeutic value of psychoanalytic observation (Rustin, 2006, p. 46). Although it is a lot to ask a family to commit to such extended observations, the implication of the observer's commitment is the profound value and interest of what is to be observed. The regularity and consistency of the observation process and the observer's disposition to understand rather than to criticise often seem to be valued by families and to facilitate their thinking and reflection about family interactions too. A therapeutic aspect of observation pioneered in France has been movingly demonstrated in the UK by a participant observer of a mother and her 18-month-old son diagnosed to become fully autistic by the age of 3 (Gretton, 2006). The capacity of the observer to be receptive to and contain intense communications of emotion from both mother and son had, over an extended period of time, modelled for the mother a way of responding to her child's communications and developing hopefulness of a more ordinary interaction.

Lastly, Rustin identifies (2006, p. 46) the contribution of psychoanalytic observation to revealing cross-cultural variations in psychic development; for example, Maiello reflects on her observations in the Eastern Cape of a baby's resilient transition from care by his mother to that of others:

> I came to think that our concept of separation, connected with the Western nuclear family structure... might be only one way of looking at the event.... In African tradition in fact, the uniqueness of the mother as a person is of lesser importance than in Western culture.
> (Maiello, 2000, pp. 88–89)

This interpretation strengthens our capacity to identify the way in which patterns of interaction vary between cultures and the extent to which such variations may be considered variations of a 'type' or examples of a different cultural norm.

Extending psychoanalytically informed observation from family to institutional contexts

Psychoanalytic observation methods were first developed in nursery contexts by Susan Isaacs in the 1920s and by Freud and Burlingham in the 1940s (Adamo and Rustin, 2001, p. 4). Robertson's observations in the mid-1950s of young children's responses to brief separations from their parents, including stays in hospital, employed psychoanalytic conceptions and helped secure a change in policy to allow parents to remain with their young children (1989). Psychoanalytic observations have also assisted understanding of the development of pre-term babies (Rustin, 2006, p. 47), exploration of the well-being of elderly people with dementia (Datler, Trunkenpolz, and Lazar, 2009) and the study of interactions in health-care settings (Hinshelwood and Skogstad, 2000).

More broadly, there is a growing body of psychosocial writing documenting the capacity of psychoanalytic methods to explore the interplay of the internal world of the individual, conscious and unconscious, and the culture of social organisations (see, for example, Clarke and Hoggett, 2009; Froggett, 2002; Huffington, Armstrong, Halton, Hoyle, and Pooley, 2004; Obholzer and Roberts, 1994). This work has drawn on the psychoanalytic concept of the 'defended subject', who will present, partly unconsciously, a particular version of her or his experience and feeling (Hollway and Jefferson, 2000; Wengraf and

Chamberlayne, 2006). Hollway (2007) and Urwin (2007) have explored women's transitions to motherhood and the mutual role of mothers and babies in shaping each other's identity.

The possibility of developing psychoanalytic observation as a research tool was first set out by Rustin (1989). He drew attention to the value of detailed case studies of individual infants in particular social contexts analogous to well-established ethnographic, life-history, and case-study methods used by observers in sociology and anthropology (1989, p. 56). Nearly a decade later, in arguing for the legitimacy of psychoanalytic observation as a research method, he develops the analogy with ethnographic work and proposes that they share an epistemological approach based on a search for common theoretical models underpinning quite different types of group behaviours (for example, street gangs, classroom peer groups, and factory workers) (1997, p. 98).

Despite this productivity, two lines of argument have been made against the use of psychoanalytic observation as a research tool. Fonagy comments on a fault line between the generation of theory based on psychoanalytically informed research and the empirical laboratory-based work of neuroscientists and developmental psychologists:

> The chief problem with using clinical experience as research is the well known one of induction... In our clinical activity we mostly tend to concentrate on confirming our theory-based expectations from our patient's material...
>
> (Fonagy, 2009, p. 22)

From the opposite direction, Groarke (2008) argues that psychoanalytic observation will always be weak as a research tool compared with clinical work. His central argument is that transference and countertransference, central in clinical work, and essential to exploration and development, can exist only in weak and generalised forms in psychoanalytic observation research. Rustin comprehensively rebuts this argument, identifying four dimensions of transference and countertransference in observation research and detailing the processes of interpretation and triangulation developed to enable rigorous scrutiny and exploration of the hypotheses generated in interpretations of observation narratives (Rustin, 2011).

Clinically trained observers using the Tavistock Observation Method in nursery contexts

There is a considerable body of work examining young children's interactions in nursery developed by external observers, that is, not nursery staff themselves and who have been fully trained in the method through participating in the Masters-level training at the Tavistock and Portman NHS Trust. My review of this literature shows five themes of investigation in young children's response to nursery life:

1. how children manage transitions to and from, and within, nursery (Adamo, 2001; Buck and Rustin, 2001; Dechent, 2008; Wittenberg, 2001);
2. attachment, individuation, and the development of self in nursery (Catty, 2009; Dennis, 2001; Meltzer and Gelati, 1986);
3. social interaction within nursery in friendships and group interactions (Urwin, 2001);
4. the significance of containment, physical holding, and touch in early development (Barnett, 2005; Tarsoly, 1998).
5. the emotional impact on staff of close interactions with other people's children (Datler, Datler, and Funder, 2010; Dechent, 2008; Monti and Crudeli, 2007).

The fifth theme of work complements the work of Bain and Barnett (1986) and Hopkins (1988) who have shown the way in which nursery staff, partly unconsciously, may adopt policies and practices (social defences) to protect themselves from the emotional stress of their work (including the challenge of making close interactions with other people's children entailing close emotional attachments and the loss of repeated separations as children move on from nursery).

The above five themes show that there is a considerable body of inquiry in the psychoanalytic literature, underpinned by psychoanalytic conceptions, and exploring the role of emotion in nursery interaction from this theoretical perspective. However, the early childhood care and education literature has not so far given any attention to this theoretical approach or its possible value in addressing current issues and dilemmas of nursery policy and organisation. Two such current issues of debate in this latter literature seem likely to benefit from exploration using psychoanalytically informed observation methods, as complementary to existing observation methodologies focused on external behaviours. These two issues are:

How to effectively take account of the 'voice' of the baby?

A prominent theme of discussion in the early childhood care and education literature is how to listen to the voice of the young child in developing policy and in shaping daily pedagogic practice. Alison Clark has pioneered one approach to do this through the development of the 'mosaic approach', so called because of its reliance on assembling together different modes of creativity that young children might use to represent their feelings and ideas (Clark and Moss, 2011). This work has achieved a great deal in enabling the voices of 3- and 4-year-olds to be much better taken into account. There is also emergent work on methodologies to enable the voices of 1- and 2-year-olds to be expressed (see, for example, Licht et al., 2008; Musattie and Mayer, 2011; Rechia, 2012; Kalliala, 2014). It is, however, much more challenging to encourage the view that babies under 12 months also have feelings and experiences that can actively be heard and included in developing policy and in pedagogy. Harrison and Sumsion (2014) have brought together a collection of different theoretical approaches to conceptualising nursery organisation and pedagogy for babies. However, this collection does not yet include psychoanalytically informed observation methodologies, with their unique capacity to address the subtle communications of feeling evoked by babies in sensitively receptive observers and their possible meanings.

How babies' interactions with peers should be balanced with encouraging attachment interactions with nursery staff?

Government standards (DfES, 2014) require nurseries to allocate small groups of babies and young children to the care of particular staff in order to facilitate attachments between particular nursery staff and individual children (the 'key person' relationship). However, the need for attachment experience in nursery is contested (Dahlberg, Moss, and Pence, 1999) on the grounds that it is unnecessary for young children who already experience close family attachments. Such attachments in nursery are seen as risking limiting children's opportunities for developing interactions with peers in friendship pairs and within groups, realising their own social life at nursery, different from but complementary to their social life in the family.

Certainly in relation to the question of babies' peer interactions and the priority that may be given to facilitating these compared to facilitating attachments with nursery staff, the task of nurseries is to find an optimal balance between the two polarities. Finding such a balance requires observational data that include not only measures of cognitive and social outcomes but also a high degree of sensitivity to children's emotional reactions. Very sensitive observational methods are required to be able, for example, to distinguish when a young child can manage without the immediate intimate attention of his chosen staff member, strengthening his own sense of agency, and when such attention is necessary to avoid feelings of rejection or a collapse of self-esteem. It is for these reasons that psychoanalytic observation methods are proposed as an essential complement to existing methods of behavioural observation in nurseries.

Adapting the Tavistock Observation Method for use in the nursery by non-clinically trained observers

The research reviewed above appears to have been highly productive in the new understandings it has opened up about the emotional processes of young children in nursery. This research has been mainly conducted by observers visiting the nursery but who are not employed there, who have trained or are training as child psychotherapists undertaking clinical work, and who have had a two-year training in infant observation methodology prior to their clinical training.

An exciting possibility arises as to whether psychoanalytically informed observation methods might be adapted for use in nursery organisations by non-clinically trained observers, including nursery staff themselves. This possibility includes observers using the method as both a research tool in nursery and as a pedagogic tool.

Adapting the Tavistock Observation Method as a research tool

As a non-clinically trained external observer, I adapted the Tavistock Observation Method as part of the data collection for a case study research project exploring nursery organisation and its impact on staff interactions (Elfer, 2009). Three to four observations, of around one hour each, were conducted at one- to two-week intervals, focused on a single child. The observations were conducted without any recording device or notebook but were written up, with attention to emotional experience, immediately after each observation. The observations were written in as free-flowing, holistic, and detailed way as possible. They were then analysed using grounded theory, first at a thematic level and then as a line by line microanalysis, each triangulated internally and with other observation data. The analysis was scrutinised by independent evaluators experienced in the observation method. Particular attention was given in the analysis to my own subjectivity and the variety of ways in which it may have influenced interpretation. This reflexive process has been very well illustrated, for example in the work of Brown (2006) and Gadd (2004). Observation data were supplemented with staff interviews, staff questionnaires, and a fieldwork diary.

I want to illustrate the potential of the methodology through data from a case vignette. The data illustrated is of Graham, 18 months old, attending a 65-place private nursery from 8 a.m. to 5 p.m. on 4 days each week. Interviews with the staff in Graham's room showed their concern to allow the children some expression of attachment to particular staff members and the mutual pleasure of this:

> Graham loves Vicky..... he goes straight to Vicky, he loves her and when he's upset... it's nice for you it makes you feel wanted and needed I think in a way

Yet the concern about preventing the children from becoming too attached to any one member of staff was common in the staff interviews and is evident here.

> ... we try and spread them round. If a person's not there then it is unsettling for them but....

The observations reveal how Graham responds to these carefully calibrated interactions. In the first observation, mid-morning, Graham is lively and feisty in defence of attention he is already receiving or in pursuit of it elsewhere:

> ... slipping off Vicky's lap he moves to Ann's... he crawls off but turns and wriggles back. She grimaces and smiles as he tramples across her, but she turns him to a more comfortable position ready to read... When this is completed, he crawls off to search for yet another book. But immediately, Luke claims the vacant lap so Graham sits on the floor next to Ann, his hand on her leg and she strokes his hand as she reads...

The second observation, at the beginning of the day, includes Graham's arrival at nursery when he struggles to part from his father:

> .... warmly greeted by Katy and Vicky, Graham marches in with a big smile... he and Katy embrace. He seems very pleased to see his friends. His dad is cheerful, laughing..... Suddenly Graham seems to get a little anxious, whimpers and runs back to his father as if his enthusiasm to come into the room has rather overtaken him. He has a hug and this enables him to turn back into the room. Vicky picks him up and dad once more says goodbye to him. Graham refuses to look round from Vicky's arms... His dad laughs 'Oh he's giving me the cold shoulder' and he calls again and again to Graham... He comments to Vicky that perhaps Graham is cross because they took away his dummy 'for the last time' last night – 'Bit of a battle of wills but we won' ... Eventually Graham does glance in his direction and dad seems to feel that is enough and says goodbye again very warmly and leaves. At breakfast, Graham sat with five other children:
> .... sociable and looking round with pleasure at the other children, reaching out to touch the children either side as if in greeting... a group decision seems to be made to scrape their chairs backwards. They smile together as they express their collective protest at having to wait for toast...

After breakfast and a first round of nappy changes, there was reading and the same jostling for lap space. The staff worked together to tidy up and then brought the children together as a group for nursery rhymes. Graham sat on the edge of the group, half joining in, particularly when his attention was caught by a particular line or the climax of a rhyme, but then his attention drifted away.

The third and fourth observations, both towards the end of the day, show a rather different picture of Graham. He did not seem as composed and buoyant as I had seen him in the mornings, as though he might just start to cry. However, his resilience and capacity to 'bounce back' that had surprised me before surprised me again:

> ... his demeanour seems to lift and, taking the brick trolley, he starts to wheel it around the room... with it, his energy levels seem to rise still further and he runs whole lengths of the room... finding a pathway through

all the children and toys scattered on the floor... he makes me feel that he is strong and confident, self-contained and clear about what he wants to do.

By that time, the mood of the room seemed like one of waiting, and it was striking that the children seemed adrift and not sure what to do with themselves. The four staff, all busy engaged on practical tasks, stopped only to intervene if there was a dispute between children. The equal sharing of tasks was consistent with this team's work culture of roles and relationships being interchangeable.

Each time a parent arrived, it seemed exciting for the other children to be reminded of going home, but also difficult to have to wait still for their own collection. Graham's response became familiar, each time running to the door and placing his bottom against it to block any departures until he was gently but firmly removed by a member of staff. Once, when the most recently arriving set of parents had also left, I thought that

> ... Graham has recovered his equilibrium but suddenly he sweeps a toy off a surface and it drops, crashing to the floor, Graham laughing at it loudly.....

One way of understanding this action could be as a representation of his feelings of being 'dropped', forgotten, swept to one side? Shortly afterwards, he came close to me, staring hard:

> Then suddenly he lifts his arm as if to throw something or to strike me, with a little smile of half amusement and half curiosity. Most of all, I feel he just wants to provoke a reaction, perhaps to feel intimidating when he is beginning to feel vulnerable.... he cuddles another little boy... in an act that seems genuinely affectionate.

I was not sure if he had a brick in his hand, and I flinched slightly to one side feeling vulnerable to his gesture and slightly helpless. I wondered if my feeling of vulnerability and helplessness, although partly based on the perceived threat from his raised arm, was also partly projected by Graham. One interpretation of his behaviour is as a communication of his own vulnerability and helplessness, as he had to wait to be collected whilst others went home. Unable to express or contain his vulnerability and helplessness at having to wait to be collected and inability to stop others leaving, it is split off and projected into me. The very distressed rather than dominant part of him remaining is then revealed by the collapse in his composure when Vicky picks him up to change his nappy:

> This marks a collapse in his composure. Vicky is the most gentle of staff... he begins to cry... only whimpering/moaning crying to begin with, but when he is put down, he cries more loudly and persistently. However, Vicky is now getting Christmas cards ready for each parent to take

home.... As Graham cries bitterly reaching up to her, she steadfastly continues this job.... Brigid intervenes to take Graham away, explaining to him that Vicky is busy just now... he cries all the louder though, wriggling and turning to try and get away. Eventually, Vicky completes the Christmas cards and comes to Graham. He lies in her arms and seems to immediately settle...

Even with these relatively short extracts of observation data on one child in nursery, the material illustrates the rich potential of the methodology, as enabling exploration of the kinds of issues current in contemporary debate about nursery organisation and practice. The data is effective in giving Graham a voice about his experience at nursery in a way that is more receptive to his deeper experience than observations of behaviour alone might provide. Second, the observations suggest the significance of Graham's attachment to Vicky in particular, and whilst the data show he gains considerably from all the staff in the room, it is Vicky who has special meaning for him. Third, in the morning, when the children are waiting for their breakfast, the observations show the richness of peer experience in groups and Graham's emergent role as a leader.

In addition to a deepened understanding of Graham, there is the question of the emotional experience of the staff. How do staff balance the reality of staff shifts and not being available for the children with the desire of the children (and their own desire or absence of it) to develop individual attachments with particular children? This group of staff seemed to manage the balance of individual and team care skilfully. However, Vicky did end her shift in the last observation by leaving quietly, without any goodbyes to the children and when Graham was not looking, perhaps fearful of his distress.

What about the contribution of an adapted form of the Tavistock Observation Method for use by nursery staff themselves to support their pedagogy?

Psychoanalytically informed observation methods as a pedagogic tool

A new study, recently completed (Elfer, 2017) investigated whether the Tavistock Observation Method could be adapted as a research tool for use by nursery practitioners themselves, either as part of their own action research or as part of the gathering of observational material to inform their professional discussions. A full discussion of this is beyond the scope of this chapter. However, in brief, two key issues arise. First, nursery staff are not there only to observe, leaving the situation once the observation is complete, as an external observer would do. They have a pre-existing and continuing role in working with the children and nursery colleagues they have been observing, and the distance necessary for thoughtful observation is thus ethically and practically more difficult to maintain – young children want to interact! Second, nursery staff are accountable to the nursery head for their day-to-day work, including observation. Asking them to discuss their observations with their head, where colleagues may be included in the observation material, is very challenging. Nevertheless, the evaluation showed that both these dilemmas could be managed with sensitivity and in an ethical way. The full findings are recorded as above.

Conclusion

First, I have endeavoured to show that psychoanalytic observation methods, entailing particular ontological and epistemological assumptions, offer a potentially valuable observation methodology, in this case in a nursery, for accessing the emotional communications in the interpersonal field. By strengthening attention to the possible meanings of observed participants, including very young children at a pre-verbal age, psychoanalytic observation methods will considerably strengthen our psychosocial understanding.

There seems, then, to be a clear and worthwhile case for developing the methodology of psychoanalytically informed observation as both a research and pedagogic tool. By making the interpretation of data as transparent as possible with researcher attention to subjectivity open to external scrutiny, the findings of intensive nursery case studies may be compared more systematically in pursuit of a detailed sociology of nursery.

Note

This chapter is based on an earlier paper published in the *International Journal of Social Research Methodology*:
Elfer, P. (2012), Psychoanalytic methods of observation as a research tool for exploring young children's nursery experience. International Journal of Social Research Methodology, 15(3): 225–238.

References

Adamo, S. (2001), 'The house is a boat': the experience of separation in a nursery school. *Infant Observation*, 4: 3–22. DOI: 10.1080/13698030108401620

Adamo, S., and Rustin, M. (2001), Editorial. *Infant Observation*, 4: 3–22. DOI: 10.1080/13698030108401620

Bain, A., and Barnett, L. (1986), *The Design of a Day Care System in a Nursery Setting for Children under Five*. London: Tavistock Institute of Human Relations.

Barnett, L. (2005), Keep in touch: the importance of touch in infant development. *Infant Observation*, 8(2): 115–123. DOI: 10.1080/13698030500171530

Belsky, J., Burchinal, M., McCartney, K., Vandell, D., Clarke-Stewart, K., and Owen, M. T. (2007), Are there long term effects of early child care? *Child Development*, 78(2): 681–701. doi:10.1111/j.1467-8624.2007.01021.x

Bick, E. (1964), Notes on infant observation in psychoanalytic training. *International Journal of Psycho-Analysis*, 45: 558–566.

Bion, W. R. (1962), *Learning from Experience*. London: Karnac.

Brown, J. (2006), Reflexivity in the research process: psychoanalytic observations. *International Journal of Social Research Methodology*, 9(3): 181–197. doi:10.1080/1364557 0600652776

Buck, L. T., and Rustin, M. (2001), Thoughts on transitions between cultures: Jonathan moves from home to school and from class to class. *Infant Observation*, 4(2): 121–133. DOI: 10.1080/13698030108401627

Catty, J. (2009), In and out of the nest: exploring attachment and separation in an infant observation. *Infant Observation*, 12(2): 151–163. DOI: 10.1080/136980 30902991923

Chamberlayne, P., Bornat, J., and Wengraf, T. (eds.) (2000), *The Turn to Biographical Methods in Social Science*. London. Routledge.

Clarke, S., and Hoggett, P. (2009), *Researching beneath the Surface: Psycho-Social Research Methods in Practice*. Normal View Series. London: Karnac.

Dahlberg, G., Moss, P., and Pence, A. (1999), *Beyond Quality in Early Childhood Education and Care: Postmodern Perspectives*. London: Falmer Press.

Datler, W., Datler, M., & Funder, A. (2010), Struggling against a feeling of becoming lost: a young boy's painful transition to day care. *Infant Observation*, 13(1): 65–87. DOI: 10.1080/13698031003606659

Datler, W., Trunkenpolz, K., and Lazar, R. (2009), An exploration of the quality of life in nursing homes: the use of single case and organisational observation in a research project. *Infant Observation*, 12(1): 63-82. DOI: 10.1080/13698030902731733

Dechent, S. (2008), Withdrawing from reality: working with a young child through his difficulties in attending nursery and the separation from his parents. *Infant Observation*, 11: 25–40. DOI: 10.1080/13698030801940567

Dennis, E. (2001), Seeing beneath the surface: an observer's encounter with a child's struggle to find herself at nursery. *Infant Observation*, 4(2): 107–120. DOI:10.1080/13698030108401626

Department for Education and Skills (2007), *The Early Years Foundation Stage*. London: DfES Publications.

Emanuel, L. (2006), Disruptive and distressed toddlers: the impact of undetected maternal depression on infants and young children. *Infant Observation*, 9(3): 249–259. DOI: 10.1080/13698030601070722

Fenech, M., Sweller, N., and Harrison, L. (2010), Identifying high-quality centre-based childcare using quantitative data-sets: what the numbers do and don't tell us. *International Journal of Early Years Education*, 18: 283–296.

Fonagy, P. (2009), Research in child psychotherapy: progress, problems and possibilities? In N. Midgley, J. Anderson, E. Grainger, T. Nesic-Vuckovic, and C. Urwin (eds.), *Child Psychotherapy and Research: New Approaches, Emerging Findings* (pp. 19–34). London: Routledge.

Froggett, L. (2002), *Love, Hate and Welfare: Psychosocial Approaches to Policy and Practice*. Bristol: The Policy Press.

Gadd, D. (2004), Making sense of interviewee–interviewer dynamics in narratives about violence in intimate relationships. *International Journal of Social Research Methodology*, 7(5): 383–401. doi:10.1080/1364557092000055077

Gentleman, A. (2010), The great nursery debate. *The Guardian*, 2 October.

Groarke, S. (2008), Psychoanalytic infant observation: a critical assessment. *European Journal of Psychotherapy and Counselling*, 10(4): 299–321. doi:10.1080/13642530802577042

Hascher, T. (2010), Learning and emotion: perspectives for theory and research. *European Educational Research Journal*, 9(1): 13–28. doi: 10.2304/eerj.2010.9.1.13

Hinshelwood, R. D., and Skogstad, W. (eds.) (2000), *Observing Organisations: Anxiety, Defence and Culture in Health Care*. Hove and New York: Brunner-Routledge.

Holland, J. (2007), Emotions and research. *International Journal of Social Research Methodology*, 10(3): 195–209. doi:10.1080/13645570701541894

Hollway, W. (2007), Afterword. *International Journal of Infant Observation and its Applications*, 10(3): 331–336. doi:10.1080/13698030701698075

Hollway, W., and Jefferson, T. (2000), *Doing Qualitative Research Differently: Free Association, Narrative and the Interview Method*. London: Sage.

Hopkins, J. (1988), Facilitating the development of intimacy between nurses and infants in day nurseries. *Early Child Development and Care*, 33: 99–111.

Huffington, C., Armstrong, D., Halton, W., Hoyle, L., and Pooley, J. (2004), *Working below the Surface: The Emotional Life of Contemporary Organizations*. London: Karnac.

Maiello, S. (2000), The cultural dimension in early mother–infant interaction and psychic development: an infant observation in South Africa. *Infant Observation*, 3(2): 80–92. DOI: 10.1080/13698030008406149

Meltzer, D., with Gelati, M. (1986), *A One Year Old Goes to Day Nursery: A Parable of Confusing Times in Studies in Extended Metapsychology*. Perthshire: Clunie Press.

Miller, L. (1999), Babyhood: becoming a person in the family. In D. Hindle & M. V. Smith (eds.), *Personality Development: A Psychoanalytic Perspective* (pp. 33–47). London: Routledge.

Monti, F., and Crudeli, F. (2007), The use of infant observation in nursery (0–3 years). *Infant Observation*, 10(1): 51–58. DOI: 10.1080/13698030701234749

Robertson, J., and Robertson, J. (1989), *Separation and the Very Young*. London: Free Association Books.

Rustin, M. E. (2009), Esther Bick's legacy of infant observation at the Tavistock – some reflections 60 years on. *International Journal of Infant Observation and its Applications*, 12(1): 29–41. doi:10.1080/13698030902731691

Rustin, M. J. (1989), Observing infants: reflections on methods. In L. Miller, M. E. Rustin, M. J. Rustin, and J. Shuttleworth (eds.), *Closely Observed Infants* (pp. 52–75). London: Duckworth.

Rustin, M. J. (1997), What do we see in the nursery? Infant observations as 'laboratory work'. *International Journal of Infant Observation and its Applications*, 1(1): 93–110. doi:10.1080/13698039708400828

Rustin, M. J. (2001), *Reason and Unreason: Psychoanalysis, Science and Politics*. London: Continuum.

Rustin, M. J. (2006), Infant observation research: what have we learned so far? *International Journal of Infant Observation and its Applications*, 9(1): 35–52. doi:10.1080/13698030600593856

Rustin, M. J. (2011), In defence of infant observational research. *European Journal of Psychotherapy and Counselling*, 13(2): 153–167. Doi:10.1080.13642537.2011.572444.

Rutter, M. (2002), Nature, nurture and development: from evangelism, through science towards policy and practice. *Child Development*, 73(1): 1–21. doi:10.1111/1467-8624.00388

Shuttleworth, J. (1989), Theories of development. In L. Miller, M. E. Rustin, M. J. Rustin, and J. Shuttleworth (eds.), *Closely Observed Infants* (pp. 22–51). London: Duckworth.

Sorenson, P. (2000), Observations of transition-facilitating behaviour: developmental and theoretical implications. *International Journal of Infant Observation and its Applications*, 3(2): 46–54.

Stanley, K., Bellamy, K., and Cooke, G. (2006), *Equal Access? Appropriate and Affordable Childcare for Every Child*. London: Institute for Public Policy Research.

Tarsoly, E. (1998), The relationship between failures in containment and early feeding difficulties a participant observational study in a Hungarian residential nursery. *Infant Observation*, 2(1): 58–78. DOI: 10.1080/13698039808404699

Urwin, C. (2001), Getting to know the self and others: babies' interactions with other babies. *Infant Observation*, 4(3): 13–28. DOI: 10.1080/13698030108401634

Urwin, C. (2006), Exploring the unexpected: transference phenomena in a research setting. *Infant Observation*, 9(2): 165–177. DOI: 10.1080/13698030600818931

Urwin, C. (2007), Doing infant observation differently? Researching the formation of mothering identities in an inner London borough. *International Journal of Infant Observation and its Applications*, 10(3): 239–251. doi:10.1080/13698030701706753

Waddell, M. (1999), *Inside Lives: Psychoanalysis and the Growth of the Personality*. Tavistock Clinic Series. London: Duckworth.

Wengraf, T., and Chamberlayne, P. (2006), Interviewing for life histories, lived situations and personal experience: the biographical-narrative-interpretive method (BNIM). Short guide to BNIM interviewing. Available at tom@tomwengraff.com

Wittenberg, I. (2001), The transition from home to nursery school. *Infant Observation*, 4(2): 23–35. DOI: 10.1080/13698030108401621

Part III

Psychoanalytic methods in data handling and data analysis

Visual methods

Chapter 8

Social photo-matrix and social dream-drawing

Rose Redding Mersky and Burkard Sievers

Theoretical background

In order to introduce the reader to these two methods, we offer first a brief theoretical background to their development and some more specific theory related to each one. Both are related to a broader set of socioanalytic approaches to organisations. The term 'socioanalysis' denotes a field of study based on the concepts of psychoanalysis applied to organisations and society. As Bain (1999) describes it, it 'combines and synthesises methodologies and theories derived from psycho-analysis, group relations, social systems thinking, and organisational behavior' (p. 14).

Susan Long (2013, p. 307) has since described it as follows:

> a science of subjectivity, devoted to understanding how subjectivity works collectively in groups, organizations and society, recognizing that the collective comes before the individual and that subjectivity and mind are formed and shaped in the social.

This field takes as its basic tenet that not only do individuals have an unconscious, but groups, organisations, and cultures have what Susan Long (2010) describes as an '"associative unconscious"… a matrix of thought that links members of a community at an unconscious level'. Long and Harney (2013) capture this conceptual duality of the unconscious:

> Here, then, is a formulation of the unconscious as a mental network of thoughts, signs, and symbols or signifiers, able to give rise to many feelings, impulses, and images. The network is between people, but yet within each of them.
>
> (p. 8)

As in psychoanalysis, so in socioanalysis is dreaming of major importance. Organisational role-holders dream about their organisations and their roles. Their dream material is not always just personal, but also collective. As Bain has noted: 'There is a waking life relationship with the Organisation, and a dream life relationship to the Organisation' (2005, p. 1), and 'the dreams of members of an organisation contribute to an understanding of that organisation, and its unconscious' (p. 5).

Gordon Lawrence's praxis of social dreaming is based on this premise. Lawrence's insight is that organisations have an unconscious that can be accessed through associations to and amplifications of dreams that organisational role-holders share with one another. The 'container' in which these dreams are shared and associated to is termed the 'matrix'.

He pioneered the concept of using individual dreams and dream material to illuminate social processes and, with many colleagues, developed the social dreaming praxis (Lawrence, 1999).

Participants in the matrix are invited to share recent dreams. Members of the matrix work with this dream material in two ways. One way is by free association. Free association comes from psychoanalysis and means anything that comes to one's mind, for example an earlier experience related to the content of a dream, such as an accident or an exam. Very often, associations are recent dreams. The other way participants work with the dream material is by offering amplifications. These are those cultural and political elements that come to mind, such as current events, music, literature, and film.

Since Gordon Lawrence's discovery of social dreaming in the early 1980s (Lawrence, 1998), various socioanalytic methodologies have been developed and continue to evolve. What they all have in common is 'the intent to access a group's unconscious thinking, whether related to a pre-identified theme or a particular organisational or social issue' (Mersky, 2012, p. 20) and to generate data to be later developed into working hypotheses.

Underlying theory and description of each method

The social photo-matrix

The social photo-matrix (SPM) was developed by Burkard Sievers (2008a, 2008b, 2013), as an experiential learning method for understanding organisations in depth. Its aim is to experience, through collective viewing of digital photos taken by the participants (and subsequent associations, amplifications, and reflections), the hidden meaning of what in an organisation usually remains unseen and, thus, unnoticed and unthought.

This praxis is based on the idea that when one takes a photograph, there is a relationship between what is being photographed and the inner world of the photographer. To apply that to socioanalytic thinking, this means that photographs taken by members of a group (subsequently to be shared in the SPM) can be thought of as being taken on behalf of the collective inner world of that group. Photographs in the SPM are not mere replicas of 'reality', but means for opening up the transitional space between the real and the unreal, the finite and the infinite, the known and thoughts that have not been thought so far.

In offering free associations and amplifications to such photos, the thoughts in the associative unconscious are made available for thinking. Contrary to the common assumption that photographs are owned by the photographer, in the SPM the photograph, not the photographer, is the medium of discourse. Thus the photos speak for themselves, and we associate to them and not to the photographer.

This experience of a collective identity is often unfamiliar to first-time participants. It is the experience of a 'we-identity' (Elias, 1987/1981), in comparison to an 'I-identity'. The photos help to 'bridge the gap between the apparently individual, private, subjective and apparently collective, social, political' (Vince and Broussine, 1996, p. 8, with reference to Samuels, 1993).

In an organisational context, the photos allow access to the 'organisation-in-the-mind' (Hutton, Bazalgette, and Reed, 1997) or the 'institution-in-the-mind' (Armstrong, 2005) or the 'institution-in-experience' (Long, 1999, p. 58), all of which are notions that refer to the inner landscape of organisations, that is, to the person's inner experience and perception of the organisation. These concepts contain, so to speak, an inner psychic model of organisational reality. This inner object forms and shapes the psychic space and thus influences actual behaviour.

Organisation, in this sense, can be perceived as not just something 'external', but also as an accumulation of experience and images that structures both the psychic space of a person and the social one of the organisation. In taking up a role in organisations, we introject parts of external reality and transform them into inner objects and part-objects. These objects build an inner matrix, which is only partly conscious, and, not least because of its often frightening character, partly remains unconscious. The photographs can be a medium through which these inner objects and part-objects can be 'externalised' and become objects for associations and sources for further thoughts and thinking. In this sense, the photographs are transitional objects (Winnicott, 1953).

The workshop event takes place as follows. Participants are invited to take photos either before the workshop or after the beginning of the workshop. They are asked to take photos that relate to a pre-identified theme. These photos are sent directly to a technical assistant, whose role it is to organise them into an archive and develop a system by which they are randomly shown during the workshop. Those who actually host the workshops, like the other participants, never see these photos in advance. They work with the photographs, and the photographers are not identified.

The workshop has two key components, that is, the matrix, where participants (including the hosts) offer associations and amplifications to the photographs, and a subsequent reflection session, whose task is to focus on the meaning of the photographs in relation to the chosen theme. The matrix lasts one hour, during which approximately six to eight photos are shown. The reflection group is usually a smaller group and takes an hour. It is facilitated by one of the hosts of the matrix.

In 2013, Burkard and Rose were invited by a colleague, who runs a series of professional development workshops in Belgrade, to offer a one-day social photo-matrix as part of these offerings. The theme for this workshop was 'Who am I as leader and follower?'. This theme was chosen in discussion with our colleague, who felt it would offer very useful insights regarding leadership in their client organisations.

Figure 8.1 from that workshop depicts the feet of some students on a sign that says 'From Vardar to Triglav'. As the technical assistant explained in an email:

> Those were the borders of [the] former Yugoslavia, the river Vardar in Macedonia at the south and Triglav, the highest mountain in Slovenia at the north. There was even a popular song in the 1980s with those lyrics, often considered [the] unofficial Yugoslav anthem that celebrated [the] unity and diversity of many nations who lived in the country.
>
> (Ristovic, 2014)

Figure 8.1 Photo, 'From Vardar to Triglav'

After many years of co-hosting social photo-matrix workshops around the world, we have learned that one can never predict in advance the associations to photos. Even though this methodology can be used in any culture or country, the photos themselves always have different connotations. For example, Figure 8.2, a photo of a trust exercise in a park, which, to Rose, as an American who has participated in this sort of exercise, would seem to say something positive about leadership, was instead associated to in a quite sceptical and somewhat cynical fashion in Serbia.

This experience reminded us that one cannot approach a socioanalytic methodology with a theory already in one's head, seeking to confirm it by the evidence. Instead, one forms one's theories or hypotheses based on the data that are generated in the matrix and later reflected upon in the smaller session. If we had gone to Serbia, a country we know very little about, with a theory in our heads related to the theme 'Who am I as leader and follower?' that we sought to prove, Rose, as an American, and Burkard, as a German, would have been woefully inadequate. Our 'theories' about Serbian leadership would have come from what we had read in the news or heard in discussions and would have been naturally influenced by our own cultural and national perspectives. One does not set out to 'prove' one's theory by finding it in the data.

Figure 8.2 Trust exercise in the park

Interestingly, however, even the Serbians in the workshop were surprised at what emerged in the matrix in relation to the theme, which were feelings of sadness and depression. In the small reflection groups, the participants shared the impact of so many years of betrayal by their leadership, whom many felt they could not trust. Thus, it is difficult for them to identify with either the idea of follower or leader, as both roles have been so contaminated.

As we always do, the theme for this SPM was chosen in collaboration with our Serbian colleague, who sponsored this event. We worked with a group of 48 participants, but only half of them sent photos. What we subsequently learned was that many in the workshop had difficulty taking a picture relating to the theme. For example, the photographer of Figure 8.3 told us that he had great difficulty finding an appropriate subject. In this photo matrix, there were many photos taken from people's personal archives, such as photos of an Egyptian statue, a famous architectural house in Barcelona, someone's daughter dressed in summer clothes (which could not have been taken for the matrix, as it occurred in March). Other photos seemed to be pulled from the internet, such as Figure 8.4, of five baby geese following their mother.

This was for us also data that the theme was very difficult to relate to.

Social dream-drawing

Social dream-drawing (SDD) was developed over a period of seven years by Rose Redding Mersky (2013, 2017) and subsequently researched from a

Figure 8.3 Boys in the gymnasium

Figure 8.4 A mother duck and her five ducklings

psychosocial perspective (Clarke and Hoggett, 2009). Research has demonstrated that participation in SDD can be a valuable individual professional learning experience, as well as an important resource for those going through major transitions in their working and personal lives (Mersky, 2017). What particularly distinguishes SDD from social dreaming and the social photo-matrix is the intensive associative work done with the dream-drawings of individual participants. It is through the associative work of the group that the individual dreamer becomes more and more aware of the deeper issues reflected in the original dream material.

SDD is based both on theories of drawing and on specific research on the drawing of dreams. It is important to keep in mind that dreams themselves, as ineffable as they are and as difficult as they are to get hold of, are visual. The dream-drawer is not sketching from a model before him or her, nor is he or she painting an object or scene from visual memory of external reality. The drawing is not an imitation and is not designed as a reproduction. Instead, the drawer is using what one might term his or her inner perception, an 'inner eye' that, in the dreaming state, registers various images that are then transformed into physical representations.

There are many advantages to the drawing of dreams. As Taylor (2012) has noted, drawing is 'an investigative, transformative and generative tool' (p. 9). Drawing allows one to document and understand a significant internal experience that might soon fade from memory. Thus, one is not only representing a visual, but, in fact, is discovering something by making it able to be seen.

To say that a picture is worth a thousand words is not an exaggeration. As Arnheim (1969) has noted: 'All is present at once in the visual and its contents are not presented linearly but rather in a complex interrelatedness, opening up possibilities for understanding and... having the potential for very complex content' (p. 249). Drawing a dream often brings back dream material that one had forgotten and neglected to mention in the verbal telling.

Stephen Hau (2004), a researcher at the Sigmund Freud Institute in Frankfurt, demonstrates that when dreamers draw their dreams, they regress to an earlier period of development. The drawings tend to be more primitive and simple than those drawings done in full consciousness and contain only the basic elements. The drawer regresses to an 'earlier developmental state' (p. 242) typified by a more primitive thought, perception, and process mode.

Hau considers drawings of dreams to be more abstract and metaphorical than a verbal telling (2004, pp. 120–131). Arnheim (1969) points out that words suggest permanency and stand for a 'fixed concept' (p. 244). They are essentially 'conservative and stabilizing' (p. 244). They are static. Walde (1999, p. 131) also notes: 'When dream images, usually consisting of pictures, are transformed into language, the interpreter is already working with a mediated and rationalized construct.' As such, drawings have the capacity to help the dreamer access more of the original primitive material in the dream.

Hau's research shows that the combination of both verbal and drawn dreams is the best way to work with dream material. These two modes complement and support one another and provide a fuller and more whole 'picture' of the dream. He cites Sendak's picture book *Where the Wild Things Are* (1963). Here, the scary drawings are mediated and contextualised by the written words, appearing in clear and comprehensible English, telling a linear story.

Thus, the combination of two forms of representation (verbal and drawn) creates a kind of 'transitional space' between the awake world and the dream world, whereby the full dream experience is revisited and where more of the original and primitive dream material becomes available. In the drawn portrayal of the dream, phantasies come closer to the 'original imagination process' than the spoken dream, which stands nearer to structured reality with its 'objective references' (Hau, 2004, p. 248).

The structure of social dream-drawing is very straightforward. In a sense, the workshop begins before we meet, because participants are asked to start drawing their dreams as soon as they learn the theme and to bring one of them to the workshop. We work for approximately an hour with each dream-drawing. After telling one's dream, the dreamer shows a drawing. We offer associations and amplifications. For the last 20 minutes, we switch seats and reflect on the theme, similarly to the reflection session in the social photo-matrix.

Although both the social photo-matrix and social dream-drawing are based on the same underlying theories, they have their differences. For example, in the photo-matrix, we associate to the photograph, and not the photographer. We do not know who took which photos. In contrast, with social dream-drawing, as with organisational role analysis (Newton, Long, and Sievers, 2006) and role biography (Long, 2006), we know whose drawing we are working with.

Another important difference is that the SPM can involve large groups. We once undertook one in Chile with over 50 participants and 4 reflection groups. In contrast, SDD works with groups of 3 or 4 participants.

In 2009, Burkard and Rose were invited by a colleague to offer a SPM workshop at a business school in Santiago, Chile. In conjunction with that invitation, another Chilean colleague, who knew of Rose's research into social dream-drawing, invited her to co-host such a workshop with a small number of colleagues. One was recently promoted to a teaching position at the business school, another was an organisational consultant, and the third was a human resources professional in a large corporation. All three were very interested in understanding and working with organisations from a psychoanalytic perspective. As part of our discussion, Rose received permission to use this workshop as part of her ongoing research. The theme 'What do I risk in my work?' was chosen, because it was the theme of other groups being researched using SDD.

Figure 8.5 is from a social dream-drawing workshop that Rose co-hosted in Chile in 2009. The theme for this workshop was 'What do I risk in my work?'. In this case, each participant was from a different organisational context, so while each dream-drawing expressed an issue relating to the individual dreamer, what eventually emerged from the collective unconscious were societal and cultural issues relating to working in Chile.

This first drawing contains images from two different dreams, which the dreamer had three days apart. The first dream, which is reflected on the left side of Figure 8.5, was about losing his hair. The second related to erotic feelings towards students who approach him after giving a lecture. The associations and reflections regarding being exposed and naked led to the discussion of the role of 'masks as a characteristic of the Chilean society, specifically of the Chilean

Figure 8.5 Social dream-drawing: no hair and university students

oligarchy, where one has the feeling of wearing masks since it is important – in order to survive – to have a certain social and family origin, to study at specific universities, etc. You must have what they call "social credentials'" (Social Dream-Drawing Transcript, 2009, p. 8).

Figure 8.6, by a self-employed consultant, reflected another kind of anxiety, that of getting sick and not being able to support the family. As the dreamer put it: 'The obligation of producing, generating, reaching stability, having material assets and power beyond a healthy level' (2009, p. 11). The cross drawn on the bed turned out to be an important element that probably would never have been revealed without the drawing. This led to associations to the role of the Knights Templar Trust in Chile, a charity which was then working in the San Juan de Dias children's hospital in Santiago. The question of how much one could or should risk, how far one should go to help others, was related also to the demands on a self-employed consultant. As was said in the reflection group: 'You have to establish certain limits regarding risks. Templars, for example, gave their lives but you don't need to go that far' (p. 12).

Lastly, Figure 8.7 is a dream-drawing by a female human relations executive working in a private enterprise. Her boss had just called her into his office to tell her she must take care of his children and that she would recognise them 'because they had blue eyes just like him' (2009, p. 15). The theme of elitism in Chile returned, since 'the most important corporate groups belong to two of the main Catholic Church collectivities: the Opus Dei and The Legionnaires of Christ' (p. 15).

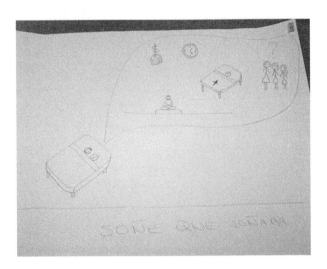

Figure 8.6 Social dream-drawing: at the hospital

Figure 8.7 Social dream-drawing: take care of my children

Connecting all three dreams was the theme of the invasion of the boundary of the role-holder in very personally vulnerable ways, leading to exposure, sickness, or humiliation. All the risks had to do with how strong a boundary one can set around one's work identity in a culture where one does not hold the elite position.

Example 1: SPM in a juvenile prison in Germany – 'A grid is a grid is a grid'

In 2007, Burkard, his colleague, and a group of university students were invited by the Catholic minister of a juvenile prison in Wuppertal, Germany, to undertake an SPM with a small group of male remand prisoners. These young men ranged in age from 14 to 20 years old and were being held in detention while awaiting trial (Sievers, 2014). This invitation came about through a student of Burkard's, who was volunteering at the prison and who recommended this idea to the minister. In order to get permission to hold this event, the minister had to negotiate with the prison administration. The results of that negotiation are described below. A simple theme of 'What is it like to be in a prison?' was decided upon, in order to emphasise that the focus was on the systemic context.

While Burkard and his colleague had previously consulted to prisons, most of the students were quite shocked when they were guided through the facility in order to take photos for the matrix. They were continually confronted with the power and authority of the state and the judiciary. The photos of the young remand prisoners often reflected the ugliness of the place and were expressions of their own despair. Both sets of photos were collected in an electronic archive to be used in the matrices. As the photographers were not known, it was not possible to differentiate between prisoner and student photographs.

The SPM took place in the chapel of the prison, which was the only place suitable for such a venture, as it was perceived by the prisoners as a 'neutral' space, where they would dare speak openly. Whereas the prisoners were at first delighted to be released from the solitude of their cells and meet 'normal' people – especially the young women – this enthusiasm soon dwindled once they were confronted with the task of associating to the photos on the screen.

For them, learning from experience was largely limited to protecting themselves from attacks by other prisoners and the punishments of wardens. The photos showed 'reality' and using the photos for a wider range of thoughts and fantasies was mere nonsense. From their perspective, as one put it, 'a grid is a grid is a grid' and not a source of free association. At the same time, the more the students became aware of the gap between themselves and the prisoners, and the enormous differences in verbal competence, the more restricted and sanitised became their free associations.

The more the prisoners became confused and frustrated by the associations of the students and our ongoing invitation to freely associate, the more stuck they became in their own 'reality principle'. They wanted to first explain every photo before we associated to it. They did not realise that once the meaning of the photos had been nailed down, any other possible meanings would be eliminated.

One hypothesis for the narrow-minded rigidity of the prisoners is that instead of allowing space for associations, which would lead to various other thoughts and meanings, they were longing for our sympathy for the mistreatment they experienced in the prison. It appeared as if their undermining of the given task was driven by the desire to escape the reality of the matrix – and the prison – and the hope that they could establish closer social and personal relationships with the students. Peer pressure was probably also a factor.

Burkard, his colleague, and the students soon realised that the invitation to freely associate, in the context of a largely totalitarian institution, was not possible. Even though a prisoner may be free to think whatever he wants, it is more often than not more appropriate to keep one's thoughts to oneself.

During the reflection sessions in mixed groups of prisoners and students following the matrices, the former talked at times about their anxieties. Their main fear was the uncertainty as to whether or not they would be convicted – and if so, how long the sentence would be and what kind of life they would be able to lead afterwards. Their reactions to some of the photos revealed ongoing anxieties relating to the violence in the system and the ongoing rejection of relatives and friends.

As it was difficult to achieve a 'good enough' SPM workshop in this context, the hosts were tempted to end the experiment after the second session. However, with the encouragement of the minister, they proceeded by slightly changing the design. Instead of reflecting in two heterogeneous groups, two homogenous reflection groups were formed. The prisoners worked with the minister and the students with Burkard and his colleague. This not only provided an opportunity for all to express their displeasure and annoyance with the previous sessions and the method, it also allowed some thinking and reflection on the sources of their disappointment.

As it turned out, the prisoners felt somehow betrayed by our invitation to work together – because we did not sufficiently fulfil their desire to socialise with them, to provide opportunities to get to know one another and to exchange experiences. It appeared that the prisoners often felt helpless in the matrices and didn't think they could cope with it:

> If one does not have any thoughts one prefers to stay silent. ... No feelings with some of the photos; anxieties to say something wrong. ... We the inmates are seeing these pictures day in and day out. ... One is thinking less in reaction to familiar images, new photos would have been better. ... One had to force oneself just to express one's current thoughts. ... The two parties do not start on the same level.

The students, on the other hand, expressed their disappointment and anger about the restricted free associations of the prisoners, but also showed some understanding of what made it so difficult for them to commit to the given task and method:

> The very first photo in the first matrix was too difficult at the beginning; if the shower room represents the epicentre of violence ... Free associations: suddenly the opinion of the inmates does count. ... If I hear too much of the individual fate I no longer can work; I don't want to give up the hope that it still will work well.

Despite reservations, another compromise for the last two sessions was made that allowed the prisoners to first explain the photos before the matrix began. Even though this may be seen as a shabby compromise, it was an opportunity for the prisoners to be listened to and to be taken seriously and to make an impact on the event. It would enable the project to come to a 'good enough' end.

Though the matrix is designed as a democratic event where all are equal, this SPM more often than not turned into an intergroup event and tended to be dominated by tyrannical dynamics among the subgroups and/or between individuals. In a sense, despite our 'good intentions', we were enacting the fundamental split of 'them and us', which characterised the relatedness (and non-relatedness) between wardens and prisoners – and, not least, that of society and prisoners.

It soon became evident that the original design of the SPM, its given task – the focus on the prison as a social system (instead of individuals) and the strict time frame of the sessions – reminded the prisoners all too well of the rigidity with which the rules and the daily schedule were enforced by the prison staff. It seems that with the SPM we unconsciously enacted the total institution.

This prison SPM made obvious the limited extent to which feelings and emotions could be experienced, admitted, endured, contained, and reflected upon by the prisoners, in particular, and by 'us' as well. The university group became aware again and again how much this 'institutionalised insensitivity' restricted, if not destroyed, the participants' capacity to think.

On the other hand, it seems very likely, from what some prisoners said at the very last session in the prison, that the SPM had set some of them to thinking:

> I felt inclined to think more intensively. ... The thoughts that one had kept to oneself got confirmed. ... Therefore my own thoughts can't be totally wrong. ... There were similar thoughts from both sides (prisoners and students) even though one group is not living in the slammer.

In hindsight, despite all the difficulties and the ongoing threat of a premature ending, the priest viewed the experience as very different from what transpires when groups of visitors come to get an impression of the prison or to 'entertain' the prisoners by liberating them temporarily from their daily experience. As the minister wrote, 'Particularly on the side of the prisoners I experienced a depth of and change in thinking which I so far would not believe to be possible. Even long after the end of the SPM it remained a topic of conversation and had meaning to the juveniles' (Uellendahl, 2014, p. 129).

Example 2: SDD in a post-doctoral course: 'We are at the extremes, really'

At the invitation of the instructor of a post-doctoral graduate course entitled 'Researching the Unconscious' at the University of the West of England (UWE), I conducted a session of SDD with my fellow students in 2010. This invitation was made with two goals in mind. It was an opportunity for Rose to research yet another group for my doctoral studies, and it was an opportunity for the students to learn more about unconscious processes in groups that can be accessed through dream-drawings. The students readily agreed to participate.

Although the focus of my doctoral research was to learn what value SDD had for participants, this experience helped me discover its value in helping groups become aware of their own underlying dynamics. The group consisted of six female participants. Three were over fifty years old (including myself; I was the oldest), two were in their early twenties, and one was in her mid-thirties. These participants had no developed knowledge of unconscious processes in groups. Their main interest and specialty was individual psychology and psychotherapy. After agreeing to participate, one of the youngest participants suggested the following theme: 'To what extent does generation play a role in research?' In this way, she set the scene for the discoveries about our dynamics as a group.

Social photo-matrix and dream-drawing 159

The next day, the participant in her mid-thirties brought the dream-drawing in Figure 8.8. (Please note that all quotations from this session are to be found in Mersky, 2017.)

This drawing depicts a very big space, with hospital beds suspended from the ceiling. The dreamer is lying in one of the beds. When her doctor enters, she starts to feel 'uncomfortable' and 'vulnerable'. Her doctor in the dream is actually (in real life) the dreamer's therapy client, who in reality is older than the dreamer.

Associations to the dream-drawing were connected to this relationship, that is, 'inferiority', 'mother and child', 'parent and child', 'the mother putting you to bed'. Here, the doctor is both patient and healer, and the dreamer is both patient and healer. There is a 'role reversal'. It is 'spooky', 'complicated', and

Figure 8.8 Social dream-drawing: hospital beds suspended from the ceiling

'awkward'. Mention was made of the movie *Atonement* and to a war-time hospital ward.

The discussion following the free associations helped to crystallise one of the major dynamics in the group, that is, the generational differences between the two sub-groups. As one of 'the oldies' noted, 'we are at the extremes, really'. One older participant noted: 'One of the things you learn as you grow older is that you can survive what you didn't think you can survive.' Another said that it is 'hard to be an older learner'. Younger participants had their say as well. As one stated: 'just because I'm younger doesn't mean I don't know what I want'. They want to say to their elders (and all three of us older women could have been their parents) 'you don't know how it works'. However, for one older participant, noting this difference was not easy: 'there's some reluctance to, to think about you as being different because you're younger.... maybe it's just my, my reluctance to acknowledge difference... cause difference can lead to conflict'. This comment seemed to touch on the underlying dynamic in the group, which had not been spoken.

The second dream-drawing was by one of the youngest participants, and depicted her in a swimming pool with a shark nearby. Here perhaps the conflict was more in the open. An older woman noted: 'You could be out of your depth in certain ways.' And there were the following comments by two participants, first the younger and then the older:

> I really enjoy people that are older than me talking about their experiences, what they've learned, how they've dealt with situations, because I can really learn from that. But on the other hand, I kind of feel sad because although I can still live it, like that time is over for them.... I kind of feel sad or guilty that I like can do it now, but that time is gone for them.
>
> I really know what that phrase being 'over the hill' means. I really have that experience inside, you know. The feeling that actually I've reached my zenith and now there is no other way but down, down all the way to the bottom.... which is a scary sort of feeling.... The arc that I'm on in life and there is that sense that... there is that sense that...uh... I can't actually go back, you know. It has to carry on to the end of that arc, wherever that may be.

My own experiences during the group session seem related to this theme. During the workshop, I took a particularly motherly role with one of the youngest participants. Although it was she who had suggested the theme, she was very withdrawn during the workshop. My motherly role was noted by the other participants. This was definitely an act of going out of role, which could be seen as an enactment of the generational issues in the group. By behaving in a motherly way, I was falling into a familiar generational dynamic and creating a private pair, which might have felt comfortable to me and to us, but was against the task of the work. So I was enacting the very issue of the group, the generational divide (Mersky, 2001).

In fact, it seemed that we as a group all participated in creating a split between the generations. We all colluded in having the participant in the middle of our ages present the first dream-drawing. She served as a mediating figure in that sense, and perhaps it was easier to work first with her dream-drawing, rather than the one by the younger woman. Nevertheless, although the first dream-drawer was easily ten years older than the two youngest ones, we lumped them all together as the young group. She herself colluded with this, noting in her interview that she was 'feeling myself a lot younger than I was'.

Thus, as Bion (1961) theorised, we could say that the group was in a basic assumption mode, that it had created a set of defensive groupings to avoid its task and to avoid anxiety. What is very interesting is that before this session, most participants were having difficulty identifying a research question to explore for their paper on this course. Following the session, almost all were able to do so. This leads to the very tentative (but not provable) hypothesis that generational issues were impeding the group's ability to get on with the task, and that in the workshop, where these issues could be explored, enough anxiety was alleviated for participants to focus on the assignment for the course.

Discussion

From our experience, SDD and the SPM (along with its root SDM) can be (and are being) utilised in a number of different ways. In each case, they access the unconscious dynamics both in individuals and in groups/systems. How they are utilised depends partly, but not entirely, on the purpose for which they are intended by those who are facilitating and sponsoring them.

All of them can be offered as one-time, stand-alone workshops, either with ongoing groups or with participants unknown to one another. The SPM in Serbia, the SDD in Chile, and the SDD at UWE in Bristol are all examples of that. In these examples, participants gain their own individual insights and collectively develop insights into their group issues, for example, Serbia and leadership, Chile and the elite leadership class, tensions between different generations in the UK group. The workshops are offered with no particular goal in mind other than to offer a creative experience, usually related to a theme important to the system where they are held, that is, 'What do I risk in my work?', 'Who am I as leader and follower?', 'To what extent does generation play a role in research?'.

Secondly, these methodologies can be used as part of a larger process of organisational development in a system. Here, the goal is to generate data relating to a problem that has stymied a system and for which consultation has been sought. The workshop generates such data for later consideration and, at the same time, functions as an intervention in the existing system. While this was not the stated purpose of the SDD workshop in the university class in

Bristol (see above), the workshop did help the group identify an underlying dynamic that was impacting the group dynamic. The use of socioanalytic methodologies in organisations is extensively covered in an article by Rose, entitled 'Contemporary methodologies to surface and act on unconscious dynamics in organizations: an exploration of design, facilitation capacities, consultant paradigm and ultimate value' (Mersky, 2012).

Thirdly, these methodologies can be utilised as action research methods, whose purpose is to investigate a certain issue in a system to better understand it, but not necessarily with the intention to bring about change in the organisation. A good example of such a process is the SPM in the prison, which revealed the way in which totalitarian dynamics hinder free association. Although the SPM in the prison was not designed as an action research project, one could say that it took an action research function in making explicit the experience of an authoritative state of mind. The theme used in this case was 'What does it mean to be in a prison?' Other examples of an action research question could be 'How is diversity managed here?', 'What characterises leadership in this organization?', or 'transitional spaces'. These may be questions that very well suit a socioanalytic approach, as the data are often not available in more quantitative ways, having to do with culture, attitudes, values, and organisational history.

Fourthly, these methodologies can be used in order to conduct academic research, which is the focus of this volume. Due to the academic rigour of their underlying theory and the wealth of publications regarding their implementation, they can be relied upon, when facilitated properly, to access data not otherwise made available in research situations. Naturally, this would involve paying close attention to issues such as sampling, ethics, data collection and data analysis, and building in the appropriate research protocols for such a study. We hesitate to draw too fine a line between action research and academic research, in that the academic research community is more and more amenable to new, innovative forms of qualitative inquiry that seek to access otherwise unavailable data. The key aspect is that these are forms of inquiry.

Lastly, these methodologies can be included in ongoing professional development programmes for organisational development consultants who wish to learn innovative and creative ways of working with their client organisations. This was the case, for example, with the social photo-matrix in Serbia.

SDD, with its intensive exploration of individual dream-drawings in a group setting, can also be a resource for various forms of professional development. This can include:

- coaching programmes for organisational development professionals and other related professions;
- ongoing supervision or training programmes for professional cohorts, such as groups of social workers, doctors, managers, or teachers;

- seminars and ongoing supervision with people going through major life transitions, such as those relocating their homes and/or switching jobs or going into retirement.

Because it is conducted in the spirit of creative fun, it has a user-friendly aspect that, over time, helps participants become aware of ongoing patterns worth investigating and perhaps changing. A good example of this is the workshop in Chile described above.

Just to note there are other emerging and creative uses of these methodologies. The SPM, for example, is being utilised as part of an overall training programme in the understanding of unconscious processes in organisations. SDM have taken place in group relations conferences, and soon either SDD or SPM may follow. Often, these methodologies take on an afterlife. One group in Sofia that participated in an SPM in 2013 continues to meet over time to use the methodology for their own learning. In their last session, in January 2016, they used the theme 'The things I reject'. As one of the hosts wrote: 'It seems that the potentials of the method are quite large but still we have to keep the boundaries of the philosophy and rational on which it was developed... Well, you can feel as parents of a new baby Bulgarian SPM Group!' (Mateeva, 2016). A group in Pretoria that participated in a SDD workshop entitled 'Who am I as a researcher?', continues to meet and will be presenting their learning at an international conference in September. The title of their presentation is: 'Social dream-drawing: using the creativity of the unconscious to enhance women's leadership capacities'. Over the years, we have worked with three different groups of doctoral candidates at the University of Humanistic Studies in Utrecht, who have used the SPM workshops to explore their doctoral material.

Key to the use of any of these methodologies in any of the four ways identified above is that they are implemented with a clear understanding of their theoretical underpinnings and the extremely important role of containment of the group and the task at hand. As Rose has written elsewhere (Mersky, 2012, p. 35), critical to leading such a workshop is 'keeping in mind the delicate balance between the need for clarity of task and boundaries and the fluidity and regression necessary for unconscious processes to emerge'. Facilitators must not only manage the sessions, but manage their own experiences, since they 'are entering something totally new and infinite each and every time. They associate and amplify, as well as contain and lead' (ibid.).

Here, it is important to emphasise what Julian Manley has called the 'side effects' (2016) that arise when using these praxes. What he was explicitly referring to here were the findings of a section of his doctoral research whose goal was to examine the creativity of the SDM as a praxis. To this end, in 2007, he and a colleague hosted a series of four social dreaming matrices in connection with an exhibition that marked the bicentenary of the 1807 Act that abolished the British slave trade: 'Breaking the chains: the fight to end slavery' at the British Empire and Commonwealth Museum (BECM) in Bristol (Manley,

2010). However, the side effect that his research unexpectedly unearthed was related not just to social dreaming, but to its potential for contributing to research into 'the evolving purposes and mission of museums and their role in society', particularly as it relates to visitors' reactions to disturbing material (Manley and Trustram, 2016). This side effect is similar to my discovery that SDD could be used as a means to unearth dynamics in a group (i.e., the post-doctoral class) that could, in retrospect, be thought of as undermining the group's ability to undertake its task (see the UWE example).

Lawrence has linked the unconscious thoughts that emerge in social dreaming to Bollas' (1987) concept of the 'unthought known', that is, what is somehow 'known' in the system but not available for thinking and reflection. In Rose's own thinking (Mersky, 2015), she has linked this concept to Peirce's notion of 'the strange intruder' (Peirce, 1992–1998, p. 154), the totally unexpected association or image that appears in such a praxis. One could say that both Bollas and Peirce would argue that instead of viewing these submerged and not yet integrated images as intrusions, they could, in fact, be an opening to the complicated unconscious reality of the group, such as the hospital beds hanging by the ceiling, in the UWE example, and the red cross on the bedsheets, in the Chile example.

Over the course of our experiences with both SPM and SDD, we have witnessed countless examples of these side effects, not only in relation to images, but in relation to actual experiences. For example, although the SPM is not designed as a therapeutic intervention, participants often have deep emotional experiences during the workshops. Sometimes participants get in touch with painful experiences (the recent death of a family member, a family's historical exclusion from its adopted culture, or the lost world of pre-communist society). This is a natural, so to say, side effect of immersing oneself in such a deep experience that also encourages regression in service of the task. One bears in mind always that this individual could be experiencing this very strong reaction on behalf of the group as a whole. And this is an important example of accessed data that, if contained, can (and does) inform the group learning. Conceptually, these deep experiences can also be thought of as enactments of the underlying issues that the praxis is designed to discover and work with. This was very well illustrated by the experiences of the student group undertaking the SPM at the juvenile prison. Therefore, it is not sufficient just to have the experience without processing it in the reflection session and attempting sense-making. Otherwise participants and groups may be left with an overabundance of unintegrated and fragmented affect.

Also related to the issue of side effects is the question of where and in which contexts these praxes are most appropriately utilised. Rose's research on SDD revealed that SDD does not work well with participants who are going through extremely traumatic events. The nature of regression in the group experience cannot easily be contained when one is in bereavement or when one is experiencing a deep loss. In addition, this work is not for everyone. Participants must have an ability to work with unconscious forces without feeling so vulnerable that they cannot think (as was the case with the prisoners). Therefore, this is not for every group, every research subject, or every organisation.

Conclusion

We conclude this chapter with the following recommendations for the utilisation of such methodologies:

1. The role of the facilitator is important to contain the learning and to integrate the inevitable strange intruder.
2. These methodologies are not for very vulnerable or very resistant systems or participants.
3. Both the matrix and the reflection sections must take place, for sense-making and for laying the ground for future actions.
4. These methods are based on a strong tradition and on specific theory which serve as inspiration and guidance.
5. Keeping in mind that free association can sometimes be defensive, as hosts, we work to continually bring participants back to the original dream material and the visual elements of the photographs.
6. Their use needs to be sufficiently grounded for it to have its full impact. A stand-alone event may be an interesting and pleasant experience but ultimately nothing more. Grounding includes, for example, being part of a larger organisational development process, an ongoing professional conference, a training programme in these processes, or a research question.
7. In any case, whether used as a stand-alone event, an action research process, an organisation intervention, or a research method, any falling out of role (whether by participant or by facilitator – see the UWE example) could be an enactment of the unconscious dynamic of the group and important data relating to that dynamic (Mersky, 2001).

In conclusion, one thing that seems clear to us is that no matter what the stated intention of using such a method, that is, a stand-alone learning experience, an organisational intervention, a part of an ongoing professional development programme, or an action/academic research method, their use in any setting produces outcomes that cannot be predicted and that can extend far into the future.

Both the SPM and SDD are based on specific theory and have been carefully developed over many years. They stand in connection with other carefully and fully developed methodologies. Much has already been published on their underlying theory and the ways one must think about facilitating them. This is extremely important, given the ethical issues related to participation and facilitation of these workshops. While not therapeutic in intent, they do have a therapeutic effect. It may seem at first glance something fun and interesting to do (which they often are), but they are more than just fun. They involve profound processes.

Using these methodologies, the frontiers of what is often considered accepted qualitative research may be extended to surface and make available for thinking even more data hitherto unreachable and for opening up new lines of inquiry to understand what we didn't know (consciously) before.

References

Armstrong, D. (2005), The 'organization-in-the-mind': reflections on the relation of psychoanalysis to work with institutions. In R. French (ed.), *Organization in the Mind: Psychoanalysis, Group Relations and Organizational Consultancy* (pp. 29–43). London: Karnac.

Arnheim, R. (1969), *Visual Thinking*. Berkeley: University of California Press.

Bain, A. (1999), On socio-analysis. *Socio-Analysis*, 1(1): 1–17.

Bain, A. (2005), The organisation containing and being contained by dreams: the organisation as a container for dreams. Unpublished manuscript.

Bion, W. R. (1961), *Experiences in Groups, and Other Papers*. London: Tavistock Publications.

Bollas, C. (1987), *The Shadow of the Object: Psychoanalysis of the Unthought Known*. New York: Columbia University Press.

Clarke, S., and Hoggett, P. (2009), *Researching beneath the Surface: A Psycho-Social Approach to Research Practice and Method*. London: Karnac.

Elias, N. (1987), Changes in the we–I balance. In *The Society of Individuals* (pp. 153–237). New York: Continuum, 1991.

Hau, S. (2004), *Träume zeichnen: Über die visuelle Darstellung von Traumbildern* [*Drawing Dreams: On the Visual Representation of Dream Images*]. Tübingen: edition diskord.

Hutton, J., Bazalgette, J., and Reed, B. (1997), Organisation-in-the-mind: a tool for leadership and management of institutions. In J. E. Neumann, K. Kellner, and A. Dawson-Shepherd (eds.), *Developing Organizational Consultancy* (pp. 113–126). London: Routledge.

Lawrence, W. G. (1998), Social Dreaming as a tool of consultancy and action research. In W. G. Lawrence (ed.), *Social Dreaming @ Work* (pp. 123–140). London: Karnac.

Lawrence, W. G. (1999), The contribution of Social Dreaming to socio-analysis. *Socio-Analysis*, 1(1): 18–33.

Long, S. (1999), Who am I at work? An exploration of work identifications and identity. *Socio-Analysis*, 1(1): 48–64.

Long, S. (2006), Drawing from role biography in Organizational Role Analysis. In J. Newton, S. Long, and B. Sievers (eds.), *Coaching in Depth: The Organizational Role Analysis Approach* (pp. 127–143). London: Karnac.

Long, S. (2010), Re: ISPSO: Working Note on Social Dreaming, 8 May. ISPSO@lists.oakland.edu, accessed 22 August (online).

Long, S. (2013), Using and creating socioanalytic methods. In S. Long (ed.), *Socioanalytic Methods: Discovering the Hidden in Organisations and Social Systems* (pp. 307–314). London: Karnac.

Long, S., and Harney, M. (2013), The associative unconscious. In S. Long (ed.), *Socioanalytic Methods: Discovering the Hidden in Organisations and Social Systems* (pp. 3–22). London: Karnac.

Manley, J. (2010), The slavery in the mind: inhibition and exhibition. In W. G. Lawrence (ed.), *The Creativity of Social Dreaming* (pp. 65–83). London: Karnac.

Manley, J. (2016), Skype conversation with Rose Mersky, 8 February.

Manley, J., and Trustram, M. (2018), 'Such endings that are not over': the slave trade, social dreaming and affect in a museum. *Psychoanalysis, Culture and Society*, 23(1): 77–96.

Mateeva, T. (2016), Email to Rose Redding Mersky, 1 February.

Mersky, R. (2001), 'Falling from grace' – when consultants go out of role: enactment in the service of organizational consultancy. *Socio-Analysis*, 3: 37–53.

Mersky, R. (2012), Contemporary methodologies to surface and act on unconscious dynamics in organizations: an exploration of design, facilitation capacities, consultant paradigm and ultimate value. *Organisational and Social Dynamics*, 12(1): 19–43.

Mersky, R. (2013), Social Dream-Drawing: 'drawing brings the inside out'. In S. Long (ed.), *Socioanalytic Methods: Discovering the Hidden in Organisations* (pp. 153–178). London: Karnac.

Mersky, R. (2015), How can we trust our research and organisational praxes? A proposed epistemology of socioanalytic methodologies. *Organisational and Social Dynamics*, 15(2): 279–299.

Mersky, R. (2017), Social Dream-Drawing (SDD): praxis and research. Doctoral dissertation.

Newton, J., S. Long, and B. Sievers (eds.) (2006), *Coaching in Depth: The Organizational Role Analysis Approach*. London: Karnac.

Peirce, C. S. (1992–1998), *The Essential Peirce: Selected Philosophical Writings (EP)*, Vol. 2, 1893–1913. The Peirce Edition Project. Bloomington, IN: Indiana University Press.

Ristovic, N. (2014), Personal email to Rose Mersky, 16 April.

Samuels, A. (1993), *The Political Psyche*. London: Routledge.

Sendak, M. (1963), *Where the Wild Things Are*. New York: Harper & Row.

Sievers, B. (2008a), Pictures from below the surface of the university: the Social Photo-Matrix as a method for understanding organizations in depth. In M. Reynolds and R. Vince (eds.), *Handbook of Experiential Learning and Management Education* (pp. 241–257). Oxford: Oxford University Press.

Sievers, B. (2008b), 'Perhaps it is the role of pictures to get in contact with the uncanny': the Social Photo-Matrix as a method to promote the understanding of the unconscious in organizations. *Organisational and Social Dynamics*, 8(2): 234–254.

Sievers, B. (2013), Thinking organizations through photographs: the Social Photo-Matrix as a method for understanding organizations in depth. In S. Long (ed.), *Socioanalytic Methods: Discovering the Hidden in Organisations* (pp. 129–151). London: Karnac.

Sievers, B. (2014), It is difficult to think in the slammer: a Social Photo-Matrix in a penal institution. In K. Kenny and M. Fotaki (eds.), *The Psychosocial and Organization Studies: Affect at Work* (pp. 129–157). Basingstoke, Hampshire: Palgrave Macmillan.

Social Dream-Drawing Transcript (2009), Santiago, Chile. 2 November.

Taylor, A. (2012), Forward – re: positioning drawing. In S. Garner (ed.), *Writing on Drawing: Essays on Drawing Practice and Research* (pp. 9–11). Bristol: Intellect.

Uellendahl, K. (2014), Was hat es gebracht? Versuch eines Resumees. In B. Sievers (ed.), *Hier drinnen sind irgendwie alle Türen zu. Eine Soziale Photo-Matrix in einer Justizvollzugsanstalt* (pp. 125–135). Münster: Agenda Verlag.

Vince, R., and Broussine, M. (1996), Paradox, defense and attachment: accessing and working with emotions and relations underlying organizational change. *Organization Studies*, 17: 1–21.

Walde, C. (1999), Dream interpretation in a prosperous age? In D. Shulman and G. G. Stroumsa (eds.), *Dream Cultures: Explorations in the Comparative History of Dreaming* (pp. 121–142). New York: Oxford University Press.

Winnicott, D. W. (1953), Transitional objects and transitional phenomena: a study of the first not-me possession. *International Journal of Psycho-Analysis*, 3: 89–97. [Reprinted in *Playing and Reality* (pp. 1–25). London: Routledge, 1991.]

Operationalisation

Chapter 9

Is it a bird? Is it a plane?
Operationalisation of unconscious processes

Gillian Walker and R. D. Hinshelwood

> When I see a bird that walks like a duck and swims like a duck and quacks like a duck, I call that bird a duck.
>
> (credited to) James Whitcomb Riley (1849–1909)

If psychoanalysis and allied work is to make claims about 'states' of mind, and especially the functioning and processes of the 'unconscious mind', how is that to be done, how can those 'unknowns' be 'inferred'? Mostly, psychoanalytic researchers attempt to identify the subjective states of mind and associated mental processes (including unconscious ones) using a method of operationalisation.

The so-called 'duck-test' has been a popular way of expressing the common process of recognition. Our epigraph quotes the original formulation attributed to the Indiana poet James Whitcomb Riley, and later attributed to Emil Mazey, secretary treasurer of the Auto-Workers Union (USA) who, at a labour meeting in 1946, used the phrase to accuse individual members of communism. This kind of apperception was described by the American philosopher C. S. Peirce (see Burks, 1946) as a process of 'abduction', or abductive reasoning or abductive inference. Published in *On the Natural Classification of Arguments*, Peirce stated that hypothetical inferences always dealt with a cluster of characteristics (X, Y, Z) known to occur when a certain event occurs (A). Without thinking about it, we identify things according to their most characteristic features; though we don't always get it right, it is good enough, mostly. An alternative term is the 'elephant test' – 'it is hard to describe it, but you know it when you see it'.

In effect, natural scientists use this method quite deliberately to identify phenomena in the material world. Using a mathematic model Peter Higgs had hypothesised the existence of a subatomic particle in 1964. This particle subsequently termed the Higgs Bosun, was not demonstrable until 2012. The Hadron Collider or particle accelerator was able to identify characteristics theoretically deemed to infer the presence of the phenomenon. Mostly scientists today invent special machinery like the particle accelerator that will display those characteristics of material objects that are not visible to our ordinary senses.

Cognitive psychology has used a similar principle in 'schema theory'. The idea of schemata was postulated by the philosopher Kant and then adopted by the gestalt psychologists, and also later by Piaget (1923). A schema, or in some schools of thought an 'archetype' or an 'imago' or a stereotype, is a psychically created framework, a way of ordering and categorising incoming information about the world, its contents, and the way it behaves. Schema, once established, can be difficult to change; in fact, new information, even that which would qualify as 'evidence', may be distorted to 'fit the frame', so to speak. However, it is a way of describing how the world is 'seen' and understood, it doesn't always have to be correct, of course. A newly discovered animal that looks and behaves like a cat will be deemed a cat until proved to be otherwise. The point is a set of characteristics appearing or occurring together suggest a specific entity or family of entities.

Psychologists go through a comparable process to make states of mind comparably 'visible'. Their instruments are often questionnaire-type studies which reveal characteristic states, such as a depression score, or they observe gross behaviour, like increased salivation, as Pavlov did when he discovered the conditioned reflex in dogs.

Psychoanalysis has a more difficult problem in that *unconscious* states of mind are not so easily accessed and not clearly identifiable by questionnaire data without a considerable degree of inference. Many psychologists would say the extensive degree of psychoanalytic inference is in itself wholly suspect; however, inference is not an invalid logic in psychology any more than it is in the natural sciences. Darwin (1872), in identifying facial expressions in animals and humans, may happily have relied on subjective reactions, but more is required than that sort of evidence.

Josef Breuer used inference from his data when he sought evidence for the cause of Anna O's multiple hysterical symptoms. Anna O, Breuer's patient, was unaware of how her symptoms were determined and that these originated inside her. Breuer used a particular instrument to enhance what could be 'seen'. The instrument that Breuer decided to try out was the hypnotic trance. Through this technique, Breuer was indeed able to gain evidence from Anna O's conscious utterances of what just might be the cause of her manifest symptomatology. Famously, Breuer inferred it was the trauma of nursing her dying father. Freud was impressed that there were non-conscious domains of mental influences the content of which could be inferred. And further, when consciously explained to the patient, the symptoms were ameliorated or even disappeared. For these non-conscious domains, Freud and Breuer adopted the (already existing) term 'the Unconscious mind' (Breuer and Freud, 1893).

Freud decided he was not good at hypnotism and invented another method for observing this mental domain outside of a person's subjective understanding of themselves. This was his association method for analysing dreams (Freud, 1900). His instrument was his own mental associating, generating data which were strings of ideas arising from each individual element of the dream. This associative data he then subjected to analysis – what we would now call a 'thematic analysis'.

The issue for psychoanalysis is what sort of a 'duck test' can be applied to unconscious subjective processes? The suspicion is that the object of study is resistant to formal research. This is because the characteristic features of 'a state of mind' are known from subjective experience(s). Such experience(s) are not available to the senses, but are instead inferred by intuition (Bion, 1970).

Briggs (1997) conducted an extensive and complex study of the interactions of the states of minds of mothers and infants. His method attempted to correlate those interactions with processes that might be observed in clinical situations. Clinical work uses, as we say, 'the third eye' which has led to increasing sensitivity to subjective data from psychoanalytic treatments. Such data is gained by inference from two sources: (i) the thematic analysis of the content of free associations; and (ii) the directly apprehended experience of the analyst – his or her countertransference. These methods may be much less applicable to non-clinical research; however, there are some possible initiatives (Kvale, 1996; Holway and Jefferson, 2000; Holmes, 2014).

Operationalisation

Operationalisation of terms is a process that forms a schema, a set of characteristics or features that can be 'inferred' or, if directly observable themselves, can infer the presence of other indirectly observable features, characteristics, functions, or processes. That is, identifying the features of a duck enables the opportunity to see if, or say whether, a duck is present (or not).

Operationalisation of terms involves several formal steps:

1. Identifying the significant features of the conceptual entity that is the subject of research.
2. Extracting from the existing literature the significant features that will be visible to observation.
3. Selecting those features, or patterns of features, that appear to be most crucial to the mental entity.
4. Gathering relevant data that is both relevant for the research question, and will reveal the necessary features; most often, these are (i) observational process notes, or (ii) recorded free association narrative interviews.
5. Searching for moments that satisfy the conjunction of a minimum set of the selected significant features.

These steps will allow specific and key characteristics to be identified that will define a phenomenon, material or psychological. It may be that a phenomenon must have all the characteristics (as Example 1, below) or just a specific proportion, or one or two obligatory criteria and a certain number of possible ones. The result is a schedule of criteria necessarily present to specify a particular phenomenon, a material thing, a state of mind, a process in transition, and so on.

Three brief accounts of differing research projects will now be given, followed by a more detailed account that operationalises the container–contained relationship.

Brief illustrations

Example 1: Differentiating anxiety, defence, and work-related functioning in the psychodynamics of social systems

First is an observational study by Dimitris Vonofakos (2009) in British psychiatry, focusing on the question 'When is practice reality-oriented, and when is practice distorted by culturally organised defences?'.

This was an investigation of institutional mental health-care cultures by applying the theory of social defence systems (Jaques, 1955). Social defences are organisational modes of practice, usually within a working organisation, which have the function of enabling members of the organisation to evade intolerable anxiety, anxiety that itself has been created by the work (Jaques, 1955; Menzies, 1959). These psychological demands on the staff may lead to the distortion of the task, and a decline in the effectiveness of the results of the work; for example, the institutionalised practice of removing social responsibilities from psychiatric inmates leading to the phenomenon of chronicity. The theoretical background of this work was based on the Kleinian theory of anxiety and defence, and Klein's description of mature, reality-oriented functioning (Klein, 1935, 1946). The original classic study was an investigation of the social defence system in the practices of a nursing service (Menzies, 1959).

Vonofakos studied mental health care, identifying three constellations of psychic functioning: schizoid defences against paranoid anxiety (operationalised as splitting, projection, idealisation, and denial); manic defences against depressive anxiety (operationalised as disparagement, denial, control, and self-idealisation); or more mature, reality-oriented functioning (operationalised as introjection and reparation).

Three sets of significant operationalised features were worked out from the literature. In a 'paranoid working culture', the significant features were:

1. collective suspicions and paranoid fears;
2. polarised splitting of intra-institutional groups into opposites;
3. intellectual incoherence and breakdown of communication.

In a 'manic working culture', they were:

1. idealisation of staff group and/or unit;
2. indifference and belittlement towards the care and rehabilitation of patients;
3. exercising tight control over the performance of work-related tasks.

And in 'reality-oriented working culture' ('thinking windows'), they were:

1. facilitating interpersonal communication and the exchange of mental elements;
2. expressing concern and curiosity;
3. surviving anxiety-provoking situations without making them static.

Observational data were collected from two studies of mental hospital wards, using the method of observation outlined and exemplified in Hinshelwood and Skogstad (2000).

Using the identified operational criteria, it was possible to show moments of interaction between staff and patients that were aligned with one or other of these functions: the more reality-based (reparative) and those less reality-based (schizoid and manic defences).

The result showed it was possible to infer a prevalent fear for survival and fear of invasion in the professional staff, a fear, however, that varied in its level of intensity. As that intensity reduced, it was possible to show that some reality-oriented thinking could occur (called, in this thesis, 'thinking windows').

Example 2: Art psychotherapy and the formation of the creative relationship metaphor

This thesis by Dominik Havsteen-Franklin (2016) examined first interviews with potential art therapy patients in a psychiatric unit. The question was to pinpoint those patients most suited to art therapy. In particular, the aim was to identify patients who showed a potential for developing a capacity for metaphor in the relationship (a 'creative relationship metaphor', CRM), a capacity that showed an elementary potentiality for reflective thinking.

To this end, a mental entity called a proto-metaphor was identified from art therapy and other literature sources, and its significant features selected as the operational definition of proto-metaphor. A typical metaphor, for example 'it's raining cats and dogs', was defined by five essential criteria:

1. non-literal (figurative) content;
2. transposition of one object onto another to create a novel meaning;
3. mentalized communication to another;
4. affectively bound image;
5. context contingent.

In some instances, perhaps in a small number of the severely disturbed psychiatric admissions, this phenomenon of the proto-metaphor existed. Subjects identified by these criteria would be able to develop some creative relationship potential. They would otherwise have had to rely solely on major anti-psychotic tranquillising medication.

Example 3: Repression and splitting

In a trial use of operationalisation, process material from a clinical setting was used as data to identify two terms: 'repression' and 'splitting'. The aim was to assess whether both terms were simply used by different psychoanalytic schools of thought for the same thing, or if the terms actually indicated different clinical phenomena, each being emphasised by separate schools of thought (Hinshelwood, 2008).

The literature was surveyed for visible differences in the appearance of the two phenomena. That is to say, the literature was analysed to reveal the significant characteristics that could differentiate between moments when one or other, repression or splitting, were operating in the session. Then, simply, it could be determined if these operational criteria (the significant characteristics) of each coincided at the same moments in the session, or if they identified temporally quite distinct moments. If at the same moment, then it pointed to the two terms having identical usage; if at different moments, that they must refer to different occurrences.

The literature produced an alternative and significant characteristic for each term. Repression left a trace in the form of a 'substitute idea', as Freud called it, whilst splitting left a sense of blankness or meaninglessness, an absence. Clearly where one characteristic applied, the other characteristic could not. Moreover, they were sufficiently visible to be observable in sessional process notes. The result of that investigation was that quite different moments were indeed observable in the material – in fact, in the material of a single session. It could then be inferred that different defence mechanisms were operating at different moments in the session.

A further research project will be examined in more detail which operationalises the phenomenon of the unconscious container–contained relationship.

The operationalisation of container–contained

A research project (unpublished as yet by one of us, GPW) investigated the hypothesis that people engage in BDSM (bondage, discipline, dominance, submission, sadism, masochism) practices because they provide some degree of containment of unmanageable experiences. Data was drawn from several sources; an email questionnaire, a published volume drawn from interviews, and a publicly shown BBC documentary of a commercial fetishistic 'dungeon' catering for these sexual tastes.

The analysis of the data proceeded with a conceptual analysis from the published literature of the containing process. This determined a sequence of steps to be found in an ordered progression in the data. The conceptual analysis started with Bion's first clear – and succinct – description of the container–contained process:

> The analytic situation built up in my mind a sense of witnessing an extremely early scene. I felt that the patient had experienced in infancy a mother who dutifully responded to the infant's emotional displays. The

dutiful response had in it an element of impatient 'I don't know what's the matter with the child'. My deduction was that in order to understand what the child wanted the mother should have treated the infant's cry as more than a demand for her presence. From the infant's point of view, she should have taken into her, and thus experienced, the fear that the child was dying. It was this fear that the child could not contain. He strove to split it off together with the part of the personality in which it lay and project it into the mother. An understanding mother is able to experience the feeling of dread that this baby was striving to deal with by projective identification, and yet retain a balanced outlook.

(Bion, 1959, pp. 312–313)

From Bion's description, a series of sequential steps were identified:

1. an intolerable anxiety (equivalent to the fear of dying);
2. the subject splits off that fear;
3. and in the process splits off a part of the ego;
4. the experience and the specific ego-function producing the experience is projected into the object.

In the analytic situation, Bion continued with a brief description of the mechanism of growth that results (in the analytic setting):

When the patient strove to rid himself of fears of death which were felt to be too powerful for his personality to contain he split off his fears and put them into me, the idea apparently being that if they were allowed to repose there long enough they would undergo modification by my psyche and could then be safely reintrojected.

(Bion, 1959, p. 312)

This leads to two further steps:

5. modification by the introjecting container (subsequently Bion, 1962) said to be in a state of reverie, and operating alpha-function as a process of modification;
6. re-projection of the modified experience, plus new understanding with a re-introjection by the subject of its lost ego-function.

Although psychoanalysis has subsequently been especially interested when the last two steps fail (either in infancy, or in the clinical situation), this particular research project was itself mostly concerned with the first four steps.

There appears to be a set of specific occurrences that we could expect to observe. First of all an intolerable experience, and second a loss of that and of a specific ego-function.

The case of Michael a client of Pandora's Box, a professional 'House of Domination'

Nick Broomfield (2005) is the documentary maker. In *Fetishes*, Broomfield tells us that the client (Michael) reports having thoughts and fantasies about killing and genocide and that Michael has come for 'total degradation'. Michael is naked on full view to the camera. When one of the leather-clad Dominatrices 'Mistress Delilah' arrives, Michael falls quickly to his knees. In the next scene, he is on all fours and Mistress Delilah is riding him side-saddle, he is having his buttocks flogged as he walks (on all fours). Michael is led by collar and leash to the bathroom, specifically the lavatory (toilet bowl). Mistress Catherine (similarly attired) joins the party. Taking Michael into the bathroom Mistress Delilah gently speaks to him, *I know how much you love this, look what's waiting for you* (she indicates the toilet bowl), *a nice big bowl huh, it's really dirty, there have been people in and out of here all day today, its full of stuff, did you look under the toilet rim?* Michael lifts the toilet seat with his teeth. He licks inside the toilet seat. Mistress Delilah softly tell him to *use that tongue, we'll get you to do the floor later*, she then commands *LICK*. Mistress Catherine asks Michael why he is shaking so much, he replies, *in anticipation, I can't believe how lucky I am*, his voice trembles. Mistress Delilah tells him she wants the toilet shining, Mistress Catherine puts her booted foot on the back of Michael's neck, pushing his head further into the toilet bowl. Mistress Delilah flushes the toilet. Both ladies give jolly laughter. As the bowl fills, Michael is told to *keep his head in there*. The seat and lid are dropped onto Michael's head, both ladies laugh.

After a moment, it is deemed Michael is ready for an interview and the ladies move away. Still with his head down the pan vomiting, Michael remains with his head under the lid and seat whilst Nick and the camera man mouth and whisper to each other about what to do. Nick looks uncomfortable, there are low voices and lots of (perturbed) facial expressions between film crew members. There is concern that there might be 'trouble with the sound' because his head is in the toilet and so on. The client Michael remains on his knees with his head down the pan.

Nick eventually approaches Michael (head still in the toilet).

Nick. *Michael, can I talk to you?*

Michael. *Yeah.*

Nick lifts the lid and seat. Michael is heaving and vomiting.

Nick. . . . *so. . . . . what. . . . . what is it that. . . . that you, you errrrr. . . . enjoy here particularly?*

Michael. . . . . .*doing what the Mistress makes me to do. I feel relieved* (he says this with feeling).

Nick. . . ..*in what way. . .what's. . . ..*

Michael. . . . *I feel like as though I have done all that craziness out. . . ... you know, I mean I just, you know, it's like you have all these impulses to do like crazy things. . . ...*

Nick. *What kind of impulses?*

Michael. . . . .. *you know, like getting into brawls and stuff, and like, and you know. . . ... like* (incomprehensible) *and war crimes. . . ... genocide, all the things that get inside your head, your head, like you know, like freaky thoughts go through my head all the time, thoughts . . . freaky thoughts, so when I get freaky I like, expunge that.*

Broomfield introduced this scene by saying that the Dominatrices had told him they provided a valuable service, to which he had been sceptical. Following this session, Broomfield reflected that he had absolutely changed his mind, to agree. That is, Pandora's Box does indeed provide a valuable service, and to someone like Michael a very valuable service indeed.

(Walker, 2018)

Data analysis

The analysis needs to conform to the conceptual steps isolated above:

1. an intolerable anxiety (equivalent to the fear of dying);
2. the subject splits off the anxiety;
3. and in the process splits off a part of his ego;
4. the experience and the specific ego-function producing the experience is projected into the object.

The first step is the intolerable experience, which appears to be Michael's own horrified knowledge of his wish to see or experience a genocide (though we know no details).

The second step is the repudiation of his own agency. His initial act on entering the premises is to fall on his knees as an abject servant or slave. This loss of agency can be seen as a combination of steps two and three. He has repudiated a major aspect of his ego-function which is his capacity to form and act on his own decision-making. It is not difficult to see that this state must relieve him of any risk or responsibility for accomplishing the harm that he says is in his mind.

This is then enacted in a very concrete way as a bodily projection – of vomit – into a literal container of unwanted refuse. This bodily expression and expulsion is a correlate of a psychological projection of some psychic refuse that nauseates Michael. His revulsion at his genocidal fantasies is manifest at the expulsion of his vomit and the export of the key ego-function of self-determination and autonomy. He is better off without those functions which, at some unconscious level, are close to bodily impulses, and revolt him.

Michael's violent repudiation of his fantasies and his autonomy result not just in a mess in the lavatory, but in his objects acquiring the ego-functions of determining his actions. The Dominatrices *become* his self-will. In other words, he has projected his ego-function into them, and they have introjected it, to literally become that function of determining what he will/ must do.

In the case of Michael, the process of containing is swiftly accomplished. In all the data used in this research, this same projective process is ubiquitous. That process wherein the subject accepts a servile position whilst the object determines his actions, what he can do, not do, or even what he may suffer. Indeed, there is a standard term used by people who frequent this lifestyle which is 'power-exchange'. It is a simple expression that conveys the basic psychological dynamic of these practices – the projection of the subject's autonomy and self-determination into the object. This key process of a significant ego-function passing over from subject to object is a core element of container–contained. Michael's 'intolerable thought' (step 1 above) of genocide seems to be the probable instigator of this unconscious psychic manoeuvre. The outcome of this manoeuvre is revealed in Michael, head in the toilet, physically vomiting out the revolting contents of his psyche.

Though it is not clear if steps 5 and 6 operate, one can see that there are two possible modifications: first is the conversion of something psychologically toxic to a bodily level; and the second is the high level of sexualisation introduced into the process. Both the regression to the bodily level and the hyper-eroticism (with even an addictive quality) are neither of them modifications that would normally be associated with growth, and it may be that these sexual practices represent a less successful form of container–contained, a cul-de-sac.

The main point of the case of Michael is that in a form of intense relating, and indeed of love, there is a particular form of containment for an intolerable and unmanageable idea. The research design used conceptually based criteria to operationalise the model of container–contained. The method of analysis produced plausible inference with explanatory power over a perplexing phenomenon.

Discussion and conclusions

The capacity to use significant features of states of mind as operational criteria for identifying subjective data, even unconscious subjective data, for research purposes has been demonstrated, with studies such as those exemplified here (see also Stamenova, Chapter 10).

For this research method to be used, certain conditions should apply:

- The criteria should not be derived from the data to be analysed, but from the literature defining the concept to be observed.

- Criteria should be discernible fairly unequivocally in whatever data are used.
- The data should be sufficiently transparent for readers of a published account to be able to confirm the observation/analysis.
- Where a constellation of several criterion has been established from the conceptual literature, then a minimum number of criteria for a positive observation should be set as the requirement at the outset.
- It may be that certain criteria are essential, and additional ones optional up to the minimum that have been set as required.
- In reporting the results of this kind of analysis, it is advisable to report moments that do not reach the required number of criteria as well as those that do.

But there are issues of validity and reliability that need further elucidation. Some of these studies have used more than one set of data to increase these requirements – in fact, the first study was employed in two psychiatric wards, and the fourth used three data sets.

This employment of the 'duck test' has an intuitive validity, providing that the initial conceptual definition and criteria are sufficiently appropriate and visible. Once a constellation of criteria has been identified as sufficiently visible for one study, it should be possible to apply the same criteria to other data samples, and by other researchers. A degree of reliability can therefore be claimed.

References

Bion, W. R. (1959), Attacks on linking. *International Journal of Psycho-Analysis*, 40: 308–315. [Reprinted in Bion, W. R. (1967), *Second Thoughts* (pp. 93–109). London: Heinemann; and in Elizabeth Bott Spillius (1988), *Melanie Klein Today*, Volume 1. London: Routledge.]

Bion, W. R. (1962), *Learning from Experience*. London: Heinemann.

Bion, W. R. (1970), *Attention and Interpretation*. London: Tavistock.

Bloomfield, N. (dir.) (2005), *Fetishes*. DVD. London: HBO.

Breuer, J., and Freud, S. (1893), On the psychical mechanism of hysterical phenomena. *The Standard Edition of the Complete Works of Sigmund Freud*, Volume 2: 3–17. London: Hogarth.

Briggs, S. (1997), *Growth and Risk in Infancy*. London: Jessica Kingsley.

Burks, A. W. (1946), Pierce's theory of abduction. *Philosophy of Science*, 13: 301–306.

Darwin, C. (1872), *The Expression of the Emotions in Man and Animals*. London: John Murray.

Freud, S. (1900), *The Interpretation of Dreams. The Standard Edition of the Complete Works of Sigmund Freud*, Volumes 4–5. London: Hogarth.

Havsteen-Franklin, D. (2016), When is a metaphor?: Art psychotherapy and the formation of the creative relationship metaphor. PhD thesis, University of Essex. Available at Ethos, British Library, http://ethos.bl.uk/OrderDetails.do?did=1&uin=uk.bl.ethos.695085

Hinshelwood, R. D. (2008), Repression and splitting: towards a method of conceptual comparison. *International Journal of Psycho-Analysis*, 89: 503–521.

Hinshelwood, R. D. (2016), *Research on the Couch: Subjectivity, Single Case Studies and Psychoanalytic Knowledge*. London: Routledge.

Hollway, W., and Jefferson, T. (2000), *Doing Qualitative Research Differently: Free Association, Narrative and the Interview Method*. London: Sage.

Holmes, J. T. (2014). Countertransference in qualitative research: a critical appraisal. *Qualitative Research*, 14(2): 166–183.

Jaques, E. (1955), Social systems as a defence against persecutory and depressive anxiety. In M. Klein, P. Heimann, and R. Money-Kyrle (eds.), *New Directions in Psycho-Analysis* (pp. 478–498). London: Tavistock.

Klein, M. (1935), A contribution to the psychogenesis of manic-depressive states. *International Journal of Psycho-Analysis*, 16: 145–174. [Republished in *The Writings of Melanie Klein*, Volume 1 (pp. 262–289). London: Hogarth, 1975.]

Klein, M. (1946), Notes on some schizoid mechanisms. *International Journal of Psycho-Analysis*, 27: 99–110. [Republished in *The Writings of Melanie Klein*, Volume 3, *Envy and Gratitude* (pp. 1–24). London: Hogarth, 1975.]

Kvale, S. (1996), *InterViews: An Introduction to Qualitative Research Interviewing*. London: Sage.

Menzies Lyth, I. (1959), The functioning of social systems as a defence against anxiety: a report on a study of the nursing service of a general hospital. *Human Relations*, 13: 95–121. [Republished in I. E. P. Menzies, *Containing Anxiety in Institutions*. London: Free Association Books, 1988; and in Trist and Murray (eds.), *The Social Engagement of Social Science*. London: Free Association Books, 1990.]

Vonofakos, D. (2009), Differentiating anxiety, defence and work-related functioning in the psychodynamics of social systems: observing the unconscious cultures of psychiatric organisations. PhD thesis, University of Essex. Available at Ethos, British Library, 1867.

Walker, G. P. (2018), Masochism as container. PhD thesis in preparation, University of Essex.

Chapter 10

Comparative analysis of overlapping psychoanalytic concepts using operationalization

Kalina Stamenova

> *I get so sick and tired of hearing about the various different schools of psychoanalysis and their great superiority to the other one – whichever it is. The possibility of arguing about their various merits is simply endless – as long as you don't anchor any of it to facts. I don't know of any scientific work that is not based on observation.*
>
> (Bion, 2005, p. 39)

During its development, psychoanalysis has generated a number of theoretical concepts, creating a pluralistic psychoanalytic world. While this is a natural and enriching development in any scientific discipline, the conceptual elaborations can sometimes be overlapping, with different schools within psychoanalysis claiming that their conceptualisations are the precise ones without actually engaging in finding the similarities as well as the differences. Debates based only on what a particular psychoanalytic school believes to be true can be endless, unjustified, often confusing, and counterproductive, ultimately leading to a Tower of Babel. The dangers of such proliferation of psychoanalytic theoretical conceptualisations are that they may lead to more confusion in the theory and in research as to what means what. Therefore, there is a growing need of comparative methodology to differentiate confusing and overlapping concepts and to allow the differences to enrich rather than confuse the psychoanalytic understanding of the unconscious, and a number of studies (Hinshelwood, 2008; Abram and Hinshelwood, 2018; Thomä and Kächele, 2007; Tuckett et al., 2008; Vonofakos, 2009) have been trying to create paradigms for comparative psychoanalysis.

Perhaps, as Bion (2005) points out, we need to ground our claims in facts. The aim of this chapter is to present a method of comparing two overlapping psychoanalytic concepts – envy and frustration – in a psychoanalytically informed observational research in education by using operationalised criteria. Operationalising the two concepts allows for establishing the similarities and differences on a conceptual level, which can then be observed empirically. The steps in operationalisation, as elaborated by Walker and Hinshelwood in Chapter 9, involve 1) identifying and extracting the important characteristics of the concept from the theory, and 2) selecting those characteristics, or patterns, which appear essential to the concepts to develop operationalised minimum sets of criteria. After the differences are established on a theoretical and conceptual level, the operationalised criteria can be used to analyse data and pinpoint occurrences of mental states in empirical observations.

The theoretical debate around envy and frustration

From a Kleinian perspective, envy is clearly a manifestation of the death instinct deflected towards the good object; the aggression is anti-growth and anti-development and attacks the links with the good object and with learning, a motivation for –K (Klein, 1957; Bion, 1959, 1962a, 1962b; Rosenfeld, 1971; Segal, 1983; Joseph, 1986; Spillius, 1993). More recently, Roth and Lemma (2008) re-examine the concepts of both envy and gratitude in the light of recent developments and highlight their clinical value. For example, Polmear (2008) maintains that Klein's and Winnicott's theories of early development can co-exist in the clinical setting. Steiner (2008) relates envy to Freud's concept of repetition compulsion and claims that the two might be aspects of the same thing. Feldman (2008) claims that envy is not an expression of the death instinct but rather an instigator of its sadistic impulses. Britton (2008) maintains that envy should be considered a complex that arises with the aggregation of a number of elements – destructiveness, recognition of the separateness of the self and object, and disappointment with self-idealisation.

Klein's opponents are inclined to see aggression as motivated predominantly from environmental frustration or maternal failure to contain the baby's painful experiences. They view destructiveness and self-destructiveness as stemming from frustration in all its forms – penis envy, jealousy, rivalry, feelings of exclusion, deprivation, and lack of good-enough mothering or containment. Racker (1960) argues that envy stems from lack and deprivation, feelings prior to the appreciation of the good object. Winnicott (1959), similar to Racker (1956), claims that with her concept of envy, Klein overlooks the role of the environment and argues that the envious attacks observable in clinical settings are a result of the analyst's or mother's failure to be available for the patient/child when they are needed or as a result of the inability of the mother/analyst to adapt to the needs of the patient/child. Ogden (1979) claims that envy is inseparable from jealousy and cannot exist in a pure form but later points out that there is 'interplay of these forms of relatedness' (Ogden, 1986, p. 79). In his criticism of the concept of envy, Kernberg (1980) points out that Kleinians attempt to attribute all negative therapeutic reactions to primary envy. Perhaps the most meticulous critique of envy is made by Joffe (1969), who repudiates the concept on the grounds that envy implies object relations from birth, and this contradicts Freud's conceptualisations of primary narcissism, a state without object relations, hence the ego does not come into existence until after the phase of primary narcissism.

So it seems an unresolved ongoing debate, with envy and frustration used interchangeably and psychoanalytical discussions claiming that only one or the other mental state can be observed in the clinical setting. The study presented in this chapter contributes to the debate by developing operational definitions of the concepts, elaborating the differences on a theoretical level and then using operationalised observable criteria to pinpoint occurrences of envy and frustration in educational observational research.

Conceptual analysis

The detailed conceptual analysis of the psychoanalytic literature on the two concepts can be summarised as follows:

In frustration

1. There is a relationship with a frustrating object, an object obstructing gratification of needs or withholding the goodness for itself. Frustration can also be linked to the phantasy of the Oedipus situation with its concomitant feelings of being excluded from the parental couple (Britton, 1989). Being able to experience frustration presupposes tolerance of separateness between self and object, that is to say, the ego may experience frustration only if it experiences itself as separate from the object. 'Awareness of separation immediately leads to feelings of dependence on an object and therefore to inevitable frustrations' (Rosenfeld, 1971, p. 172).
2. The aggressive attacks aim to destroy the frustrating object *because* it is perceived as bad by frustrating, obstructing, and denying gratification. The attacks are *not* on the goodness of the object.

> In states of frustration and anxiety the oral sadistic and cannibalistic desires are reinforced, and then the infant feels that he has taken in the nipple and the breast, in bits. Thus in addition to the division between one good and one bad breast in the young infant's phantasy, the frustrating breast – attacked in oral-sadistic phantasies – is felt to be in bits; while the gratifying breast, taken in under the dominance of the sucking libido, is felt to be complete.
>
> (Klein, 1946, p. 101)

Later, Klein (1957) elaborates that attacks stemming from frustration in relation to the object are less intensive and do not completely destroy it, so that a frustrating object may be perceived as good once it gives gratification, and the attacks usually stop once the frustration is overcome. 'Observations of babies show us something of these underlying unconscious attitudes. As I have said above, some infants who have been screaming

with rage appear quite happy soon after they begin to feed. This means that they have temporarily lost but regained their good object' (Klein, 1957, p. 186).
3. In relation to the ego, *the frustrated part of the self is repressed rather than split and there is a substitute formation.* Freud elaborates on symptom formation, 'I have only given you one piece of information about this: namely that people fall ill of a neurosis if they are deprived of the possibility of satisfying their libido – that they fall ill owing to "frustration", as I put it – and that their symptoms are precisely a substitute for their frustrated satisfaction' (Freud, 1917, p. 344). Frustration belongs to the neurotic spectrum of psychic phenomena, and the defence against frustration is more likely to be repression rather than splitting. As a result, the core of the ego is left intact. The self is less damaged and feels itself to be loving, not hating, and the ego is felt more alive and not annihilated.

On the other hand, the analysis of the theoretical conceptualisations on envy can be summarised as follows:

In envy

1. There is 'a destructive attack on the sources of life, on the *good* object, not on the bad object, and it is to be distinguished from ambivalence and frustration' (Hinshelwood, 1991, p. 167). In psychoanalytic terms, a good object can broadly be described as an object that is perceived as gratifying needs, promoting personal development, growth, and learning.
2. As a defence, the envied object is devalued or denigrated, since the subject feels belittled by its love for the good feeding object. 'The object which has been devalued need not be envied any more' (Klein, 1957, p. 217). Segal (1962) claims that 'devaluation, which defends against envy and expresses it, spoils all good experiences' (p. 213).
3. Another important defence is stirring envy in others and 'reversing the situation in which envy is experienced' (Klein, 1957, p. 218) and thus protecting the ego from its own envy. As envy is split off and projected on external objects, the self feels as if surrounded by envious objects (Spillius, 1993). This may lead, in extreme cases of projective identification, to merging with the object, and loss of identity and differentiation. The proliferation of envy obstructs the introjection of good objects and through splitting and projective identification may lead to serious ego depletion, manifested lack of energy, and indifference.

Based on the conceptual analysis, I have extracted the following observable minimum sets of criteria for differentiating frustration and envy.

Criteria for frustration

Criterion F 1. Observable aggressive attacks against frustrating objects, in other words objects obstructing gratification and perceived as bad, punishing, or frustrating. Unlike envy, the attack is on the *badness* of the object. Such attacks could be manifested as jealousy, feeling excluded, reluctance to participate, and withdrawal because of feelings of exasperation or fear of being criticised; rivalry, rebellion, or competitiveness.

Criterion F 2. Presence of substitute formations (substitute objects or sublimations) in relation to the repressed experiences. *Key discriminating criterion.*

Criterion F 3. Unlike envy, the emotion is still present – energy and liveliness in the interaction are palpable despite the negativity of the aggression. *Key discriminating criterion.*

Any of the above criteria will indicate occurrences of aggression stemming from frustration. A conjunction of two or more will be a strong indicator of frustration.

Criteria for envy

Criterion E 1. Aggressive attacks against objects perceived as helpful and caring; hostility against learning which is needed. Aggressive attacks against authority figures; for instance, in the context of educational settings, hostility against teachers, particularly when they are experienced as helpful. The attacks are carried out in the form of covert undermining or devaluing such helpful authority figures, for example, ridiculing what the teacher is offering, and spoiling the quality of teaching and learning, thus resulting in anti-learning or anti-understanding.

Criterion E 2. Lack of awareness about the emotional experience related to learning, so learning is neither accepted nor actively rejected, for example, detachment, or blankness of expression; wiping of mental contents, manifested lack of energy and stifling of emotions, atmosphere of flatness. *Criterion E 2 is a key discriminating criterion, particularly in conjunction with criterion E 1.*

Criterion E 3. Manifested lack of energy and stifling of emotions; atmosphere of deadness; lack of differentiation and/or ensuing lack of rivalry and competitiveness. *Key differentiating criterion.*

Any of the key discriminating criteria would suggest occurrences of envious attacks, but a particular conjunction of two or all three criteria will suggest strong evidence.

Comparative analysis using the operationalised criteria

Using the above operationalised criteria, the collected data were analysed for occurrences of two types of attacks, those stemming from frustration and those stemming from envy.

An adaptation of infant observation method (see Hinshelwood and Skogstad, 2000; Skogstad in Chapter 6, and Elfer in Chapter 7 in this book) was used for data collection, as its relative unobtrusiveness and regularity of observations within definite parameters allows for direct observations of subtle emotional processes developing in their ordinary environments (Urwin, 2007). During the data analysis phase of the study, the two concepts of envy and frustration were operationalised and two sets of criteria were used to pinpoint occurrences in the observational reports for the data analysis.

The weekly psychoanalytic observations were conducted in a higher education institution in the UK. I began the observations with a loose set of theoretical conceptions and refrained consciously from making theoretical conclusions during the observations. I wrote detailed process notes after each observation in the form of a narrative, using everyday language. It is important to point out that the observation, the data collection, and the data analysis were conducted in relatively separate stages.

Data analysis

The observation reports constituted the primary data for analysis. The data analysis began after the observations were completed to avoid premature reference to the theoretical elaborations and to remain open to the evolving experience. The extracts below are used for the analysis of the two mental states.

Feeling excluded

In Observation 5, the teacher organised the group in a familiar manner – the students worked collaboratively with neighbouring students in pairs on a learning task, often checking and comparing answers. This time the task was to do a short test together and discuss their answers. Susan (the teacher) divided the group in three. Two of the pairs were obviously quite happy with the arrangement, while the third one gave signs of annoyance.

> She [the teacher] rearranged them and asked Blanche and the French girl to work together, then the boy and the Austrian girl, together and then Dimitrina and the Polish girl. The atmosphere changed immediately, there was excitement and the first two pairs seemed quite happy with the new arrangement, particularly the Austrian girl and the boy. The third pair though seemed a bit reluctant. They started chatting with the teacher sitting in the middle and listening. The boy told a story to the Austrian, which was quite funny. He was explaining how he was running for the bus on the high street and then I did not hear very well and the Austrian girl and the teacher started laughing a lot. They obviously found it very funny.
>
> Then the teacher asked everyone to check their answers together. She went on to check in a familiar manner 1-b, 2-a. I still could not understand what the

nature of the exercise was. The teacher then asked 'What are the first two questions about?' One of the students said 'IQ. She asked, 'Do you know what IQ is?' They said, 'Yes'. 'Have you ever done such a test?' the teacher asked. Most said they have. The Romanian girl, Dimitrina, went on to say they had to take a similar test for a job in the USA or Romania and went on explaining in details of the test. It was to do with money and different banknotes in America and Romania. I could not understand what she was trying to explain. She was talking to the teacher. I looked around the group. The white girl was withdrawn and making slow movements with her legs crossed.

The Polish girl was looking at a point in the wall opposite and not listening.
....

The teacher then said the second part of the test was to do with EQ, which she went on, was emotional intelligence and asked for the correct answers. All but Dimitrina gave the correct answers. The teacher started explaining what emotional intelligence was and stopped and asked the boy to tell his story, which was quite funny, she added. He happily took the floor and told everyone how he was running for the bus, missed it, but went on running slowly because he wanted the people at the bus station to think he was just jogging. It was funny and everybody but the Polish girl laughed. She did not seem entertained a bit. Her face remained serious. I suddenly thought she was missing Michael. I noticed they were very close the previous time. She obviously did not like this boy. While he was talking, she rolled her eyes, it was as if, 'oh, no, not him again'.

Then the French girl said she had a similar funny story to tell and started explaining how she slipped and fell down but was still smiling although it hurt. While she was talking, the boy and the Austrian girl were talking so much that the teacher had to stop the French girl and made him (not them both) a remark that he was interfering and not listening. The French girl finished and the teacher also said she once fell and hurt herself badly, and tears were rolling down her cheek but she still tried to smile. There was an atmosphere of sharing and warmth. I looked around the group. The white girl was still looking distracted and withdrawn, her expression emotionless. I also did not feel any sympathy for the group members' misfortunes.

(Observation 5)

The above vignette plots a sequence of interactions in which, at the beginning, the students in two of the pairs are obviously quite keen on working with each other. They seem content with the teacher's instructions and the follow-up rearrangement. The third pair, however, is somewhat dissatisfied with the pairing. When one of the pairs gets involved in an enjoyable conversation with the teacher, the conversation seems to stir curiosity; my subjective feelings seem to confirm that as well because I also find myself wondering about the end of the story. At the same time, however, the engagement with the teacher seems to evoke different feelings in some of the other students. The interactions show various degrees of involvement with the teacher and learning – while some of the students, such as the one from Romania, seem quite engaged, others, such as Blanche and one of the students from Poland, show different reactions. They look quite disconnected from the conversation, the learning, and from the group and the teacher. Blanche looks rather detached and withdrawn, and the student from Poland looks as if she is studying a point in the wall. Her mind seems unaware of what is going on in the group. It could be that when students are not connected to the teacher, they emotionally leave the room and disengage. The sequence of interactions seems to indicate that the students in the group are witnessing the involvement of their peers with the teacher from a place where they might feel excluded, which might also transform the scene in their minds as bad or frustrating. Such phantasies of inclusion/exclusion seem to be confirmed by the story of the boy who runs after the bus but is left out. The story seems to represent a substitute for the repressed feelings of being excluded.

However, despite the feelings of detachment, the whole atmosphere in this vignette is livelier, students seem more connected to each other and learning, and this is reflected in their desire to link their stories. It seems that rivalry is sublimated here into a more productive competition and, in the context of learning, into a fruitful discussion despite the ensuing negativity.

The vignette also suggests that some students might feel envy of a good object – the learning, which is needed, or the teacher who is trying to help them and engage them in the process. For example, Blanche, who completely disconnects from the activity and her face goes blank. However, other students, such as the Polish girl, do not join the laughter and show annoyance with the boy's story, and although they do not engage, they retain their feelings; they look irritated. The vignette might therefore be good at illustrating the difference between the two types of aggressive attacks. With the first type of aggression, the emotion is absent which might suggest a splitting process, the student's face goes blank and emotionless, while with the second type of aggression, the emotion is present and the hostility and annoyance is visible – the girl rolls her eyes.

The interactions meet the following criteria for frustration.

Criterion F 1 – feeling excluded

The example suggests evidence for attacks due to feelings of exclusion. Rivalry and competition are observable – rivalry towards those included in the interactions with the teacher by those excluded.

Criterion F 2 – a substitute formation

The feelings of exclusion in this occurrence are represented symbolically by the story of the boy who runs after the bus but misses it. This is a very important differentiating criterion. Unlike envious attacks where the feelings are often split with frustration, the negativity is repressed and substituted.

Criterion F 3 – observable energy

There is palpable energy in the interactions – liveliness and engagement despite the negativity of feeling excluded. This is another important differentiating criterion.

To sum up, the vignette meets three of the criteria and suggests occurrences of aggressive attacks stemming from frustration.

The second extract below comes from the ninth observation (Observation 9).

Undermining the teacher

At the beginning of the class, the teacher expressed concern about one particular student, who was lightly dressed. The teacher was worried that the girl might be cold and made a somewhat motherly comment. This comment was taken by the group and the students made about people feeling warm and then they associated the idea of warmth with the feeling of being in love. The teacher seemed to be able to connect to the students as well as engage them in a lively conversation with each other. As I note in the process notes, the atmosphere felt to me quite 'playful'. The theme of play was reflected and somehow naturally led to the topic of the lesson related to sports and sports activities. The teacher asked the students to guess the names of different sports. There was a considerable degree of excitement in the room as the students were quite involved in finding out different sports. They were clearly enjoying the lesson, and there were excitement and observable energy as they were speaking in a lively manner and seemed engaged in the learning activity. As I point out in the observation notes, I found myself visualising girls 'jumping for the ball' and obviously competing for an award and perhaps for the attention of the teacher and her recognition.

The teacher then asked the students to work in small groups and match sports in their textbooks, when there seemed to be some attacks against her.

> The teacher was explaining some words related to sports equipment and the Austrian kept asking her as if disbelieving that that was the meaning. For a brief moment, I thought the teacher actually hesitated and was not sure about the word. Nevertheless she suggested a word, but then the Austrian girl opened the dictionary and started looking as if double checking the meaning of the word. Then the teacher was explaining vocabulary about football and the shin pads footballers wear and the next words were about 'guard', collocations with guard, and then the teacher said it was similar in boxing, what they put in their mouths. I am not sure if the teacher suggested the word or it was one of the students who asked her about it, but Susan [the teacher] suddenly said 'Oh, what was the word?' And she

could not remember. She was sitting in her chair, looked down for a few moments and could not remember the word. She said it was something to do with guard and added she would check it later. The Austrian started leafing through the dictionary.

She asked the girls then to read something in the books. The class was silent again. Susan went to the opposite corner and tried to log onto a computer. She then left it and walked back to the centre of the room. At this point, I finally caught her look and stood up slowly. She came to me and I whispered in her ear. 'It's very interesting here. Can I stay till 11.30?' She smiled and said 'Of course, yes.' I sat back.

Susan went back and sat in the middle and started asking the students again and checking answers. She then suddenly remembered the word 'chin shield' and jumped to write it on the whiteboard. Then she went on to discuss new words. Now Dimitrina asked her with a slightly disbelieving expression on her face. As if she did not believe that the teacher was right. Immaculate Maria was looking through the window now and then with blank eyes, and Rickey next to her remained throughout most of the time detached.

(Observation 9)

The vignette seems to indicate a series of aggressive attacks at the teacher who is trying to explain and feed in some new vocabulary and who seems caring about the students. It appears that her confidence is subtly undermined through a sequence of peculiar attacks which are covert and disguised as questioning – both verbal, questioning her, and non-verbal, manifested as looks of disbelief – with a rather ridiculing or doubtful quality. The student from Austria, who appears only with her nationality in the process notes, repeatedly questions her and does not seem to accept what the teacher has to offer – she dismisses the teacher's authority and decides to double check the meaning of the word in the dictionary. While, on the one hand, it might be argued that checking up words in the dictionary could be viewed as an attempt for independent learning in the context of the interactions and the obvious suspicion, it seems more that the student refuses to acknowledge the authority of the teacher. In other words, it seems that the looks of disbelief are aimed to weaken the teacher's authority. This seems to lead to the teacher's confidence being *undermined*, and in the next moment the teacher first hesitates about a word and then she cannot remember the word! Her mind seems to go blank. As a result of the peculiar questioning and lack of trust in what the teacher is offering, the word seems to be wiped out from the mind of the teacher. The student somewhat triumphantly returns to the dictionary and resumes looking up the word. She also seems to reverse the position of teacher and student to show superiority towards her. In the student's mind, the teacher's capacity to feed in new words seems to be destroyed.

In addition, my subjective experience seems also indicative of what is happening in the group. I clearly experience the situation as embarrassing and try to mobilise my efforts to encourage and support the teacher. My identification with the teacher might have been so painful that I perform a small act – stepping out of my role as an unobtrusive and non-interfering observer, I stand up and, by asking quietly to stay longer, I imply that what I find in the room is stimulating for learning. I emphasise that 'it's *very interesting*'. The act seems helpful and the teacher looks more able to integrate her fragmented mind, revive the links within it, and thinking seems repaired, so a little later she restores her capacity to think and remembers the word.

Attacks, however, do not seem to stop, and another student, Dimitrina, clearly shows with a look of suspicion that she *doubts* the teacher's capacity to explain new vocabulary even when the teacher is able to recall and provide the word. I also notice how at this point a third student, Maria, emotionally leaves the room – she looks absent-minded, her eyes are empty, watching something through the window. One more student, Rickey, seems to join her, she too seems to disconnect from the learning process and looks detached. Once the students perceive the teacher as a failure, it seems to reinforce their own incapacity to take in new words from her. Ultimately, they are unable to learn. The aggression seems to have a peculiar quality, and it looks as if the minds of the group members are being sliced and students get isolated within their minds.

Alternatively, it might be argued that the teacher is attacked and undermined because the students are experiencing some anxiety related to not knowing the new words; their attacks could be directed against the painfulness of not knowing. The interactions, however, indicate a lack of struggle and conflict. The teacher is not being confronted openly or asked with genuine curiosity for further explanations. Ideas are not debated or discussed. On the contrary, it seems here that the satisfaction to the students' questioning – in this case, the teacher managing to remember and provide the word – triggers more demands and disbelief, and the students quietly and subversively continue to look up words in the dictionary.

The vignette seems to meet the following criteria for envy.

Criterion E 1 – *attacks on a helpful authority figure*

The interactions in this vignette, both verbal and non-verbal, meet criteria E 1. The teacher clearly expresses concern about the students, she attempts to create a lively and engaging atmosphere at the beginning of the class and tries to teach new words and collocations, yet her efforts and confidence are being continuously undermined. Her authority seems to be withheld from the students, who now distrust her and feel that she is perhaps not a good enough teacher. There are observable looks of mistrust and disbelief at what the teacher is trying to teach or the knowledge she is trying to offer. The occurrence seems to fulfil criteria E 1.

Criterion E 2 – *wiping of mental contents*

The vignette clearly shows how the results of the verbal and non-verbal interactions affect the mind of the teacher and the links with its contents.

The looks of disbelief from the students seem to affect the teacher, and she suddenly forgets words in her own language! As a result of the subtle attacks, her mind seems destroyed and suddenly a word is deleted. The vignette fulfils criterion E 2, namely wiping of mental contents, and suggests the operation of projective identification aimed to disturb and dismantle the teacher's mind.

Criterion 3 – lack of energy

The vignette also fulfils criterion E 3. Throughout the class, the energy, which was quite palpable at the beginning of the lesson, seems to drain, and by the end of the session the work of the group has become somewhat sluggish as students have disconnected and emotionally left the room.

To sum up, the vignette has met three of the criteria for envious attacks, which is a strong indicator for occurrences of primary envy.

Conclusion

The research has a number of important contributions:

1. The research is important from a methodological perspective since it has demonstrated that a comparison of controversial and debatable psychoanalytic concepts based on operationalised criteria is possible.
2. It contributes to the understanding of envy and frustration as different concepts. The differentiation between the two psychic phenomena is an important contribution to psychoanalytic theory, in particular the debates about the death instinct, primary narcissism, and pathological organisations. The theoretical analysis has indicated differences between the two concepts which are also observable and can be differentiated by using the operationalised criteria in the analysis of the empirical data.
3. The study shows that manifestations of primary envy are observable not only in the clinical setting but also in ordinary life, that is to say, in extra-clinical settings.

References

Abram, J., and Hinshelwood, R. D. (2018), *The Clinical Paradigms of Melanie Klein and Donald Winnicott: Comparisons and Dialogues*. New York: Routledge.

Bion, W. R. (1959), Attacks on linking. *International Journal of Psycho-Analysis*, 40: 308–315.

Bion, W. R. (1962a), The psycho-analytic study of thinking. *International Journal of Psycho-Analysis*, 43: 306–310.

Bion, W. R. (1962b), *Learning from Experience*. London: Maresfield Library.

Bion, W. R. (2005), *The Italian Seminars*. London: Karnac.

Britton, R. (1989), The missing link: parental sexuality in the Oedipus complex. In R. Britton, M. Feldman, and E. O'Shaugnessy (eds.), *The Oedipus Complex Today: Clinical Implications* (pp. 1–150). London: Karnac Books.

Britton, R. (2008). He thinks himself impaired: the pathologically envious personality. In P. Roth and A. Lemma (eds.), *Envy and Gratitude Revisited*. London: Karnac.

Feldman, M. (2008), Envy and the negative therapeutic reaction. In P. Roth and L. Alessandra (eds.), *Envy and Gratitude Revisited*. London: Karnac.

Freud, S. (1917), Introductory lectures on psycho-analysis. *The Standard Edition of the Complete Psychological Works of Sigmund Freud*, Volume 16: 241–463. London: Hogarth.

Hinshelwood, R. D. (1991), *A Dictionary of Kleinian Thought*, 2nd edn. London: Free Association Books.

Hinshelwood, R. D. (2008), Repression and splitting: towards a method of conceptual comparison. *International Journal of Psycho-Analysis*, 89: 503–505.

Hinshelwood, R. D., and Skogstad, W. (2000), *Observing Organisations: Anxiety, Defence and Culture in Health Care*. Hove and New York: Brunner-Routledge.

Joffe, W. (1969), A critical review of the status of the envy concept. *International Journal of Psycho-Analysis*, 50: 533–545.

Joseph, B. (1986), Envy in everyday life. *Psychoanalytic Psychotherapy*, 2: 13–22.

Kernberg, O. (1980), *The Internal World and External Reality*. New York: Jason Aronson.

Klein, M. (1946), Notes on some schizoid mechanisms. *International Journal of Psycho-Analysis*, 27: 99–110.

Klein, M. (1957), Envy and gratitude. In *Envy and Gratitude, and Other Works, 1946–1963* (pp. 176–236). London: Hogarth Press.

Ogden, T. (1979), On projective identification. *Internationa Journal of Psycho-Analysis*, 60: 357–373.

Ogden, T. (1986), *The Matrix and the Mind: Object Relations and the Psychoanalytic Dialogue*. London: Karnac.

Polmear, C. (2008), An independent response to envy and gratitude. In P. Roth and A. Lemma (eds.), *Envy and Gratitude Revisited*. London: Karnac.

Racker, H. (1960), A study of some early conflicts through their return in the patient's relation with the interpretation. *International Journal of Psycho-Analysis*, 41: 47–58.

Rosenfeld, H. (1971), A clinical approach to the psychoanalytic theory of the life and death instincts: an investigation into the aggressive aspects of narcissism. *International Journal of Psycho-Analysis*, 52: 169–178.

Roth, P., and Lemma, A. (2008), *Envy and Gratitude Revisited*. London: Karnac.

Segal, H. (1962), The curative factors in psycho-analysis. *International Journal of Psycho-Analysis*, 43: 212–217.

Segal, H. (1993), On the clinical usefulness of the concept of death instinct. *International Journal of Psycho-Analysis*, 74: 55–61.

Segal, H. (1998), The importance of symbol-formation in the development of the ego – in context. *Journal of Child Psychotherapy*, 24: 349–357.

Spillius, E. (1993), Varieties of envious experience. *International Journal of Psycho-Analysis*, 74: 1199–1212.

Steiner, J. (2008), The repetition compulsion, envy and the death instinct. In A. Lemma and P. Roth (eds.), *Envy and Gratitude Revisited*. London: Karnac.

Thomä, H., and Kächele, H. (2007), Comparative psychoanalysis on the basis form of treatment report. *Psychoanalytic Enquiry*, 27(5): 650–689.

Tuckett, D. (2008), *Psychoanalysis Comparable and Incomparable: The Evolution of a Method to Describe and Compare Psychoanalytic Approaches*. Hove and New York: Routledge.

Urwin, C. (2007), Doing infant observation differently? Researching the formation of mothering identities in an inner London borough. *Infant Observation: International Journal of Infant Observation and its Applications*, 10(3): 239–251.

Vonofakos, D. (2009), Differentiating anxiety, defence and work-related functioning in the psychodynamics of social systems: observing the unconscious cultures of psychiatric organisations. University of Essex, unpublished PhD thesis.

Winnicott, D. (1959), Melanie Klein: on her concept of envy. In C. Winnicott, R. Shepherd, and M. Davis (eds.), *Psycho-Analytic Explorations*. London: Karnac, 1989.

Narrative analysis

Chapter 11

Psychoanalysis in narrative research

Lisa Saville Young and Stephen Frosh

Introduction

With the growing awareness during the 1990s and 2000s in the social sciences of the value of qualitative research – an awareness that had long been evident in anthropology but absent in most other areas – psychoanalysis became more available as a reference point both for theory and for the methodology of research practice. This can be seen in such diverse fields as politics (Austed, 2012), geography (Kingsbury, 2007), and even computer science (Turkle, 2004); but more relevantly in qualitative and discursive psychology (Hollway and Jefferson, 2013), psychoanalytic sociology (Roseneil, 2006), and psychosocial studies (Frosh, 2010). The interest in psychoanalysis was helped by an initial 'turn' to language, reflected in the growth of discourse and narrative analysis as methodological approaches in psychology (Potter and Wetherell, 1987; Riesmann, 2008), and more recently in the 'affective turn' (Blackman and Venn, 2010). Whilst much work in these areas has actually been ambivalent about psychoanalysis (Wetherell, 2012, for example, is markedly critical and much of 'affect theory' is Deleuzian), there has been considerable interest in how psychoanalysis might offer concepts and approaches that thicken out notions of the subject that appear in such work, and also in how the practices of psychoanalytic interpretation might interleave with those of qualitative research. In this chapter, we explore the employment of psychoanalytic ideas in one important area of social research, narrative research, beginning with a discussion of the continuities between psychoanalytic thinking and the narrative turn, briefly reviewing selected work that has drawn on both these paradigms. We emphasise the way in which psychoanalysis provides conceptual and methodological tools for reinserting the focus on subjectivity, and in particular the affective dimensions of subjectivity, in the narrative domain. In the second part of the chapter, we provide a worked example of how psychoanalysis might be employed alongside a critical narrative focus to analyse an interview extract. In doing so, we hope to demonstrate, in an empirically grounded way, that bringing psychoanalysis into the frame alongside narrative work allows for the emergence of nuanced understanding and interpretation, while at the same time 'interrupting' – that is, offering a reflexive space for – the research project itself.

Psychoanalysis and narrative research: form, performance, and context

For the purposes of this chapter, narrative research is positioned as research that is based on social constructionist assumptions and therefore engages with talk or text not as representative of reality but rather as constructed by and constructive of the social and historical context. From this perspective, narrative research is less interested in reading text for what it says about mental states or cognitive processes, than in the social and personal realities that are constructed through talk, and in how these constructions shift and change both temporally and contextually.

There are various ways in which narrative researchers have approached this concern with what people *do* with words. One way is through analysing the form (the saying) alongside the content (the said) of narratives, investigating the grammatical structure and rhythm of a story with the view that it is as much of a construction as, and in that respect lends an additional range of 'meanings' to, the content of the story. Gee (1991) argues that the linguistic structure of a story provides us with information about how the teller wants his or her story to be heard. Narrative work of this kind interrogates form in order to find central and recurrent storylines. Especially where the form of a narrative has not been constrained by a structured questioning or interview technique – that is, where there is some approximation to the 'free association' that Freud (1912) claimed as the 'fundamental rule' of psychoanalysis – the idea that the manner in which something is expressed will be revelatory of its significance to the speaker has a number of parallels with psychoanalytic approaches. In particular, it suggests a path towards 'reading' the speaker as more than what she or he consciously intends to say; that is, the form of a narrative is often taken to embody pressure points at which 'unintended' (or unconsciously intended) messages are expressed. In contrast, therefore, to the traditional research emphasis on what is dominant in the structure of the narrative (reflected in thematic and discursive modes of analysis), a psychoanalytic reading is specifically attuned to breakdowns in narrative form – moments that are marginal, isolated, and contradictory, based on the understanding that affect is disruptive (Nobus and Quinn, 2005). Emerson and Frosh (2004) demonstrate the usefulness of this emphasis on form in their critical narrative analysis of interviews with boys: close analysis of the 'structural' features of texts (breaks, pauses, and other 'breaches' in smooth sense-making) shows them to have emotional resonance that contribute to a rounded understanding of speakers' narratives, allowing a set of 'bottom-up' interpretive moves that avoid some of the heavy-handedness that can come with a 'top-down' theoretical psychoanalytic reading. Moreover, a psychoanalytic emphasis on the form or structure of people's talk draws attention to the ways in which language 'uses' us, limiting what we can and cannot say (hence narrative's breaches or tendency to 'burst at the seams') – an emphasis that is congruent with Lacanian psychoanalysis and has been claimed as a 'method' of Lacanian discourse analysis (Parker, 2010).

Another way narrative researchers have analysed narratives is by paying attention to the *performative* aspects of the text for the interaction it constructs between the interviewer and the interviewee, for the social actions that it accomplishes, and for how this reflects the cultural and political context in which it is spoken (see Riessman, 2003, for example). Embedded in this is an understanding of reflexivity that links the psychosocial approach to narrative (as subjects speak, so they constitute themselves relationally) with the psychoanalytic approach to intersubjectivity. The latter tends to be codified in the language of transference and countertransference, with the various meanings of these terms in psychoanalysis' different schools (Frosh, 2012); but what is shared is the understanding that psychoanalytic discourse is relational discourse: it affects, and can only be understood within, a specific relational context, usually the peculiar one of the analyst and patient in the clinical consulting room. Psychoanalytic approaches to narrative have extended this into the research domain by understanding the relationship that develops with the research participant and/or with the analysed text as one that is reflexive in this same, 'clinical' way. Specifically, psychoanalytically inflected research of this kind emphasises the interview as an intersubjective encounter. Hollway (2010), for example, in her work on first-time mothering, in this case by a mother called Justine, writes:

> Elements belonging to Justine's relationships with her mother are unconsciously transferred to the interview, which therefore holds meanings in excess of what the relationship with the interviewer would otherwise produce.
> (p. 145)

Here, the performance is read for what it tells us about Justine's typical way of relating to others, based on her most significant relationship (with her mother). Hollway suggests that her performance in this particular research context is indicative of a way of being in the world that might tell us something about the emotional function of her narrative – the story she tells to this particular listener (the researcher) meets particular intersubjective needs. While the use of notions of transference and countertransference in this way has been critiqued for suggesting that they can be transferred relatively unproblematically from clinic to research environment, despite the radical differences of context (for example, that the research interview is commonly a once-off event, not allowing for the kinds of relational development that underpin clinical transference), and also for presenting an image of an 'expert' researcher who is somehow more able to 'look past' his or her own unconscious (Frosh and Baraitser, 2008), it nevertheless stages two important psychoanalytic notions. Firstly, the conceptualisation of the other as always implicated in subjectivity (Laplanche, 1997); and secondly, an emphasis on knowing (though never fully) through emotional structures with which we experience ourselves and others (Davies, 2011).

A further way that narrative researchers have analysed narratives is through consideration of the socio-cultural context in which the story is told and the ways in which the narrator resists or engages with dominant discourses of the social context. Here, the notion of 'positioning' has been employed in narrative work, disrupting the idea that pre-existing roles and grammar shape forms of talk in deterministic ways, and rather foregrounding language as always coming into being through interaction (Davies and Harré, 1990). From this perspective, our own subjective histories intersect with the narrative forms with which we are most familiar (the dominant discourses) constructing particular subject positions for others and ourselves. The emphasis here is on the individual agency of participants who 'accept, negotiate, challenge, or even actively resist the positioning provided for them by dominant discursive forms' (Andrews et al., 2000, p. 194), emphasising a crucial inter-relationship between self and society. Psychoanalytic approaches have similarly and explicitly aimed to reinsert subjective agency into what has been referred to as the 'empty subjectivity' (Gough, 2004, p. 247) of discursive work; as Wetherell (2012, p. 128) comments (prior to offering a critique of what she terms 'social psychoanalysis'): psychoanalysis 'suggests that who performs affect, and their particular history, matters, and offers ways to think about this mattering'. However, a psychoanalytic view of agency is of a different kind to that conceptualised for narrative subjectivity. In particular, it is an agency that is fuelled by mental states and affects that are not immediately visible in texts, and it is an agency that is dynamic in its resistance to being known. In addition, in response to critiques that have pointed to the individualistic and reductionist tendencies of the psychoanalytic emphasis on the personal unconscious, recent work has conceptualised this agency as produced not solely within individuals but in interpersonal contexts *and* societal contexts. With regard to the latter, the concept of a social unconscious is particularly useful in referring to:

> the existence and constraints of social, cultural and communicational arrangements of which people are unaware. Unaware, in so far as these arrangements are not perceived (not 'known'), and if perceived not acknowledged ('denied'), and if acknowledged, not taken as problematic ('given'), and if taken as problematic, not considered with an optimal degree of detachment and objectivity.
>
> (Hopper, cited in Weinberg, 2007, p. 311)

Employing this notion, Saville Young and Jearey-Graham (2015), for example, read into the analysis of narratives the traces of disavowals in the socio-historical context that are played out in the interpersonal situation that mediates meaning-making. Such a psychoanalytic approach, rather than viewing the unconscious as individual in operation, deploys the notion of the unconscious in ways that perceive it as socially produced.

Employing psychoanalysis responsively

We have been arguing that psychoanalysis and narrative work have significant continuities that make a rapprochement productive, particularly in relation to their shared emphasis on looking beyond the content of what is said to include the form, the performance, and the context of narratives. Yet, psychoanalysis is not a unified field, and researchers have not always agreed on the purpose of utilising psychoanalysis. Those drawing on the work of Kleinian theorists, or taking a specifically object relations approach, aim to build a nuanced interpretative 'model' of participants' talk (see Hollway and Jefferson, 2005, 2013), recognising the shared meanings that participants draw on as a function of their social context and their biographical maps, such that these shared meanings perform particular psychic functions. The risk here is splitting the social from the psychological, and conducting the reading from the 'inside out', thereby prioritising the internal world (Wetherell, 2012). The social then becomes a space onto which internal functions are projected, but with relatively little 'agency' of its own. In addition, as the interpretation of psychic functions has sometimes been done in a manner that suggests that researchers know participants better than they know themselves, there is always a risk of a pathologising emphasis creeping in (Frosh and Baraitser, 2008). Those researchers drawing on Lacanian ideas have emphasised 'interruption' rather than 'interpretation' of meanings, with psychoanalysis under deconstruction such that it is itself interrogated for how it structures readings and for what it leaves outside of the frame. In Lacanian-influenced work, however, psychoanalysis has sometimes been reduced to the production of knowledge about the process of conducting research, emphasising the limits of what can be said about phenomena without psychoanalysis imposing its own particular meaning system (see Saville Young, 2013). This may be salutary, but it does not always fulfil the intentions of research projects aiming to 'find something out'.

In this chapter, we advocate an integrated use of psychoanalysis in narrative research, one that argues for the usefulness of interpretation alongside interruption, in other words, viewing psychoanalysis as useful in narrative work for its theoretical richness in relation to intersubjectivity and affective encounters, as well as for its insistence that there is always something that resists being known within, between, and around subjects. Thus, while psychoanalysis reclaims the agency that discursive work has been criticised for losing, it is an agency that does not reflect a 'choosing subject'. Rather, our unconscious or our defended and yet structuring emotional life is simultaneously expressed and never fully known. It is also not an emotional life that is located 'in' individuals, but it is in process between (interpersonal) and around (societal) subjectivities in relation to one another. Employing psychoanalysis in this way is responsive to what Butler (2005) describes as our constitution in relationality, 'implicated, beholden, derived, sustained by a social world that is beyond us and before us' (p. 64). As such, it is also responsive to accepting the limits of knowability in ourselves and others, even as we employ psychoanalysis. Psychoanalytic work in narrative research is therefore understood as always 'in fragments'.

Below, we demonstrate in outline a particular psychoanalytic approach to narrative work by analysing an extract from an interview conducted by Lisa (a white, English-speaking academic in her thirties) as part of a broader study carried out in the Eastern Cape of South Africa on men's narratives of their relationships with their brothers. The men interviewed for the study were labourers, all of them having grown up in a semi-urban part of South Africa during apartheid. Lonwabo (a pseudonym) is a black, Xhosa-speaking man in his thirties who left school at the age of 16 years after his girlfriend fell pregnant with their first child. He describes being unemployed for many years after leaving school, reflecting the particularly high unemployment levels in the part of South Africa he is from. At the time of the interview, he had worked as a labourer for four years. The extract focuses on the beginning of the second interview where Lonwabo describes being prompted by the first research interview to visit his brother in prison. This brother had been jailed for murder and Lonwabo, in the first interview, described his anger and disappointment with him, to the extent that he had not visited him since his incarceration 13 years previously.

Extract

```
1   INTERVIEWER: There we go. So it's our second interview, and I wonder if you've had any
2                thoughts since we last met, Lonwabo?
3   LONWABO:     Hmm, if I tell you my dear, I was thinking after I talked to you, I was thinking to
4                myself, 'No, I must go to my brother in prison.' I go there, he is there at [prison name],
5                ay we meet, we talk, I explain what is my problem to him, then we try each other, just go
6                down and talk, and talk, and talk until I ask him 'Do you want to be a person or do you
7                want to be somebody just in and out in the street?' I just, 'no I want to change myself.'
8                I say 'okay you can change yourself, if you want to change yourself it is good, yeah. I
9                saw somebody carrying some books what about you?' He said, no he's doing standard
10               one. I was surprised because he didn't go to school at all. He said to me he's doing
11               standard one now. I said 'Yow that's number one.' Then I ask another prison warder,
12               'Are those books for prison warders?' He said, 'Listen about him', he said 'no, he's
13               a good man now, he's changed. He knows about, what you call, plumbing.' Said 'Yow,
14               good he's coming, he's coming, yes he's coming.' Even if a guard knows it,
15               something's changed from him. And I said thank you to you, just to talk to me then, and
16               to explain what my problem is. I think, I'm just praying, if you want to change you can
17               change, you can change it. And then there's another guy that's a prison warder there,
18               he's a preacher and he said they do something to the church, he's going there, he's a,
19               I'm glad, you know I'm glad and I want to thank you first.
20  I:           Oh why, why?
21  L:           You gave me something.
22  I:           That made you think about it
```

23	L:	Yah made me think about first because I, I, that time I never ever talked to him, I was
24		angry with him, I just put him away from me, that's something you gave me, I changed.
25	I:	What made you think, what made you think 'oh I must go visit him,' what was it, because
26		it wasn't something, I mean I didn't tell you to?
27	L:	Yah it's that question you asked when, oh about us, about my family, said we are three,
28		there's a one chair, our community. If I forget about my brother, who's going to make
29		him happy one day, or when he dies, who's going to, what you call it, to bury him? It's
30		me, it's only me who's big at home. My sister is there you see, no, no I must go, I must
31		go and see him and talk to him. We talked to each other seriously, we talked.
32	I:	Was it difficult for you?
33	L:	It was difficult at first, it was difficult, it was very, very difficult.
34	I:	Why, were you, why was it?
35	L:	I was angry, I was angry, seriously I was angry. Talking about it, ha it's not good, it's not
36		good, seriously, but when I met you, you asking about my family then I keep on thinking
37		about God, God knows, I must go and talk to him. I did, I did.
38	I:	And so how do you feel now that you've been?
39	L:	I'm, I'm trying to take these things out, I was thinking about him, you know, I'm trying,
40		but I promised myself 'no he's going to change' maybe I will be not angry with him, you
41		see, I don't know. But that, that after that talk about that staff told me that he's
42		changed, he's doing, he's coming like a human being, said thank you, thank you, thank
43		you.

Our approach to this extract is to conduct multiple readings with an emphasis on conceptualising the text as meaningful for a) *what* it is saying (content) and for b) *how* it is said (process), generating both narrative and psychoanalytic understandings. In relation to process, the reading focuses respectively on i) the form or structure of the text including its linguistic style; ii) the performance of the text in a particular interpersonal context; and iii) the ventriloquation of the socio-historical context in the text. The emphasis throughout is on what language fails to symbolise, to 'the space between what can be said and what cannot' (Frosh, 1997, p. 174), including the language of the interpretation we are making.

At the level of content, Lonwabo narrates a story of change, both in his imprisoned brother and in himself. The story describes a change in his brother, moving from 'somebody just in and out in the street' (l.7) to a 'person' (l.6) or a 'good man' (l.13) through the valuing of education and religious faith. The story also describes a change in Lonwabo's feelings towards his brother, moving from anger to potential forgiveness, initiated through talking about his thoughts and feelings in the interview with Lisa and in jail with his brother, as well as prompted by a sense of allegiance to cultural values ('who's going to... bury him', l.29). At the level of content, Lonwabo's story is also one of gratitude towards Lisa for prompting him to undergo this change.

Moving to the level of process and looking firstly at the structure of the narrative, the extract begins with Lisa inviting Lonwabo to share his thoughts (l.1–2), leading to a long uninterrupted narrative where Lonwabo describes visiting his brother in prison, addressing 'my problem' (l.5), talking, listening, and noticing a change in his brother. This event is narrated as significant in terms of Lonwabo's relationship with Lisa by its introduction with 'If I tell you my dear' (l.3) and conclusion with 'I want to thank you first' (l.19). This structure invites the reader to view this event as a 'revelation' such that Lonwabo has achieved something surprising which is in turn attributed to Lisa. There is then some negotiation around this attribution, with short interactions between the participant and the interviewer where we note a linguistic shift in the description of Lisa's role in the narrative of events from Lisa giving him something (l. 21) to Lisa asking questions (l.27). The narrative then moves to describing a difficulty for Lonwabo, specifically angry feelings towards his brother which he is trying to 'take...out' (l.39), made easier by the change he sees in his brother. This structure follows a pattern of the introduction of a complication followed by a resolution of this complication, both in lines 1–19 and again in lines 35–43. In the midst of this is an evaluative section, specifically a negotiation of evaluation between the speaker/Lonwabo and the audience/Lisa (l. 20–31) – an attempt to understand these resolutions ('why?', l.20). Arguably, this evaluation is not necessarily prominent in its meaning within the text; certainly, the description of the content of the story above did not even include this aspect of the text. Nevertheless, we argue that it is, in particular, this marginal moment that provides clues about what remains hidden and yet structuring of the narrative.

Secondly, attending to the performance of the text draws attention to this active negotiation of meaning in the middle of the extract specifically in relation to the interview/er's role in the unfolding of events. What does this performance say about the meaning of the story? Tracking the interaction, Lonwabo describes Lisa as giving him something (l.24) and Lisa resists this construction, specifically denying instructing Lonwabo to visit his brother ('I mean, I didn't tell you to', l.26). Lonwabo then seems to retract this placing of direct responsibility on Lisa and provides a rationale for his visit, linking it to his role in the family as the oldest brother and his sense of obligation to his brother based on cultural values (l. 28–9). The extract ends with a return to the gratitude of the early part of the exchange (l. 42), although this time the gratefulness is non-specific: it could be directed towards Lisa or towards God, the prison warders or staff (l. 41), or even towards his brother.

Paying attention to the feelings evoked by this interaction in the interviewer gives us further insight into this performance. Lisa recalls having two very different emotions around this exchange and cycling alternately from one to the other. Firstly, she remembers experiencing intense anxiety at the idea that the research interview had made an impact in Lonwabo's 'real life', as if it/she was not being ethical in doing so. Secondly, she recalls feeling immensely proud of the research interview's/her ability to bring about significant transformations in perspectives and relationships, as if the interview/she was indeed solely responsible for the events. There is thus an ambivalence towards her agency in the research relationship alternating between a defensive desire to repudiate any responsibility and a narcissistic impulse to take ownership of Lonwabo's experiences.

Considering how the socio-cultural context is both spoken and unspoken in the text may shed further light on the meaning of the affective encounter described above and the ways in which the particular structure of the text both reveals and conceals meaning. Exploring the shared meanings that Lonwabo draws on in the extract, we can read traces of a dominant discourse of morality that he employs throughout his interview in order to describe living a 'good' life, like a 'good' man. He draws on this discourse in commenting that his brother is '(be)coming like a human being' (l. 42), like a 'good man' (l. 13). A second discourse traced in the extract is one of rationality, upholding humans as thinking and learning beings who are able to verbalise their thoughts, talk through any difficulties, and influence others – the words 'thinking' and 'talking' are repeatedly employed throughout the extract. Given the specific context of South Africa, with its highly salient racist history and its powerful racialisation of contemporary society, it is also reasonable to hear in these two ideologically laden discourses echoes of colonialism, which aimed to transform the primitive/bad into the civilised/good through the primacy of masculine 'reason' (Frosh, 2013). From this perspective, in the encounter we can trace in the text a colonising process that is rooted in racist paradigms: the story is one of how two black men change their 'primitive' and 'unreasonable' ways under a magnanimous white gaze.

Returning to the analysis of the performance and the affect evoked within Lisa during the encounter, we might see both the resistance (defensive desire) and enjoyment (narcissistic impulse) of the coloniser position as two distinct states of mind that reflect the psychic configurations that support the colonising process read out above. Significantly, neither state of mind allows for thinking about the other as subject, but rather the other is an object to defensively reject or narcissistically claim in a move to bolster individual agentic control. In the text itself, Lonwabo might be understood as similarly resisting being constructed as the speaker/subject even while being interviewed; rather, he attributes a considerable portion of the agentic impulse in his narrative to Lisa, to whom he listened while she identified his problem or asked him a question. He takes on the position of the object of enquiry, feeding into the colonising process of othering. It is possible here too to understand these psychic configurations as being partly his response to the murderousness of his brother. Throughout the text, the emphasis is very much on change being from within ('change yourself', l.8), such that his brother's murderousness is located 'inside' and not in the violently oppressive context in which both he and his brother grew up. Placing this murderousness within his brother, emphasising inner life over social context, in some ways relieves Lonwabo of being potentially subject to the same kinds of hatred that his brother enacted through murder – it is his brother that is primitive and not him. However, this othering of his brother through a suppression of the contribution of social context is an echo of the colonialist discourse that maintains his own oppression.

We are arguing here that both Lisa and Lonwabo are 'in love with the lie' of colonialism (see Frosh, 2013), re-enacted in the text and held on to through an emphasis on the singular agentic self, for to be open to the influence of the other and to recognise the interpenetration of this other in our lives, is to face the otherness within us. A further significant social feature of this material, lying outside the discourses of morality and rationality that so strongly constitute this text, are the sociopolitical processes that fuel Lonwabo's own personal story of bettering himself in a context of high unemployment and Lisa's desire to produce research, an increasingly valuable commodity in university settings. These individualising processes reassert the concept of a singular self and belie the ways in which our narratives are always built on the social other. Finally, it is worth noting that psychoanalysis itself, even as it is employed reflexively in the interpretation above, is arguably rooted in a colonial mentality where rationality is valued and primitive impulses are repudiated (Frosh, 2013). In other words, the interpretation has a tendency to reify logical argument which has now made sense of the given text. In doing so, it elides the way in which only one participant reflected in the extract is giving her contribution to the analysis. Lonwabo continues to be spoken for.

Conclusion

This chapter has presented some of the context for the dialogue between psychoanalysis and narrative analysis, and has offered an example of a piece of psychoanalytically inflected narrative work. We have tried to show that psychoanalysis can 'thicken' narrative analytic accounts of interview material by directing attention to affective elements in that material, and that it can also work along 'the line of the Symbolic' (Parker, 2005, p. 177) to make the research enterprise itself subject to reflexive critique. This means that psychoanalytic narrative work does not have to be individualising or psychologising; indeed, we have tried to show that opening up texts in this way can lead quite far afield to interrogations of interpersonal, intersubjective, and social processes – not always comfortable ones. This does not fully remedy some specific difficulties produced by the psychoanalytic mind-set (most of which are not actually unique to psychoanalysis): for example, a set of rationalist assumptions that are politically narrower than they might seem; a faith in expertise that reproduces 'top-down', alienating discourses familiar from much traditional social science; and a constant pull back towards colonialist impulses in both the form and content of the work. Nevertheless, our claim is that the kind of psychoanalysis that we are advocating here – a 'deconstructing' rather than integrating one (Frosh and Baraitser, 2008) – contributes considerably to a wider psychosocial project of developing theories and methods that can encompass both 'inner' states of mind and the social process with which they are continuously and irrevocably entwined.

References

Andrews, M., Day Sclater, S., Squire, C., and Treacher, A. (eds.) (2000), *Lines of Narrative: Psychosocial Perspectives*. London: Routledge.

Austed, L. (ed.) (2012), *Psychoanalysis and Politics*. London: Karnac.

Blackman, L., and Venn, C. (eds.) (2010), Special Issue: Affect. *Body and Society*, 16(1).

Butler, J. (2005), *Giving an Account of Oneself*. New York: Fordham University Press.

Davies, B., and Harré, R. (1990), Positioning: the discursive production of selves. *Journal for the Theory of Social Behaviour*, 20: 43–63.

Davies, J. E. (2011), Cultural dimensions of intersubjectivity: negotiating 'sameness' and 'otherness' in the analytic relationship. *Psychoanalytic Psychology*, 28(4): 549–559.

Emerson, P., and Frosh, S. (2004), *Critical Narrative Analysis in Psychology: A Guide to Practice*. London: Palgrave.

Freud, S. (1912). The dynamics of transference. *The Standard Edition of the Complete Psychological Works of Sigmund Freud*, Volume XII: *The Case of Schreber, Papers on Technique, and Other Works*: 97–108. London: Hogarth.

Frosh, S. (1997), *For and Against Psychoanalysis*. London: Routledge.

Frosh, S. (2010), *Psychoanalysis Outside the Clinic*. London: Palgrave.

Frosh, S. (2012), *A Brief Introduction to Psychoanalytic Theory*. London: Palgrave.

Frosh, S. (2013), Psychoanalysis, colonialism, racism. *Journal of Theoretical and Philosophical Psychology*, 33(3): 141–154.

Frosh, S., and Baraitser, L. (2008), Psychoanalysis and psychosocial studies. *Psychoanalysis, Culture and Society*, 13: 346–365.

Gee, J. P. (1991), A linguistic approach to narrative. *Journal of Narrative and Life History*, 1(1): 15–39.

Gough, B. (2004), Psychoanalysis as a resource for understanding emotional ruptures in the text: the case of defensive masculinities. *British Journal of Social Psychology*, 43: 245–267.

Hollway, W. (2010), Conflict in the transitions to becoming a mother: a psycho-social approach. *Psychoanalysis, Culture and Society*, 15: 136–155.

Hollway, W., and Jefferson, T. (2005), Panic and perjury: a psychosocial exploration of agency. *British Journal of Social Psychology*, 44: 147–163.

Hollway, W., and Jefferson, T. (2013), *Doing Qualitative Research Differently* (second edition). London: Sage.

Kingsbury, P. (2007), Psychoanalytic approaches. In J. Duncan, N. Johnson, and R. Schein (eds.), *A Companion to Cultural Geography*. Oxford: Blackwell.

Laplanche, J. (1997), The theory of seduction and the problem of the other. *International Journal of Psycho-Analysis*, 78: 653–666.

Nobus, D., and Quinn, M. (2005), *Knowing Nothing, Staying Stupid: Elements for a Psychoanalytic Epistemology*. London: Routledge.

Parker, I. (2005), Lacanian discourse analysis in psychology: seven theoretical elements. *Theory and Psychology*, 15: 163–182.

Parker, I. (2010), Psychosocial studies: Lacanian discourse analysis negotiating interview text. *Psychoanalysis, Culture and Society*, 15(2): 156–172.

Potter, J., and Wetherell, M. (1987), *Discourse and Social Psychology*. London: Sage.

Riessman, C. (2003), Performing identities in illness narratives: masculinity and multiple sclerosis. *Qualitative Research*, 31(1),5–33.

Riessman, C. (2008), *Narrative Methods for the Human Sciences*. London: Sage.

Roseneil, S. (2006), The ambivalences of Angel's 'arrangement': a psycho-social lens on the contemporary condition of personal life. *The Sociological Review*, 54(4): 846–868.

Saville Young, L. (2014), Becoming other to oneself: misreading the researcher through Lacanian discourse analysis. In I. Parker and D. Pavon-Cuellar (eds.), *Lacan, Discourse, Event: New Psychoanalytic Approaches to Textual Indeterminacy* (pp. 279–290). London: Routledge.

Saville Young, L., and Jearey-Graham, N. (2015), 'They're gonna come and corrupt our children': a psychosocial reading of South African xenophobia. *Psychoanalysis, Culture and Society*, 20(4): 395–413.

Turkle, S. (2004), Whither psychoanalysis in computer culture? *Psychoanalytic Psychology*, 21(1): 16–30.

Weinberg, H. (2007), So, what is this social unconscious anyway? *Group Analysis*, 40: 307–322.

Wetherell, M. (2012), *Affect and Emotion: A New Social Science Understanding*. London: Sage.

Chapter 12

Researching dated, situated, defended, and deciding/evolving subjectivities by biographic-narrative interview[1]

Psychoanalysis, the psycho-societal unconscious, and biographic-narrative interview method and interpretation[2]

Tom Wengraf

Introduction

I use the loose concept of the 'psycho-societal unconscious' deriving from the 'social unconscious' of Hopper in 2003:

> the concept of the social unconscious refers to the existence and constraints of social, cultural and communications arrangements of which people are unaware – unaware, insofar as these arrangements are not perceived (not 'known') and, if perceived, not acknowledged ('denied') and, if acknowledged, not taken as problematic ('given'), and, if taken as problematic, not considered with an optimal degree of detachment and objectivity.
> (Earl Hopper, 2003, p. 11, cited in Saville Young and Kearney-Graham, 2015, p. 406)

The personal dynamically repressed 'unconscious' (the Freudian 'unconscious') may be seen as embedded within Hopper's rather weak formulation 'not perceived (not "known")'.

Roy Bhaskar, the founder of critical realism, declared that the accounts of actors form the starting point:

> In contrast to the hermeneutical perspective... actors' accounts [and deliberations] are both corrigible and limited by the existence of unacknowledged conditions, unintended consequences, tacit skills *and unconscious motivations*; but, in opposition to the positivist view, actors' account for the indispensable starting point of social enquiry.
> (Bhaskar, 1998, p. xvi; italics and materials in square brackets added TW; cited in Wengraf with Chamberlayne, 2013, pp. 63–64)

Contra Hopper's useful emphasis in the paragraph cited above, psychoanalysts emphasise the personal 'unconscious motivations and internal contradictions' that meet, and usually not in an easy way, Hopper's 'social, cultural and communications arrangements'. BNIM fosters the in-interview expression of lived experience that enables both the personal and societal to be expressed, detected, and psycho-societally interpreted.

The contribution of the macro-societal

The contribution of the macro-societal (history and sociology) might be seen as complementing an otherwise too narrow psychoanalytical focus which is expanded by the BNIM imperative that the researcher should sufficiently explore and articulate the geo-historical context(s) and time-period situatedness through which the situated subjectivity moves and evolves.

Early purist psychoanalysis as a therapy was sometimes accused, and with some justification, of ignoring 'outer world realities'. Jewish analysts and analysands in New York in 1946 explored 'Oedipus complexes' without reference to the Holocaust. Freud's creative but also destructive 'rejection of the seduction theory' implied either that no male relatives ever sexually abused female children, or at least whether or not they did was not the concern of psychoanalysts. 'Historical truth', as one theorist (Spence, 1982) said, is not our concern. Those psychoanalysts (or indeed sociological social-constructionists) who subscribe implicitly to such one-sidedness are not concerned with what really happened, but only with the client's perceptions, fantasies, and ideas about what happened. They will not be happy with BNIM's demand that the 'outer world realities' be researched and identified.

In the *Journal of Psycho-Social Studies*, 5(1), I asked 'Can psychoanalysts think about the psycho-societal?'.

The importance of the real history (dated, situated) is particularly stressed by sociologists and historians. Nancy Hollander (2010), herself a psychoanalyst as well as an historian, provided a fascinating account, in her *Uprooted Minds*, of the responses of psychoanalysts, their institutions, and their clients to the US-backed military coups and political cleansings in Latin America that started (or re-started) in the last half of the twentieth century. If I were to recommend one book to embody 'psycho-societal understanding', it would be this one.

The macro-societal and the long-term historical both tend to fade into the background from the point of view of the *therapy* of a particular client. Sometimes, this may be more plausible than at other times. But.

Consider those migrating from one civilisation to another under conditions of traumatic danger; or internal 'migrants' who have suffered or are suffering a dramatic or covert transformation of societal regime around them (from the welfare state of the people to the illfare state of the 1 per cent; from social democratic to neoliberal authoritarian regimes). The mutations of such 'dated re-situated subjectivities' cannot be understood without a serious understanding of the mutations [re-situatedness] of their 'outer worlds'. And most of us, including those who agree to be BNIM-interviewed, in this period during-the-ongoing-wars within our countries and across the planet, struggle to identify what is really going on where (as the cliché has it) there is 'rapid and uncertain change'.

In BNIM research, *both* types of one-sided account must (iteratively) go on – that is, the positivist history ignoring for the (first methodological) moment of subjectivity; and then the reconstruction of states of successive subjectivity ignoring for the (second methodological) moment outer-world historical realities. So it must continue till the period of one-sided work can give way to a psycho-societally sophisticated synthesis-history of the case evolution.

Some BNIM studies are of long periods of time – family histories over time. Multi-generation case studies are labour-intensive, but very fruitful. For instance, Gabrielle Rosenthal – an originator of BNIM – edited a collection of case studies by herself and others, entitled *The Holocaust in Three Generations: Families of Victims and Perpetrators* (1998). Although not friendly to psychoanalysis, that text is all about situated and defended subjectivities over a very large number of economically described cases of family transmission in hard times and harsh conditions.

Psychoanalysis, BNIM interpretation, and the psycho-societal

BNIM psycho-societal interpretation procedure

The distinction in the social sciences, and in BNIM practice, between two different foci and specialisations – 'inner world' and 'outer world' – can be summarised by an earlier survey:

> [W]e mostly have... either (i) *complex dynamic sociologies spoiled by a simplifying commonsense psychology;* or (ii) *complex dynamic psychologies spoiled by a simplifying commonsense sociology.* In addition, we mostly have them seriously weakened by an *unhistorical – or insufficiently historical* – approach.
> (Wengraf with Chamberlayne, 2013, pp. 69–70; italics mine)

They are not just 'insufficiently historical' but also 'insufficiently comparative', given the lack of training in languages other than English.

To consider the practice of BNIM interpretation from both psychoanalytic and psycho-societal viewpoints, I use two binaries: (i) the inner world–outer world specialisation; (ii) the policy adviser–expert practitioner specialisation.

They apply to the psychoanalytic/psycho-societal viewpoint on

- the kickstart panels which start the process of BNIM individual case interpretation; and
- the history of the case evolution.

The individual case-history interpretation of a 'dated situated subjectivity' is the proximate goal, but it may then be used to study non-individual realities such as institutions, regimes, sub-cultures, historical transitions, policy and processes practice research at different levels, depending on sufficient, adequate 'case interpretation'. BNIM research can and does also focus on practices within a profession, an institution, or some other 'situating situation' in order to see more clearly how these work or don't work, and how policy at different levels might be modified to improve practices, including the practices of policy-making and policy-implementing themselves.

This gives us then two binaries:

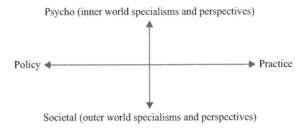

Figure 12.1 Inner/outer and policy/practice

Policies and practices stay constant for a short while and then mutate. The same is true for the inner and outer worlds of the individual and the collective. For social science, reality is profoundly historical, so this third dimension may be indicated thus, moving from past into possible futures, evolving:

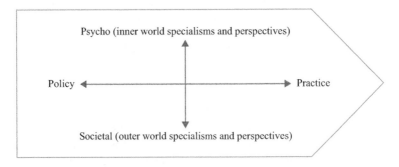

Figure 12.2 Inner/outer and policy/practice in uneven historical mutation

The hotspot/blindspot groupthink of the one-speciality researcher

It is a truism in contemporary sociology and social science more generally that the researcher should examine him- or herself for prejudice or bias whilst collecting data (in interviews in the selection of questions and responses to the interviewee, both overt and covert) and particularly interpreting collected data. In BNIM terms, I like to think of these as individual and collective 'hotspots and blind spots'.

The notion of 'dated situated defended evolving/deciding subjectivity' necessarily suggests that our research activity is limited by the epoch or period in which we are living, and by our own local institutional and disciplinary 'situatedness'. This is both collective, but also highly individual. Very often, at least in sociology, this 'self-examination for prejudice and bias' has been fairly nominal and superficial; whilst insight into *them*, those we are arguing with and researching (those others), is usually much more systematic and pains-taking, not to say pains-giving!

Psychoanalysis and its attempt to research seriously 'hotspots and blind spots' (defendedness) as an ongoing process within its practice demands a constant monitoring of transference and countertransference. It has contributed immeasurably to deepening simultaneously our self-understanding as researchers and consequently our understanding of our interview partners/interview subjects. As psychoanalyst Wilfred Bion wrote, 'it takes two people to think one's most difficult thoughts'.

The individual researcher – particularly one without close supervision – is normally at the mercy of their bias and prejudice. However, the BNIM kickstart panel, a panel of other people that kickstarts at least two of the BNIM interpretation procedures – 'living of the lived life', and 'telling the told story' (see Table 12.1) tracks – can become and generate the informal equivalent of a close attention to our own unconscious hotspots and blindspots.

Now to the 'methodology of BNIM interpretation' considered in the light of psychoanalysis and vice versa (see Wengraf, 2001, 2017a, 2017b).

The BNIM kickstart panel and psychoanalysis

BNIM interpretation of each track always starts with a kickstart panel (four to five people, three hours). The panel's heterogeneity of life experiences, of their memories and desires, their disciplines and trainings and life-journeys, are positive resources that create contrasting 'hypothesising about the interviewee's experiencing in and at that moment', or 'counter hypothesising' and 'tangential hypothesising'; it leads to a mutual self-education, through the surfacing of unconscious assumptions and desires as the associative chunk-by-chunk hypothesising and counter-hypothesising happens.

This kind of psychoanalytic prevention of 'consensual closure' is helpful in training and guidance to BNIM researchers. Sociologists and social scientists as well as BNIM in its early days tended to have group discussion in order to come to a majority or unanimous decision; however, becoming psychoanalytically informed has clearly justified the practice of *non*-closure with not just tolerance of all differences, but *the 'treasuring' of such differences*.

One particular device may be mentioned for surfacing and detecting something like countertransference. I now suggest that the facilitator at given moments ask the panel members to quietly think which hypotheses they would privately prefer to be correct and which hypotheses (not infrequently put forward by others) they would prefer to be not correct, and, indeed, would prefer not have been put forward in the first place.

This self-inspection enables the panel members to be clearer privately, and sometimes publicly, about the operation of their hotspots and blindspots within the panel itself and regarding the interviewee.

The kickstart panel has to be deliberately future-blinded, and open to think anew prior to 'the next future chunk' about to be posted on the flip-chart. This future-blindness permits 'fresh thinking' after each 'next data-chunk moment' is presented. Step-by-step. (For details of procedures, see Wengraf, 2001, chapter 12, and Wengraf, 2017b).

Method of BNIM interviewing

The three sub-sessions

How are the interview data elicited?

Gabriele Rosenthal in Germany created the original 'mix of methods' (Quatext) out of which BNIM developed. Based on the work of Fritz Schütze, the BNIM interview consists of three sub-sessions, with a focus mostly on the first two. The initial narrative sub-session is entirely improvised – after the posing one initial question. The cue-phrases noted down during the initial narration provide the *à la carte* menu from which the interviewer selects cue-phrases. They are used for formulating further narrative questions in sub-session two; and in which the interviewer selects the best words, known informally as 'magic words', with which to ask them. I will spell this out.

Sub-session one

The first interview elicits a single self-improvised answer by the interviewee to a carefully designed single question posed by the interviewer; and then not expanded or added to in any way during sub-session one.

The simplest form of the sub-session one narrative question is this:

> As you know, I'm researching X.... So can you please tell me the story of your life/in respect of X/during Y period...., all the experiences and events that have been important for you personally......... Tell me when you've finished.... I'll listen first; I won't interrupt.... I'll just take some notes in

case I have any questions for when you've finished telling me about it all.... So, let's begin... please tell me your story... Start wherever you like, and take the time you need....

This question is known as a *SQUIN*, a single question aimed at inducing narrative. The response might take two minutes or two hours; it is the interviewee who decides when to complete the sub-session.

When the interviewee declares that they have finished their story, there is then a space, and then a pause-and-coda-question, 'Anything else you'd like to add?'.

Interlude

Unless the first sub-session is extremely short (say, under ten minutes), the interviewer then asks for some time to review their notes and think of any further questions they wish to ask. This interlude might last between five and fifteen minutes.

The interviewer is selecting which of the noted-down cue-phrases that he or she is choosing to work with in sub-session two, and a selection of the 'magic words' to use. It is likely that the interviewee also reflects during that interlude. It provides a moment of distraction and escape, as can the interlude between psychoanalytic sessions. It is, typically, longer than the pause-and-coda at the end of sub-session one. Both psychoanalytic therapy and BNIM research work provide '*private* spaces for free-associative reflection'.

Sub-session two

After the interlude, the interviewer then uses a selection of the most promising cue-phrases used in sub-session one as a basis for further narrative questioning. The order of the delivery of the cue-phrases in the initial narration must be completely respected, as must their integrity as 'quotations of speech'. Topics not mentioned (but in the mind of the interviewer) cannot be asked about. Although typically some cue-phrases will be missed out, or selected out, they can never be returned to (at least in sub-session two). The 'order' of the delivery must be completely respected: 'you can miss things out; you cannot go back or the gestalt goes crack'.

Example of the pushing-for-PINs sub-session two interviewing

In their initial narration, the interviewee may have referred to a general state of mind or mode of subjective experiencing ('*I was always happy when we went on holiday.....*') and later to a particular period or series of events ('*After that, then came a set of difficulties*'). In the interlude, the interviewer may then single out these two main-narration items (cue-phrases) for following up in sub-session two.

The simplest form of the sub-session two narrative question runs typically like this, using a slightly special voice to indicate the quotations: ('/' are alternatives between which the interviewer has to choose):

> You said 'XXX' [quotation of their cue-phrase or short cue-sentence]...... Can you remember/a/any/particular example when this was the case/more detail about this/how it all happened?

Applying this to our two examples, the interviewer might improvise as follows:

> You said 'You were always happy when we went on holiday'.... Can you remember an example of a particular holiday when you were particularly happy?....

And later on, the interviewer will ask:

> You said 'After that, then came a set of difficulties'..... Can you remember any particular moment of the coming of that 'set of difficulties', how all that/it all/happened?....

The key imperative in sub-session two is that the interviewer always pushes towards a unique particular incident, in as much detail as possible. In BNIM speak, we call this 'pushing pausefully and gracefully towards a PIN', particular incident narratives; short form, 'pushing for PINs'.

A schematic example of pushing for PINs:

> You said 'You were always happy when you went on holiday'.... Can you remember an example of a particular holiday when you were particularly happy?....

Which particular holiday the interviewee leaves completely free.

> No, I can't. But I do remember one when I was particularly unhappy.
> You said there was one 'when you were particularly unhappy'. Do you remember any details about that particular holiday?
> Yes. I remember that I lost my bicycle and later on that my parents left me alone in the hotel.
> You said that 'you lost your bicycle'. Do you remember any details about the day when you lost your bicycle? ....

This might go on for several rounds till the PIN is fully told. The interviewer then goes back to the second item (cue-phrase) in the menu provided by the interviewee.

> You said earlier on that 'then your parents left you alone in the hotel'. Do you remember any details about how all that happened?

This too might go on for several rounds till the PIN is fully told.

> When you were telling me your main story, you said that 'After that, then came a set of difficulties'…... Can you remember the coming of that 'set of difficulties', how all that happened? ….

At the end of the last item of sub-session two, the interviewer adds a coda after a pause:

> Anything more you would like to add?', or 'anything else come to mind?'

This summary example should show how the BNIM interview sub-session two proceeds.

Note that BNIM distinguishes between two types of particular incident narrative (PIN). The first is an 'about-PIN' in the second is an 'in-PIN'.

The 'about-PIN' is the story of a particular incident but told from a state of mind pretty firmly in the present. It might, for example, be the story of the childhood humiliation told from the point of view of the current adult conveying 'aren't children/wasn't I/bloody hyper-sensitive!'. The story is told from today's perspective, at an emotional distance from the child's perspective at the time.

We want to get to in-PINs. The interviewer puts great emphasis on pushing deeper, towards an in-PIN account. We want to reconstruct the earlier mode of experiencing; *so that, when we come to interpret the material in the interview, we have material to identify states of mind earlier than the state of mind dominant at the time of the interview itself.* This is achieved by pushing for more detail, and yet more detail again, about the incident. At some point, if we are lucky, the interviewee will be plunged back into the original lived experiencing, or something much more like it.

We say that the person is – as they give in-PIN detail to the interviewer – half in and half out of that earlier lived experiencing, and can then convey something of its quality.

> You said that you 'lost your bicycle'. Do you remember any details about the particular day when you lost your bicycle?
>
> No. I don't. I just went round the corner to get some ice-cream and when I got back it was gone. Kids are just stupid. Nothing more to be said.

This is a very short about-pin. To get to in-PIN detail, the interviewer ignores the 'nothing more to be said', and pushes for 'any more detail'. A lot more may be said, in fact:

> That sounds as if it must have been quite a shock. Do you remember any details at all from that time when it all happened, when 'you got back and it was gone'?
>
> My parents were furious. First with me, well my mother certainly, and then with each other. I felt terrible, I usually did. First she had a go at me. 'You are such a stupid girl, you know you shouldn't leave expensive things lying around for people to steal, blah-blah-blah' [imitates screams, high-pitched voice]. Then my father came in and tried to defend me a little. I remember him saying to her in his bluff soothing voice 'come on, Susan, it's a shame it happened but don't be too hard on her. Remember you lost a bike the same way, I remember you telling me, when you were two years older'. But then, of course, she flew into a temper with him 'you're always defending her, how is she ever going to remember to look after herself carefully if you....', and I was left in the corner of the hall, not able to leave, not able to say 'sorry'. I think they eventually forgot I was even there. It was a horrible moment. I remember they separated the following year, two years later, I suddenly had the thought that it was because I had my bike stolen that they separated. I felt so guilty and ashamed. Of course, I stopped thinking that after a while..... Kids are pretty daft, aren't they? ... I suppose you're thinking badly of me too about losing the bike?

This shows how the sub-session two slogan *'push towards an in-pin'* can powerfully transform a brief allusion, to a bare-bones about-PIN, and then – at least for a time – into a rich in-PIN narration of then-experiencing.

Sub-session three

This is optional later. It is normally designed and undertaken a week or a month after. After reviewing the first two narrative sub-sessions, it is a space to do anything that seems needed or useful: fully structured or semi-structured, a conversation about the preliminary findings or a puzzle from the first two sub-sessions, things that your interviewee thinks that they want to say now, and so on (see Wilkinson et al., 2017).

After pushing-for-(in)-PINs with the given cue-phrase, the interviewer, after the traditional pause, will give the free-associative prompt, *'does anything else come to mind?'*. That can allow further thinking and feeling, and, if fortunate, allows the interviewee to think of further particular related incidents.

> In one case, the interview was about 'bullying at work' and the interviewee had given a very strong, precise, and detailed description of an unpleasant incident with a superior at work. When asked 'does anything else come to mind?', he instantly gave a vivid picture of being bullied forty years before by a school teacher in primary school. Probed for detail in turn, this was the basis for a further set of free-associative material.

Illustrative excerpt from the transcript

BNIM interpretation is based (i) to some extent on the researcher's fieldnotes before, during, and after the interview moment, and (ii) to the largest extent on the digital recording of the interview turned into a verbatim transcript. The transcript might look like this:

> – and I thought to myself (2) well, I'd like to see what this man's got to say for himself, so I went out, and I said, *'yeah, wh- (1) so what have you got to say'*
>
> – and he said *'I know your mother's poisoned your mind against me ((abrupt, rushed)'*
>
> – I was like 'my *mum's not said* **anything** *about* **anything** *that's gone on, but all* **I** *want to know is* **regardless** *of whether my mum* **did** *say anything or* **didn't** *say anything, at the age of sixteen you could have done anything you wanted to do and you* **didn't**
>
> – and I said *'for all of those years you can't get that time back, for all of the years that have gone past you can't get that time back at all [Interviewer: yeah, yeah] so what do you want* **now, why**, *why come back* **now**, *why not whenever [Interviewer: mhm] and what do you hope (2) for now?*
>
> – and he was like well he
>
> – *'just wanted to see you after all this time'*
>
> – and I said *'ok, we've been seen (1), bye'*
>
> – you know… 'so that was it, I didn't feel anything for him, I……
>
> (Excerpted chunk from verbatim 'Janette' interview, typography imagined and clarified, numbers in brackets indicate pauses in seconds)

This is an example from the verbatim transcript of a BNIM interview. Janette's interview was sixty-six pages long. In technical terms, the excerpt is part of a sub-session two PIN (particular incident narrative).

If this is the sort of unprocessed raw material that BNIM interpretation starts with, what does it look like towards the end? The original default BNIM research question is:

> How did a person who lived their life for a period of their life like *this* come in the BNIM interview to tell the story of their life, or of that period of their life, like *that*?

The default outcome is a researcher-constructed history of the case evolution (HCE).

Examples of a history of the case evolution (HCE) can be found in Wengraf (2017) *Detailed Manual*, volume 4, and in the items within the BNIM bibliography. What we can do is to give an indication of how the results of previous stages of the BNIM interpretation process can be summarised.

Interpretation of interview material

Overall view of the two tracks

The interviews are summarised in a twin-track, three-column construct, as in Table 12.1.

The life-chronology of column one (forty-five years) is not the same as the interview-chronology of column three (three hours); and the inferable 'objectivity' phases of column one are not the same as the 'subjectivity' phases of column two (though both cover the forty-five years). The 'case-phases' of the history of the case evolution have not yet been worked up, but the diagram should show how generating the three columns helps.

The diagram represents the 'two-tracks, three-column summary sheet' that the researcher completes on which to base and help think out his or her history of the case evolution (HCE). There are two basic tracks: one is the (longer) historical line of Ben's life, his living (track one); and the other, the sequence of the data provided by the digital recorder in the interview, the (shorter) historical line of the historical telling (track two).

The objective living of the lived life

Left-hand column: A sparse record of hard 'objective data' about the life period, an uncontroversial in-principle-verifiable record as in a truthful-factual CV. This is the BDC, the biographical data chronology. From this, the researcher derives, with a kickstart panel, a fairly minimal BDA, biographical data analysis (BDA), which is a slightly worked-up first-approximation 'researcher's narrative' of phases of the evolution of the 'objective living of the life' over the life period.

The 'chronology chunks' are derived mostly, but not necessarily solely, from the interview, reorganised chronologically, but just stripped of subjectivity (attributions of meaning or cause and effect). At the space at the bottom of Ben's BDC, the researcher (ignoring other data) might just note 'early divorce and separation; wild period around university and drinking; joins AA and works as a bank manager for 20 years'. So much for a three-phase BDA.

The question arises: How might we start thinking about the possible *dated situated subjectivity* of the case, given only this pattern of the 'objective' living in the life period?

The subjective telling of the told story

The concept of sequentialisation chunks

Right-hand column: We have a very full record (on the voice recorder) of everything that was said in the BNIM interview. This audio-record is turned into a transcript, which is itself condensed and processed into a sequentialisation.

Table 12.1 Ben – three-column summary

Track One	Track Two	
I	II	III
Lived-life phases over the (life) period 1960 to 1995	State of subjectivity phases over the (life) period 1960 to 1995	Teller flow phases over the (two-hour interview) telling period 12 September 2005
• 1960: born London -> early family life – one younger brother born 1965 • 1968: parents' divorce – Ben goes to live with mother in Edinburgh • 1980: Ben goes to university – starts drinking, is arrested • 1981: Ben leaves university • 1983: Ben joins Alcoholics Anonymous • 1984: Ben buys a house • Barclays Bank manager 1985–2005	1. 'Hates' younger brother from the word 'go' – Hates primary school 2. Blames himself and younger brother for divorce 3. 1977+: 'Understands' his father's difficulties; fears his mother's 'flattery' 4. 1979: feels 'betrayed' by his father's 'objective dishonesty' 5. 1980–1982: 'I despise my mother' 6. 1983: Sees 'God' in a vision, who tells him to 'change his life'. Becomes very penitent; 'I was the creature of the devil: my parents, they were and are always angels' 7. 1985–2005: 'I'm a saved man' (but confused)	Sub-session one phases I. My life in the last two years: "I'm a changed man" (report of the two years) II. Long PIN of seeing God in a vision when he was 21 III. Short report of wicked early life up to mid-university (expanded at length in ss2) IV. Lengthy argumentation about being a victim of his parents and younger brother and of society as a whole V. Empassioned argumentation that he was the cause of his parents' divorce, and that/but that/ in God's eyes, nobody is beyond forgiveness VI. Confused PINs about his first day at school, fights with younger brother in his 20s Sub-session two to be added
Summary theorisation	Summary theorisation	Summary theorisation

Rather like a chapter and contents page, this text structure sequentialisation (TSS) is then turned, starting with another kickstart panel, into a researcher-narrative's interpretive narrative of the interview, a teller flow analysis (TFA).

Let's look at this in a little more detail.

BNIM breaks up the transcript of the telling into 'chunks', characterised by topic talked about (conventional) and by textsort (unconventional), the *way* in which the topic is talked about. The importance of *way* is well conveyed by the following summary of Rosenthal's brilliant study – previously referred to, astonishingly neglected – of families over three generations (Rosenthal, 1998, pp. 4–5):

> We identify: (a) at what point of the text, (b) in what sequence, they speak about (c) certain parts of their lives. Then we reconstruct the mechanisms (pattern of selection/action) behind the themes they choose to talk about and the experiences they choose to tell, and the way they choose to tell them.
>
> As regards the way the told story is told, we assume that it is by no means coincidental and insignificant when self-biographers: (a) argue about one phase of their lives (ARG), (b) get stuck at the level of generic or typical accounts (GINs) but speak about something else, (c) narrate a PIN at great length and with much feeling, and (d) then give only a brief report of yet another part of their lives (REP), or (e) describe the circumstances of their lives in detail or omit some significant feature altogether (DESCR).
>
> And if their evaluation(s) of their narrative or narratives – the moral(s) that they draw from their life as a whole and from particular events (EVALs) – differs from our own, that is also important.
>
> We also assume that how we are positioned by the interviewee and our fluctuations of 'felt lived experiencing' during the interview are important clues as aspects of the intersubjective interaction certainly and at least one default mode of the interviewee subjectivity possibly [*last paragraph and extra material added*].

Example of six chunks of a sequentialisation (TSS)

What are the 'chunks' of a telling?

In Table 12.2 is an example of a sequentialisation, of 'Janette'.

From the verbatim transcript, the researcher works out an appropriate level of sequentialising. Janette's extract is very detailed. The researcher deems a new sequentialisation chunk to have started if one of three things happen: (i) the speaker changes (as from chunk I to chunk II), (ii) the topic changes (as from chunk II to chunk V), or (iii) the textsort changes (chunk II to IV, chunk V to VI). The topic remains the same between chunk V and VI, but then a new chunk is started because the textsort (the manner used to deal with the topic) has changed from report to evaluation. The topic, in the right-hand column, is

Table 12.2 Extract from Janette's sequentialisation (contrived for illustrative purposes)

	Page/line no's	PLine bulk	PTextsort/speaker Can be mixed, e.g. REP/desc; DESCR/rep DESCRIP/ REP	PGist/Topic– brief indication of content Can be with single quotation marks [""] Mostly will be your paraphrase summary [no quotes] Give a theme heading, and then topics in order
I	59/15-17	3	Int: Q	You mentioned you became a proper housewife: how did that happen?
II	59/18 - 26	8	J: Generic incident narrative (GIN)	I remembered myself every Sunday – Ironing from morning to evening Cooking for his friends, back to ironing Everything down to handkerchiefs and underwear
III	59/28 – 6-/2	4	J: Self-questioning	I don't know what I was trying to achieve, don't know what happened to me, was I trying to please?
IV	60/3-5	2	J: Condensed situation (CS)	When I woke up from it, I felt suffocated
V	60/7-13	6	J: REPORT	I used to iron for him when he went out with friends, and I knew they were going to meet other women Iron clothes for him Stop him at door to change his tie for a better one 'Use this other aftershave, not that one'
VI			J: EVALUATION	'There was nothing of me in that person, that dolly'

straightforward. What is distinctive to BNIM and to its sequentialisation is its concern for the 'manner in which the topic is treated', the textsorts.

Interpreting by chunk-by-chunk new hypothesising and retro-checking in the kickstart panels

When doing the biographical data analysis (BDA – the 'objective' life happenings over the period of the lived life – first column) and when doing the teller flow analysis (TFA – the subjective telling of the told story over the period of the interview – third column), the BNIM researcher deals with them in the same way, yet for each of them asks different questions.

Chunks are presented to the collective panel of researchers in historical sequence and are 'future blind': that is, the collective researcher in principle does not know and cannot find out what the future chunks will be.

> A BDC example. If one BDC chunk is that somebody left school at 16, then the future BDC chunks might indicate that they go back to school at 17; or that they never go back to any education at all; or that they go back to education after they retire; or when they found no jobs available. When dealing with a given chunk, the panel knows nothing of future-chunks. This future-blindness chunk-by-chunk method is central to the BNIM panel method.

Just as we all live our lives and tell our stories not knowing what will happen next, so the researcher simulates for the whole kickstart panel the same lack of knowledge. Panel members will imagine different alternative versions of the interviewee's state of mind at a given historical moment, and without knowing what will happen next.

This is an insistence on 'historicity first' as a way of understanding people: '*Unless you know my history, how can you know who I am?*'. As a result, even if we want to understand something as present-centred as patient compliance with medical prescriptions, we use the BNIM interview to interpret the tracks; the living of the lived life, and the telling the told story. We then move to construct the successive states of subjectivity (SSS), and thus our own narrative of the case-phases (the history of the case evolution, the HCE) in order to better understand what is happening in the current phase when this particular person is or isn't unevenly complying with medical prescriptions.

If you look back at the three columns in the diagram (Table 12.1), you will notice that there is a large space to identify at the bottom of each column, and then *a small space in which some sort of structural or compressed-dynamic conclusion/theorisation* can be drawn from the history in the column. So, historicity comes first, theorisation second. Only afterwards is the eventual case-phased HCE used for particular theoretical, practical, or policy purposes.

This deliberate one-sidedness continues until the three-column summary is constructed. Only then, through the writing/synthesising of the history of the case evolution (HCE) is there an attempt to reconcile the aspects.

The pull within the BNIM interpreter towards a premature impressionist synthesis is very powerful. Therefore, BNIM encourages storing away any writing of 'dated, situated theoretical side-notes' that are not about the current focus, and which will be looked at only at the time when the other note-relevant column is considered.

This compares with the practice of psychoanalysts who deliberately and consciously bracket away the aspect of reality which is not the current focus of attention and about which the analyst knows little. However, the BNIM researcher perhaps goes further: when also doing track one (column one), 'the objective living of the lived life' (BDA), he or she will bracket out the subjective-reporting side.

The question arises: What can we say about the dated, situated subjectivity of the teller, given all this very rich subjective data from the voice recorder showing how, during the interview, they told that story in this way (and not another) at this point in their life?

The left- and the right-hand columns in Table 12.1 summarise the material relevant to answering the question:

> How did a person who lives a period of their life like *this* (column one) come in the BNIM interview to tell the story of their life, or of that period of their life, like *that* (column three)?

These two columns represent the two tracks, and tasks, of the researcher. That teller flow analysis (TFA) must eventually be made sense of in terms of the objective geo-historical (BDC) data of the period of the interviewee's life he or she is telling.

The similarity of the questions that the researcher asks him- or herself when faced with a new chunk can be exemplified by 'Ben buys house'. The researcher/panel members will first of all explore how this event was experienced by Ben, and will set out a number of alternative 'experiencing hypotheses'. The collective researcher assumes a variety of different experiences. For the sake of example, I shall give three 'experiencing hypotheses' about the buying of the house:

- Did he experience it as at last achieving a firm basis for being a traditional career person and breadwinner? (EH1)
- Did he experience it as a final nail in any hopes he might have had for emancipation? (EH2)
- Did he experience it as a mere convenience with no symbolic value? (EH3)

The collective researcher then puts forward a number of alternative 'following hypotheses'; that is, hypotheses about what might happen next if a given 'experiencing hypothesis' turned out to be true. These might be called, in terms of the philosophy of science of Karl Popper, 'risky following hypotheses'. This may help us to infer which of our chosen experiencing hypotheses are more likely to be wrong and which right. This future-blind chunk-by-chunk procedure, involving 'experiencing hypotheses' and 'risky FH predictions' is common to both the biographical data analysis and to the teller flow analysis.

It is reasonable to assume that each chunk, each event such as buying a new house, is experienced *at the time* in one way, however complex or contradictory, as a single experiencing. On the other hand, it is also reasonable to assume that the interviewee – *recalling later a particular earlier experiencing* such as the purchasing of the house – has always, at least in principle, *in the interview* a 'double experiencing'.

The '*double experiencing is in the interview*'; and it occurs because the original experience of buying the house is recalled, together with an experiencing from their now-perspective, affected by all the things that happened afterwards and by the current experiencing of the actual interview itself. He or she had to decide whether to say anything at all about the house-buying, and if so *how*, given the lived experience of the interview interaction at that particular moment – with the degree of trust/suspicion/self-knowledge that the interview has reached. This means there is always a double experiencing by the teller telling the story in interview about the past that needs to be thought about.

The kickstart panel interprets

Finally, an important feature of BNIM interpretation practice is the use of the kickstart panel to start this process of future-blind chunk-by-chunk interpretation. Researchers have both hotspots and blindspots. There are things that their perspective and position and history in the world make it easy for them to see and others that are made difficult (or even virtually impossible) for them to see. To rectify this, the heterogeneous panel is assembled.

The individual researcher does not, on their own, start to generate experiencing hypotheses about the single experiencing, nor about the double experiencing of talking in the interview to the interviewer about past moments of the lived life. In this sense, 'the panel researcher' is (initially) a collective researcher, a panel. It is a panel of different sorts of people – as different as possible – in which the physical researcher is the facilitator but otherwise has no special status. The BNIM researcher will be more interested in listening to the hypotheses that are quite different from the ones that he or she would spontaneously put forward. This is a way of recognising his or her own hotspots and blindspots, and obliges him to take into account 'experiencing hypotheses' that he or she would much prefer (for cultural or countertransference reasons, or others) not to think, or would much prefer not to be true. *The importance of cultivating and treasuring differences.*

The rule for selecting panel members is that of necessary heterogeneity and desirable complementarity. Both of these criteria are always only partially satisfied, but it is good to have them in mind.

- *Necessary heterogeneity*: Apart from one member of the panel who should be significantly like the interviewee and so able to comment knowledgeably on his or her local life-world and time, the other members of the panel should be pretty unlike the interviewee, and unlike each other. This will maximise the degree of different perspectives and life experiences which can be drawn upon to correct the limitations of the 'perspective of the interviewee', and above all of the 'perspective of the interviewer/researcher'.
- *Desirable complementarity*: The two tracks of interpretation of BNIM require sufficient interest in both the inner worlds and the outer histories of the interviewee. Just psychologists or just sociologists/historians would prioritise/over-emphasise inner or outer worlds. The panel needs sufficient multi-perspective complementarity to make the different perspectives on the interviewee as a dated situated subjectivity work well together in the panel interaction.

After each chunk, panel members are invited to put forward 'experiencing hypotheses' (single in the BDA panel; double in the TFA panel). All hypotheses put forward – the experiencing ones together with the risky following hypotheses (or future predictions) are noted and registered; but they are not decided upon, as it is the flow of 'chunks still to come' that will decide which earlier ones become less plausible and which become more convincing (for an example of a panel at work with insight into countertransference, see Froggett and Wengraf, 2004, pp. 100–114).

Over the three hours of the typical kickstart panel, a large number of hypotheses flourish at first, but gradually fewer and fewer remain plausible in the light of the accumulating evidence.

States of successive subjectivity (SSS, middle column)

Nearly all BNIM case accounts have used these rich resources to infer *past states of situated subjectivity*. Evidence for them is always there in the digital record – sometimes very explicitly, as in '*I used to think this; now I realised I was wrong and I now think that*'. Sometimes much more implicitly, particularly among those who pride themselves on never changing their mind; and sometimes denied, in ways either subtle or not.

Nearly all BNIM case accounts, right from the start, pay attention to such earlier 'past states of dated situated subjectivity', whether they were an explicit part of the person's biographic narrative ('how I changed my mind at this turning point in my life') or whether they could be detected only in a very implicit state.

Because of this, the third, middle column was added around 2010, so the 'subjective track' now includes this middle column (SSS – successive states of subjectivity). It is always completed *after* the right-hand column about the TFA, which infers the present-day perspective or subjectivity derived from the flow of the telling in interview.

This new middle column, developed later in their process of 'doing the columns', invites the researcher to infer a succession of earlier states of subjectivity, for which varied amounts of evidence exist in the interview. That is, in addition to the 'present state of situated subjectivity' in the interview, for which its contents provide normally ample evidence.

To the extent it is possible to infer 'past states of subjectivity' from the evidence, we have a basis for a fuller answer to the original research question: *'how did a person who lived their life like this .... come at the point of interview to tell their story like that?'* We have the researcher's narrative of the 'objective' life, and, next to it, the researcher's inferred narrative of the successive states of subjectivity, both covering the same life period. Developing this history of the case evolution (HCE) involves the researcher in thinking about the first two columns and how best to interrelate the two of them, bearing in mind that the most recent state-of-subjectivity is that embodied in column three, the interview-telling of the told story.

History of the case evolution (HCE)

This HCE is conceived in terms of the researcher's appropriate case-phases, in which those 'objective phases' suggested in the descriptions of the lived life and the 'subjective phases' suggested by describing the successive states of subjectivity over that period have to be rethought and synthesised together. What emerges is a case synthesis: the case-phased history of the case evolution. We cannot expand on this synthesising of columns one and two. There are examples in the BNIM and other literature.

BNIM interview and psychoanalysis

Four major differences

From the above description, four major differences from psychoanalytic sessions may be discerned:

1. The psychoanalytic client is there for the purpose of self-understanding and therapy and pays for this over a large number of sessions; the BNIM interviewee is recruited to aid the social-science researcher, and typically has one three-sub-session BNIM interview, and does not pay for it.
2. For the psychoanalyst, the task of systematic interpretation is fairly constant during each and every session, but for BNIM, systematic interpretation is

left till after the interview as a whole, or at least until after the first two sub-sessions.
3. Intervention practices are very different.

   a. The psychoanalyst is free to intervene in any session in any way he or she thinks analytically and therapeutically appropriate. They may bring together things said at different moments in the session, introduce an apparently new topic, talk in their own words, etc. Contrariwise, in the first two BNIM sub-sessions, the BNIM interviewer is bound by very tight rules which give in principle very little discretion as to how she or he intervenes: only one narrative question (the SQUIN) at the start of sub-session one, and no further questions after that; in sub-session two, a tight sequence of narrative questions, 'pushing for PINs' on a single interviewee cue-phrase in turn. There always has to be a 'pause-and-coda'; there always has to be a serious interlude between the first two sub-sessions. The sequence of telling must be respected.

   b. For psychoanalysts, the particular intervention of 'interpreting to the client' is an essential part of achieving therapeutic effects; the BNIM researcher is not trained to make, and is barred from making, such 'improving interventions'. The BNIM interview must rigorously avoid 'nudges to consciousness', whether critical or therapeutic.

4. The recording and making notes is very different. The psychoanalyst typically does not digitally record sessions, and does not make notes during the session, but may make notes after the session. The BNIM researcher digitally records all sessions and also makes a constant stream of in-session cue-phrase notes in the rigid order of the sequence of when they were said.

Discussion

Thus, with the four major differences, BNIM interviews have something like a 'narrative past-incident-focused constrained' free association pattern, with some more classic 'open, free-associative moments'. In a psychoanalytical session, particularly where present interaction in the transference/countertransference is the focus, remembering and history are a way to evoke and understand present feelings and relationships. BNIM, however, is concerned with these, but not to modify them; it is not a therapy. In addition to evoking *present* states of subjectivity, it aims to *in part re-evoke past states of mind and situations* (dated, situated deciding/evolving subjectivities), in order to describe and understand the sequence leading into the present dynamically.

Both identify 'free association' as the key movement of mind and foster it. Both tolerate, welcome, or structure in 'pauses' (private thinking time) as key to the practice. Therapy wants to get at now-feelings and perspectives, moving forwards; BNIM researchers want to elicit now-feelings to enrich then-remembering, going backwards.

Different from psychoanalytic practice, BNIM seeks single-mindedly to revive and relive past lived experiences in in-PIN detail, avoiding all other intervention (e.g., interpretations and the like) and pushes, pausefully and gracefully, towards in-PINs.

In the psychoanalytic session, the analyst tends to stress that the session is necessarily one-sided, and that he or she does not know what the 'real situation' is that the client is talking about. The analyst may say:

> Obviously, I don't know whether your father did behave to you in the way that you said he behaved. But what we can work with, and this is all we can work with, is your feelings and your perception then and now which lead you to say that he behaved in the way that you represent him as behaving.

This overt and careful limiting of what is being dealt with – namely, one person's perception and fantasy – is paralleled in BNIM by the difference between the work done in relationship to the two tracks and the three columns (see Table 12.2). When doing each of these, the BNIM interpreter carefully focuses on one aspect only, to the exclusion of the other or others.

> This is the way the interviewee told the story. What is true and false, what is omitted, we have to say at this point (in this column) we don't know.
>
> These are the known objective facts of what happened, as far as we can see. How the interviewee told the story in the interview, what significance he attaches to them there, we have to say at this point (in this column) we don't know.

But in each case, when working on any one track or column, the mind-set of the BNIM researcher has to be specialised and partial. She or he focuses on one aspect to be explored and written up, and is fully conscious of the partial nature of the knowledge gained and generated from that aspect. One aspect at a time, avoiding premature synthesising.

BNIM and FANI interviewing compared

To my knowledge, the only Anglophone-world biographic-narrative interviewing technique similar to BNIM is the 'free association narrative interview' (FANI). It is worth briefly comparing the two. The originators of FANI in their study of crime:

> considered asking one single question (as the German biographers do), but [say] our three-part theoretical structure.... provided a particular frame that we could not ignore. We decided, therefore, upon six questions deriving from our theoretical structure and a seventh about moving into the area ... Each

question was followed up in terms of detail and time periods, following the order of the narrative:

- Can you tell me about how crime has impacted on your life since you've been living here?
- Can you tell me about unsafe situations in your life since you've been living here?
- Can you think of something that you've read, seen or heard about recently that makes you fearful? Anything [not necessarily about crime]?
- Can you tell me about risky situations in your life since you've been living here?
- Can you tell me about times in your life recently when you've been anxious?
- Can you tell me about earlier times in your life when you've been anxious? Can you tell me what it was like moving to this area?

(Hollway and Jefferson, 2013, p. 35)

The most obvious difference to the *single SQUIN* that initiates sub-session one is what Hollway and Jefferson call attention to – *their multiplicity of opening questions*.

Contrariwise, the SQUIN required by BNIM asks for a *unified whole story of the whole person over the specified life period*.

Such a push towards a unified whole story is absent from the FANI questions. FANI questions push only towards interviewer categorisations of relevant-to-researcher 'the events and experiences', without requiring them to be set within a unified historical sequence. Asking for 'unsafe situations in your life since you been living here', for example, does not ask for any historical or chronological order of such 'unsafe situations'. Hollway and Jefferson's six-part initial sub-session is more constrained than the BNIM single question SQUIN and not oriented to obtaining a single whole-life-period history. They do not necessarily push for narrative.

The second obvious difference is between the formulation '*can you tell me about, can you think of something*' and the BNIM very precisely insisted-upon '*Do you remember any particular... How it all happened?*'.

BNIM researchers are carefully enjoined not to say '*tell me about*', but only say '*do you remember*'. The FANI '*tell me about*' allows a present-time perspective on past events; it does not push towards the past-perspectives embodied in in-PINs. It can also be answered by a completely non-narrative response, whilst the BNIM '*do you remember any particular.... How it all happened*' is more likely to elicit a narrative. The FANI interview schedule is nevertheless open for free-associative improvisation, however, the questions do not push right from the start for *narrative* free-associative improvisation.

To sum up: the FANI interview schedule allows only for free improvisation within each question, and not an overall story or narrative. It does not have a concern to explore past perspectives in the way that BNIM achieves by 'pushing forcefully towards in-PINs'. FANI also does not point right from the start towards a narrative response: 'tell me about' is less narrative-pointed than 'do you remember... how it all happened?'.

Conclusions

BNIM has produced material at a fast rate. In 2015, 2016, and 2017, the average output of reports, papers, chapters, books, or PhDs was roughly one every ten days. A constantly updated bibliography surveying the BNIM literature would take another paper. Here, to suggest the explicit use of psychodynamic and psycho-societal thinking in such work, I can only suggest a few exemplary case studies.

Exploring questions of death and dying are to be found in Kjetil Moen's 2018 'Death at work: an interpretation of biographical narratives of professionals in end-of-life and, from the point of view of the lived experience of a mother afflicted with a sudden death and variably sensitive professionals, Denise Turner, 'Telling the story: what can be learned from parents experience of the professional response following the sudden unexpected death of a child' (2013).

The study of climate change denial and activism from a biographical-narrative perspective other than the researcher's own is only just starting. Sally Weintrobe's edited collection (2013) shows the potential, and in it you will find Renee Lertzman's 'The myth of apathy: psychoanalytic explorations of environmental subjectivity' (2013) emerging from a slightly different South African research tradition.

There are many other areas in which psychodynamically informed research using biographic narratives have been developed. I'll finish by just citing three from the area of health and social care: Jane Graham (2010) on drug users; Kathleen Russell (2015), emerging from the Tavistock's professional doctorate training, on psychosocial concerns and individual anxieties for fathers with testicular cancer; Caroline Nicholson and colleagues' (2012) study of living at home with frailty in old age.

BNIM provides a powerful data-collection method for all research interviews concerned with the difficult dated situated subjectivity of individuals as their life takes them through their experiences. Its twin-track case-interpretation methodology lays down a powerful 'historicity-mindedness' to avoid both excesses of inner-world psychologism and psychoanalysis and those of outer-world sociologism, all tending to be locked into 'the present' within global society. It enables the researcher to develop a psychoanalytically and historical-cultural self-understanding, and so fosters a truly 'psycho-societal understanding' of the dated, situated, defended, and deciding/evolving subjectivities under study.

Glossary of some terms in BNIM use

biographical data analysis (BDA) – the researcher's first attempt to periodise into phases the interviewee's life period by a minimal narrative based on the *biographical data chronology*.

biographical data chronology (BDC) – a dated list of factual events over the life period, stripped of all interviewee attributions of 'meaning', 'alleged causes', and 'alleged consequences'.

biographic-narrative interpretive method (BNIM) – the biographic-narrative interpretive method has at least two distinct *sub-sessions* in the interview, and, in the case-interpretation method, with at least two distinct tracks of preliminary interpretive work prior to synthesising a *history of the case evolution* (HCE).

case-phases – in the *history of the case evolution* construction by the researcher, the phases through which the (re)constructed history of the interviewee is held to have transited. This final construction takes into account but supersedes the 'phase-modelling' that occurred earlier in the research when the researcher constructed tentative phase models for each of track one and track two treated on their own.

future-blindness – the principle of *kickstart panel* work by which panel members are only given one chunk of data at a time about which to develop experiencing hypotheses and to put forward predictive or following hypotheses about what later evidence (later chunks) would tend to confirm or disconfirm particular experiencing hypotheses.

history of the case evolution (HCE) – the final point at which the one-sided working and separate writing-up of both the 'objective situated events' track and the 'subjective experiencing' track are brought together in the researcher's account of the evolution of 'the case'.

hotspots/blindspots – a colloquial phrase to indicate that any researcher and any interviewee will have cultural and individual positive and negative 'defences' (in psychoanalytic terms) and that psycho-societally sophisticated research requires proper peer-supervisory methodology to reduce the impact of these.

in-PIN – a particular incident narrative in the recounting of which the interviewee at least in part feels as if they were back 'in' the historical experience that they are endeavouring to access so as to narrate.

kickstart panel – each of the two tracks in BNIM interpretation starts with a kickstart panel whose careful heterogeneity tends to force the researcher to go beyond the assumptions (*hotspots* and *blindspots*), shared and different, of both the interviewee and themselves. They typically last for three hours – one for the *biographical data analysis* and a different one for the *teller flow analysis*. Normally, shorter panels can be brought together to 'interpret' puzzling bits of verbatim interview transcript (micro-analysis panels).

living of the lived life – equivalent to track one, contrasted to *telling of the told story.*

pause-and-coda – the principle that at the end of each of the BNIM sub-sessions, there should always be a serious time of silence generated by the interviewer so that there is mental space for the interviewee to think about what they have and haven't said, and what they think/feel about that. After such a pause, from which both parties benefit, the interviewer offers a 'coda' space with the completely open question, '*Anything you would like to add?*', followed by another appropriate space. . ...

psycho-societal – a methodological-philosophical perspective and set of methods whereby the attempt is made to give proper weight to both the inner-world dynamics of the 'psycho' and the outer-world dynamics of the 'societal', for a proper understanding of people and regimes in historical societies, all considered to be dated, situated, and evolving.

Quatext – the German school of biographical research associated with Gabriele Rosenthal. BNIM is an Anglophone off-shoot of that tradition.

sequentialisation – the text structure sequentialisation (TSS) is carried out by the researcher on the basis of the verbatim transcript of the interview. The flow of talk from beginning to end is broken up into chunks for the purpose of chunk-by-chunk consideration needed for the *teller flow analysis*. A new chunk is held to start when one of three features can be found as you go through the verbatim transcript:(i) a new speaker starts, (ii) a new topic starts, or (iii) the manner in which a topic is treated starts (the '*textsort*' changes).

SQUIN – the prepared and tested single (and only) question aimed at inducing a (whole story) narrative with which BNIM's sub-session one starts (no further questions are added during sub-session one).

sub-sessions – BNIM has three different sub-sessions. Sub-session one is aimed at obtaining a unified, whole story of the life period in question, and is started by the *SQUIN*. Sub-session two is aimed at using cue-phrase noted during sub-session one (and then during sub-session two) in order to elicit narratives of particular incidents (PINs) associated clearly or obscurely with such chosen cue-phrases. Sub-session three may be regarded as optional, but is one that typically occurs rather later, once the researcher listens to the voice recording, consults their notes, and decides which further material she or he needs to generate to answer their original or emergent research questions.

teller flow analysis (TFA) – on the basis of the *sequentialisation* of the interview flow, the flow of the telling, the 'sequence of "chunks"', the researcher starts carefully and cautiously inferring hypotheses about the flow of the subjectivity of the teller behind the said and the unsaid of the telling. This starts with a TFA *kickstart panel*, and continues subsequently by the individual or collective researcher after the three-hour panel is over.

telling of the told story – this is voice recording of the interview, first condensed/reduced into a verbatim transcript, and then this latter is condensed/reduced into the chunk-by-chunk sequentialisation.

Textsorts – the 'manner in which' things are said and not said in the interaction sessions of both BNIM interviews and psychoanalytic therapy are of the greatest importance in understanding dated situated subjectivity and its movement. In writing up the 'telling of the told story', in the construction of the *sequentialisation*, the researcher pays great attention to identifying gross and subtle shifts in the way that the 'manner in which' topics are treated. The simplest and original distinction was three-fold: A-N-D (argumentation, narration, description). More recently, BNIM has come to subdivide narration first into broad report contrasting with particular incident narratives, and then further distinguished particular incident narratives into about-PINs and in-PINs. Rather similar to sociologist Max Weber's concept of an 'ideal type' or a 'conceptual model', the concept of a *textsort* is a clumsy but useful one for thinking beyond topic content.

Notes

1 Considering the phrase "dated, situated, defended… and deciding/evolving" whilst copy-editing, Alyson Silverwood commented beautifully "To my mind, the first three sound rather fixed and closed - and the last mutable, like a bid for freedom - or like a butterfly pinned on a scientist's board, a mere specimen of evolution, magically flexing its wings...". This grasps the matter (ontology, epistemology) wonderfully. Thanks Alyson.
2 I am indebted to Bob Hinshelwood for his re-structuring of this chapter and provision of the glossary.

References

Bar-On, D. (1995), *Fear and Hope: Three Generations of the Holocaust*. London: Harvard University Press.
Bhaskar, R. (1998), *The Possibility of Naturalism: A Philosophical Critique of the Contemporary Social Sciences*, 3rd edition. London: Routledge.
Bollas, C. (2008), *The Evocative Object World*. London: Taylor and Francis.
Carpenter, P. (2002), *Learning from Our Mistakes: Beyond Dogma in Psychoanalysis and Psychotherapy*. Hove: Brunner-Routledge.
Froggett, L., and Wengraf. T. (2004), Interpreting interviews in the light of research team dynamics. *Critical Psychology*, vol. 10: *Psychosocial Research* (pp. 93–121). London: Lawrence and Wishart.
Graham, J. (2010), *Full of empty promises? Exploring what drug use achieves for the individual*. PhD thesis, University of Central Lancashire.
Hollander, N. (2010), *Uprooted Minds: Surviving the Politics of Terror in the Americas – Psychoanalysis, History, Memoir*. New York: Routledge.
Hollway, W., and Jefferson, T. (2013), *Doing Qualitative Research Differently*, 2nd edition. London: Sage.
Lertzman. R. (2013), The myth of apathy: psychoanalytic explorations of environmental subjectivity. In S. Weintrobe (ed.), *Engaging with Climate Change: Psychoanalytic and Interdisciplinary Perspectives* (pp. 117–132). London: Routledge.

Moen, K. (2018), *Death at Work: An Interpretation of Biographical Work of Professionals in End-of-Life Care*. London: Palgrave.

Nicholson, C., Meyer, J., Flatley, M., and Holman, C. (2012), The experience of living at home with frailty in old age: a psychosocial qualitative study. *International Journal of Nursing Studies*, 50(9): 1172–1179.

Ogden, T. (2008), *Rediscovering Psychoanalysis: Thinking and Dreaming, Learning and Forgetting*. London: Routledge.

Rosenthal, G. (ed.) (1998), *The Holocaust in Three Generations: Families of Victims and Perpetrators of the Nazi Regime*. London: Cassell.

Russell, K. (2015), *Psychosocial Concerns and Individual Anxieties for Fathers with Testicular Cancer*. Professional doctorate, University of East London.

Spence, D. (1982), *Narrative Truth and Historical Truth: Meaning and Interpretation in Psychoanalysis*. New York: Norton.

Turner, D. (2015), Telling the story: what can be learned from parents' experience of the professional response following the sudden unexpected death of a child. PhD thesis, University of Sussex. [Published by Palgrave, 2017.]

Turner, D. (2016), 'Research you cannot talk about': a personal account of researching sudden unexpected child death. *Illness, Crisis and Loss*, 24(2): 73–87.

Wengraf, T. (2001), *Qualitative Research Interviewing: Biographic Narrative and Semi-Structured Method*. London: Sage Publications, chapters 6 and 12, particularly on BNIM.

Wengraf, T. (2011), Can psychoanalysts think about the psycho-societal? *Journal of Psycho-Social Studies*, 5(1): 184–195.

Wengraf, T., with Chamberlayne, P. (2013), Biography-using research (BNIM), Sostris, institutional regimes and critical psychosocietal realism. In J. Turk and A. Mrozowicki (eds.), *Realist Biography and European Policy* (pp. 63–92). Leuven: Leuven University Press.

Wengraf, T. (2017–), *BNIM Short Guide bound with BNIM Detailed Manuals*.

Wengraf, T. (2017–), *BNIM Quick Outline Sketch*.

Constantly updated: current versions always available from tom.wengraf@gmail.com

Wilkinson, K., Tomlinson J., and Gardiner, J. (2017), Exploring the work–life challenges and dilemmas faced by managers and professionals who live alone. *Work, Employment and Society*, 31(4): 640–656.

Zwerman, G. (2014), Persona: psychodynamic and sociological dimensions of a project on US activism and political violence. In L. Chancer and J. Andrews (eds.), *The Unhappy Divorce of Sociology and Psychoanalysis: Diverse Perspectives on the Psychosocial* (pp. 239–265). London: Palgrave Macmillan.

Psycho-societal ethnography

Chapter 13

Psychoanalytic ethnography

Linda Lundgaard Andersen

A brief account of my experiences of using psychoanalytic ethnography

My journey into psychoanalytic ethnography started when I was a young PhD student trying to understand and make sense of my fieldwork in which I encountered a turmoil of experiences, feelings, and information. A number of insights followed from this. The researcher's academic and life-historical subjectivity are a significant but often overlooked dimension in fieldwork. The researcher's interaction with and experiencing of the field determine field reports and analysis, and subsequently influence the development of the ethnography. However, fieldwork is also subjected to psychodynamic processes and representations. Due to its long-term presence and human interaction, fieldwork is well suited to develop psychodynamic processes (Hunt, 1989). Therefore, I have stated that ethnographic research, and researchers in general, are influenced by both recognised and unrecognised motives and forces (Andersen, 2012, p. 3). Psychodynamic processes influence sub-themes in research, such as the formulation of a research question, data production, and methodology, the choice of and relations to informants, data analysis, interpretation and writing processes.

In my initial research, which focused on the outcome and dynamics of efficiency and democracy in a number of Danish public human service organisations, I applied a number of psychoanalytic concepts that I found provided unique insight into how people and organisations interact and perform. I developed a psycho-societal approach to the micro-processes of Danish neoliberal welfare services, elaborating a learning and identity perspective. My many years of encounters with professionals in welfare services have illuminated how they display a strong identification with, but also a significant ambivalence towards, welfare service innovation, being both enthusiastic and burdened. By applying a psycho-societal conceptual approach, I have analysed how identification, ambivalence, and defence are significant features of welfare service professionals' learning and practices (Andersen, 2003a, 2015, 2016).

My theoretical and methodological approach combined a number of concepts and methods. I applied Wellendorf's concept of institutional transference and countertransference, which provided significant insight into dimensions of the research process (Wellendorf, 1986). My early encounters with the research field brought feelings of inferiority, anxiety, and rejection due to rather hostile reactions from staff (Andersen, 2003a, 2015, 2016). At a later point, I was able to understand these reactions as mirroring a gamut of emotions the staff in the human service institutions had experienced. The employees' reactions were seen as institutional transference, where they transferred the same mix of emotions to me (the researcher) that they themselves had been carrying for some time. These were emotional responses closely linked to the work-related pressure for efficiency and democracy coming from local politicians and human service administration. By examining and interpreting my own reactions and feelings through the institutional transference lens, I was able to develop a psychosocially informed analysis of these encounters. Analysis of transference between the researcher and the field thus provided insight into organisational and human dynamics that could enrich prevailing understandings of change processes and public modernisation. I subsequently validated these findings through a large amount of qualitative data. Based on these empirical findings, I was able to conclude that development and change processes related to modernising welfare services had resulted in significant levels of anxiety and unease, defensiveness and ambivalence among employees and management. Anna Freud's work on the ego and its defence mechanisms also proved useful in understanding the emotional turmoil. I was able to disentangle how the interactions were influenced by a number of mental processes such as fantasy, sublimation, displacement, densification, introjection, and projection, all of which uniquely and subjectively form the patchwork of human personality (A. Freud, 1937).

Another significant concept that I have put to work concerned how field researchers develop their fieldwork in a methodological and theoretical balance of experiencing, participating, and observing, in their attempts to make representations. A classic distinction developed by Sterba suggests that the establishment of an ego-dissociation is a precondition of successful and productive positioning in the research field. In ego-dissociation, the researcher's ego is split into the 'observing ego' and the 'experiencing ego'. The experiencing ego records and participates in the activities in the setting, while the observing ego considers and conceptualises the observations from a continuous meta-position (Friedman and Samberg, 1994; Sterba, 1934). Researchers must be both observing and experiencing; neither of these processes should predominate, since both dimensions are significant for the research process. This distinction then offers a fruitful understanding of how fieldwork can be processed and clarifies how the two positions may feed the ethnography.

A final theme to mention would be the potentials to address the interplay between power structures, relations, and subjectivity in a societal context. I have deployed the concept of ambivalence of Regina Becker-Schmidt in my ethnographies, who connects ambivalence with separation and distinction in an historical and societal context. This concept of ambivalence mirrors the dynamics of transference in the sense that the latter mediates feelings of ambivalence (Becker-Schmidt and Knapp, 1987). Ambivalence links negative and positive associations and emotions to the phenomenon in question, and arises from differentiations and contradictions contextualised by societal and historical conditions. An analysis of ambivalence involves different aspects of external and internal reality. I have applied ambivalence in several ethnographic analyses, since long-term presence strengthens the possibility for accessing data on potential conflicts or tensions. In a study of social workers and their working identities and organisational structure and collaboration, I analysed professional decision-making in casework. This worried social workers somewhat, and they withdrew from decision-making, stating a number of reasons and emotions. This withdrawal contradicted their ideal views about professional practice and case influence. The ambivalence also referred to an external reality. Management displayed an ambiguous relationship to the influence of social workers; they laid down administrative and legal guidelines for joint influence but also accused the case officers of being unable or unwilling to follow these. At the same time, they failed to establish an administrative evaluative procedure for casework. At a societal level, the ambivalence was facilitated by a social policy that provided limited options in the solving of social problems. The contrast between individual social workers' ideal work criteria and actual administrative options fertilised the ground for ambivalence (Andersen, 2005a, pp. 76ff).

In another study, I have applied a psycho-societal approach to the microprocesses of the Danish neoliberal welfare service. I have pointed out how, on the one hand, numerous organisational, financial, and cultural changes have provided more differentiated and efficient welfare services. On the other hand, I show that standardisation and quality assessment regulating daily work have led to pressure on welfare professionals, distancing them from the voices and lives of vulnerable citizens. A psycho-societal reading of neoliberal welfare services aiming at efficiency and performance management shows that the result can be anxiety, defensiveness, and ambivalence. I suggest an approach to these 'sticky constructions' as condensed points of meaning located in the many troubling encounters between welfare professionals and citizens, which will enable us to understand and learn from this phenomenon. Identification, ambivalence, and defensive reactions constitute a significant psycho-societal analytical grid through which to study welfare services (Andersen, 2016).

I draw upon a psycho-societal tradition rooted in critical theory tradition and the Frankfurter school and have applied this to a variety of studies (Andersen, 2003a, 2005b, 2012, 2013, 2015, 2016; Andersen and Dybbroe, 2011, 2017). Briefly, this situates societal processes at the core of understanding humans, related to changes in the economic, cultural, and historic conditions of society. Psycho-societal theory explores the interfaces and intertwining of the subjects and subjectivity in a societal context, and vice versa how the societal can be traced in the subjectivity (Andersen, 2013). These are often conflictual processes formed by capitalistic valorisation and profit, paid work, social class, gender, family, and upbringing that all form humans and society. These processes have a major influence on individuals' identity, as well as on the identity formation of the individual (Leithäuser, 1976; Leithäuser and Volmerg, 1988, p. 55). The concept of everyday consciousness and everyday actions are pivotal and understood as dense expressions, which link up both inwardly to the individual's particular life history, experiences, and background and outwardly to social conditions, history, and culture (Leithäuser, 1976; Leithäuser, Meyerhuber, and Schottmayer, 2009; Redman, Bereswill, and Morgenroth, 2010).

A review of comparable methodological approaches

Psychoanalytic ethnography is a label that spans a rich variety of applied concepts, methods, and methodologies. In the following, I focus on three of these: psychoanalytic reflectivity, ethnopsychoanalysis and the third space, and transference and countertransference, providing insight into (some of) the methodological approaches and practices in psychoanalytic ethnography.

Psychoanalytic reflexivity in ethnography

Psychoanalytic reflexivity in ethnographic settings stands as a pivotal axis highlighted and discussed by many scholars in the field (see, e.g., Britzman, 2012, 2013; Brown, 2006; Cargill, 2006; Froggett and Briggs, 2012; Froggett, Ramvi, and Davies, 2015; Hollway, 2011; Hollway and Jefferson, 2000). Britzman points out how Freud positioned objections, objects, and obstacles to constitute psychoanalytic movement, and thereby suggests that it seems that Freud is always addressing a learning subject from the point of view of learning from difficulties. In this way, individuals engaged in psychoanalysis place their objections to the psychoanalytic process and, in doing so, they transform this resistance or anxiety into psychoanalytic objects such as ego defences, resistance to resistance, moral anxiety, transference and love, free association, and dreams. Britzman names these phenomena 'sticky constructions' (Britzman, 2010, p. 20). In this way, she offers an entry and a cluster for psychoanalytic reflections that can be adapted to ethnography. Corin further adds that psychoanalytic approaches help to direct ethnographers' attention to subdued aspects of human communication, enhancing our capacities to grasp the significance of gestures, tones of voice, hesitations, silences, omissions, and the 'gaps and discrepancies that pierce the coherence of manifest discourse' (Corin, 2012, p. 108). In a special issue on this topic, Gammeltoft and Segal suggest that 'anthropological fieldwork can be enriched by a conscious cultivation of capacities to grasp social processes that unfold at the limits of language and at the edges of awareness. In both classic and contemporary anthropology, in short, engagements with psychoanalytic concepts have played key roles, opening new questions, new avenues of thinking, and new modes of engaging with ethnographic materials' (Gammeltoft and Segal, 2016, p. 403). Thus, we see that reflexivity is fostered by awareness, cultivation of capacities, and an open attitude to significance, subduedness, gaps, and discrepancies.

We further need to acknowledge that the combining of ethnographic methods and psychoanalysis offers much to be gained. Cargill points to how 'recent works in ethnographic psychoanalysis demonstrate how psychoanalysis stands to function better as both community intervention and participatory action research' (2006, p. 99). He underlines that the historical convergence between psychoanalysis and cultural anthropology thus situates ethnographic psychoanalysis within interdisciplinary theory and practice (Cargill, 2006, p. 99). Psychoanalytic ethnography then merges and intersects from two traditions, epistemologies, methods, and methodologies. Cargill describes this as follows:

> ethnographic psychoanalysis, then, is comprised of psychoanalysts and psychoanalytic theorists who rely on ethnographic methods, while its cousin, psychological anthropology, typically refers to the opposite: scholars trained as anthropologists who rely on psychoanalytic theories. Ethnographic psychoanalysis can be contextualised both as an interdisciplinary in its own right and as a constituent of the qualitative psychology movement.
> (Cargill, 2006, p. 102)

Several authors seek to deepen the reflexivity involved. Kenny and Gilmore pinpoint how in ethnography, 'a researcher's emotional journey tends to be seen as embarrassing and "to be avoided" in the final text', and 'given that ethnography involves a prolonged intensive immersion in a new social setting it is particularly surprising that emotions do not feature more prominently' (Kenny and Gilmore, 2014, p. 161). They advocate 'research affectivity as a social theory concept aimed at understanding how unconscious dynamics inscribe people's orientation to aspects of the social world and connect them to particular forms of power and identification' (Kenny and Gilmore, 2014, p. 167). Brown highlights what psychoanalysis can add to discussions of reflexivity and describes how psychoanalytic approaches to learning encourage a reflexive relationship to empirical and conceptual work. This psychological form of reflexivity is relevant to empirical and conceptual work and shares interesting parallels with debates about reflexivity in social research methods, while also contributing to discussions of what constitutes reflexivity. Reflexivity is often discussed in relation to a researcher's empirical work, but reflexivity is equally needed in relation to the academic context in which most research and learning takes place (Brown, 2006, p. 181).

Froggett and Briggs add another dimension in their discussion of practice-near research in human services as

> a cluster of methodologies that may include thick description, intensive reflexivity, and the study of emotional and relational processes. Such

methods aim to get as near as possible to experiences at the relational interface between institutions and the practice field. Psychoanalytically informed approaches to research are particularly fruitful here. Drawing on Clifford Geertz's distinction between experience-near and experience-distant inquiry, this article also discusses the relationship between practice-near and practice-distant approaches. These may be used in parallel to investigate different but related objects of interest and can be used to triangulate different data when focusing on the same object; finally practice-near and practice-distant methods can be combined in interpretive procedures which depend on an oscillation between immersion within and distancing from the field.

(Froggett and Briggs, 2012, p. 1)

Vignettes: how to do it

A number of in-depth hermeneutic techniques can foster and encourage psychoanalytic-ethnographic reflexivity. The hermeneutic circle refers to the idea that one understanding of the text – from fieldwork, interviews, or dialogue – as a whole is established by reference to the individual parts, and one understanding of each individual part by reference to the whole. Neither the whole text nor any individual part can be understood without reference to one another, and hence, this forms a circle. The meaning of a text must be found within its cultural, historical, and literary context.

Free-flowing attention

A free-flowing attention is inspired by the psychoanalytic clinical practice, and applied to ethnography, emphasises how and why psychoanalytic-ethnographic researchers should develop an unfocused attention, drifting intuitively and openly in their fieldwork – at the least at the beginning of a study and to some degree thereafter. In this way, the intention is to gather a large amount of data to be further processed and explored, generating interpretative thematic understandings.

Empathic sensitivity

Rubin highlights how developing an empathic sensitivity through daily informal interaction with research informants gradually enabled her to develop rapport as well as applying the concept of ambivalence and considering both verbal and non-verbal data through an in-depth analysis (Andersen, 2012, p. 3). This was provided by engaging in applying a 'near-ness' approach and understanding to the social and inner worlds of the research setting and informants – trying to understand what they understood – as opposed to unconsciously distancing oneself (Rubin, 1985).

Sticky constructions

As mentioned, Britzman suggests 'sticky constructions' (Britzman, 2010, p. 20) as condensed points of symbolisations and meanings in social world interactions. Researchers should engage their attention towards locating and inquiring into clusters of, for instance, ego defences, resistance, moral anxiety, transference and love, free association, dreams, contradictions, oppositions, and messiness. As previously mentioned, I have identified troubling encounters between welfare professionals and citizens that enabled me to understand and learn from this phenomenon. Identification, ambivalence, and defensive reactions constitute a significant psycho-societal analytical grid through which to study welfare services (Andersen, 2016).

Pair-interview method

Kenny and Gilmore suggest the 'pair-interview method' that comprises a number of features enabling a psychoanalytic-ethnographic approach. Conducting interviews in pairs strengthens processes of facilitation, containment, and patiently open-minded interpretation of affective material (Kenny and Gilmore, 2014, p. 171). Likewise, pair or group interpretation strengthens the production of data analysis that is sensitive and true to affectivity and significant meanings.

Ethnopsychoanalysis and the third space

The French psychoanalyst and ethnologist George Devereux was one of the early developers of ethnopsychoanalysis that situated the Freudian concept of transference and countertransference as a significant trait of human behaviour, also found in research encounters. He pointed out how data produced in behavioural science influence researchers in a multitude of ways and, in this context, he placed transference and countertransference as an important element of an investigative methodology. He further clarified how inquiries into human behaviour and interaction may lead to anxiety and insecurity, against which researchers find ways of protecting themselves. As an interesting elaboration, Devereux makes clear that it is not the study of the subject, but rather the observer, that provides access to the essence of the observational situation. Therefore, in research encounters, we should be sensitive to how the subject behaves, the 'disturbances' that are created by the observer's existence, and the activities and behaviour of the observer, for example her anxiety, defence manoeuvres, research strategies, decisions, and attempts to give meaning to her observations (Devereux, 1967, p. xix).

Ethnopsychoanalysis situates the psychic processes between the ethnologist and her or his informants as important material for the analysis. Content, transferences, and manifestations of these exchanges represent unique material, making it possible to 'read' cultural specificity and social structures (Nadig,

1986, p. 47). The psychoanalytic concepts of transference, countertransference, and resistance are key elements. Ethnopsychoanalytic interpretation does not attribute much importance to the identification of life and history, as in classical psychoanalysis, but applies a method in which curiosity, irritation, and free association act as focal points for the analysis (Erdheim and Nadig, 1991; Nadig and Hegener, 2013). Curiosity is the driving force and motivation behind narratives shared between informants and ethnologists. In this transfer and interaction, cultural roles and interaction patterns are repeated, and thus clarified. The ethnologist, who is not part of the given culture, serves as an irritation trigger. Uneasiness is seen as a prompt to qualify insight and analysis of the historical-ethnic context that embeds the life stories. In this way, the social environment of a particular group is reconstructed. Thus, the goal of ethnopsychoanalytic interpretation is to use the culturally specific psychodynamics and cultural environment to understand the conversation partner's unconscious and cultural dynamics. The ethnopsychoanalytic language locates a form of social interaction that is informed by drives and libido (Nadig, 1986, p. 49). People belonging to different cultures react critically to each other. Every culture structures and portrays certain emotional and libidinous needs and conflicts, and their members react in certain social situations with typical patterns and content. Clashes between different cultures trigger subjective irritation among ethnologists. These feelings serve as the basis for an analysis in an alternating movement between empathetic identification and a reflexive delimiting withdrawal (Erdheim and Nadig, 1991; Nadig, 1986, p. 49).

Nadig talks about a 'third space' as a transitional place that aims at facilitating social spaces, critical exploration, and reflection taking place in the intersection of ethnography and psychoanalysis. The data-informed collaboration between researcher and informants provides a unique venue: a transitional space offering a manageable framing that enables a multi-collaborative inquiry into the dynamics of the societal and psychosocial. The potentials of the third space, then, are to work on the national and international processes of de-symbolisation and re-symbolisation of modern life and their inconsistencies and variations (Nadig, 2000, pp. 87–88). These venues enable settings of alliances, mediation, and the construction of new meanings central to this type of work. They also mark settings as spaces for profoundly creative encounters and the development of new meanings coming 'from the margins' of societies (Sturm, Nadig, and Moro, 2010a).

Vignettes: how to do it

Researchers' affectivity: curiosity, irritation, and free associations

The ethnopsychoanalytic approach harvests material from a method in which curiosity, irritation, and free association act as focal points for the analysis (Erdheim and Nadig, 1991; Nadig and Hegener, 2013). Researchers should direct their curiosity towards significant parts of social life and make reports and narratives that can be shared and reflected between informants and researchers. The uneasiness and wonderings can lead to insights and analysis that are embedded in history, ethnicity, culture, and life stories.

Complementarist research method

In complementarist research, data are submitted to several independent rounds of analysis. The objective is to create data and data analysis that provide an interdisciplinary approach to the research theme. The research processes are performed in a number of rounds, in which the researcher uses methods and theories that belong to the disciplines he or she is referring to. At the very end of the research process, the researcher integrates the results of the different rounds of analysis into a global interpretation from an interdisciplinary perspective (Sturm, Nadig, and Moro, 2010b).

Third spaces

Third spaces are a significant part of the ethnopsychoanalytic method. A third space is a shared transitional space that can facilitate and critically explore and reflect the intersections of ethnography and psychoanalysis. Researchers then might be creative in identifying where and how they can create a third space. A third space is neither the research setting that is being investigated nor the researchers' domain – but it is the true creation of a third space that has to be invented in which a shared exploratory dialogue can take place.

Research seminars and supervision

I emphasise the importance of providing sessions in which researchers can analyse their emotional and affective reactions to the material (observations, interviews, and fieldwork) in order to avoid defensive reactions towards frightening aspects of the material. In seminars and supervisions, researchers can reflect their countertransference reactions to avoid distorted perceptions of the data they analysed, but also get hold of the unconscious aspects of their material.

Institutional transference and countertransference

My third theme brings institutional transference and countertransference to the table. Based on the positioning between the research subjects, the organisation, and the researcher in research settings, Wellendorf has developed the concept of 'institutional transference'. He suggests that transference in organisational settings tends to involve particular dynamics and positioning between the researcher and the investigated organisation. The organisation will attempt to draw the researcher into the dynamics and manifestations of institutional life to eliminate her or him as a disturbing element. Institutional transference then refers to the aspect of transference that the researcher produces in the organisation. Institutional countertransference is the researcher's reaction to transferences from the members of the organisation. The researcher's relationship thus offers a medium for organisational analysis (Wellendorf, 1986). Wellendorf uses the label 'border crosser' to stress how scholars applying psychoanalysis step out of their conventional positions and take on new tasks in complex networks of social groups and institutions. In this way, new opportunities emerge, transforming psychoanalysis into cross-disciplinary knowledge production that will provide new thinking and new discoveries (Wellendorf, 1996, p. 80).

Erhard Tietel exemplifies some possible themes for this analysis: how the members of the organisation form partnerships and further develop the relationship with the researcher, which functions the members take on, and how they position the researcher in relation to these; how the members shape and organise their common task and how they organise their borders. All these aspects produce insight into the hidden institutional dynamics and structure. Tietel (2002) therefore speaks of a projection surface for a particular organisation's culture. He then adds another dimension, stressing that an organisational culture analysis cannot be detached from the researcher's self-analysis. This self-analysis can unfold within the framework of a new psychoanalytical practice in the social sciences, namely research supervision. This is an analogue to the learning analysis in the education of psychoanalysts, implying a restructuring and deeper insight into the processes of the researcher's experience and knowledge. Psychoanalytically oriented research supervision helps the researcher to understand her or his own motives and blind spots in relation to the research field, thereby enabling a more differentiated view of the problem in question and a more open relationship to and interaction with the research field (Tietel, 1994, pp. 46ff, 2000, 2002).

Vignettes: how to do it

Ego-dissociation: observing and experiencing

Sterba unfolds how researchers can balance their positioning in the research settings in order to make representation. In ego-dissociation, the researcher's ego is split into the 'observing ego' and the 'experiencing ego'. The experiencing ego records and participates in the activities in the setting, while the observing ego considers and conceptualises the observations from a continuous meta-position. Researchers might organise their logbooks or field notes in two columns, thereby developing a nuanced understanding of how observing and experiencing their data might lead to different narratives and representations.

Border-crossing and transference

Transference and countertransference take up a key pivotal position in psychoanalytic ethnography as described. Psychoanalytic ethnographic reflectivity and ethnopsychoanalysis incorporate processes of transference and countertransference. A number of key questions can help researchers become more aware of these processes: when gaining entry, how do the field site members welcome the researcher; which aspirations, problems, and challenges are voiced? How does this affect the researcher? Along the way, how do the interactions, partnerships, collaborations, and activities develop? Which forms of criticism, distance, or ignorance are enacted towards the researcher? In which situations and interactions does the researcher feel at ease and comfortable – or the opposite, uneasy, uncomfortable, or bored? How do different members of the field site position the researcher – as a friend, enemy, spy, or co-developer? How do field members react when the researcher leaves the fieldwork?

What is psychoanalytic ethnography most appropriate for?

As mentioned earlier, fieldwork and the building and sustaining of long-term relationships is often highlighted as the royal route to applying psychoanalytic ethnography. The intention is thus to gather in-depth data in all the settings and venues relevant to the research interest and focus. As such, this method can be applied in almost every setting and every corner, with only one precondition. The inquiry should be of such a nature that the chosen method of psychoanalytic ethnography would be a good match for the purpose and research questions. These are often of an explorative kind; here, this particular method can provide the necessary techniques to clarify and unfold the research ambition.

The ambition to dig into psychoanalytic fieldwork needs further to be rooted in an urge to provide deep understandings and to be driven by an epistemological interest, that is, a search for hidden meanings, symbolic representations, and what is under the surface. As any fieldwork textbook will point out, data gathering and making reports can be tedious, difficult, and conflictual. Applying psychoanalytic ethnography, which tends to be demanding and laborious beyond ordinary fieldwork, requires patience and should be driven by an open and deep interest in people and human behaviour, of how groups, organisations, and networks function, power is taken, practised, and avoided, and how men and women work, live, compete, crave, perform, love, and fight. Additionally, it takes a willingness to let your life, feelings, and thoughts as a researcher and human being be part of your inquiry. In the psycho-societal tradition that Leithäuser and Volmerg point to, the epistemology situates a self-directed perspective. They talk about *self*-experience, *self*-analysis, *self*-reflection, and *self*-cognition as all woven into the psychoanalytic understanding. The path of knowledge is to explore what we know nothing of and what we may have an idea about. Scholars study how the traces of the unconscious, for instance in the form of the unfamiliar, can be linked to societal factors. However, the unfamiliar, being often associated with the unconscious, is a part of all of us. Thus, the processes of inquiry are closely linked to processes of self-experience, self-reflection, and introspection (Andersen and Dybbroe, 2017; Leithäuser and Volmerg, 1988, p. 9). As mentioned, this approach leads to a particular interest in the researcher's role and subjectivity, and how these influence the choice of research area, method, and theory (Andersen, 2012, 2013, p. 135).

Yet another approach could address how conflicts can be readdressed in psychoanalytic ethnography. Scholars using fieldwork in educational, social, and organisational research taking place in, for instance, learning institutions, workplaces, or human service organisations, often find themselves involved in difficult, conflicting, and complicated interactions and processes. They are embedded in significant experiences and interactions that will influence their research. In many cases, they may see their reactions to these incidents as individual and private emotional factors to be dealt with in the private sphere (and maybe even perceived as inadequacy) and consequently dismissed as irrelevant for research inquiry and analysis. Contrary to this point of view, I have pointed out the importance of these processes as a knowledge reservoir to be revealed, if these incidents become more visible and reflected upon as illuminating paths of inquiry. They are the bearers of significant information about the subject of inquiry and are therefore important contributions in creating a deeper and more nuanced research narrative (Andersen, 2012, p. 10).

Similarly, the current trend for evidence and documentation of the effectiveness of welfare services through target-driven practice and monitoring might endanger the ability to research practice-based knowledge, professional doubt, and unsuccessful work processes (Andersen and Dybbroe, 2011, p. 264). In other words, social research needs to develop and apply a methodology that is able to create representations that are multi-dimensional, and psychoanalytic ethnography should be seen as such a methodology.

Critical reflections on psychoanalytic ethnography: pros and cons

There are a number of pros and cons related to psychoanalytic ethnography. The pros relate to the following themes. Psychoanalytic ethnography is based on an epistemology that deconstructs 'the rational subject' and displays the multitude of motives, drives, and meanings that human beings attach to inner and outer worlds. In this sense, these studies often enlarge our understandings of human behaviour and interactions in the world. This also implies that psychoanalytic ethnography has a potential inherent cultural and societal critique, since current governance regimes tend to favour rational, performance-oriented behaviour that has the potential to de-humanise. For instance, in human service, education, and health, psychoanalytic ethnographies have proven to point out other readings than the dominant discourse, thus providing a critical understanding of the dynamics of changes in welfare settings, but at the same time sustaining a humane, in-depth understanding of people in crisis or change and their interactions with welfare professionals.

The cons imply that this is not a quick-fix method, but one that relies upon inquiries with a timespan that allows for immersion in the topic and presence in ways that allow multiple sensitivities. A further point mentioned above is that immersing oneself in psychoanalytic ethnography requires an ability to be introspective and to safeguard certain ethical principles.

References

Andersen, L. L. (2003a). When the unconscious joins the game: A psychoanalytic perspective on modernization and change. *Forum Qualitative Sozialforschung, 4*(3), 1–13.

Andersen, L. L. (2005a). The long gone promise of social work: Ambivalence and individualisation in social services administration. *Journal of Social Work Practice, 19* (1), 73–86. https://doi.org/10.1080/02650530500071985

Andersen, L. L. (2012). Interaction, transference, and subjectivity: A psychoanalytic approach to fieldwork. *Journal of Research Practice, 8* (2),Article M3, 1-13.

Andersen, L. L. (2013). Inner and outer life at work. The roots and horizon of psychoanalytically informed work life research. *Historical Social Research-Historische Sozialforschung, 38*(2), 124–139.

Andersen, L. L. (2015). Micro-processes of collaborative innovation in Danish welfare settings: a psychosocial approach to learning and performance. In *Collaborative Governance and Public Innovation in Northern Europe* (pp. 249–268). Bentham EBooks.

Andersen, L. L. (2016). A psycho-societal perspective on neoliberal welfare services in Denmark: Identification and ambivalence. *Journal of Psycho-Social Studies Volume, 9* (1), 94–109.

Andersen, L. L., and Dybbroe, B. (2011). The psycho-societal in social and health care: Implications for inquiry, practice and learning in welfare settings. *Journal of Social Work Practice, 25*(3), 261–269. https://doi.org/10.1080/02650533.2011.597190

Andersen, L. L., and Dybbroe, B. (2017). Introspection as intra-professionalism in social and health care. *Journal of Social Work Practice, 31*(1), 21–35. https://doi.org/10.1080/02650533.2016.1142952

Becker-Schmidt, R., and Knapp, G. A. (1987). *Geschlechtertrennerung - Geschlechterdifferenz. Suchbewegungen sozialen Lernens*. Bonn: Verlag Neue Gesellschaft GmbH.

Becker-Schmidt, R., and Knapp, G. A. (1994). Det er ikke os der har minutterne - det er minutterne, der har os. (B. S. Nielsen, K. Weber, and H. Salling Olesen, Eds.), *Arbejde og subjektivitet. En antologi om arbejde, køn og erfaring*. Viborg: Erhvervs- og voksenuddannelsesgruppen, Roskilde Universitetscenter.

Britzman, D. P. (2010). *Freud and education*. London: Routledge.

Britzman, D. P. (2012). What is the use of theory? A psychoanalytic discussion. *Changing English, 19*(1), 43–56. https://doi.org/10.1080/1358684X.2012.649143

Britzman, D. P. (2013). Between Psychoanalysis and Pedagogy: Scenes of Rapprochement and Alienation. *Curriculum Inquiry, 43*(1), 95–117. https://doi.org/10.1111/curi.12007

Brown, J. (2006). Reflexivity in the research process: psychoanalytic observations. *International Journal of Social Research Methodology*, *9*(3), 181–197. https://doi.org/10.1080/13645570600652776

Cargill, K. (2006). Off the couch and onto the streets: toward an ethnographic psychoanalysis. *Psychoanalysis, Culture & Society*, *11*(1), 99–105. https://doi.org/10.1057/palgrave.pcs.2100073

Corin, E. (2012). Commentary: Interdisciplinary dialogue: a site of estrangement. *Ethos*, *41*(1), 104–112.

Devereux, G. (1967). *From anxiety to method in the behavioral sciences* (Vol. 3). Walter de Gruyter GmbH & Co KG.

Erdheim, M., and Nadig, M. (1991). Ethnopsychoanalyse. *Ethnopsychoanalyse*, *2*, 187–201.

Freud, A. (1993). *The ego and the mechanisms of defence* (1937th ed.). Karnac Books.

Friedman, L., and Samberg, E. (1994). Richard Sterba's (1934) "The fate of the ego in analytic therapy." *Journal of the American Psychoanalytic Association*, *42*(3), 863–873. https://doi.org/10.1177/000306519404200310

Froggett, L., and Briggs, S. (2012). Practice-near and practice-distant methods in human services research. *Journal of Research Practice*, *8*(2), 1–17.

Froggett, L., Ramvi, E., and Davies, L. (2015). Thinking from experience in psychosocial practice: reclaiming and teaching 'use of self'. *Journal of Social Work Practice*, *29*(2), 133–150. https://doi.org/10.1080/02650533.2014.923389

Gammeltoft, T. M., and Segal, L. B. (2016). Anthropology and psychoanalysis: explorations at the edges of culture and consciousness. *Ethos*, *44*(4), 399–410. https://doi.org/10.1111/etho.12138

Hollway, W. (2011). Psycho-social writing from data. *Journal of Psycho-Social Studies*, *4*(2), 1–10. Retrieved from http://hls.uwe.ac.uk/research/current-volume.aspx

Hollway, W., and Jefferson, T. (2000). *Doing qualitative research differently: Free association, narrative and the interview method*. Sage.

Hunt, J. C. (1989). *Psychoanalytic aspects of fieldwork*. London: Sage Publications, Inc.

Kenny, K., and Gilmore, S. (2014). From research reflectivity to research affectivity: ethnographic research in organizations. In M. Kenny, K., & Fotaki (Ed.), *The psychosocial and organization studies: Affect at work*. (pp. 130–158). London: Palgrave Macmillan.

Leithäuser, T. (1976). *Formen des Alltagsbewusstseins*. Frankfurt: Campus.

Leithäuser, T., Meyerhuber, S., & Schottmayer, M. (2009). *Sozialpsychologisches Organisationsverstehen*. Wiesbaden: VS Verlag für Sozialwissenschaften.

Leithäuser, T., and Volmerg, B. (1988). *Psychoanalyse in der Socialforschung. Eine Einführung am Beispiel einer Sozialpsychologie der Arbeit*. Westdeutscher Verlag.

Nadig, M. (1986). Die verborgene Kultur der Frau. *Ethnopsychoanalytische Gespräche Mit Bäuerinnen in Mexiko*. Frankfurt Am Main.

Nadig, M. (2000). Interkulturalität im Prozeß. Ethnopsychoanalyse und Feldforschung als methodischer und theoretischer Übergangsraum. In L.-B. M. Lahme-Gronostaj H. (Ed.), *Identität und Differenz. Beiträge zur psychologischen Forschung* (pp. 87–101). VS Verlag für Sozialwissenschaften.

Nadig, M., and Hegener, W. (2013). Hegener Forum Qualitative Sozialforschung/Forum : Qualitative Social "Konstruktionen sind im aktiven Handeln entstanden, und wir sind nicht nur Opfer, die von der herrschenden Kultur, die sich globalisiert, erschlagen und zu etwas Farblosem geklont, *5*(3), 1–10.

Redman, P., Bereswill, M., and Morgenroth, C. (2010). Special issue on Alfred Lorenzer: Introduction. *Psychoanalysis, Culture and Society*, *15*(3), 213–220. https://doi.org/10.1057/pcs.2010.15

Rubin, L. B. (1985). Worlds of pain. In James M. Henslin (ed.), *Marriage and family in a changing society*. New York: Free Press.

Sterba, R. (1934). The fate of the ego in analytic therapy. *PEB Web: The International Journal of Psychoanalysis*, *15*, 117–126.

Sturm, G., Nadig, M., and Moro, M. R. (2010a). Current developments in French ethnopsychoanalysis. *Transcultural Psychiatry*, *48*(3), 205–227. https://doi.org/10.1177/1363461511402868

Sturm, G., Nadig, M., and Moro, M. R. (2010b). Writing therapies—An ethnographic approach to transcultural therapies. *Forum Qualitative Sozialforschung/Forum: Qualitative Social Research, Art. 1*, *11*(3).

Tietel, E. (1994). Institutionelle Übertragung und institutionelle Gegenübertragung als methodische Aspekte des Verständnisses latenter Prozesse in Organisationen. *Arbejde og teknik: kultur og bevidsthed*, 44–57.

Tietel, E. (2000). The interview as a relational space. In *Forum Qualitative Sozialforschung/Forum: Qualitative Social Research*(Vol.1).

Tietel, E. (2002). Triangular spaces and social skins in Organisations. http://psydok.psycharchives.de/jspui/handle/20.500.11780/375

Wellendorf, F. (1986). Supervision als Institutionsanalyse. In H. Pühl & W. Schmidbauer (Eds.), *Supervision und Psychoanalyse - Selbstreflexion der helfenden Berufe*. Fischer Taschenbuch Verlag.

Wellendorf, F. (1996). Der Psychoanalytiker als Grenzgänger. *Journal Für Psychologie*, *4*(4), 79–91.

Conclusion

R. D. Hinshelwood and Kalina Stamenova

The intention has been to collect as far as possible methods specifically aimed at revealing useful knowledge about the unconscious. There is no doubt much has been left out here, knowingly and inadvertently. We deliberately excluded those qualitative kind of studies in social science that are not specifically focused on the unconscious mind, methods such as grounded theory, interpretative phenomenological analysis, discourse analysis, and tried to map those that were used in combination with psychoanalytic conceptualisations. We have also excluded much of the work based on data that is simply a mechanical form of recording. This prioritises the 'recording' made by the subjective instrument of the researcher, usually interviewer or observer.

There have been a number of studies in organisational, educational, political, sociological, cultural, and historical research, outlined in the Introduction, and perhaps the scoping review is not exhaustive, as there could not have been room for further elaboration in this book. And last but not least, there have been new studies coming during the two years while the book was in the making. In fact, the abundance of studies using psychoanalytic understanding suggests that each of the sections of the book could be developed into a separate collection, for example, psychoanalysis in interviewing, observations, visual methods, and so on. Visual methods, for instance, has been a growing field, with new studies utilising social dreaming constantly emerging and developing (Froggett et al., 2015; Liveng et al., 2017; Manley and Roy, 2016). If the book could inspire such further projects that would be quite an achievement in itself.

By making these deliberate exclusions, we have entered into the debate that centres on scepticism about the researcher's subjectivity. Whilst we would not want to counter the arguments about such unreliability, we must claim that all psychological research is highly biased by researchers' interests, their funding sources, and other obvious *conscious* influences. And such biases in data gathering and in interpretation exist even in natural sciences. It may be true that the biases inherent in the researcher-as-instrument methods, which we have concentrated on here, are particularly significant; we can claim that these biases are especially acknowledged with built-in means of recognising them as far as possible. More than that, those biases that go beyond the conscious ones, such as pleasing funders or supervisors, and are genuinely unconscious can provide a particular perspective on the unconscious field in which the research activity occurs. After all, the very disturbance of reality that the unconscious creates is the prime target of psychoanalytically informed research.

We make no attempt to claim that access to the human unconscious is easy, merely that the more consciously based attempts are more likely to miss the mark. The fact that it is difficult requires more persistence, and perhaps subtlety. It requires a genuine respect for the elusiveness of unconscious dynamics, and one could say that the experience of one's own analysis is important in this respect. Only by engaging on that most personal of all researches can one recognise how cleverly the unconscious can hide itself, and moreover how explanatory it is to gain an insight into the effects it can command.

Perhaps it is also important to keep in mind the distinction between the collection of data and its analysis. In some ways, the kinds of data we need are more to hand in the experiences of subjects and their researchers. After all, it was the recognition of the opportunities given by automatic writing, dreams, and the word association test that provided the initial impetus in the last decades of the nineteenth century that made the twentieth the 'century of the unconscious', we might say. The analysis of those forms of data, with the addition of the expressive methods of art and music particularly, as well as the social dimension of groups, has led to the emergence of the unconscious in that century. And, we would argue, that form of data analysis of the unconscious should be the special preoccupation of the dynamic psychology of the twenty-first.

There are also the emerging fields of psychosocial, socioanalytic, psychosocietal, and group relations studies of which psychoanalysis is an essential part. And there are, of course, inherent complex relations within and between these fields which our book did not aim to address, although those debates and discussions could enrich research practice and help to clarify important aspects about the nature of psychoanalytic research. Our aim has been to present some current developments of innovative psychoanalytic methodologies into the unconscious and how psychoanalytic ideas can be the basis of rigorous methods of systematic research, alone or alongside other complementing methodologies. In that sense, the book has aimed at a pluralistic approach and presents a larger overview of the field.

Like any research, working on this book has been exciting, frustrating, challenging, and an immensely rewarding experience of linking and bringing together minds trying to solve intricate puzzles of the unconscious in social life by consistently and continuously elaborating methodologies. It has also been heartening to discover and map so many current developments of psychoanalytically informed studies across the world. It seems like a fertile ground right now.

References

Froggett, L., Manley, J., and Roy, A. (2015), The visual matrix method: imagery and affect in a group-based research setting. *Forum: Qualitative Social Research*, 16(3).

Liveng, A., et al. (2017), Imagining transitions in old age through the visual matrix method: thinking about what is hard to bear. *Journal of Social Work Practice*, 31(2): 155–170.

Manley, J., and Roy, A. (2016), The visual matrix: a psycho-social method for discovering unspoken complexities in social care practice. *Psychoanalysis, Culture and Society*, 22(2): 132–153.

Index

abduction 171; *see also* Peirce, C.S
abductive inference 171
abductive logic 51, 53
abductive reasoning 171
about-PIN 219, 220, 237
action research methods 162
Adorno, T.W 71, 79
affect theory 199
alpha-function 177
ambivalence 20, 24–35, 28, 241, 243, 247
analysis: *see also* data analysis; comparative 183–89; conceptual 176, 185; discursive 7; socioanalytic interviews 51; thematic 172, 173; validation of 81
analytic third 48
anthropologists 6, 7, 245
anthropology 111; psychoanalytic 6, 7
anxiety 108, 113, 127, 247; avoid 161; inferred 121; unconscious 122; defence dynamic 4, 10, 108
archetypes 2, 50, 172
association method 172
associations 146, 159, 173
associative unconscious 4, 44, 50, 145, 147
attachment 129, 133, 134, 135, 138
attitudes 113
autobiographical narratives 73
avoided relationship 88

Bain, Alistair 133, 145
basic assumption 161
beliefs 28, 46, 47, 113
Bick, Esther 8, 107, 126, 127, 130
biographical data analysis (BDA); *see also* analysis and data analysis 221, 222, 226, 227, 229, 235

Bion, Wilfred 7, 8, 43, 64, 113, 161, 176, 177, 215
BNIM default research question 221
BNIM interviewee 216–20, 224, 226–30, 232
bodily-ness 75
Bollas, Christopher 164
border crosser 250; crossing 251
Breuer, Josef 172

calamitous relationship 88
case-phases 222, 226, 230, 235
causation 52; efficient 52; final 53; formal 53; material 52
choosing subject 203
Clark, Alison 133
clinical setting 5
clinical theories 89
collective unconscious 2, 43, 50, 153
collusion 47, 48
colonialism 207, 208
communication 70, 72; child's 131; unconscious 4, 5; unconscious-to-unconscious 4; verbal 115
complementarity 229
complexity theory 122
conceptions 114
conceptual level 183
condensation 4
conflict 77, 108, 109; everyday life 84; inner 76; interpretation of 93; intrapsychic 108
conscious emotion 76
container 47, 130, 146; emotional 130; introjecting 177; literal 179

container-contained 11; analysis 180; conceptualisations 11; core element 180; less successful form of 180; operationalisation of 176; process 176; relationship 174, 176
containing 180
containment 129; *see also* container-contained
contiguity 87, 89
counterassumptive remarks *see also* 92–94, 97–100
countertransference 9, 72, 97, 108, 110, 111, 129, 132, 173; analysis of 60; dimensions of 132; experience 119; feelings 91, 95; indirect 95; institutional 249, 250; reaction 60, 91; relationship 87; researchers' 87; response 112; unrecognised material and 6; use of 5, 6
creative relationship metaphor (CRM) 175
criteria 190, 191, 193, 194; *see also* operationalisation; discriminating 187; envy 193, 194; frustration 187; minimum number of 181; observable 186; operational 175, 176, 180; operationalised 183–87; required number of 181; schedule of 173
critical social analysis 79
critical theory 243
cue-phrases 216, 217, 236
culture 121; dynamic 6; group 46; institutional 113, 122; manic working 174; paranoid working 174; psychosocial 113; unconscious 28

data: analysed 180, 184, 187; analysis 9, 176, 179, 180, 188; analysis patterns 51; associative 172; collected 175, 187; collection 9, 55, 135, 188; constructed 102; empirical 72; gathering 173; generate 1, 161; generating 172; in-depth 251; observational 175; primary 188; production 71, 79; subjective 173; transitional spaces and 162; unavailable 162; unconscious subjective 180
death instinct 184
defence(s) 49, 108, 111, 127, 241; dynamics of 84; elements of 84; mechanisms of 108; manic 174; operationalised 174; schizoid 174; systemic 49; unconscious 127
defended subject 5, 56, 57, 90, 131

defensive: reactions 247; technique 109, 113, 121
definition 64, 80, 175, 181, 185
denial 32, 49, 108, 174; as systemic defence 49; study of climate change 234
depressive position 128, 129
destructiveness 184
desymbolisation 76
Devereux, George 5, 247
discourse: alienating 207; analysis 7, 256; analysis Lacanian 201; colonialist 207; ideologically laden 207; psychoanalytic 7, 201; relational 201
discursive psychology 62, 199
displacement 4, 242
double experiencing 228
drawing(s) 8, 151, 152
dream analysis 5
dream-drawing 151, 153, 154, 159–62; social 152
dreamer 154
dreaming 145
dreams 146; analysing 172; anxiety 154; examples 153–55; reflection group 154; representation 152; researcher's 6; transitional space 152; verbal and drawn 152
drive theory 75
duck test 173, 181
dynamics 121; cultural 73; generational 160; group 158; hidden conflict 80; individual 58; institution 107; institutional 250; institutions 122; intersubjective 57; personal 60; societal 43; system-as-a-whole 43; totalitarian 162; transference-countertransference 81; unconscious 57, 59, 77, 88, 161; unconscious psychic 84; underlying 160; work life 85

education studies 8
ego 92; defences 247; depletion 186; -dissociation 242, 250; -function 177; -ideal 27, 36, 37n7
emotion 33, 49, 59, 77, 128, 133; stimulated in the interviewer 49
emotional atmosphere 113
emotional labour 8
empathic sensitivity 246
empirical research 11, 72
enactment 160, 165
engrams 58, 74

envy 184; concept of 184; conceptualisations of 186; defence 186; negative therapeutic reaction and 184; observable criteria 187; occurrences of 185; primary narcissism and 184; projective identification and 186
epistemic subject 71
ethnography 72, 242; and psychoanalysis 245; psychoanalytic 6, 7, 243, 244
ethnomethodology 21
ethnopsychoanalysis 244, 247
everyday consciousness 244
experience(s) 2, 10; bodily 71, 72; bodily-ness 70; of sociation 21; sensory 71, 74; sensual 72, 78; subjective 120
experience-distant inquiry 246
experience-near inquiry 246
experiencing ego 242, 250
Ezriel, Henry 87, 88, 91

family transmission 213
fantasy 242
Ferenczi, Sandor 71
field research 250
fieldwork 241; anthropological 111; diary 135; psychoanalytic 251
following hypotheses 227, 228, 229, 235
Foulkes, S.H. 2, 9, 43
Frankfurter school 146, 147, 243
Free Association Narrative Interview (FANI) 56, 173, 232–34; criticised 61, 62; disempowering 62; essentialising 62; pathologising 62
free associations 50, 56, 57, 87, 90, 91, 94, 156, 160, 162, 165
free associative reflection 217
free-floating attention 56, 80, 246
Freud, Anna 131, 242
Freud, Sigmund 2, 4, 5, 57, 66, 111, 244
Fromm, Eric 43
frustration 191; occurrences of 185, 187, 191; substitute formations and 186
future-blindness 216, 226, 235

genetic continuity 87, 89
geography 199; psychoanalysis and 199
geo-historical context 212
gestalt 75, 217; psychologists 172
grounded theory 102, 135, 256
group dynamic 162
group relations 145

Heimann, Paula 111
hermeneutic experiences 70
heterogeneity 215, 229, 235
historicity 239, 247, 226, 234
history 8; analyst's social and educational 31; life 83, 84, 121, 132; organisational 162; relationship with psychoanalysis 8, 36n7; subjective life 73; oral 31
History of the Case Evolution (HCE) 213, 214, 221, 222, 226, 227, 230, 235
Hollway, Wendy 56–58, 60–62, 90
hotspot/blind spot 215, 216, 228, 235
human systems 43
hypotheses 96, 122, 132, 156; based on data 149; causal 122; empirically investigated 96; experiencing 228; reformulated 95; researcher's 92; tentative 161; tested 87

identification 192, 241, 243, 247; and observer's experience 21
identity transitions 6
I-identity 147
Imago 172
imitation 26, 36n5, 151
in-depth hermeneutics 58, 75
individual 19, 23, 27–30; experience 2
individualising processes 207
infant observation 117, 121, 188
inferences 1, 5, 21, 171; body of 1; hypothetical 171
inner objects 147; world 213, 214, 229, 234, 236
in-PIN 219, 220, 232–235, 237
institution 27; psychic 27; psychoanalytic 94, 95; totalitarian 156
institution-in-the-experience 147
institution-in-the-mind 147
interaction 189; experience 76; forms 75, 78; hidden 5; non-verbal 77; patterns of 131; social 70, 71, 76
International Research Group for Psycho-Societal Analysis 73
interpersonal theory 92
interpretation 6, 71, 74, 75, 78, 114; ethnopsychoanalytic 248; examples 81; formulating 87, 115; here-and-now 87, 88; in-depth hermeneutic 80; methodology 70, 73; mutative 93; observation narratives 132; preliminary 81; primary 81; procedures 72, 80; psychoanalytic 199; psychoanalytically

informed 8; psychodynamic 73; psycho-societal 75; requirements 116
intersubjective agreement 92
intervention practices 231
interview 1, 44; elements unconsciously transferred to 201; experimental situation 87; focus group 72; in-depth 7, 63; interpersonal relations of 55; intersubjective encounter 201; narrative 72; process 7; psychoanalytic research 55; psychoanalytically informed 56; semi-structured 72; socioanalytic 43–55; theme centred 58; use of reverie 64
interview-chronology 222
interviewees 9, 55
interviewer 5, 9, 55
inter-vision 59, 60, 242
introjection 242
investigation: instrument of 4; of social defence systems 174; themes of 132
irrational 24, 27, 30, 33
Isaacs, Susan 131

Jaques, Elliot 28, 108
Jefferson, Tony 56–8, 61, 90; *see also* Free Association Narrative Interview (FANI)
Jung, Carl 2, 43, 50

Kant, Emanuel 171
kickstart panels 214, 226
Klein, Melanie 71, 128, 129, 184; theory of anxiety and defence 174
knowledge: accessing 1; constructing 55, 56; discourses 84; generation 56; inter-subjective 56
Kohte-Meyer, I. 31, 33
Kvale, Steiner 55

Lacan, Jacques 3, 8, 62
language 80, 152; acquisition 70, 76; action 76; class differences 3; fail to symbolise 205; figures 81; game 70, 76–8; implicit assumptions 3; influence of 3; object-cathexes 3; power of 76; scenic phenomena and 58; structure 2; symbol-building 77; symbolisation and 77; thing-cathexes 3; turn to 199; use 3, 70, 73, 74, 76, 83, 200; valuation of gender 3; visual representations 3; word-presentations 3
language-symbolic interaction form 76–78, 81

Lawrence, Gordon 146, 164
le tiers (the third party) 59
leadership 148
libido 248
life-chronology 222
limits of knowability 203
literary texts 79
lived-life phases 223
long-term historical 212
Lorenzer, Alfred 58, 61, 67, 71, 74–80
Lukacs, Georg 3

macro-societal 212
magic words 216, 217
manic working culture 174
Marxism 3, 62, 71
masculinity 63
matrix 2, 146–150, 155, 157; unconscious 44
meaning occurrences 94
memory traces 75
Menzies Lyth, Isabel 108
method 5, 10; complementarist 249; limitations 102; pair-interview 247; potentials of 163; practice-distant 246
methodologies: academic research and 162; contemporary 162; creative uses of 163; cultural analysis 71; hermeneutic 80; organisational development and 161; socioanalytic 146, 149, 162; use of 163
micro-sociology 20, 22, 23
mind: analyst's 4; collective 107; observer 107; states of 171, 173; subjective states of 171; unconscious states 172
multi-generation case-studies 213

narrative 82; agentic control 207; agentic impulse 207; approximation to free association 200; built on social other 208; emotional function of 201; focus 199; interpersonal contexts and societal contexts 202; interpreting 200; men's 204; psychoanalytic approaches to 201; psychoanalytic approaches to 204; psychoanalytic reading 200; recurrent storylines 200; reflexive space 200; reflexivity 201; relationship with brothers 204; research 199, 200; research constructions 200; research social and personal realities 200; research social constructionist assumptions 200; research use of psychoanalysis 203;

researchers 200–202; socio-cultural context and 207; structural semantics 73; structure of 200; transference and countertransference 201; turn 199; unintended messages 200; uninterrupted 205; work psychoanalytical inflected 208
narrative analysis 199, 200, 208; bottom-up interpretative moves 200; content 200, 205, 206; critical 200; emphasis on form 200; form 200; individual agency 202; interpretation 203; inter-relationship between self and society 202; interruption 203; language 202; linguistic structure of story 200; multiple readings 205; negotiation of meaning 206; performative aspects of text 201; positioning 202; process 204, 205; rationality 207; shared meaning 207; sociocultural context 202; structural features of texts 200; subjective agency and 202; text structure both reveals and conceals 207; use of psychoanalysis 203; utilising psychoanalysis pathologising 203; utilising psychoanalysis prioritising internal world 203
negative capability 113

object relations 88, 203; avoided relation 94, 101; avoided relationship predicted 96; calamitous relation 94; required relation 94, 97, 101; required relationship predicted 96
objective hermeneutics 58
observation: behavioural 134; direct 87; infant 127; institutional 121; instrument of 1; psychoanalytical 126; psychoanalytical 130; regularity 188
observer 5; anxieties 117; conflicts 117; countertransference 112; emotional experience 117; impact 117; persecuting 118; persecuting ego 117; persecutory transference 119; role 112, 116, 117; transference object 120; unconscious 115
observing ego 242, 250
operational criteria 175
operational definitions 175, 185
operationalisation 171, 173; container-contained 176; illustrations 174–79; steps 173; trial use of 176
operationalising 183; concept 183; pattern and 184

oppression 208
organisational role analysis 152
organisation-as-a-whole 46
organisation-in-the-mind 147
outer world 213, 214, 229; realities 212, 213

paradigms 183
paranoid working culture 174
paranoid-schizoid position 128
parataxic distortions 92
Parker, Ian 61, 62
participant observer 130
part-objects 147
patterns: analysis of 51; ongoing 163; ordering 115
pauses (private thinking time) 231
Peirce, C. 53, 164, 171
performance: analysis of 207; enjoyment 207; resistance 207
person-in-a-role 45
phantasies 111, 112, 118
photographs 146, 155–58
Piaget, Jean 172
PIN 217–19, 221, 223, 224, 231, 236
pleasure-unpleasure principle 75
policy-implementing 214
policy-making 214
positivism 72; critique of 79
post-interpretation 90; occurrence 99, 100
post-structuralism 62
power 48; structures 242
preconceptions 114
prediction 96; formulated 90; formulating 89, 94; hypothesised 89; tested 94
pre-interpretation 90
premature synthesising 232
present-time perspective 233
primal elements 25–8
projections 49, 93, 108, 109, 129, 242, 250
projective identification 26, 30, 36n5, 45, 60, 108, 110, 120, 177; process of 111
projective surface 58
proto-metaphor 175
psychoanalysis: employed reflexively 208; employing 203; Lacanian 201; social 202; utilising 203
psychoanalytic (social) object 19, 20, 30
psychoanalytic observations: arguments against 132; babies 134; life history and 132; pre-term babies 131; sociology and 132

psychoanalytic reflectivity 244
psychoanalytic sociology 199
psychology: affective turn 199; methodological approaches 199
psychosocial culture 108, 113
psychosocial studies 199
psychosocietal thinking 234
pushing for PINs 217–20, 231, 234

racism 63
rational subject 252
real history 212
reality-oriented working culture 175
re-enactment 76
reflection 82; group 148, 150; internal 76; sessions anxieties 156
reflexivity 201, 244, 245
relational scenarios 87
relationality 203
relations: matrix of 2; power 47; social 70; societal 70
relationship: internal object 111; transference-countertransference 90
reliability 4, 45, 122, 181, 256
reparation 29
repression 23, 77, 176; and splitting 176, 186; social 44, 176
required relationship 88
research: affectivity 245; design 96; educational 73; group 107; instrument group's mind 115; learning 73; object 71; practice methodology of 199; question 96; seminars 249
researcher: affectivity 248; curiosity 248; irritation 248; role 252; subjectivity 252
reverie 63–5, 177; aims 66; anticipation 65; continuity 67; facilitation of thoughts 65; linking 66; overcoming barriers 65; privacy 67; reflection 66; training 67; transference-countertransference 64; utterance 66; writing 66
risky FH predictions 228

Saussure, Ferdinand de 3, 4
scene 75
scenic compositions 60, 61
scenic drafts 78
scenic drama 58
scenic enactment 58
scenic interpretation 80
scenic understanding 58, 60, 61, 70, 78–80, 87

schema 172, 173; theory 171
Schutz, A. 21–2, 34, 35n1
second skin 130
self-analysis 251
self-cognition 251
self-experience 251
self-inspection 216
self-reflection 251
sequentialisation 222, 224–226, 236, 237
sibling rivalry 95
signifiers 44, 145
signs 44
Simmel, G. 21, 35n2
single case study 122
singular agentic self 208
situated subjectivity 212, 214, 222, 227, 229, 230, 234, 237
Smelser, N. 22–4
social agency 70, 72
social defence system 20, 28–9
social defences 43, 49, 174
social dream-drawing (SDD) 150–163; post-doctoral course 158–161; side effects 164, 165
social dreaming 146, 151, 164
social dynamics 2
social field 93
social institutions 109
social photo-matrix (SPM) 11, 146–149, 161; social photo-matrix (SPM) in prison 155–158, 162
social structures 247
social superego 30–3
social systems 49, 50
social theory 79
social unconscious 49, 202, 211
socialisation 70, 74; process 76; theory of 71, 73, 78
sociation/sociated 20, 21, 23–5, 27, 35n3
societal regime 212
socioanalysis 43, 145
sociology 8
splitting 49, 108–110, 128, 176, 181
Squid Group 74
SQUIN 217, 231, 233, 236
states of subjectivity: phases 223; situated 229; successive (SSS) 226, 229
sticky constructions 244, 247
strange intruder 164
structural model 27, 32
subjective/subjectivity 21, 23, 30

subjectivity 62, 70, 111, 135, 242; affective dimensions of 199; empty 202; focus on 199; individual specific capacity 71; interpretation of 70; psycho-societal understanding of 71; research into 74; understanding of 70
subjects 97
sublimation 242
subsession three 220, 221
subsession two 217–220
substitute formations 187, 190
Sullivan, Henry S. 92
supervision 249
supervision psychoanalytically oriented 250
symbolic interactionism 73
symbolisation 74, 77
symbols 44, 145
system-as-a-whole 43, 44
systems: socio-emotional 46; theory 43

Tavistock Observation Method (TAO) 132, 134, 135, 138
Teitel, Erhard 250
teller flow analysis (TFA) 224, 227, 236
teller flow phases 223
test data 97
text analysis 70
textsort 224–226, 236, 237
the other 207
thematic affinity 87, 89
thematic group discussion 72, 79
theme-centred interview 58
theoretical level 184
therapy 212, 217, 230, 231, 237
third position 117
third space 51, 244, 247–49

three-column summary 222, 223, 227
time-period situatedness 212
transference 9, 49, 72, 80, 87, 97, 108, 110, 129, 132; avoided relation 90, 91; calamitous relation 90, 91; dimensions of 132; dynamics of 91; figures 93; institutional 242, 249; interpretation 93; manifestations of 111; material 88; phenomena 118; required relation 90, 91; response 112
transference/countertransference 19; process 57
transferential moment 19, 31, 33
transitional space 146, 152, 162
transparent self 56
triangulation 59, 87, 89, 90, 94, 98–100, 132
twin-track methodology 234

unconscious: assumptions 113; assumptions and desires 215; meaning 81; phantasies 108; socially produced 202
unified whole story 233, 236
unthought known 164

validation 81, 93, 107
validity 94, 122, 181
verbal representation 2
verbatim transcript 221, 224, 236
verstehen 21, 29
vignettes 189–93

we-identity 147
Winnicott, Donald 45, 184
Wittgenstein, Ludwig 76, 77
working hypotheses 52

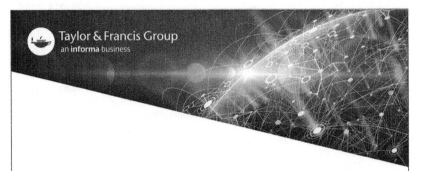